CONTEMPORARY SOCIOLOGICAL THEORY

CONTEMPORARY SOCIOLOGICAL THEORY

GEORGE RITZER
UNIVERSITY OF MARYLAND

ALFRED A. KNOPF
NEW YORK

THIS IS A BORZOI BOOK
PUBLISHED BY ALFRED A. KNOPF, INC.

First Edition

9 8 7 6 5 4 3 2 1

Copyright © 1983 by Alfred A. Knopf, Inc.

Library of Congress Cataloging in Publication Data

Ritzer, George.
  Contemporary Sociological theory.

  Bibliography
  Includes indexes.   1. Sociology—Philosophy.   I. Title.
  HM24.R4936   1983   301'.01   82-18022
  ISBN 0-394-32816-7

Manufactured in the United States of America.

Cover design by James McGuire. Composition by Dianne Rooney Enterprises, Staten Island, New York. Printed and bound by R. R. Donnelley & Sons.

PERMISSIONS ACKNOWLEDGMENTS

Text

CHAPTER 3: Quotations from Talcott Parsons, *The Social System*. Copyright © 1951 by Talcott Parsons. Reprinted by permission of The Free Press.

Autobiographical sketch of Robert K. Merton. Copyright © 1981 by Robert K. Merton. Reprinted by permission of the author.

CHAPTERS 4, 8: Quotations from Maurice Godelier, *Rationality and Irrationality in Economics*. Copyright © 1972 by NLB. Reprinted by permission of the publisher.

CHAPTER 5: Quotations from Herbert Blumer, *Symbolic Interactionism: Perspective and Method*. Copyright © 1969. Reprinted by permission of Prentice-Hall, Inc., Englewood Cliffs, N.J. 07632.

CHAPTER 6: Quotations from George Psathas, ed., *Everyday Language: Studies in Ethnomethodology*. Copyright © 1979 by Irvington Publishers, Inc. Reprinted by permission of the publisher.

CHAPTER 7: Autobiographical sketch of George Homans. Reprinted by permission of the author.

Figures 7.1 and 7.2 from Don Bushell and Robert Burgess, "Some Basic Principles of Behavior," in Robert Burgess and Don Bushell, eds., *Behavioral Sociology*. Copyright © 1969 by Columbia University Press. Reprinted by permission of the publisher.

Quotations from George Homans, *Social Behavior: Its Elementary Forms*. Copyright © 1961, 1974 by Harcourt Brace Jovanovich, Inc. Reprinted by permission of the publisher.

Quotations from Peter Blau, *Exchange and Power in Social Life*. Copyright © 1964 by John Wiley & Sons. Reprinted by permission of the publisher.

Quotations from Peter Singelmann, "Exchange as Symbolic Interaction," in *American Sociological Review* 37 (August 1972). Reprinted by permission of The American Sociological Association and the author.

Quotations from Linda Molm, "The Legitimacy of Behavioral Theory," in *The American Sociologist* 16 (1981). Reprinted by permission of The American Sociological Association and the author.

Photos

PAGE 14:   Photo: The Bettmann Archive
PAGE 20:   Photo: The Granger Collection
PAGE 26:   Photo: The Granger Collection
PAGE 30:   Photo: The Granger Collection
PAGE 46:   Courtesy, University of Chicago
PAGE 76:   Photo: The Granger Collection

PAGE   90:   Courtesy, Robert K. Merton
PAGE 131:   Photo: UPI
PAGE 150:   Courtesy, Immanuel Wallerstein
PAGE 162:   Courtesy, University of Chicago
PAGE 193:   Courtesy, Mrs. Alfred Schutz
PAGE 240:   Photo: Christopher S. Johnson
PAGE 274:   © Lilian Kemp Photography
PAGE 290:   Courtesy, Peter M. Blau

PREFACE

This book on contemporary sociological theory is derived from, and is being published simultaneously with, *Sociological Theory*, a book devoted to the entire history of the discipline's theory, both classic and contemporary. Although some historical background will be presented here, the main focus is contemporary theory.

Sociological theory (along with methods and statistics) is the most important subfield within sociology. This is not to deny the significance of the other subareas of sociology. However, theory (as well as methods and statistics) is important not only in itself, but also because it is an integral part of all other areas of sociology. A sound understanding of theory allows one to develop a deeper understanding of the discipline as a whole and all of its subareas.

Sociological theory has attracted the attention of some of the best thinkers in the history of the discipline. In this book the reader will encounter the brilliant insights of such modern theorists as Alfred Schutz, Talcott Parsons, Robert Merton, Erving Goffman, Louis Althusser, Harold Garfinkel, and Peter Blau. The theorists treated here are those whose ideas have had a profound effect on sociology and, in some cases, on humanity as a whole.

Although the text focuses on contemporary theory, I believe it is necessary to provide students with the historical background needed to understand contemporary developments. Thus, the first two chapters are devoted to an overview of the history of sociological theory.

I believe, too, that certain sociological theories have not always gotten the attention they deserve in books like this one. Very substantial chapters in *Contemporary Sociological Theory* are therefore devoted to the often-ignored neo-Marxian theories as well as phenomenology and ethnomethodology. In addition, there are the expected chapters on structural functionalism and conflict theory, symbolic interactionism, and exchange theory and behavioral sociology.

Books on sociological theory are also sometimes insufficiently attentive to recent changes in interests and fashions in sociological theory. The last chapter seeks to rectify this omission, at least in part. Much of the chapter is devoted to theories currently in fashion in sociology—sociobiology, existential sociology, macrostructural theory, and structuralism. In addition, I deal with a theory (action theory) that is currently out of fashion and one (systems theory) that experienced a meteoric rise and fall in recent years.

The reader should be aware that I have developed and used several bases for the systematic analysis of the theories discussed in this text. Some of the organizing principles are outlined in the first two chapters. Those principles are fairly straightforward and can be used by all readers of the book. An additional set of principles, derived from my previous work in metatheory, is offered in the Appendix. The material is placed in an appendix because it might not fit the backgrounds and interests of some readers. The book can be read without a knowledge of the material covered there. However, the Appendix may enhance understanding of the book and of sociological theory in general. For those interested in that material, it should be read either after the first two chapters or after completion of the book. As important as the principles discussed there were to me in organizing the book, I have tried to keep them from being too intrusive in the text. The emphasis remains on theories not the underlying metatheoretical principles. Those who wish even more material on the metatheoretical bases of this book should refer to my other works, especially *Sociology: A Multiple Paradigm Science* and *Toward an Integrated Sociological Paradigm*.

There are a number of people who deserve special recognition and thanks for their help with this project. I am grateful to Roger Reitman for coauthoring an earlier version of the section devoted to Alfred Schutz in the chapter on phenomenology and ethnomethodology. I am especially indebted to Robert J. Antonio for a large number of very useful suggestions, many of which I included in the final draft of this book. My greatest debt, however, is to my long-time colleague, and sometime coauthor, Ken Kammeyer. Ken carefully reviewed every page of this manuscript and made numerous suggestions on how better to communicate some very difficult concepts. I have not incorporated every one of his suggestions, but I probably should have, given his astuteness as an editor and a sociologist.

The final draft of this book was written at the Netherlands Institute for Advanced Study in Wassenaar, The Netherlands. I am grateful to the Institute for providing me with an ideal environment in which to finish the text. Special thanks go to Pilar van Breda and Marina Voerman, who typed the final draft of this manuscript, and to staff members at the University of Maryland—Gladys Graham, Cass O'Toole, Dorothy Bowers, and Joyce Sterling—who typed the first draft.

Finally, there is the always difficult problem of trying to express my love and appreciation to my wife, Sue, and my children, David and Jeremy. To put it simply, it is their love and affection that makes this work, indeed all my work, both possible and meaningful.

CONTENTS

Chapter Seven: Exchange Theory and Behavioral Sociology   231

PART THREE: CONCLUSIONS   263

Chapter Eight: Sociological Theory Today   265

Appendix: A Schema for Analyzing Sociological Theory   300

Bibliography   313

Name Index   335

Subject Index   340

BIOGRAPHICAL AND AUTOBIOGRAPHICAL SKETCHES

CONTEMPORARY SOCIOLOGICAL THEORY

PART ONE
INTRODUCTION

CHAPTER ONE
A Historical Sketch of Sociological Theory: The Early Years

SOCIAL FORCES IN THE DEVELOPMENT OF SOCIOLOGICAL THEORY
POLITICAL REVOLUTIONS
THE INDUSTRIAL REVOLUTION AND THE RISE OF CAPITALISM
THE RISE OF SOCIALISM
URBANIZATION
RELIGIOUS CHANGE
THE GROWTH OF SCIENCE

INTELLECTUAL FORCES AND THE RISE OF SOCIOLOGICAL THEORY
THE ENLIGHTENMENT AND THE FOUNDING OF SOCIOLOGY IN FRANCE
KARL MARX AND THE DEVELOPMENT OF GERMAN SOCIOLOGY
THE ORIGINS OF BRITISH SOCIOLOGY
ITALIAN SOCIOLOGY: PARETO AND MOSCA
TURN-OF-THE-CENTURY DEVELOPMENTS IN EUROPEAN MARXISM

THIS is a book about contemporary sociological theory. The bulk of it is devoted to well-established theories that continue to be relevant to the 1980s and to a few theories that are just coming into their own in this decade. However, an adequate understanding of today's theories requires some familiarity with the history of sociological theory. Thus, this chapter and the next will be devoted to an overview of the major theorists and theories in the history of sociology.

Although sociological ideas are traceable to the early history of humankind, sociology as a distinctive discipline is not much more than a century old. Thus, while the material discussed in the first two chapters is not contemporary, it is not exactly ancient history either. From a long-range point of view, all of sociological theory is really relatively modern.

The material to be discussed is contemporary in still another sense: the theories and theorists discussed here are, in the main, those that continue to be relevant to this day. To take just a few examples, the ideas of major thinkers like Max Weber, Karl Marx, and Emile Durkheim are still very useful, and widely used, even though they were first developed in the 1800s and early 1900s.

We need to summarize the history of sociological theory too because many contemporary theories have been with us for some time, and to understand them we have to appreciate their early roots and the historical context in which they arose. Thus, in these first two chapters we will first encounter the theories that will occupy our attention throughout the rest of this book.

Although there are many definitions of the term *sociological theory*, this book is based on the simple idea that a sociological theory is a *wide-ranging* system of ideas that deals with the *centrally important* issues of social life.[1] The theories to be dealt with throughout the body of this book have a wide range of application and they deal with centrally important social issues. Many have *stood the test of time*, and the most recent sociological theories chosen for inclusion have shown at least the potential of having lasting significance.[2]

Our focus is the important theoretical work of *sociologists* or the work done by those in other fields that has come to be *defined as important in sociology*. To put it succinctly, this is a book about the "big ideas" in sociology that have stood, or show signs of standing, the test of time, idea systems that deal with major social issues and are far-reaching in scope.

Presenting a history of sociological theory is an enormous task, but since we can devote only two chapters to that task, what follows is a highly selective historical sketch.[3] The idea is to provide the student with a historical "scaffolding" on which the later discussions of contemporary theories can be erected. As the reader proceeds through the later chapters that discuss specific theories, it might prove useful to return to these initial chapters and place topics in their historical context. (Figure 1.1 is a schematic representation of the history covered in this chapter.) It also might be useful to reread these chapters after having finished the book. Much of the material in them will then be more easily comprehended.

One cannot really establish the date when sociological theory began. People have been thinking about, and developing theories of, social life since early in history. But we will not go back to the early historic times of the Greeks or Romans or even the Middle Ages. This is not because people in these epochs did not have sociologically relevant ideas, but because the return on our investment in time would be small; we would spend a lot of time getting very few ideas that are revelant to *modern* sociology. In any case, none of the thinkers associated with those eras thought of themselves, and few are now thought of, as sociologists. It is only in the middle and late 1800s that we begin to find thinkers who can be clearly identified as sociologists. These are the sociological thinkers we shall be interested in, and we begin by examining the main social and intellectual forces that shaped their ideas.

SOCIAL FORCES IN THE DEVELOPMENT OF SOCIOLOGICAL THEORY

All intellectual fields are profoundly shaped by their social settings. This is particularly true of sociology, which is not only derived from that setting but takes the social setting

---

[1]This stands in contrast to those texts which open with such formal, "scientific" definitions as: "A theory is a set of interrelated propositions that allow one to explain and predict social life." Whatever the scientific merit of such a definition, it does not accurately describe the sets of ideas that have, throughout the history of sociology, been defined as theories.

[2]There is also an elaborate metasociological schema that is the basis of these first two chapters as well as the book as a whole. That schema is outlined in the Appendix at the end of this book.

[3]For a much more detailed historical sketch, see Jerzy Szacki (1979).

FIGURE 1.1 Sociological Theory: The Early Years

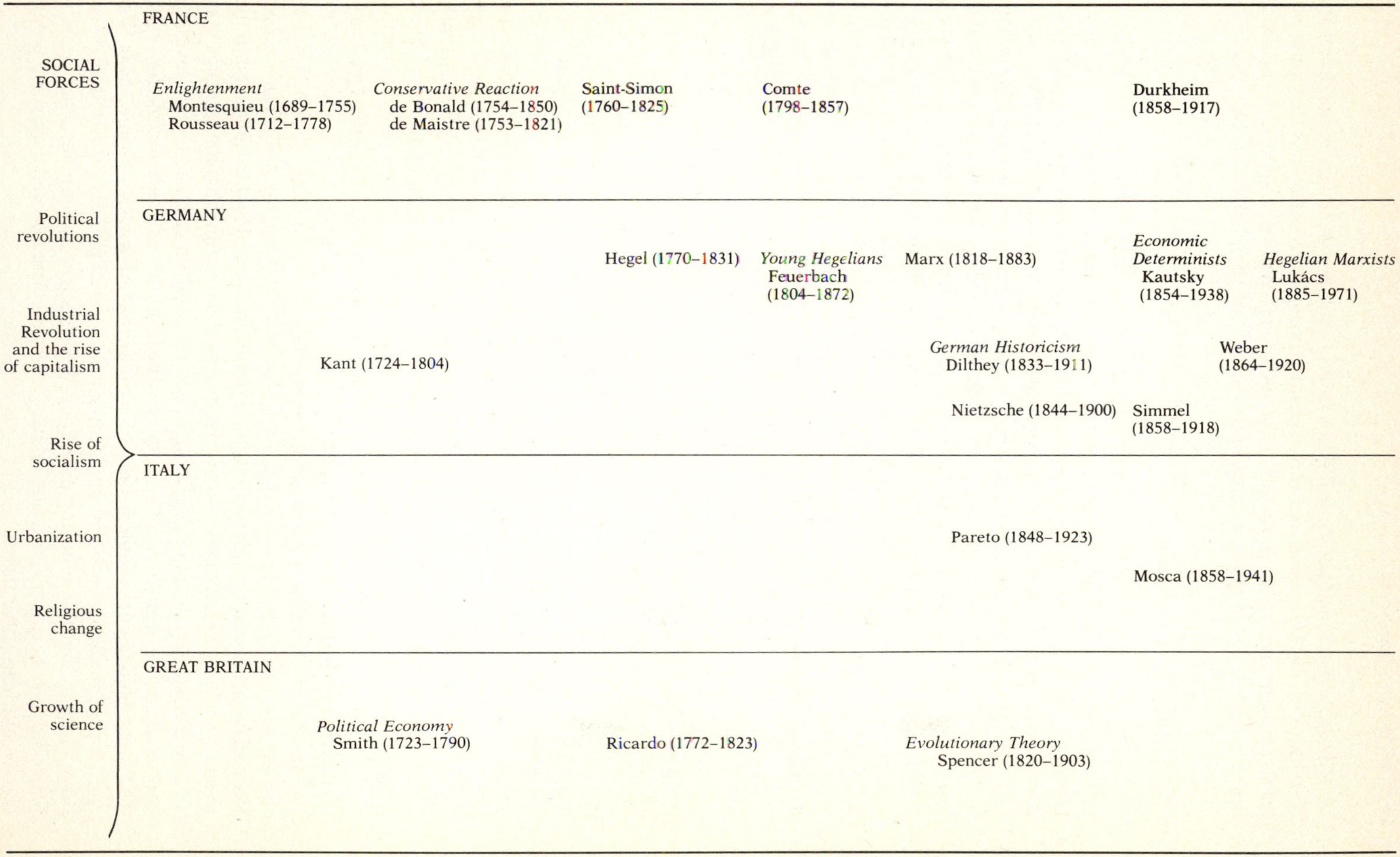

SOCIAL FORCES
- Political revolutions
- Industrial Revolution and the rise of capitalism
- Rise of socialism
- Urbanization
- Religious change
- Growth of science

FRANCE
- *Enlightenment* — Montesquieu (1689–1755), Rousseau (1712–1778)
- *Conservative Reaction* — de Bonald (1754–1850), de Maistre (1753–1821)
- Saint-Simon (1760–1825)
- Comte (1798–1857)
- Durkheim (1858–1917)

GERMANY
- Kant (1724–1804)
- Hegel (1770–1831)
- *Young Hegelians* — Feuerbach (1804–1872)
- Marx (1818–1883)
- *German Historicism* — Dilthey (1833–1911)
- *Economic Determinists* — Kautsky (1854–1938)
- Weber (1864–1920)
- Simmel (1858–1918)
- Nietzsche (1844–1900)
- *Hegelian Marxists* — Lukács (1885–1971)

ITALY
- Pareto (1848–1923)
- Mosca (1858–1941)

GREAT BRITAIN
- *Political Economy* — Smith (1723–1790)
- Ricardo (1772–1823)
- *Evolutionary Theory* — Spencer (1820–1903)

as its basic subject matter. We will focus briefly on a few of the most important social conditions of the nineteenth and early twentieth centuries, conditions that were of the utmost significance in the development of sociology. We will also take the occasion to begin introducing the major figures in the history of sociological theory.

Political Revolutions

The long series of political revolutions ushered in by the French Revolution in 1789 and carrying over through the nineteenth century was the most immediate factor in the rise of sociological theorizing. The impact of these revolutions on many societies was enormous, and many positive changes resulted. However, what attracted the attention of many early theorists was not the positive consequences, but the negative effects of such changes. These writers were particularly disturbed by the resulting chaos and disorder, especially in France. They were united in a desire to restore order to society. Some of the more extreme thinkers of this period literally wanted a return to the peaceful and relatively orderly days of the Middle Ages. The more sophisticated thinkers recognized that social change had made such a return impossible. Thus they sought instead to find new bases of order in societies that had been overturned by the political revolutions of the eighteenth and nineteenth centuries. This interest in the issue of social order persists to this day as one of the major concerns of many sociologists and several sociological theories.

The Industrial Revolution and the Rise of Capitalism

At least as important as political revolution in the shaping of sociological theory was the Industrial Revolution that swept through many Western societies, mainly in the nineteenth and early twentieth centuries. The Industrial Revolution was not a single event but many interrelated developments that culminated in the transformation of the Western world from a largely agricultural to an overwhelmingly industrial system. Large numbers of people left farms and agricultural work for the industrial work offered in the burgeoning factories. The factories themselves were transformed time and time again by a long series of technological improvements. Large economic bureaucracies arose to provide the many services needed by industry and the emerging capitalist economic system. In this economy the ideal was a free marketplace where the many products of an industrial system could be exchanged. Within this system, a few profited greatly while the majority worked long hours for low wages. A reaction against the industrial system and against capitalism in general followed and led to the labor movement as well as to various radical movements aimed at overthrowing the capitalist system.

The Industrial Revolution, capitalism, and the reaction against them all involved an enormous upheaval in Western society, an upheaval that affected sociologists greatly. The three major figures in the history of sociological theory—Karl Marx, Max Weber, and Emile Durkheim—were all preoccupied, as were many other lesser thinkers, with these changes and the problems they created for society as a whole. They spent their lives studying these problems, and in many cases they endeavored to develop programs that would help solve them.

The Rise of Socialism

One set of changes aimed at coping with the excesses of the industrial system and capitalism can be lumped under the heading of socialism. While some sociologists favored socialism as a solution to industrial problems, most were personally and intellectually opposed to it. On the one side, Karl Marx was an active supporter of the overthrow of the capitalist system and its replacement by a socialist system. Although he did not develop a theory of socialism per se, he spent a great deal of time criticizing various aspects of capitalist society. In addition, he engaged in a variety of political activities that he hoped would help bring about the rise of socialist societies.

However, Marx was atypical in the early years of sociological theory. Most of the early theorists, such as Weber and Durkheim, were opposed to socialism. While they recognized the problems within capitalist society, they sought social reform within capitalism rather than the social revolution argued for by Marx. They feared socialism more than they did capitalism. This fear played a far greater role in shaping sociological theory than did Marx's support of the socialist alternative to capitalism. In fact, as we will see, in many cases sociological theory developed in reaction *against* Marxian and, more generally, socialist theory.

Urbanization

Partly as a result of the Industrial Revolution, large numbers of people in the nineteenth and twentieth centuries were uprooted from their rural homes and moved to urban settings. This massive migration was caused, in large part, by the availability of jobs created by the industrial system in the urban areas. But it presented many difficulties for those people who had to adjust to urban life. In addition, the expansion of the cities produced a seemingly endless list of urban problems—overcrowding, pollution, noise, traffic, and so forth. The nature of urban life and its problems attracted the attention of many early sociologists, especially Weber and Georg Simmel. In fact, the first major school of American sociology, the Chicago school, was in large part defined by its concern for the city and its interest in using Chicago as a laboratory in which to study urbanization and its problems.

Religious Change

Social changes brought on by political revolutions, the Industrial Revolution, and urbanization had a profound effect on religiosity. Many early sociologists came from religious backgrounds and were actively, and in some cases professionally, involved in religion (Hinkle and Hinkle, 1954). They brought to sociology the same objectives that they had in their religious lives. They wished to improve people's lives. For some (such as Comte), sociology was transformed into a religion. For the rest, their sociological theories bore an unmistakable religious imprint. Durkheim wrote one of his major works on religion. Morality played a key role not only in Durkheim's sociology but in much of later sociological theory (for example, the work of Talcott Parsons). A large portion of Weber's work was also devoted to the religions of the world. Marx too had an interest in religiosity, but his orientation was far more critical.

The Growth of Science

As sociological theory was being developed, there was an increasing emphasis on science, not only in colleges and universities but in society as a whole. The technological products of science were permeating every sector of life, and science was acquiring enormous prestige. Those associated with the most successful sciences (physics, biology, and chemistry) were accorded honored places in society. Sociologists from the beginning were preoccupied with science, and many wanted to model sociology after the successful physical and biological sciences. However, a debate soon developed between those who wholeheartedly accepted the scientific model and those who thought there were distinctive characteristics of social life that made a wholesale adoption of a scientific model difficult and unwise. The issue of the relationship between sociology and science is debated to this day, although even a glimpse at the major journals in the field would seem to indicate the predominance of those who favor sociology as a science.

These are but a few of the major social factors that played key roles in the early years of sociological theory. The impact of these factors will become clear as we discuss the various theories throughout the body of the book. A variety of *other* social factors have also been important throughout the history of sociological theory, though it will not always be possible to point out their influence. For example, the radical movements of the 1960s and early 1970s led to a renewed interest, in the United States and in many other societies, in Marxian and other forms of radical theory. Although their impact varies in intensity, social factors are *always* implicated in the development of sociological theory.

While social factors are important, the primary focus of the first two chapters will be the intellectual forces that played a central role in shaping sociological theory. In the real world, of course, intellectual factors cannot be separated from social forces. For example, in the discussion of the Enlightenment that follows, we will find that that movement was intimately related to, and in many cases provided the intellectual basis for, the social changes discussed above.

INTELLECTUAL FORCES AND THE RISE OF SOCIOLOGICAL THEORY

The many intellectual forces that shaped the development of social theories will be dealt with in the national context where their influence was primarily felt. We begin with the Enlightenment and its influences on the development of sociological theory in France.

The Enlightenment and the Founding of Sociology in France

It is the view of many observers (Nisbet, 1967; Zeitlin, 1968; Hawthorn, 1976) that the Enlightenment constitutes a critical development in terms of the later evolution of sociology. The Enlightenment was a period of remarkable intellectual development and change in philosophical thought.[4] A number of long-standing ideas and beliefs—many of which related to social life—were overthrown and replaced during the Enlightenment. The most prominent thinkers associated with the Enlightenment were the French philosophers Charles Montesquieu (1689–1755) and Jean Jacques Rousseau (1712–1778). The influence of the Enlightenment on sociological theory, however, was more indirect and negative than it was direct and positive. As Irving Zeitlin (1968:10) puts it, "Much of western sociology developed as a reaction to the Enlightenment."

The thinkers associated with the Enlightenment were influenced, above all, by two intellectual currents—seventeenth-century philosophy and science.

Seventeenth-century philosophy was associated with the work of thinkers such as René Descartes, Thomas Hobbes, and John Locke. The emphasis was on producing grand, general, and very abstract systems of ideas that made rational sense. The later thinkers associated with the Enlightenment did not reject the idea that systems of ideas should be general and should make rational sense, but they did make greater efforts to derive their ideas from the real world and to test them there. In other words, they wanted to combine empirical research with reason. The model for this was science, especially Newtonian physics. It is at this point that we see the emergence of the application of the scientific method to social issues. At another level, not only did Enlightenment thinkers want their ideas to be, at least in part, derived from the real world, but they also wanted them to be useful to the social world, especially in the critical analysis of that world.

Overall, the Enlightenment was characterized by the belief that people could comprehend and control the universe by means of reason and empirical research. The view was that since the physical world was dominated by natural laws, it was likely that the social world was too. Thus it was up to the philosopher, using reason and research, to discover these social laws. Once they understood how the social world worked, the Enlightenment thinkers had a practical goal—the creation of a "better," more rational world.

With an emphasis on reason, the Enlightenment philosophers were inclined to reject beliefs in traditional authority. When these thinkers examined traditional values and institutions, they often found them to be irrational—that is, contrary to human nature and inhibitive of human growth and development. The mission of the practical and change-oriented philosophy of the Enlightenment was to overcome these irrational systems.

CONSERVATIVE REACTION TO THE ENLIGHTENMENT

On the surface, we might think that French sociology was directly and positively influenced by the Enlightenment. After all, didn't French sociology become rational, empirical, scientific, and change-oriented? The answer is that it did, but not before it was

---

[4]This section is based on the work of Irving Zeitlin (1968). Although Zeitlin's analysis is presented here because of the coherent image it gives of the roots of sociological theory, it has a number of limitations: there are better analyses of the Enlightenment, there are many other factors involved in shaping the development of sociology, and Zeitlin tends to overstate his case in places (for example, the impact of Marx). But on the whole, Zeitlin provides us with a useful starting point, given our objectives in this chapter.

also shaped by a set of ideas that was developed in reaction to the Enlightenment. As we will see, sociology in general, and French sociology in particular, has from the beginning been an uncomfortable mix of Enlightenment and anti-Enlightenment ideas.

The most extreme form of opposition to Enlightenment ideas was French Catholic counterrevolutionary philosophy, as represented by the ideas of Louis de Bonald (1754–1840) and Joseph de Maistre (1753–1821). These men were reacting against not only the Enlightenment but also the French Revolution, which they saw partly as a product of the kind of thinking characteristic of the Enlightenment. De Bonald, for example, was disturbed by the revolutionary changes and yearned for a return to the peace and harmony of the Middle Ages. In this view, God was the source of society; therefore, reason, which was so important to the Enlightenment philosophers, was seen as inferior to traditional religious beliefs. Furthermore, it was believed that since God had created society, people should not tamper with it and should not try to change such a holy creation. By extension, de Bonald opposed anything that undermined such traditional institutions as patriarchy, the monogamous family, the monarchy, and the Catholic Church. To call de Bonald's position conservative is to understate the case.

Although de Bonald represented a rather extreme form of the conservative reaction, his work constitutes a useful introduction to its general premises. The conservatives turned away from what they considered to be the ''naive'' rationalism of the Enlightenment. They not only recognized the irrational aspects of social life but also assigned them positive value. Thus they regarded such phenomena as tradition, imagination, emotionalism, and religion as useful and necessary components of social life. Since they disliked upheaval and sought to retain the existing order, they deplored developments such as the French Revolution and the Industrial Revolution, which they saw as disruptive forces. The conservatives tended to emphasize social order, an emphasis that continues to be one of the central themes of a major portion of sociological theory.

Zeitlin has outlined ten major propositions that he sees as emerging from the conservative reaction and providing the basis for the development, at least initially, of French sociology.

1. While Enlightenment thinkers tended to emphasize the individual, the conservative reaction led to a major sociological interest in, and emphasis on, society and other large-scale phenomena. Society was viewed as something more than simply an aggregate of individuals. Society was seen as having an existence of its own with its own laws of development and deep roots in the past.

2. Society was the most important unit of analysis; it was seen as more important than the individual. It was society that produced the individual, primarily through the process of socialization.

3. The individual was not even seen as the most basic element within society. A society consisted of such component parts as roles, positions, relationships, structures, and institutions. The individuals were seen as doing little more than filling these units within society.

4. The parts of society were seen as interrelated and interdependent. Indeed, it was these interrelationships that were a major basis of society. This view led to a conservative political orientation. That is, since the parts were held to be interrelated, it followed that tampering with one part could well lead to the undermining of other parts and ultimately of the system as a whole. This meant that changes in the social system should be made with extreme care.

5. Change was seen as a threat not only to society and its components but also to the individuals in society. The various components of society were seen as satisfying people's needs. When institutions were disrupted people were likely to suffer, and their suffering was likely to lead to social disorder.

6. The general tendency was to see the various large-scale components of society as useful for both society and the individuals in it. As a result, there was little desire to look for the negative effects of existing social structures and social institutions.

7. Smaller units, such as the family, the neighborhood, and religious and occupational groups, were also seen as essential to individuals and society. They provided the intimate, face-to-face environments that people needed in order to survive in modern societies.

8. There was a tendency to see various modern social changes, such as industrialization, urbanization, and bureaucratization, as having disorganizing effects. These changes were viewed with fear and anxiety, and there was an emphasis on developing ways of dealing with their disruptive effects.

9. While most of these feared changes were leading to a more rational society, the conservative reaction led to an emphasis on the importance of nonrational factors (ritual, ceremony, and worship, for example) in social life.

10. Finally, the conservatives supported the existence of a hierarchical system in society. It was seen as important to society that there be a differential system of status and reward.

These ten propositions, derived from the conservative reaction to the Enlightenment, should be seen as the immediate intellectual basis of the development of sociology in France. Many of these ideas made their way into early sociological thought, although some of the Enlightenment ideas (empiricism, for example) were also influential. We turn now to the actual founding of sociology as a distinctive discipline—specifically, to the work of three French thinkers, Claude Saint-Simon, Auguste Comte, and especially Emile Durkheim. There is general agreement that they were the founders of sociology.

CLAUDE HENRI SAINT-SIMON (1760–1825)   Saint-Simon was older than Auguste Comte, and in fact Comte, in his early years, served as Saint-Simon's secretary and disciple. There is a very strong similarity between the ideas of these two thinkers, and yet a bitter debate developed between them that led to their eventual split (K. Thompson, 1975). Since Comte is generally considered to be more important to the founding of sociology, we need say only a few words about Saint-Simon's thinking.

The most interesting aspect of Saint-Simon was his significance to the development of *both* conservative sociological theory (like Comte's) *and* Marxian theory, which was in many ways the opposite of conservative sociology. On the conservative side, Saint-Simon wanted to preserve society as it was, but he did not seek a return to life as it was in the Middle Ages, as did de Bonald and de Maistre. In addition, he was a *positivist*, which meant that he believed the study of social phenomena should employ the same scientific techniques as the natural sciences. On the radical side, Saint-Simon saw the need for socialist reforms, especially the centralized planning of the economic system. But Saint-Simon did not go nearly as far as Marx did later. Although he, like Marx, saw the capitalists superseding the feudal nobility, he felt it inconceivable that the working class would come to replace the capitalists. Many of Saint-Simon's ideas are found in Comte's work, and we now turn to a brief examination of it.

AUGUSTE COMTE (1798—1857)   Comte was the first to use the term *sociology*. He had an enormous influence on early sociological theorists (especially Herbert Spencer and Emile Durkheim). And he believed that the study of sociology should be scientific, just as many contemporary sociologists do. Nevertheless, Auguste Comte is no longer a powerful influence on sociology. This remains the case even though several recent publications have tried to rekindle an interest in his work (for example, Andreski, 1974; Lenzer, 1975).

Comte's work can be seen, at least in part, as a reaction against the French Revolution and the Enlightenment, which he saw as its main cause. He was greatly disturbed by the anarchy that pervaded society and was critical of those French thinkers who had spawned both the Enlightenment and the Revolution. He developed his scientific view, called "positivism," or "positive philosophy," to combat what he considered to be the negative and destructive philosophy of the Enlightenment. Comte was in line with, and influenced by, the French counterrevolutionary Catholics (especially de Bonald and de Maistre). However, his work can be set apart from theirs on at least two grounds. First, he did not think it possible to return to the Middle Ages; advances of science and industry made that impossible. Second, he developed a much more sophisticated theoretical system than his predecessors, one that was adequate to shape a good portion of early sociology.

Comte developed *social physics*, or what he was later to call "sociology," to combat the negative philosophies and the anarchy that in his view pervaded French society. The use of the term "social physics" made it clear that Comte sought to model sociology after the "hard sciences." This new science, which in his view would ultimately become *the* dominant science, was to be concerned with both social statics (existing social structures) and social dynamics (social change). While both involved the search for laws of social life, he felt that social dynamics was more important than social statics. This focus on change reflected his interest in social reform, particularly of the ills created by the French Revolution and the Enlightenment. Comte did not urge revolutionary change, because he felt the natural evolution of society would make things better. Reforms were needed only to assist the process a bit.

This leads us to the cornerstone of Comte's approach—his evolutionary theory, or the *law of the three stages*. The theory proposes that there are three intellectual stages through which the world has gone throughout its history. According to Comte, not only did the world go through this process, but groups, societies, sciences, individuals, and even minds went through the same three stages. The *theological* stage was the first, and it characterized the world prior to 1300. During this period the major idea system emphasized the belief that supernatural powers, religious figures modeled after humankind, were at the root of everything. In particular, the social and physical world was seen as produced by God. The second stage was the *metaphysical* stage, which occurred roughly between 1300 and 1800. This era was characterized by the belief that abstract forces like "nature," rather than personalized gods, explain virtually everything. Finally, in 1800 the world entered the *positivistic* stage, characterized by belief in science. People now tended to give up the search for absolute causes (God or nature) and concentrated instead on observation of the social and physical world in the search for the laws governing them.

It is clear that in his theory of the world Comte focused on intellectual factors. Indeed, he argued that intellectual disorder was the cause of social disorder. The disorder stemmed from earlier idea systems (theological and metaphysical) that continued to exist in the positivistic (scientific) age. Only when positivism gained total control would social upheavals cease. Since this was an evolutionary process, there was no need to foment social upheaval and revolution. Positivism would come, although perhaps not as quickly as some would like. Here Comte's social reformism and his sociology coincide. Sociology could help expedite the arrival of positivism and hence bring order to the social world. Above all, Comte did not want to seem to be espousing revolution. There was, in his view, enough disorder in the world. In any case, from Comte's point of view it was intellectual change that was needed, so there was little reason for social and political revolution.

We have already encountered several of Comte's positions that were to be of great significance to the development of sociology—his basic conservatism, reformism, and scientism, and his evolutionary view of the world. Several other aspects of his work deserve mention since they also were to play a major role in the development of sociology. For example, his sociology does *not* focus on the individual but rather takes as its basic unit of analysis larger entities such as the family. He also urged that we look at *both* social structure and social change. Of great importance to later sociological theory, especially structural functionalism, is Comte's stress on the systematic character of society—the links among and between the various components of society. He also accorded great importance to the role of consensus in society. He saw little merit in the idea that society is characterized by inevitable conflict between workers and capitalists. In addition, Comte emphasized the need to go out and do sociological research rather than engage in abstract theorizing. He urged that sociologists use experimentation and comparative-historical analysis. Finally, Comte was an elitist; he believed that sociology would ultimately become the dominant scientific force in the world because of its distinctive ability to interpret social laws and to develop reforms aimed at patching up problems within the system.

Comte published his most important works between 1830 and 1854. Although he was a prolific writer, Comte never held a regular academic post, and his occasional part-time employment at the Ecole Polytechnique came to an end, rather typically for him, after a row with its administrators. Comte lived a good portion of his life in poverty, surviving on the money earned by his prostitute wife and on donations from scholars such as John Stuart Mill (Andreski, 1974). Even though Comte lacked a solid academic base on which to build a school of Comtian sociological theory, he nevertheless laid a basis for the development of a significant stream of sociological theory. But his long-term significance pales in comparison with that of his successor in French sociology and the inheritor of a number of his ideas, Emile Durkheim.

EMILE DURKHEIM (1858–1917)   Although for Durkheim, as for Comte, the Enlightenment was a negative influence, it also had a number of positive effects on his work (for example, the emphasis on science and social reformism). However, Durkheim is best seen as the inheritor of the conservative tradition, especially as it was manifested in Comte's work. But while Comte had remained outside of academia, Durkheim developed an increasingly solid academic base as his career progressed. It was Durkheim who legitimized sociology in France and whose work ultimately became a dominant force in the development of sociology in general and of sociological theory in particular.

EMILE DURKHEIM: A Biographical Sketch

Emile Durkheim was born on April 15, 1858, in Epinal, France. He was descended from a long line of rabbis and himself studied to be a rabbi, but by the time he was in his teens he had rejected his heritage and become an agnostic. From that time on, his lifelong interest in religion was academic rather than theological. He was dissatisfied not only with his religious training but also with his general education and its emphasis on literary and esthetic matters. He longed for schooling in scientific methods and in the moral principles needed to guide social life. He rejected a traditional academic career in philosophy and sought instead to acquire the scientific training needed to contribute to the moral guidance of society. Although he was interested in scientific sociology, there was no field of sociology at that time, so between 1882 and 1887 he taught philosophy in a number of provincial schools in the Paris area.

His appetite for science was whetted further by a trip to Germany, where he was exposed to the scientific psychology being pioneered by Wilhelm Wundt. In the years immediately after his visit to Germany, Durkheim published a good deal, basing his work, in part, on his experiences there. These publications helped him gain a position in the department of philosophy at the University of Bordeaux in 1887. There Durkheim offered the first course in social science in a French university. This was a particularly impressive accomplishment, since only a decade earlier a furor had been caused in a French university by the mention of Auguste Comte in a student dissertation. Durkheim's main responsibility, however, was the teaching of courses in education to schoolteachers, and his most important course was in the area of moral education. His goal was to communicate a moral system to the educators, who he hoped would then pass it on to young people in an effort to help reverse the moral degeneration he saw around him in French society.

The years that followed were characterized by a series of personal successes for Durkheim. In 1893 he published his French doctoral thesis, *The Division of Labor in Society*, as well as his Latin thesis on Montesquieu and Rousseau. His major methodo-

Durkheim was politically liberal, but he took a more conservative position intellectually. Like Comte and the Catholic counterrevolutionaries, Durkheim feared and hated social disorder. In fact, most of his work was devoted to the study of social order His view was that social disorders were *not* a necessary part of the modern world and could be reduced by social reforms. While Marx saw the problems of the modern world as inherent in society, Durkheim (along with Comte, Weber, and others) did not. As a result Marx's ideas on the need for social revolution stood in sharp contrast to the reformism of Durkheim and the others. As sociological theory developed, it was the Durkheimian interest in order and reform that came to dominate, while the Marxian position was eclipsed for many years.

In two books published in the late 1800s, Durkheim developed a distinctive conception of the subject matter of sociology and then tested it in an empirical study. In *The Rules of Sociological Method* (1895/1964) Durkheim argued that it is the special task

logical statement, *The Rules of Sociological Method,* appeared in 1895, followed (in 1897) by his empirical application of those methods in the study of *Suicide*. By 1896 he had become full professor at Bordeaux. In 1902 he was summoned to the famous French university, the Sorbonne, and in 1906 he was named professor of the science of education, a title that was changed in 1913 to professor of the science of education *and sociology*. The other of his most famous works, *The Elementary Forms of Religious Life*, was published in 1912.

Durkheim is most often thought of today as a political conservative, and his influence within sociology has certainly been a conservative one. But in his time he was considered a liberal, and this was exemplified by the active public role he played in the defense of Alfred Dreyfus, the Jewish army captain whose court-martial for treason was felt by many to be a result of anti-Semitism. To Durkheim, this was an outrage against individual rights that reflected the broader moral crisis in society, and he played an active role in Dreyfus's defense.

Durkheim's interest in socialism is also taken as evidence against the idea that he was a conservative, but his kind of socialism was very different from the kind that interested Marx and his followers. In fact, Durkheim labeled Marxism as a set of "disputable and out-of-date hypotheses" (Lukes, 1972:323). To Durkheim, socialism represented a movement aimed at the moral regeneration of society through scientific morality, and he was not interested in short-term political methods or the economic aspects of socialism. He did not see the proletariat as the salvation of society, and he was greatly opposed to agitation or violence. Socialism for Durkheim was very different from what we usually think of as socialism; it simply represented a system in which the moral principles discovered by scientific sociology were to be applied.

Durkheim, as we will see throughout this book, had a profound influence on the development of sociology, but his influence was not restricted to it. Much of his impact on other fields came through the journal *L'annee sociologique*, which he founded in 1898. An intellectual circle arose around the journal with Durkheim at its center. Through it, he and his ideas influenced such fields as anthropology, history, linguistics, and —somewhat ironically, considering his early attacks on the field—psychology.

Durkheim died on November 15, 1916, a celebrated figure in French intellectual circles, but it was not until over twenty years later, with the publication of Talcott Parsons's *The Structure of Social Action* (1937), that he became a significant influence on American sociology.

of sociology to study what he called *social facts*. He conceived of social facts as forces and structures that are external to, and coercive of, the individual. The study of these large-scale structures and forces—for example, institutionalized law and shared moral beliefs—and their impact on people became the concern of many later sociological theorists. Durkheim was not content simply to define the subject matter of sociology; he sought through sociological research (Durkheim, 1897/1951) to demonstrate the utility of such a focus. He chose as his subject suicide. He reasoned that if he could link such an individual behavior as suicide to social causes (social facts), he would have made a persuasive case for the importance of the discipline of sociology. But Durkheim did not examine why individual *A* or *B* committed suicide; rather he was interested in the causes of differences in suicide rates among groups, regions, countries, and different categories of people (for example, married and single). His basic argument was that it was the nature of, and changes in, social facts that led to differences in suicide rates. For example, a war or an economic depression would create a collective mood of depression that would in turn lead to increases in suicide rates. There is much more to be said on this subject, but the key point for our purposes here is that Durkheim developed a distinctive view of sociology and sought to demonstrate its usefulness in a scientific study of suicide.

In *The Rules of Sociological Method* Durkheim differentiated between two types of social facts—material and nonmaterial. Although he dealt with both in the course of his work, his main focus was on *nonmaterial social facts* (for example, culture, social institutions) rather than *material social facts* (for example, bureaucracy, law). This concern for nonmaterial social facts was already clear in his earliest major work, *The Division of Labor in Society* (1893/1964). His focus there was a comparative analysis of what held society together in the primitive and modern cases. He concluded that earlier societies were held together primarily by nonmaterial social facts, specifically, a strongly held common morality, or what he called a strong "collective conscience." However because of the complexities of modern society, there had been a decline in the strength of the collective conscience. The primary bond in the modern world was an intricate division of labor, which tied people to others in dependency relationships. However, Durkheim felt that the modern division of labor brought with it several "pathologies"; it was, in other words, an inadequate method of holding society together. Given his conservative sociology, Durkheim did not feel that revolution was needed to solve these problems. Rather, he suggested a variety of reforms that could "patch up" the modern system and keep it functioning. Although he recognized that there was no going back to the age when a powerful collective conscience predominated, he did feel that the common morality could be strengthened in modern society and that people could thereby cope better with the pathologies they were experiencing.

In his later work nonmaterial social facts occupied an even more central position. In fact, he came to focus on perhaps the ultimate form of a nonmaterial social fact—religion—in his last major work, *The Elementary Forms of Religious Life* (1912/1965). In this work Durkheim examined primitive society in order to find the roots of religion. He believed that he would be better able to find those roots in the comparative simplicity of primitive society than in the complexity of the modern world. What he found, he felt, was that the source of religion was society itself. Society comes to define certain things as religious and others as profane. Specifically, in the case he studied, the clan was the source of a primitive kind of religion, *totemism*. Totemism, in turn, was seen as a specific type of nonmaterial social fact, a form of the collective conscience. In the end Durkheim came to argue that society and religion (or, more generally, the collective conscience) were one and the same. Religion was the way society expressed itself in the form of a nonmaterial social fact. In a sense, then, Durkheim came to deify society and its major products. Clearly, in deifying society Durkheim took a highly conservative stance: one would not want to overturn a deity *or* its societal source. Since he identified society with God, Durkheim was not inclined to urge social revolution. Instead, he was a social reformer seeking ways of improving the functioning of society. In these and other ways Durkheim was clearly in line with French conservative sociology. The fact that he avoided many of its excesses made him the most significant figure in French sociology.

Karl Marx and the Development of German Sociology

While the early history of French sociology is a fairly coherent story of the progression from the Enlightenment and the French Revolution to the conservative reaction and to the increasingly important sociological ideas of Saint-Simon, Comte, and Durkheim, German sociology was fragmented from the beginning. A split developed between Marx (and his supporters), who remained on the edge of sociology, and the early giants of mainstream German sociology, Max Weber and Georg Simmel. However, although Marxian theory itself was deemed unacceptable, its ideas found their way in a variety of positive and negative ways into mainstream German sociology. Our discussion here will be divided between Marxian and non-Marxian theory in Germany.

THE ROOTS OF MARXIAN THEORY

The dominant intellectual influence on Karl Marx was the German philosopher G. W. F. Hegel (1770–1831). Marx's education at the University of Berlin was shaped by Hegel's ideas as well as by the split that developed among Hegel's followers after his death. The "Old Hegelians" continued to subscribe to the master's ideas while the "Young Hegelians," although still working in the Hegelian tradition, were critical of many facets of his philosophical system. Among the Young Hegelians was Ludwig Feuerbach (1804–1872), who tried to revise Hegel's ideas. Marx was influenced by both Hegel's ideas and Feuerbach's revisions, but he extended and combined the two philosophies in a novel and insightful way.

Two concepts represent the essence of Hegel's philosophy—the dialectic and idealism. The idea of the dialectic is very complicated, but a few introductory words are needed at this point. The *dialectic* is both a way of thinking and an image of the world. On the one hand, it is a way of thinking that stresses the importance of processes, relations, dynamics, conflicts, and contradictions—a dynamic rather than a static way of thinking about the world. On the other hand, it is a view that the *world* is made up not of static structures but of processes, relationships, dynamics, conflicts, and contradictions. Although the dialectic is generally associated with Hegel, it certainly predates him in philosophy. Marx, trained in the Hegelian tradition, accepted the significance of the dialectic. However, he was critical of some aspects of the way Hegel used it. For example, Hegel tended to apply the dialectic only to ideas while Marx felt that it applied as well to more material aspects of life, for example, the economy.

Hegel is also associated with the philosophy of *idealism*, which emphasizes the importance of the mind and mental products rather than the material world. It is the social definition of the physical and material worlds that matters most, not those worlds themselves. In its extreme form, idealism asserts that *only* the mind and psychological constructs exist. Some idealists believed that their mental processes would remain the same even if the physical and social worlds no longer existed. Idealists emphasize not only mental processes but also the ideas produced by these processes. Hegel paid a great deal of attention to the development of such ideas, especially to what he referred to as the "spirit" of society.

In fact, Hegel offered a kind of evolutionary theory of the world in idealistic terms. At first, people were endowed only with the ability to acquire a sensory understanding of the world around them. They could understand things like the sight, smell, and feel of the social and physical world. Later, people developed the ability to be conscious of, to understand, themselves. With self-knowledge and self-understanding people began to understand that they could become more than they were. In terms of Hegel's dialectical approach, a contradiction developed between what people were and what they now felt they could be. The resolution of this contradiction lay in the development of an individual's awareness of his or her place in the larger spirit of society. Individuals come to realize that their ultimate fulfillment lies in the development and the expansion of the spirit of society as a whole. Thus, individuals in Hegel's scheme evolve from an understanding of things, to an understanding of self, to an understanding of their place in the larger scheme of things.

Hegel, then, offered a general theory of the evolution of the world. It is a subjective theory in which change is held to occur at the level of consciousness. However, that change occurs largely beyond the control of actors. Actors are reduced to little more than vessels swept along by the inevitable evolution of consciousness.

Ludwig Feuerbach was an important bridge between Hegel and Marx. As a Young Hegelian, Feuerbach was critical of Hegel for, among other things, his excessive emphasis on consciousness and the spirit of society. Feuerbach's adoption of a materialist philosophy led him to argue that what was needed was to move from Hegel's subjective idealism to a focus not on ideas but on the material reality of real human beings. In his critique of Hegel, Feuerbach focused on religion. To Feuerbach, God is simply a projection by people of their human essence onto an impersonal force. People set God over and above themselves, with the result that they become alienated from God and project a series of positive characteristics onto God (perfect, almighty, and holy) while they reduce themselves to being imperfect, powerless, and sinful. Feuerbach argued that this kind of religion must be overcome and that its defeat could be aided by a materialist philosophy in which people (not religion) became their own highest object, an end in themselves. Real people, not abstract ideas like religion, are deified by a materialist philosophy.

Marx was simultaneously influenced by, and critical of, *both* Hegel and Feuerbach. Marx, following Feuerbach, was critical of Hegel's adherence to an idealist philosophy. Marx took this position not only because of his adoption of a materialist orientation but also because of his interest in practical activities. Social facts like wealth and the state are treated by Hegel as ideas rather than as real, material entities. Even when he examined a seemingly material process like labor, Hegel was looking only at abstract mental labor. This is very different from Marx's interest in the labor of real, sensuous people. Thus Hegel was looking at the wrong issues as far as Marx was concerned. In addition, Marx felt that Hegel's idealism led to a very conservative political orientation. To Hegel, the process of evolution was occurring beyond the control of people and their activities. In any case, since people seemed to be moving toward greater consciousness of the world as it could be potentially, there seemed no need for any revolutionary change; the process was already moving in the ''desired'' direction. Whatever problems did exist lay in consciousness, and the answer therefore seemed to lie in changing thinking.

Marx took a very different position, arguing that the problems of modern life can be traced to real, material sources (for example, the structures of capitalism), and the solutions, therefore, can *only* be found in the overturning of those structures by the collective action of large numbers of people. Here is the way Marx put his basic critique of Hegel:

> Hegel makes man *the man of self-consciousness* instead of making self-consciousness the *self-consciousness of man,* man living in a real objective world determined by that world. He stands the world *on its head* and can therefore dissolve *in the head* all of the limitations which naturally remain in existence . . . for *real man.*
>
> (Marx and Engels, 1845/1956:254)

While Hegel stood the world on its head (that is, focused on consciousness, not the real material world), Marx firmly embedded his dialectic in a material base.

Marx applauded Feuerbach's critique of Hegel on a number of counts (for example, its materialism and its rejection of the abstractness of Hegel's theory), but he was far from fully satisfied with Feuerbach's own position. For one thing, Feuerbach focused on the religious world while Marx believed that it was the entire social world, and the economy in particular, that must be analyzed. Although Marx accepted Feuerbach's materialism, he felt that Feuerbach had gone too far in focusing one-sidedly, nondialectically, on the material world. Feuerbach failed to include the most important of Hegel's contributions, the dialectic, in his materialist orientation, particularly the relationship between people and the material world. Finally, Marx argued that Feuerbach, like most philosophers, failed to emphasize praxis—practical activity—in particular, revolutionary activity. As Marx (cited in Tucker, 1970:109) put it, "The philosophers have only *interpreted* the world, in various ways; the point, however, is to *change* it."

Marx extracted what he considered to be the two most important elements from these two thinkers—Hegel's dialectic and Feuerbach's materialism—and fused them into his own distinctive orientation, *dialectical materialism*, which focuses on dialectical relationships within the material world.

Marx's materialism, and his consequent focus on the economic sector, led him rather naturally to the work of a group of *political economists* (for example, Adam Smith and David Ricardo). Marx was very attracted to a number of their positions. He lauded their basic premise that labor was the source of all wealth. This ultimately led Marx to his *labor theory of value,* in which he argued that the profit of the capitalist was based on the exploitation of the laborer. Capitalists performed the rather simple trick of paying the workers less than they deserved, because they received less pay than the value of what they actually produced in a work period. This *surplus value,* which was retained and reinvested by the capitalist, was the basis of the entire capitalist system. The capitalist system grew by continually increasing the level of exploitation of the workers (and therefore the amount of surplus value) and investing the profits in the expansion of the capitalist system.

Marx was also affected by the political economists' depiction of the horrors of the capitalist system and the exploitation of the workers. However, while they depicted the evils of capitalism, Marx criticized the political economists for seeing these evils as inevitable components of capitalism. Marx deplored their general acceptance of capitalism and the way they urged people to work for economic success within it. He was also critical of the political economists for failing to see the inherent conflict between capitalists and laborers and for denying the need for a radical change in the economic order. Such conservative economics was obviously hard for Marx to accept, given his commitment to a radical change from capitalism to socialism. With this intellectual background, we can turn briefly to Marx himself and to the reasons for the negative reaction to him among mainstream sociologists.

KARL MARX (1818−1883)   Marx was not a sociologist and did not consider himself to be one. While his work is too broad to be encompassed by the term "sociology," there *is* a sociology to be found in Marx's work. From the beginning, there were those who were heavily influenced by Marx, and there has been a continuous strand of Marxian sociology, primarily in Europe, but for the majority of early sociologists his work was a negative force, something against which to shape their sociology. Until very recently, sociological theory, especially in America, has been characterized by either hostility to, or ignorance of, Marxian theory. This has, as we will see, changed dramatically in the last decade or two, but the negative reaction to Marx's work was a major force in the shaping of much of sociological theory (Gurney, 1981).

KARL MARX: A Biographical Sketch

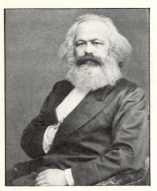

Kark Marx was born in Trier, Prussia, on May 5, 1818. His father, a lawyer, provided the family with a fairly typical middle-class existence. Both parents were from rabbinical families, but for business reasons the father had converted to Lutheranism.

In 1841 Marx received his doctorate in philosophy from the University of Berlin, a school heavily influenced by Hegel and his critics, the Young Hegelians. Marx's doctorate was a dry philosophical treatise that bore little resemblance to his later, more radical and more pragmatic work. After graduation he became a writer for a liberal-radical newspaper and within ten months had become its editor-in-chief. However, because of its political positions the paper was closed shortly thereafter by the government. The early essays published in this period began to reflect a number of the positions that would guide Marx throughout his life. They were liberally sprinkled with democratic principles, humanism, and idealism. He rejected the abstractness of Hegelian philosophy, the naive dreaming of utopian communists, and those activists who were urging what he considered to be premature political action. In rejecting these activists, Marx laid the groundwork for his own life's work:

> Practical attempts, even by the masses, can be answered with a cannon as soon as they become dangerous, but ideas that have overcome our intellect and conquered our conviction, ideas to which reason has riveted our conscience, are chains from which one cannot break loose without breaking one's heart; they are demons that one can only overcome by submitting to them.

(Marx, 1842/1977:20)

Marx married in 1843 and soon thereafter left Germany for the more liberal atmosphere of Paris. There he continued to grapple with the ideas of Hegel and the Young Hegelians, but he also encountered two new sets of ideas—French socialism and

The basic reason for this rejection of Marx was ideological. Many of the early socio-logical theorists were inheritors of the conservative reaction to the disruptions of the Enlightenment and the French Revolution. Marx's radical ideas and the radical social changes he foretold and sought to bring to life were clearly feared and hated by such thinkers. Marx was dismissed as an ideologist. It was argued that he was not a serious sociological theorist. However, ideology per se could not have been the real reason for the rejection of Marx, since the work of Comte, Durkheim, and other conservative thinkers was also heavily ideological. It was the nature of the ideology, not the exist-ence of ideology as such, that put off many sociological theorists. They were ready and eager to buy conservative ideology wrapped in a cloak of sociological theory, but not the radical ideology offered by Marx and his followers.

There were, of course, other reasons why Marx was not accepted by many early theorists. He seemed to be more an economist than a sociologist. While the early soci-ologists would certainly admit the importance of the economy, they would also argue that it was only one of a number of components of social life.

Another reason for the early rejection of Marx was the nature of his interests. While the early sociologists were reacting to the disorder created by the Enlightenment, the

---

English political economy. It was the unique way in which he combined Hegelianism, socialism, and political economy that shaped his intellectual orientation. Also of great importance at this point was meeting the man who was to become his lifelong friend, benefactor, and collaborator—Friedrich Engels. The son of a textile manufacturer, Engels had become a socialist critical of the conditions facing the working class. Much of Marx's compassion for the misery of the working class came from his exposure to Engels and his ideas. During this period Marx produced academic works (many unpublished in his lifetime) that were mainly concerned with sorting out his link to the Hegelian tradition (for example, *The Holy Family* and *The German Ideology*), but he also produced *The Economic and Philosophic Manuscripts of 1844,* which better inte-grated all of the intellectual traditions in which he was immersed and which fore-shadowed his increasing preoccupation with the economic domain.

Because some of his writings had upset the Prussian government, the French gov-ernment (at the request of the Prussians) expelled Marx, and he moved to Brussels. His radicalism was growing, and he had become an active member of the international revolutionary movement. He also associated with the Communist League and was asked to write a document (with Engels) expounding its aims and beliefs. The result was the *Communist Manifesto* of 1848, a work that was characterized by ringing political slogans.

In 1849 Marx moved to London, and, in light of the failures of the political revolutions of 1848, he began to withdraw from active revolutionary activity and to move into serious and detailed research on the workings of the capitalist system. In 1852 he began his famous studies in the British Museum of the working conditions in capitalism. These studies ultimately resulted in the three volumes of *Capital,* the first of which was published in 1867, while the other two were published posthumously. He lived in pov-erty during these years, barely managing to survive on a small income from his writings and the support of Engels. In 1863 Marx began to become reinvolved in political activ-ity by joining the *International,* an international movement of workers. He soon gained dominance within the movement and devoted a number of years to it. He began to gain fame both as leader of the *International* and as the author of *Capital.* But the disintegration of the *International* by 1876, the failure of various revolutionary move-ments, and personal illness took their toll on Marx. His wife died in 1881, a daughter in 1882, and Marx himself on March 14, 1883.

French Revolution, and later the Industrial Revolution, Marx was not upset by these disorders—or by disorder in general. Rather, what interested and concerned Marx most was the oppressiveness of the capitalist system that was emerging out of the Industrial Revolution. Marx wanted to develop a theory that explained this oppressiveness and that would help overthrow that system. Marx's interest was in revolution, which stood in contrast to the conservative concern for reform and orderly change.

Another difference worth noting is the difference in philosophical roots between Marxian and conservative sociological theory. Most of the conservative theorists were heavily influenced by the philosophy of Immanuel Kant. Among other things, this led them to think in linear, cause-and-effect terms. That is, they tended to argue that a change in *A* (say, the change in ideas during the Enlightenment) leads to a change in *B* (say, the political changes of the French Revolution). In contrast, Marx was most heavily influenced, as we have seen, by Hegel, who thought in dialectical rather than cause-and-effect terms. Among other things, the dialectic attunes us to the ongoing reciprocal effects of social forces. Thus, a dialectician would reconceptualize the example discussed above as a continual, ongoing interplay of ideas and politics. It is admittedly difficult to get a feel for the complicated differences between Kantian and Hegelian philosophy, but the crucial point for our purposes is that these basic philosophical differences were an important source of the negative reaction of early sociological theorists to Marxian theory.

Many volumes have been written about the substance of Marx's theory; in fact, the theory itself is found in a number of volumes written by Marx over a period of many years. Thus, as is the case with most major theorists, we cannot do justice to Marx's theory in a few paragraphs. But in order to orient the reader we need to say something substantive, albeit sketchy, about his theory at this point.

To oversimplify enormously, Marx offered a theory of capitalist society based on his image of the basic nature of human beings. Marx believed that people are basically productive; that is, in order to survive people need to work in, and with, nature. In so doing they produce the food, clothing, tools, shelter, and other necessities that permit them to live. Their productivity is a perfectly natural way by which they express basic creative impulses. Furthermore, these impulses are expressed in concert with other people; in other words, people are inherently social. They need to work together in order to produce what they need to survive.

Throughout history this natural process has been subverted, at first by the mean conditions of primitive society and later by a variety of structural arrangements erected by societies in the course of history. In various ways these structures interfered with the natural productive process. However, it is in capitalist society that this breakdown is most acute; the breakdown in the natural productive process reaches its culmination in capitalism.

Basically capitalism is a structure (or, more accurately, a series of structures) that erects barriers between an individual and the production process, the products of that process, and other people; ultimately, it even divides the individual himself. This is the basic meaning of the concept of *alienation*: it is the breakdown of the natural interconnection between people and between people and what they produce. Alienation occurs because capitalism has evolved into a two-class system in which a few capitalists own the production process, the products, and the labor time of those who work for them. Instead of naturally producing for themselves, people produce unnaturally in capitalist society for a small group of capitalists. Intellectually Marx was very concerned with the structures of capitalism and their oppressive impact on actors. Politically he was led to an interest in emancipating people from the oppressive structures of capitalism.

This brings us to Marx's ideas on the future state of socialism. Marx actually spent very little time dreaming about what a utopian socialist state would look like. He was more concerned with helping bring about the demise of capitalism. He believed that the contradictions and conflicts within capitalism would lead dialectically to its ultimate collapse, but he did not think the process was inevitable. People had to act at the appropriate times and in the appropriate ways in order for socialism to come into being. The capitalists have great resources at their disposal to forestall the coming of socialism, but they could be overcome by the concerted action of a class-conscious proletariat. What would the proletariat create in the process? What is socialism? Most basically it is a society in which for the first time people could approach Marx's ideal image of productivity. With the aid of modern technology, people could interact harmoniously with nature and other people to create what they needed to survive. To put it another way, in socialist society people would no longer be alienated.

THE ROOTS OF GERMAN SOCIOLOGY

Although Marx and his followers in the late nineteenth and early twentieth century remained outside of mainstream German sociology, to a considerable extent early German sociology can be seen as developing in opposition to Marxian theory. In the view of some, this explains a large part of the theory of the early giant of German sociology, Max Weber. Albert Salomon (1945:596), for example, claimed that Weberian theory developed ''in a long and intense debate with the ghost of Marx.'' This is probably an exaggeration, but in many ways Marxian theory did play a negative role in Weberian theory. In other ways, however, Weber was working *within* the Marxian tradition, trying to ''round out'' Marx's theory. Also, there were many inputs into Weberian theory other than Marxian theory (Burger, 1976). We can clarify a good deal about the sources of German sociology by outlining each of these views of the relationship between Marx and Weber.

Weber *did* tend to view Marx and the Marxists of his day as economic determinists who offered single-cause theories of social life. That is, Marxian theory was seen as tracing all historical developments to economic bases and viewing all contemporaneous structures as erected on an economic base. While this is not true of Marx's own theory, it was the position of many later Marxists.

One of the examples of economic determinism that seemed to rankle Weber most was the view that ideas are simply the reflections of material (especially economic) interests, that material interests determine ideology. From this point of view, Weber was supposed to have ''turned Marx on his head'' (much as Marx had done to Hegel). Instead of focusing on economic factors and their effect of ideas, Weber devoted much of his attention to ideas and their effect on the economy. Rather than seeing ideas as simple reflections of economic factors, Weber saw them as fairly autonomous forces capable of having a profound effect on the economic world. Weber certainly devoted a lot

of attention to ideas, particularly systems of religious ideas, and he was especially concerned with the impact of religious ideas on the economy. In *The Protestant Ethic*
(1904–1905) he was concerned with Protestantism, mainly as a system of ideas, and its
impact on the rise of another system of ideas, the ''spirit of capitalism,'' and ultimately
on a capitalist economic system. Weber had a similar interest in other world religions,
looking at how their nature might have obstructed the development of capitalism in
their respective societies. On the basis of this kind of work some scholars came to the
conclusion that Weber developed his ideas in opposition to those of Marx.

A second view of Weber's relationship to Marx, as mentioned earlier, is that he did
not so much oppose Marx as try to round out his theoretical perspective. Here Weber is
seen as working more within the Marxian tradition than in opposition to it. His work on
religion, interpreted from this point of view, was simply an effort to show that not only
do material factors affect ideas, but ideas themselves affect material structures. This interpretation of Weber's work obviously places it much closer to, in fact in line with,
Marxian theory.

A good example of the view that Weber was engaged in a process of rounding out
Marxian theory is in the area of stratification theory. In his work on stratification, Marx
focused on social *class,* the economic dimension of stratification. While Weber accepted the importance of this factor, he argued that other dimensions of stratification
were also important. He argued that the notion of social stratification should be extended
to include stratification on the basis of prestige (*status*) and *power*. The inclusion of
these other dimensions does not constitute a refutation of Marx but is simply an extension of his ideas.

Both of the views outlined above accept the importance of Marxian theory for Weber.
There are elements of truth in both positions; at some points Weber *was* working in opposition to Marx, while at other points he was extending Marx's ideas. However, a
third view of this issue may best characterize the relationship between Marx and Weber.
In this view, Marx is simply seen as but one of many influences on Weber's thought.

We can identify a number of sources of Weberian theory, including German
historians, philosophers, economists, and political theorists. Among those who influenced Weber, the philosopher Immanuel Kant (1724–1804) stands out above all the
others. But we must not overlook the impact of Friedrich Nietzsche (1844–1900)—especially his emphasis on the hero—on Weber's work on the need for individuals to
stand up to the impact of bureaucracies and other structures of modern society.

The influence of Immanuel Kant on Weber, and on German sociology generally,
shows that German sociology and Marxism flowed from different philosophical roots.
As we have seen, it was Hegel, not Kant, who was the important philosophical influence on Marxian theory. While Hegel's philosophy led Marx and the Marxists to look
for relations, conflict, and contradictions, Kantian philosophy led at least some German sociologists in a more static direction. To Kant the world was a buzzing confusion
of events that could never be known directly. The world could only be known through
thought processes that filter, select, and categorize these events. The content of the real
world was differentiated by Kant from the forms through which that content can be
comprehended. The emphasis on these forms gave the work of those sociologists
within the Kantian tradition a more static quality than that of the Marxists within the
Hegelian tradition.

German sociology emerged in a complex interplay with Marxian theory and a variety of other intellectual currents. The foremost exponents of early German sociology are two figures whom we need to deal with in a little more detail at this point—Max Weber and Georg Simmel.

MAX WEBER (1864–1920) While Karl Marx offered basically a theory of capitalism, Weber's work was fundamentally a theory of the process of rationalization (Kalberg, 1980). *Rationalization* was fundamentally a process by which the modern Western world came to emphasize acting in the most efficient manner to achieve its goals. Weber was interested in the general issue of why institutions in the Western world had grown progressively more rational while powerful barriers seemed to prevent a similar development in the rest of the world.

Weber developed his theories in the context of a large number of comparative-historical studies he undertook of the West, China, India, and many other regions of the world. In these studies he sought to delineate the factors that helped bring about, or impede, the development of rationalization.

Weber never offered a simple definition of rationalization; in fact, at one point or another in his work it encompassed a number of types (Kalberg, 1980) and subdimensions (Eisen, 1978). But rationalization was most frequently taken to mean a progressive emphasis on efficiency, calculability, and demystification as well as the resulting dehumanization of life. In emphasizing *efficiency*, a society focuses on the quickest and most direct route from one point to another. *Calculability* means an interest in predictability as well as in those things that can be quantified as opposed to the more qualitative aspects of life. *Demystification* implies the elimination of magical elements from society and their replacement by more logical components. Finally, rationalization leads to progressive *dehumanization*; we become preoccupied with getting the most from the least effort; we care less and less about the negative impact of such policies on people. Weber saw the bureaucracy as a classic example of rationalization, but rationalization is perhaps best illustrated today by the Nazi concentration camp. The emphasis there was on dispatching as many people as possible in the most efficient manner, and the result was perhaps the ultimate expression of dehumanization—the murdering of millions of people in the most demeaning of circumstances. Although Weber saw many positive characteristics in rationalization, he perhaps foresaw the development of such things as concentration camps and sought to warn his readers by emphasizing its negative effects.

Weber embedded his discussion of the process of bureaucratization in a broader discussion of the political institution. He differentiated between three types of authority systems—traditional, charismatic, and rational-legal. Only in the modern Western world can a rational-legal authority system develop, and only within that system does one find the full-scale development of the modern bureaucracy. The rest of the world remains dominated by traditional or charismatic authority systems, which generally impede the development of a rational-legal authority system and modern bureaucracies. Briefly, *traditional* authority stems from a long-lasting system of beliefs. An example would be a leader who comes to power because his or her family or clan has always provided the group's leadership. A *charismatic* leader derives his or her authority from extraordinary abilities or characteristics, or more likely simply from the *belief* on the part of followers that the leader has such traits. While these two types of authority are of historical importance, Weber believed that the trend in the West, and ultimately in

MAX WEBER: A Biographical Sketch

Max Weber was born in Erfurt, Germany, on April 21, 1864, into a decidedly middle-class family. There were important differences between his parents that had a profound effect upon both his intellectual orientation and his psychological development. His father was a bureaucrat who rose to a relatively important political position. He was clearly a part of the political establishment and as a result eschewed any activity or idealism that would require personal sacrifice or threaten his position within the system. In addition, the senior Weber was a man who enjoyed earthly pleasures, and in this and many other ways he stood in sharp contrast to his wife. Max Weber's mother was a deeply religious woman, a devout Calvinist, a woman who sought to lead an ascetic life largely devoid of the pleasures craved by her husband. Her concerns were more otherworldly; she was disturbed by the imperfections that were signs that she was not destined for salvation. These deep differences between the parents led to marital tension, and both the differences and the tension had an immense impact on Weber.

Since it was impossible to emulate both parents, Weber was presented with a clear choice as a child. He first seemed to opt for his father's orientation to life, but later he drew closer to his mother's approach. Whatever the choice, the tension produced by the need to choose between such polar opposites negatively affected Max Weber's psyche.

At age eighteen Max Weber left home for a short time to attend the University of Heidelberg. Weber had already demonstrated intellectual precocity, but on a social level he entered Heidelberg shy and underdeveloped. However, that quickly changed after he gravitated toward his father's way of life and joined his father's old dueling fraternity. There he developed socially and physically, at least in part because of the huge quantities of beer he consumed. In addition, he proudly displayed the dueling scars that were the trademarks of such fraternities. Weber not only manifested his identity with his father's way of life in these ways, but also chose, at least for the time being, the same career—the law.

After three terms Weber left Heidelberg for military service, and in 1884 he returned to Berlin and to his parents' home to take courses at the University of Berlin. He remained there for most of the next eight years as he completed his studies, earned his Ph.D., became a lawyer, and started teaching at the University of Berlin. In the process his in-

the rest of the world, is toward systems of *rational-legal* authority. In such systems authority is derived from rules legally and rationally enacted. Thus, the president of the United States derives his authority ultimately from the laws of society. The evolution of rational-legal authority, with its accompanying bureaucracies, is but one part of Weber's general argument on the rationalization of the Western world.

Weber also did detailed and sophisticated analyses of the rationalization of such phenomena as religion, law, the city, and even music. But we can illustrate Weber's mode of thinking with one other example—the rationalization of the economic institution. This discussion is couched in Weber's broader analysis of the relationship terests shifted more toward his lifelong concerns—economics, history, and sociology. During his eight years in Berlin, Weber was financially dependent on his father, a circumstance he progressively grew to dislike. At the same time he moved closer to his mother's values, and his antipathy to his father increased. He adopted an ascetic life style and plunged deeply into his work. For example, during one semester as a student his work habits were described as follows: "He continues the rigid work discipline, regulates his life by the clock, divides the daily routine into exact sections for the various subjects, saves in his way, by feeding himself evenings in his room with a pound of raw chopped beef and four fried eggs" (Mitzman, 1970:48). Thus Weber, following his mother, had become ascetic and diligent, a compulsive worker—in contemporary terms a "workaholic."

This compulsion for work led in 1896 to a position as professor of economics at Heidelberg. But in 1897, with Weber's academic career blossoming, his father died following a violent argument between them. Shortly thereafter Weber began to manifest symptoms that were to culminate in a nervous breakdown. Often unable to sleep or to work, Weber spent the next six or seven years in near-total collapse. After a long hiatus, some of his powers began to return in 1903, but it was not until 1904, when he delivered his first lecture in six and one-half years (in the United States), that Weber was able to begin to return to active academic life. In 1904 and 1905 he published one of his best-known works, *The Protestant Ethic and the Spirit of Capitalism*. It was in this work that Weber announced the ascendance of his mother's religion on an academic level. Weber devoted much of his time to the study of religion, though he was not personally religious.

Although he continued to be plagued by psychological problems, after 1904 Weber was able to function, indeed to produce some of his most important work. In these years Weber published his studies of the world's religions in world-historical perspective (for example, China, India, and ancient Judaism). At the time of his death (June 14, 1920), he was working on his most important work, *Economy and Society*. Although this book was published, and subsequently translated into many languages, it was unfinished.

In addition to the voluminous writings produced in this period, Weber undertook a number of other activities. He helped found the German Sociological Society in 1910. His home became a center for a wide range of intellectuals, including sociologists such as Georg Simmel, Robert Michels, and Georg Lukacs. In addition, Weber was active politically and wrote essays on the issues of the day.

There was a tension in Weber's life, and more important in his work, between the bureaucratic mind, as represented by his father, and his mother's religiosity. This unresolved tension permeates Weber's work as it permeated his personal life.

between religion and capitalism. In a wide-ranging historical study Weber sought to understand why a rational economic system (capitalism) had developed in the West and why it had failed to develop in the rest of the world. Weber accorded a central role to religion in this process. At one level he was engaged in a dialogue with the Marxists in an effort to show that, contrary to what many Marxists of the day believed, religion was not merely an epiphenomenon. Instead, it had played a key role in the rise of capitalism in the West and in its failure to develop elsewhere in the world. Weber argued that it was a distinctively rational religious system (Calvinism) that played the central role in the rise of capitalism in the West. In contrast, in the rest of the world that he studied, Weber found more irrational religious systems (for example, Confucianism, Taoism, Hinduism), which helped to inhibit the development of a rational economic system. However, in the end, one gets the feeling that these religions provided only temporary barriers, for the economic systems—indeed, the entire social structure—of these societies would ultimately become rationalized.

There is a great deal more to Weberian theory than this. For example, his work on rationalization has much more historical detail and innumerable theoretical insights. Beyond that, although rationalization lies at the heart of Weberian theory, it is far from all there is to the theory. But this is not the place to go into that rich body of material. Instead, let us return to the development of sociological theory. A key issue in that development is: Why did Weber's theory prove more attractive to later sociological theorists than Marxian theory?

One reason is that Weber proved to be more acceptable politically. Instead of espousing Marxian radicalism, Weber was more of a liberal on some issues and a conservative on others (for example, the role of the state). While he was a severe critic of many aspects of modern capitalist society, and came to many of the same critical conclusions as did Marx, he was not one to propose radical solutions to problems. In fact, he felt the radical reforms offered by many Marxists and other socialists would do more harm than good.

Later sociological theorists, especially Americans, saw their society under attack by Marxian theory. Largely conservative in orientation, they cast about for theoretical alternatives to Marxism. One of those who proved attractive was Max Weber. (Durkheim and Vilfredo Pareto were others.) After all, rationalization was a process affecting not only capitalist but also socialist societies. Indeed, from Weber's point of view, rationalization constituted an even greater problem in socialist than in capitalist societies.

Also in Weber's favor was the form in which he presented his judgments. He spent most of his life doing detailed historical studies, and his political conclusions were often made within the context of his research. Thus they usually sounded very scientific and academic. Marx—although he did much serious research—also wrote a good deal of explicitly polemical material. Even his more academic work is laced with acid political judgments. For example, in *Capital* (1867/1967) he described capitalists as ''vampires'' and ''werewolves.'' Weber's more academic style helped make him more acceptable to later sociologists.

Another reason for the greater acceptability of Weber was that he operated in a philosophical tradition that also helped shape the work of later sociologists. That is, Weber operated in the Kantian tradition, which meant, among other things, that he tended to think in cause-and-effect terms. This kind of thinking was more acceptable to later sociologists, who were largely unfamiliar and uncomfortable with the dialectical logic that informed Marx's work.

Finally, Weber appeared to offer a much more well-rounded approach to the social world than Marx. While Marx appeared to be almost totally preoccupied with the economy, Weber was interested in a wide range of social phenomena. This diversity of focus seemed to give later sociologists more to work with than the apparently more single-minded concerns of Marx.

Weber produced most of his major works in the late 1800s and early 1900s. Early in his career Weber was identified more as a historian who was concerned with sociological issues, but in the early 1900s his focus grew more and more sociological. Indeed, he became the dominant sociologist of his time in Germany. Although his work was broadly influential in Germany, it was to become even more influential in the United States, especially after Talcott Parsons introduced Weber's ideas (and those of other European theorists) to a large American audience. While Marx's ideas did not have a significant positive effect on American sociological theorists until the 1960s, Weber was already highly influential by the late 1930s.

GEORG SIMMEL (1858—1918)   Simmel was a somewhat atypical sociological theorist (Levine, Carter, and Gorman, 1976a; 1976b). For one thing, he had an immediate and profound effect on the development of American sociological theory, while Marx and Weber were largely ignored for a number of years. Simmel's work helped shape the development of one of the early centers of American sociology—the University of Chicago—and its major theory, symbolic interactionism. The Chicago school and symbolic interactionism came, as we will see, to dominate American sociology in the 1920s and early 1930s. Simmel's ideas were influential at Chicago mainly because the dominant figures in the early years of Chicago, Albion Small and Robert Park, had been exposed to Simmel in Berlin in the late 1800s. They were instrumental in bringing Simmel's ideas to students and faculty at Chicago, in translating some of his work, and in bringing it to the attention of a large-scale American audience.

Another atypical aspect of Simmel's work is his "level" of analysis, or at least that level for which he became best known in America. While Weber and Marx were preoccupied with large-scale issues like the rationalization of society and a capitalist economy, Simmel was best known for his work on smaller-scale issues, especially individual action and interaction. He became famous early for his thinking, derived from Kantian philosophy, on *forms* of interaction (for example, conflict) and *types* of interactants (for example, the stranger). Basically, Simmel saw that understanding interaction among people was one of the major tasks of sociology. However, it was impossible to study the massive number of interactions in social life without some conceptual tools. This is where forms of interaction and types of interactants came in. Simmel felt that he could isolate a limited number of forms of interaction that could be found in a large number of social settings. With these forms in hand we could then analyze and understand these different interaction settings. The development of a limited number of types of interactants could be similarly useful in helping us understand interaction settings. This work had a profound effect on symbolic interactionism, which, as the name suggests, was focally concerned with interaction. One of the ironies, however, is that Simmel also was concerned with large-scale issues similar to those that obsessed Marx and Weber. However, this work was much less influential than his work on interaction, although there are contemporary signs of a growing interest in the large-scale aspects of Simmel's sociology.

It was partly Simmel's style in his work on interaction that made him accessible to early American sociological theorists. While he wrote heavy tomes like Weber and Marx, he also wrote a set of deceptively simple essays on such interesting topics as poverty, the prostitute, the miser and the spendthrift, and the stranger. The brevity of such essays and the interest of the material made the dissemination of Simmel's ideas much easier. Unfortunately, the essays had the negative effect of obscuring Simmel's

GEORG SIMMEL: A Biographical Sketch

Georg Simmel is an unusual figure in the history of sociology. Despite his central role in contemporary thought, he was in his own time an outsider in many ways:

He was a Jew in a nineteenth-century Germany rife with anti-Semitism.

He had a wide range of interests while academic success is usually associated with a narrow focus.

He did not receive a professorship until late in his life; he was a marginal figure in German academic life.

Instead of heavy philosophic tomes, his best-known works were a series of clever essays on commonplace phenomena (fashion, the city, and so forth).

Simmel's marginality may have been a strain to him during his lifetime, but it can be argued that it served to give him unusual insights into, and a heightened perception of, social life.

Simmel was born in Berlin on March 1, 1958. He studied a wide range of subjects at the University of Berlin, including history, art, philosophy, anthropology, and psychology, and received his doctorate in philosophy in 1881. He remained at the university in a teaching capacity until 1914, although he occupied a relatively unimportant position on the faculty as a *privatdocent* from 1885 to 1901. There is no parallel to this position in the American university system, but it is basically that of an unpaid lecturer whose livelihood is dependent on student fees. Despite his marginality, Simmel did rather well in this position, largely because he was an excellent lecturer and attracted large numbers of students. His style was so popular that even the cultured members of Berlin society were drawn to his lectures, which became public events.

Simmel wrote innumerable articles and books, was well known in German academic circles, and even had an international following, especially in the United States, where his work was of great significance in the birth of sociology. Finally, in 1901 Simmel received some official recognition, but it was only the minimal bestowal of a purely honorary title that still did not give him the right to engage fully in academic life at the University of Berlin. Simmel tried to obtain many academic positions, but he failed in spite of the support of scholars such as Max Weber. This failure is traceable to a number of factors, especially anti-Semitism and his wide array of interests, which defied easy classification and evaluation.

Ironically, when in 1914 Simmel finally obtained a regular academic position, a full professorship at the University of Strasbourg, his ability to teach was severely restricted. World War I started soon afterward; lecture halls were turned into military hospitals, and students went off to war. In a very real sense, Simmel remained a marginal figure to his death in 1918—he never did have a normal academic career. But, in spite of, or perhaps because of, his peripheral position, Simmel attracted a large academic following in his day, and his fame as a scholar has if anything grown over the years.

more massive works (for example, the recently [1978] translated *Philosophy of Money*), which were potentially as significant to sociology. Nevertheless, it was partly through the short and clever essays that Simmel had a much more significant effect on early American sociological theory than either Marx or Weber.

We should not leave Simmel without saying something about *Philosophy of Money* since its recent English translation is likely to make Simmel's work attractive to a whole new set of theorists interested in culture and society. Although this macro-orientation is clearer in *Philosophy of Money*, it always existed in Simmel's work. For example, it is clear in his famous work on the dyad and the triad. Simmel thought some crucial sociological developments take place when a two-person group (or *dyad*) is transformed into a *triad* by the addition of a third party. Social possibilities emerge that simply could not exist in a dyad. For example, in a triad one of the members can become an arbitrator or mediator of the differences between the other two. More important, two of the members can band together and dominate the other member. This represents on a small scale what can happen with the emergence of large-scale structures that become separate from individuals and begin to dominate them.

This theme lies at the base of *Philosophy of Money*. Simmel was primarily concerned with the emergence in the modern world of a money economy that becomes separate from the individual and predominant. This theme, in turn, is part of an even broader and more pervasive one in Simmel's work, the domination of the culture as a whole over the individual. As Simmel saw it, in the modern world the larger culture and all of its various components (including the money economy) expands, and as it expands the importance of the individual decreases. Thus, for example, as the industrial technology associated with a modern economy expands and grows more sophisticated, the skills and abilities of the individual worker grow progressively less important. In the end, the worker is confronted with an industrial machine over which he or she can exert little, if any, control. More generally, Simmel's thought that in the modern world the expansion of the larger culture leads to the growing insignificance of the individual.

While sociologists have become increasingly attuned to the broader implications of Simmel's work, his early influence was primarily through his studies of small-scale social phenomena, such as the forms of interaction and types of interactants.

The Origins of British Sociology

We have been examining the development of sociology in France (Comte, Durkheim) and Germany (Marx, Weber, and Simmel). We turn now to the parallel development of sociology in England. As we will see, Continental ideas had their impact on early British sociology, but more important were native influences.

POLITICAL ECONOMY, AMELIORISM, AND SOCIAL EVOLUTION

Philip Abrams (1968) contended that British sociology was shaped in the nineteenth century by three often conflicting sources—political economy, ameliorism, and social evolution.[5] Thus when the Sociological Society of London was founded in 1903, there were strong differences over the definition of sociology. However, there were few who doubted the view that sociology could be a science. It was the differences that gave British sociology its distinctive character, and we will look at each of the sources of these differences briefly.

---

[5]For more recent developments in British sociology, see Philip Abrams et al. (1981).

We have already touched on *political economy*, which was a theory of industrial and capitalist society traceable largely to the work of Adam Smith (1723–1790). As we saw, political economy had a profound effect on Karl Marx. However, while Marx studied political economy closely, he was critical of it. But that was not the direction taken by British economists and sociologists. They tended to accept Smith's idea that there was an "invisible hand" that shaped the market for labor and goods. The market was seen as an independent reality that stood above individuals and controlled their behavior. The British sociologists, like the political economists and unlike Marx, saw the market as a positive force, as a source of order, harmony, and integration in society. Since they saw the market, and more generally society, in a positive light, the task of the sociologists was not to criticize society but simply to gather data on the laws by which it operated. The goal was to provide the government with the facts it needed to understand the way the system worked and to direct its workings wisely.

The emphasis was on facts, but which facts? While Marx, Weber, Durkheim, and Comte looked to the structures of society for their basic facts, the British thinkers tended to focus on the individuals who made up those structures. In dealing with large-scale structures they tended to collect individual-level data and then combine them to form a collective portrait. In the mid-1800s it was the statisticians who dominated British social science, and it was this kind of data collection that was deemed to be the major task of sociology. The objective was the accumulation of "pure" facts without theorizing or philosophizing. Instead of general theorizing, the "emphasis settled on the business of producing more exact indicators, better methods of classification and data collection, improved life tables, higher levels of comparability between discrete bodies of data, and the like" (Abrams, 1968:18).

It was almost in spite of themselves that these statistically oriented sociologists came to see some limitations in their approach. A few sociologists began to feel the need for broader theorizing. To them, a problem such as poverty pointed to failings in the market system as well as in the society as a whole. But most, focused as they were on individuals, did not question the larger system; they turned instead to more detailed field studies and to the development of more complicated and more exact statistical techniques. To them, the source of the problem had to lie in inadequate research methods, *not* in the system as a whole. As Philip Abrams (1968:27) noted: "Focusing persistently on the distribution of individual circumstances, the statisticians found it hard to break through to a perception of poverty as a product of social structure. . . . They did not and probably could not achieve the concept of structural victimization." In addition to their theoretical and methodological commitments to the study of individuals, the statisticians worked too closely with government policy makers to arrive at the conclusion that the larger political and economic system was the problem.

Related to, but separable from, political economy was the second defining characteristic of British sociology—*ameliorism,* or a desire to solve social problems by reforming individuals. Although British scholars began to recognize that there were problems in society (for example, poverty), they still believed in that society and wanted to preserve it. They desired to forestall violence and revolution and to reform the system so it could continue essentially as it was. Above all, they wanted to prevent the coming of a socialist society. Thus, like French sociology and some branches of German sociology, British sociology was conservatively oriented.

Since the British sociologists could not, or would not, trace the source of problems such as poverty to the society as a whole, the source had to lie within the individuals themselves. This was an early form of what William Ryan (1971) later called "blaming the victim." Much attention was devoted to a long series of individual problems— "ignorance, spiritual destitution, impurity, bad sanitation, pauperism, crime, and intemperance—above all intemperance" (Abrams, 1968:39). Clearly, there was a tendency to look for a simple cause for all social ills, and the one that suggested itself before all others was alcoholism. What made this perfect to the ameliorist was that this was an individual pathology, not a social pathology. The ameliorists lacked a theory of social structure, a theory of the social causes of such individual problems.

But a stronger sense of social structure was lurking below the surface of British sociology, and it burst through in the latter part of the nineteenth century with the growth of interest in *social evolution*. One important influence was the work of Auguste Comte, part of which had been translated into English in the 1850s. Although Comte's work did not inspire immediate interest, by the last quarter of the century a number of thinkers had been attracted to it and to its concern for the larger structures of society, its scientific (positivistic) orientation, its comparative orientation, and its evolutionary theory. However, a number of British thinkers sharpened their own conception of the world in opposition to some of the excesses of Comtian theory (for example, the tendency to elevate sociology to the status of a religion).

In Abrams's view the real importance of Comte lay in his providing one of the bases on which opposition could be mounted against the "oppressive genius of Herbert Spencer" (Abrams, 1968:58). In both a positive and a negative sense, Spencer was a dominant figure in British sociological theory, especially evolutionary theory.

HERBERT SPENCER (1820—1903)   In attempting to understand Spencer's ideas it is useful to compare and contrast them with Comtian theory. Spencer is often categorized with Comte in terms of their influence on the development of sociological theory, but there are some important differences between them. For example, it is less easy to categorize Spencer as a conservative. In fact, in his early years Spencer is better seen as a political liberal, and he retained elements of liberalism throughout his life. However, it is also true that Spencer grew more conservative during the course of his life and that his basic influence, as was true of Comte, was conservative.

One of his liberal views that coexisted rather uncomfortably with his conservatism was his acceptance of a laissez-faire doctrine: he felt that the state should not intervene in individual affairs, except for the rather passive function of protecting people. This meant that Spencer, unlike Comte, was not interested in social reforms; he wanted social life to evolve free of external control.

This difference points to Spencer as a *Social Darwinist*. As such, he held the evolutionary view that the world was growing progressively better. Therefore, it should be left alone; outside interference could only worsen the situation. He adopted the view that social institutions, like plants and animals, adapted progressively and positively to their social environment. He also accepted the Darwinian view that a process of natural selection, "survival of the fittest," occurred in the social world. That is, if unimpeded by external intervention, people who were "fit" would survive and proliferate while the "unfit" would eventually die out. Another difference was that Spencer emphasized the individual, whereas Comte focused on larger units such as the family.

While there are important differences between Comte and Spencer, their shared orientations, or at least the similar ways in which they were interpreted, proved to be more important than their differences for the development of sociological theory.

Comte and Spencer shared with Durkheim and others a commitment to a science of sociology, which was a very attractive perspective to early theorists who were intrigued by that possibility. Another influence of Spencer's work, shared with both Comte and Durkheim, was his tendency to see society as an *organism*. In this, Spencer borrowed his perspective and concepts from biology. He was concerned with the overall structure of society, the interrelationship of the *parts* of society, and the *functions* of the parts for each other as well as for the system as a whole.

Most important, Spencer, like Comte, had an evolutionary conception of historical development. However, Spencer was critical of Comte's evolutionary theory on several grounds. Specifically, he rejected Comte's law of the three stages. He argued that Comte was content to deal with evolution in the realm of ideas, in terms of intellectual development. Spencer, however, sought to develop an evolutionary theory in the real, material world.

Although Spencer is best remembered as an evolutionary theorist, his theory is highly complex, takes varied forms, and is often unclear and ambiguous. Robert Perrin (1976) has performed a useful service by pointing out that in fact Spencer held four different, although sometimes overlapping, theories of social evolution.

In his first theory Spencer argued that social evolution involved progress toward an ideal social state. As Perrin (1976:1343) described it, this future society was to be based upon friendship, altruism, elaborate specialization, recognition for achievements rather than characteristics one is born with, "and, primarily, a voluntary cooperation among highly disciplined individuals." Such a society would be held together by voluntary contractual relations and, more important, by a strong common morality. Although normative restraint from without would still be necessary, the government's role would be restricted to determining what people ought *not* to do, rather than mandating what they should do. These modern, industrialized societies would be less warlike than the militant types that preceded them.

Spencer's second evolutionary theory is a bit more theoretical and slightly less ideological. It proposes that society is evolving in the direction of the progressive differentiation of a variety of *structures* that fulfill the various *functional* requirements of society. Modern societies develop increasingly differentiated structures to handle such functional problems as procreation, production, exchange, communication, position-role placement, and control over individual behavior. This is in line with what we now call *structural-functional theory*, an approach we will have more to say about later.

In his third theory Spencer, much as Durkheim was to do later, equated social evolution with the increasing division of labor. Basically, Spencer argued that increasing population growth necessitates increasing social differentiation. Increasing numbers disturb social equilibrium and make necessary a variety of social adjustments. One of those adjustments is an increasing division of labor. The homogeneity of primitive societies is forced to give way to the heterogeneity of more modern societies.

Finally, Spencer adopted a model of social evolution based on the model of biological evolution. In fact, it was Spencer who coined the phrase "survival of the fittest" several years *before* Darwin's work on natural selection. In this theory Spencer was concerned with why some societies survive and others do not. Basically, his view was that the fittest societies survive, thereby leading to an adaptive upgrading of the world as a whole. A variety of factors are identified as being involved in a society's probability of success: size, fertility levels, efficiency of communication, degree of public control of resources, military organization, and so forth.

Thus Spencer offered a rich and complicated set of ideas on social evolution. As we will see, his ideas first enjoyed great success, then were rejected for many years, and have recently been revived with the rise of neoevolutionary sociological theories.

THE REACTION AGAINST SPENCER IN BRITAIN

Despite his emphasis on the individual, Spencer was best known for his large-scale theory of social evolution. In this, he stood in stark contrast to the sociology that preceded him in Britain. However, the reaction against Spencer was based more on the threat that his idea of survival of the fittest posed to the ameliorism so dear to most early British sociologists. Although Spencer later repudiated some of his more outrageous ideas, he *did* argue for a survival-of-the-fittest philosophy and against government intervention and social reform. He did say things like:

> Fostering the good-for-nothing at the expense of the good, is an extreme cruelty. It is a deliberate stirring-up of miseries for future generations. There is no greater curse to posterity than that of bequeathing to them an increasing population of imbeciles and idlers and criminals. . . . The whole effort of nature is to get rid of such, to clear the world of them, and make room for better. . . . If they are not sufficiently complete to live, they die, and it is best they should die.
>
> (cited in Abrams, 1968:74)

Such sentiments were clearly at odds with the ameliorative orientation of the British reformer-sociologists.

Italian Sociology: Pareto and Mosca

We can close this sketch of early, primarily conservative European sociological theory with brief mention of two Italian sociologists, Vilfredo Pareto (1848–1923) and Gaetano Mosca (1858–1941). These two sociologists were influential in their time, but their contemporary relevance is minimal. Few people read Mosca today. There was a brief outburst of interest in Pareto's work in the 1930s when the major American theorist, Talcott Parsons, devoted as much attention to him as he gave to Weber and Durkheim. However, in recent years, except for a few of his major concepts, Pareto has also receded in importance and contemporary relevance.

Zeitlin (1968:169) said of Pareto that "the entire structure of his general 'sociology' is shaped by his debate with Marxism." In fact, Pareto was rejecting not only Marx but also a good portion of Enlightenment philosophy. For example, while the Enlightenment philosophers emphasized rationality, Pareto emphasized the role of nonrational factors such as human instincts. This emphasis also was tied to his rejection of Marxian theory. That is, since nonrational, instinctual factors were so important *and* so unchanging, it was unrealistic to hope to achieve dramatic social changes with an economic revolution.

Pareto also developed a theory of social change that stood in stark contrast to Marxian theory. While Marx's theory focused on the role of the masses, Pareto offered an elite theory of social change, which held that society is inevitably dominated by a small elite that operates on the basis of enlightened self-interest. It rules over the masses of people, who are dominated by nonrational forces. Because they lack rational capacities, the masses, in Pareto's system, were unlikely to be a revolutionary force. Social change occurs when the elite begins to degenerate and is replaced by a new elite derived from the nongoverning elite or higher elements of the masses. Once the new elite is in power, the process begins anew. Thus, we have a cyclical theory of social change instead of the directional theories offered by Marx, Comte, Spencer, and others. In addition, Pareto's theory of change largely ignores the plight of the masses. Elites come and go, but the lot of the masses remains the same.

This theory, however, was not Pareto's lasting contribution to sociology. That lay in his scientific conception of sociology and the social world: ''My wish is to construct a system of sociology on the model of celestial mechanics [astronomy], physics, chemistry'' (cited in Hook, 1965:57). Briefly, Pareto conceived of society as a system in equilibrium, a whole consisting of interdependent parts. A change in one part was seen as leading to changes in other parts of the system. Pareto's systemic conception of society was the most important reason Parsons devoted so much attention to Pareto's work in his 1937 book, *The Structure of Social Action,* and it was Pareto's most important influence on Parsons's thinking. Fused with similar views held by those who had an organic image of society (Comte, Durkheim, and Spencer, for example), Pareto's theory played a central role in the development of Parsons's theory and more generally in structural functionalism.

While few modern sociologists now read Pareto's work, virtually none ever read Mosca's. But his work can also be seen as a rejection of the Enlightenment and of Marxism. The important point is that Mosca, like Pareto, offered an elite theory of social change that stands in opposition to the Marxian perspective.

Turn-of-the-Century Developments in European Marxism

While many nineteenth-century sociologists were developing their theories in opposition to Marx, there was a simultaneous effort by a number of Marxists to clarify and extend Marxian theory. Between roughly 1875 and 1925 there was little overlap between Marxism and sociology. (Weber is an exception to this.) The two schools of thought were developing in parallel fashion with little or no interchange between them.

After the death of Marx, Marxian theory was first dominated by those who saw in his theory scientific and economic determinism. Friedrich Engels, Marx's benefactor and collaborator, lived on after Marx's death and can be seen as the first exponent of such a perspective. Basically, this view was that Marx's scientific theory had uncovered the economic laws that ruled the capitalist world. Such laws pointed to the inevitable collapse of the capitalist system. Early Marxian thinkers like Karl Kautsky sought to gain a better understanding of the operation of these laws. There were several problems with this perspective. For one thing, it seemed to rule out political action, a cornerstone of Marx's position. That is, there seemed no need for individuals, especially workers, to do anything. Since the system was inevitably crumbling, all they had to do was sit back and wait for its demise. On a theoretical level, deterministic Marxism seemed to rule out the dialectical relationship between individuals and larger social structures.

These problems led to a reaction among Marxian theorists and the development of "Hegelian Marxism" in the early 1900s. The Hegelian Marxists refused to reduce Marxism to a scientific theory that ignored individual thought and action. They are labeled Hegelian Marxists because they sought to combine Hegel's interest in consciousness (which some view Marx as sharing) with the determinists' interest in the economic structures of society. The Hegelian theorists were significant for both theoretical and practical reasons. Theoretically, they reinstated the importance of the individual, consciousness, and the relationship between thought and action. Practically, they emphasized the importance of individual action in bringing about a social revolution.

The major exponent of this point of view was George Lukács. He had begun in the early 1900s to integrate Marxism with sociology (in particular, Weberian theory). This integration was soon to accelerate with the development of critical theory in the 1920s and 1930s.

SUMMARY

This chapter sketches the early history of sociological theory in two parts. The first, and much briefer, section deals with the various social forces involved in the development of sociological theory. Although there were many such influences, our focus is the impact of political revolution, the Industrial Revolution and the rise of capitalism, socialism, urbanization, religious change, and the growth of science on sociological theory. The second part of the chapter examines the influence of intellectual forces on the rise of sociological theory in various countries. We begin with France and the role played by the Enlightenment, stressing the conservative and romantic reaction to it. It is out of this interplay that French sociological theory developed. In this context, we examine the major figures in the early years of French sociology—Claude Henri Saint-Simon, Auguste Comte, and Emile Durkheim.

Next we turn to Germany and a discussion of the role played by Karl Marx in the development of sociology in that country. We discuss the parallel development of Marxian theory and sociological theory and the ways in which Marxian theory influenced sociology, both positively and negatively. We begin with the roots of Marxian theory in Hegelianism, materialism, and political economy. Marx's theory itself is touched upon briefly. The discussion then shifts to the roots of German sociology. Max Weber's work is examined in order to show the diverse sources of German sociology. Also discussed are some of the reasons that Weber's theory proved more acceptable to later sociologists than did Marx's ideas. This section closes with a brief discussion of Georg Simmel's work.

The rise of sociological theory in Britain is next considered. The major sources of British sociology were political economy, ameliorism, and social evolution. In this context we touch on the work of Herbert Spencer as well as on some of the controversy that surrounded it.

This chapter closes with a brief discussion of Italian sociological theory, especially the work of Vilfredo Pareto, and the turn-of-the-century developments in European Marxian theory, primarily economic determinism and Hegelian Marxism.

CHAPTER TWO
A Historical Sketch of Sociological Theory: The Later Years

IN the preceding chapter we discussed the development of sociological theory, largely in nineteenth-century Europe. We move now to more late nineteenth- and twentieth-century developments, with particular attention to developments in the United States. Figure 2.1 shows the important intellectual influences on this development as well as the major theories and theorists.

EARLY AMERICAN SOCIOLOGICAL THEORY

It is difficult to give a precise date for the founding of sociology in the United States. There was a course in social problems taught at Oberlin as early as 1858; Comte's term "sociology" was used by George Fitzhugh in 1854; and William Graham Sumner taught social science courses at Yale beginning in 1873. During the 1880s courses specifically bearing the title sociology began to appear. The first department with sociology in its title was founded at the University of Kansas in 1889. At the same time Albion

FIGURE 2.1 Sociological Theory: The Later Years

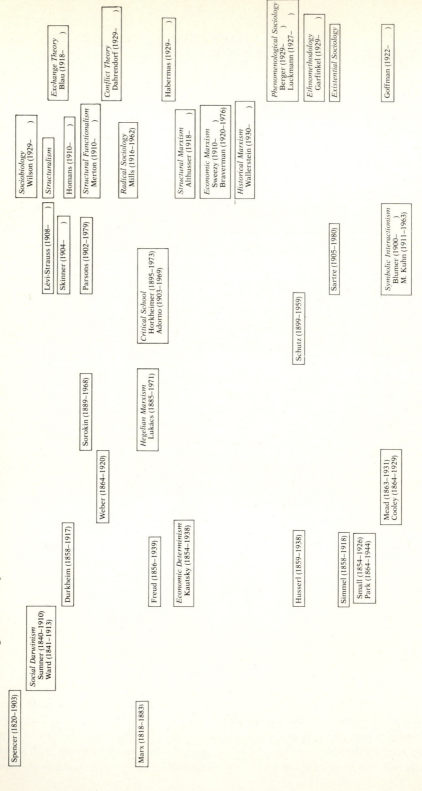

Small moved to the University of Chicago and set up the new department of sociology. The Chicago department became the first important center of American sociology in general and of sociological theory in particular (Matthews, 1977).

The Politics of Early American Sociology

Before we discuss the specific people associated with early American sociology, it would be useful to return to some of the themes that have run through much of this discussion of the history of sociological theory. One such theme is that sociology has been, from the beginning, highly political. That theme carries over into early American sociological theory.

A major study of the politics of early American sociological theory (Schwendinger and Schwendinger, 1974) argued that the early sociologists are best described as political liberals and not, as was true of most early European theorists, as conservatives. The liberalism characteristic of early American sociology had basically two elements. First, it operated with a belief in the freedom and welfare of the individual. In this, it was far more influenced by Spencer's orientation than by Comte's more collective position. Second, many sociologists associated with this orientation adopted an evolutionary view of social progress. However, they split over how best to bring about this progress. Some argued that steps should be taken by the government to aid social reform, while others pushed a laissez-faire doctrine, arguing that the various components of society should be left to solve their own problems.

Liberalism, taken to its extreme, comes very close to conservatism. The belief in social progress—in reform or a laissez-faire doctrine—and the belief in the importance of the individual both lead to positions supportive of the system as a whole. The overriding belief is that the social system works or can be reformed to work. There is little criticism of the system as a whole; in the American case this means, in particular, that there is little questioning of capitalism. Instead of imminent class struggle, the early sociologists saw a future of class harmony and class cooperation. Ultimately this meant that early American sociological theory helped to rationalize exploitation, domestic and international imperialism, and social inequality (Schwendinger and Schwendinger, 1974). In the end, the political liberalism of the early sociologists had enormously conservative implications.

Social Change, Intellectual Currents, and Early American Sociology

In his recent analysis of the founding of American sociological theory, Roscoe Hinkle (1980) outlines several basic contexts from which that body of theory emerged. Of utmost importance are the social changes that occurred in American society after the close of the Civil War. In Chapter One we discussed an array of factors involved in the development of European sociological theory; several of these factors were also intimately involved in the development of theory in America. Hinkle singles out the Industrial Revolution and urbanization as major forces in the development of American sociological theory. He also adds a factor, immigration, that helped shape American theory, even though it played little or no part in the development of theory in other societies.

Another major factor discussed by Hinkle is the simultaneous emergence, in the late 1800s, of both sociology and the modern university system in America. In Europe, on the other hand, the university system was already well established *before* the emergence of sociology. While sociology had a difficult time becoming established in Europe, it found the going easier in the more fluid setting of the new American university system.

Although Hinkle outlines a number of other factors, we need mention only one more —the impact of already established European theory on American sociological theory. European theorists largely created sociological theory, and the Americans were able to rely on this groundwork. The Europeans most important to the Americans were Spencer and Comte. Durkheim was of some importance in the early years, while the influence of Weber and Marx was not to have a dramatic effect for a number of years. As an illustration of the impact of early European theory on American sociology, the history of the ideas of Herbert Spencer is interesting and informative.

HERBERT SPENCER'S INFLUENCE ON SOCIOLOGY

No sociologist had a more dramatic rise and fall in influence on American sociology than Herbert Spencer. Even before his ideas reached America and sociology, he was already a major popular figure in Britain and in many other parts of the world. His work was reportedly much read by British officers on India's northern frontier, and J. D. Y. Peel (1971) reports that three farm laborers and a minister were heard discussing one of his works on a train in northern Scotland. Spencer and his ideas even found their way into popular short stories and novels, such as Anton Chekhov's "The Duel" and Jack London's *Martin Eden.* This popular success was, if anything, exceeded by Spencer's influence on the European intellectuals of his day.

By the late 1800s Spencer's ideas had crossed the ocean and were having a significant impact on both laypeople and academics. Hundreds of thousands of his books were sold in this country. As Richard Hofstadter (1959:33) put it: "In the three decades after the Civil War it was impossible to be active in any field of intellectual work without mastering Spencer." Among his supporters was the important industrialist Andrew Carnegie, who was almost nauseatingly obsequious in his admiration for Spencer. Note the following letter to Spencer during his last illness in 1903:

> Dear Master Teacher, . . . you come to me every day in thought, and the everlasting "why" intrudes—Why lies he? Why must he go? and I follow. . . . The World jogs on unconscious of its greatest mind . . . lying silently brooding. But it will wake some day to its teachings and decree Spencer's place is with the greatest.
>
> I am gratefully, My Master, Your Devoted pupil
> Andrew Carnegie
> (Peel, 1971:2)

Why were Spencer's ideas so much more influential than those of Comte, Durkheim, Marx, and Weber? Hofstadter offered several explanations. To take the easiest first, Spencer wrote in English while the others did not. In addition, Spencer did not write very technically, thereby making his work broadly accessible. Indeed, some have argued that the lack of technicality is traceable to Spencer's *not* being a very sophisticated scholar. But there are other, more important reasons for Spencer's broad appeal. He offered a scientific orientation that was attractive to an audience becoming enamored of science and its technological products. He offered a comprehensive theory that seemed to deal with the entire sweep of human history. The broadness of his ideas, as well as the voluminous work he produced, allowed his theory to be many different things to many different people. Finally, and perhaps most important, his theory was soothing and reassuring to a society undergoing the wrenching process of industrialization—society was, according to Spencer, steadily moving in the direction of greater and greater progress.

Spencer's most famous American disciple was William Graham Sumner, who accepted and expanded upon many of Spencer's Social Darwinist ideas. Spencer also influenced other early American sociologists, among them Lester Ward, Charles Horton Cooley, E. A. Ross, and Robert Park.

But by the 1930s Spencer was in eclipse in the intellectual world in general, as well as in sociology. His Social Darwinist, laissez-faire ideas seemed ridiculous in the light of massive social problems, a world war, and a major economic depression. In 1937 Talcott Parsons announced Spencer's intellectual death for sociology when he echoed historian Crane Brinton's words of a few years earlier, "Who now reads Spencer?" Today Spencer is of little more than historical interest, but his ideas *were* important in shaping early American sociological theory. Let us look briefly at the work of two American theorists who were influenced, at least in part, by Spencer's work.

WILLIAM GRAHAM SUMNER (1840–1910) It is convenient to start a discussion of early American sociological theorists with William Graham Sumner, since he was the person who taught the first course in the United States that could be called sociology. Sumner was the major exponent of Social Darwinism in the United States, although he appeared to change his view late in life (N. Smith, 1979). The following exchange between Sumner and one of his students illustrates his "liberal" views on the need for individual freedom and his position against government interference:

"Professor, don't you believe in any government aid to industries?"
"No! It's root, hog, or die."
"Yet, but hasn't the hog got a right to root?"
"There are no rights. The world owes nobody a living."
"You believe then, Professor, in only one system, the contract-competitive system?"
"That's the only sound economic system. All others are fallacies."
"Well, suppose some professor of political economy came along and took your job away from you. Wouldn't you be sore?"
"Any other professor is welcome to try. If he gets my job, it is my fault. My business is to teach the subject so well that no one can take the job away from me."
(Phelps, cited in Hofstadter, 1959:54)

Sumner basically adopted a survival-of-the-fittest approach to the social world. Like Spencer, he saw people struggling against their environment, and the fittest were those who would be successful. Thus Sumner was a supporter of human aggressiveness and competitiveness. Those who succeeded deserved it, and those who did not succeed deserved to fail. Again like Spencer, Sumner was opposed to efforts, especially government efforts, to aid those who had failed. In his view such intervention operated against the natural selection that, among people just as among lower animals, allowed the fit to survive and the unfit to perish. This theoretical system fit in well with the development of capitalism since it provided theoretical legitimacy for the existence of great differences in wealth and power.

Sumner is of little more than historical interest for two reasons. First, his orientation, and Social Darwinism in general, has come to be regarded as little more than a crude legitimation of competitive capitalism and the status quo. Second, he failed to build a solid enough base at Yale to build a school of sociology with many disciples. That kind of success was to occur some years later at the University of Chicago (Heyl and Heyl, 1976).

LESTER F. WARD (1841–1913)   Another sociologist of note in his time, but of little lasting significance, is Lester Ward. He had an unusual career in that he spent most of it as a paleontologist working for the federal government. During that time, Ward read Spencer and Comte and developed a strong interest in sociology. He published a number of works in the late 1800s and early 1900s in which he expounded his sociological theory. As a result of the notoriety that this work achieved, Ward was elected the first president of the American Sociological Society in 1906. It was only then that he took his first academic position, at Brown University, a position he held until his death.

Ward, like Sumner, was influenced by the ideas of Herbert Spencer. He accepted the idea that people had evolved from lower forms to their present status. He believed that early society was characterized by its simplicity and its moral poverty, while modern society was more complex, happier, and offered greater freedom. One task of sociology, *pure sociology,* was to study the basic laws of social change and social structure. But Ward was not content simply to have sociology study social life. He believed that sociology should have a practical side; there should also be an *applied sociology.* This involved the conscious use of scientific knowledge to attain a better society. Thus, Ward was not an extreme Social Darwinist: he believed in the need for, and importance of, social reform.

Although of historical significance, Sumner and Ward have not been of long-term significance to sociological theory. We turn now, however, to some theorists and to a school, the Chicago school, that came to dominate sociology in America. The tradition started at the University of Chicago is of continuing importance to sociology and its theoretical status.

The Chicago School

The department of sociology at the University of Chicago was founded in 1892 by Albion Small. Small's intellectual work is of less contemporary significance than the key role he played in the institutionalization of sociology in the United States (Faris, 1970; Matthews, 1977). He was instrumental in creating a department at Chicago that was to become the center of the discipline in the United States for many years. Small collaborated on the first textbook in sociology in 1894. In 1895 he founded the *American Journal of Sociology*, a journal that to this day is a dominant force in the discipline. In

1905 Small cofounded the American Sociological Society, *the* major professional association of American sociologists to this date (Rhoades, 1981). (The embarrassment caused by the initials of the American Sociological Society, A.S.S., led to a name change in 1959 to the American Sociological Association—A.S.A.)

DISTINCTIVE CHARACTERISTICS OF EARLY CHICAGO SOCIOLOGY

The early Chicago department had several distinctive characteristics. For one thing, it had a strong connection with religion. Some members were ministers themselves, while others had fathers who were ministers. Small, for example, believed that "the ultimate goal of sociology must be essentially Christian" (Matthews, 1977:95). This opinion led to a view that sociology must be interested in social reform, and this was combined with a belief that sociology should be scientific.[1] Scientific sociology with an objective of social amelioration was to be practiced in the burgeoning city of Chicago, which was beset by the positive *and* negative effects of urbanization and industrialization.

We might note here the contributions of one of the earliest members of the Chicago sociology department, W. I. Thomas (1863–1947). In 1895 Thomas became a fellow at the Chicago department, where he wrote his dissertation in 1896. Thomas's lasting significance was in his emphasis on the need to do scientific research on social psychological issues. Although he championed this position for many years, its major statement came in 1918 with the publication of *The Polish Peasant in Europe and America*, which he coauthored with Florian Znaniecki. The book was the product of eight years of research in both Europe and the United States and was primarily a study of social disorganization among Polish migrants. The data were of little lasting importance. However, the methodology was significant, involving the use of a variety of data sources, including autobiographical material, paid writings, family letters, newspaper files, public documents, and institutional letters. One other item of consequence emerged from this work. When questioned about the truthfulness of some of the self-reported data, Thomas responded, "If men define situations as real, they are real in their consequences" (Thomas and Thomas, 1928:572). The emphasis was on the importance of what people think and how this affects what they do. This microscopic, social-psychological focus stood in contrast to the macroscopic, social-structural and -cultural perspectives of such European scholars as Marx, Weber, and Durkheim. It was to become one of the defining characteristics of Chicago's theoretical product— symbolic interactionism.

Another figure of significance at Chicago was Robert Park (1864–1944). Park had come to Chicago as a part-time instructor in 1913 and quickly worked his way into a central role in the department. As was true of Small, Park's long-term significance was not simply in his intellectual contributions. His importance for the development of sociology lay in several areas. First, he became the dominant figure in the Chicago department, which, in turn, dominated sociology into the 1930s. Second, Park had studied in Europe and was instrumental in bringing Continental thinkers to the atten-

---

[1] As we will see, however, the Chicago school's conception of science was to become too "soft," at least in the eyes of the positivists who later came to dominate sociology.

tion of Chicago sociologists. Of particular theoretical importance, Park had taken courses with Simmel, and Simmel's ideas, particularly his focus on action and interaction, were instrumental in the development of the Chicago school's theoretical orientation. Third, prior to becoming a sociologist Park had been a reporter, and this experience gave him a sense of the importance of urban problems and of the need to go out into the field to collect data through personal observation. Out of this emerged the Chicago school's substantive interest in urban ecology. Finally, in 1921, Park and Ernest W. Burgess published the first truly important sociology textbook, *An Introduction to the Science of Sociology*. It was to be an influential book for many years and was particularly notable for its commitments to science, to research, and to the study of a wide range of social phenomena.

Beginning in the late 1920s and early 1930s, Park began to spend less and less time in Chicago. Finally, his lifelong interest in race relations (he had been secretary to Booker T. Washington before becoming a sociologist) led him to take a position at the black Fisk University in 1934. Although the decline of the Chicago department was not

ROBERT PARK: A Biographical Sketch

Robert Park did not follow the typical career route of an academic sociologist—college, graduate school, professorship. Instead, he led a varied career before he became a sociologist late in his life. Despite his late start, Park had a profound effect on sociology in general and on theory in particular. Park's varied experiences gave him an unusual orientation to life, and this view helped to shape the Chicago school, symbolic interactionism, and ultimately a good portion of sociology.

Park was born in Harveyville, Pennsylvania, on February 14, 1864 (Matthews, 1977). As a student at the University of Michigan he was exposed to a number of great thinkers, such as John Dewey. Although he was excited by ideas, Park felt a strong need to work in the real world. Upon graduation, he began a career as a journalist, which gave him this real-world opportunity. He particularly liked to write about city life in vivid detail. He would go into the field, observe and analyze, and finally write up his observations. In point of fact, he was already doing essentially the kind of research that came to be one of the hallmarks of Chicago sociology—that is, urban ethnology using participant observation techniques.

Although the accurate description of social life remained one of his passions, Park grew dissatisfied with newspaper work, since it did not fulfill his familial or, more important, his intellectual needs. Furthermore, it did not seem to contribute to the improvement of the world, and Park had a deep interest in social reform. In 1898, at age thirty-four, Park left newspaper work and enrolled in the philosophy department at Harvard. He remained there for a year but then decided to move to Germany, at that time the heart of the world's intellectual life. In Berlin he encountered Georg Simmel, whose work was to have a profound influence on Park's sociology. In fact, Simmel's lectures were the *only* formal sociological training Park received. In 1904 Park submitted his completed doctoral dissertation to the University of Heidelberg. Characteristically, he caused solely or even chiefly by Park's departure, its status began to wane in the 1930s. But before we can deal with the decline of Chicago sociology and the rise of other departments and theories, we need to return to the early days of the school and the two figures whose work was to be of the most lasting theoretical significance— Charles Horton Cooley and, most important, George Herbert Mead.

CHARLES HORTON COOLEY (1864—1929)   The association of Cooley with the Chicago school is interesting in that he spent his career at the University of Michigan, not the University of Chicago. But Cooley's theoretical perspective was in line with the theory of symbolic interactionism that was to become Chicago's most important product.

Cooley received his Ph.D. from the University of Michigan in 1894. He had developed a strong interest in sociology, but there was as yet no department of sociology at Michigan. As a result, the questions for his Ph.D. examination came from Columbia University, where sociology had been taught since 1889 under the leadership of Frank-

---

was dissatisfied with his dissertation: "All I had to show was that little book and I was ashamed of it" (cited in Matthews, 1977:57). At this point he refused a summer teaching job at the University of Chicago and turned away from academe as he had earlier turned away from newspaper work.

His need to contribute to social betterment led him to become secretary and chief publicity officer for the Congo Reform Association, which was set up to help alleviate the brutality and exploitation then taking place in the Belgian Congo. During this period he met Booker T. Washington, and he was attracted to the cause of improving the lot of black Americans. He became Washington's secretary and played a key role in the activities of the Tuskegee Institute. In 1912 he met W. I. Thomas, the Chicago sociologist, who was lecturing at Tuskegee. Thomas invited him to give a course on "The Negro in America" to a small group of graduate students at Chicago. It was successful and he gave it again the next year, to an audience twice as large. At this time he joined the American Sociological Society, and only a decade later he became its president. Park gradually worked his way into a full-time appointment at Chicago, although he did not get a full professorship until 1923, when he was fifty-nine years old.

Over the approximately two decades that he was affiliated with the University of Chicago, he played a key role in shaping the intellectual orientation of the sociology department. Among the characteristics of Chicago sociology that bore his imprint were a reportorial style that led to participant observation; an interest in social problems, especially race relations; a concern for the city, both substantively and as an area in which to do sociological research; and an interest in Simmel's theory and its relationship to the emerging theory of symbolic interactionism. Although he was not a prolific writer, Park became a national figure in sociology, as reflected by his presidency of the American Sociological Society. His textbook, coauthored with E. W. Burgess, was the most important sociology text for many years and shaped the orientation of many students.

Park remained peripatetic even after his retirement from Chicago in the early 1930s. He taught courses and oversaw research at the primarily black Fisk University until he was nearly eighty years old. He also traveled extensively after his departure from Chicago. He died on February 7, 1944, one week before his eightieth birthday.

lin Giddings. Cooley began his teaching career at Michigan in 1892 prior to completion of his doctorate, and he remained there throughout his career.

Although Cooley had a wide range of views, he is mainly remembered today for his insights into the social-psychological aspects of social life. His work in this area is in line with that of George Herbert Mead, although Mead was to have a deeper and more lasting effect on sociology than Cooley. Cooley had an interest in consciousness, but he refused (as did Mead) to separate consciousness from the social context. He saw consciousness as being shaped by social interaction. This is best exemplified by a concept of his that survives to this day—the *looking-glass self.* As Cooley (1902/1964: 184) saw it, the looking-glass self involved three phases. First, we imagine how we appear to others. Then we imagine how others judge our appearance. Finally, we develop some sort of self-feeling such as pride or mortification on the basis of what we perceive others' judgments to be. The crucial point here is that Cooley understood that people possess consciousness and that it is shaped in continuing interaction.

A second basic concept that is illustrative of Cooley's social-psychological interests, and which is also of continuing interest and importance, is that of the primary group. *Primary groups* are for Cooley intimate, face-to-face groups that play a key role in linking the actor to the larger society. Especially crucial are the primary groups of the young—mainly the family and the peer group. Within the context of these groups the individual grows into a social being. It is basically within the primary group that the looking-glass self emerges and that the ego-centered child learns to take others into account and thereby to become a contributing member of society.

One other point about Cooley's approach needs to be mentioned. Both Cooley and Mead rejected a psychological *behavioristic* view of human beings, the view that people blindly and unconsciously respond to external stimuli. On the positive side, they believed that people had consciousness, a self, and that it was the responsibility of the sociologist to study this aspect of social reality. Cooley urged sociologists to try to put themselves in the place of the actors they were studying, to use the method of *sympathetic introspection,* in order to analyze consciousness. By analyzing what they as actors might do in various circumstances, sociologists could understand the meanings and motives that are at the base of social behavior. The method of sympathetic introspection seemed to many to be a very unscientific approach. In this area, among others, Mead's work represents an advance over Cooley's. Nevertheless, there is a great deal of similarity in the interests of the two men, not the least of which is their shared view that sociology should focus on such social-psychological phenomena as consciousness, action, and interaction.

GEORGE HERBERT MEAD (1863—1931) The most important thinker associated with the Chicago school and symbolic interactionism was not a sociologist but a philosopher, George Herbert Mead. Mead started teaching philosophy at the University of Chicago in 1894, and he taught there until his death in 1931. He is something of a paradox, given his central importance in the history of sociological theory, both because he taught philosophy, not sociology, and because he published very little during his lifetime. The paradox is, in part, resolved by two facts. First, Mead taught courses in social psychology in the philosophy department, which were taken by many graduate students in sociology. His ideas had a profound effect on a number of them. These students combined Mead's ideas with those they were getting in the sociology depart-ment from people like Park and Thomas. Although there was no theory known as sym-bolic interactionism at the time, it was created by students out of these various inputs. Thus Mead had a deep and personal impact on the people who were later to develop symbolic interactionism. Second, these students put together their notes on Mead's courses and published a posthumous volume under his name. The work, *Mind, Self and Society* (1934/1962), moved his ideas from the realm of oral to that of written tradition. Widely read to this day, this volume forms the main intellectual pillar of sym-bolic interactionism.

We will deal with Mead's ideas in Chapter Five, but it is necessary at this point to underscore a few points in order to situate him historically. Mead's ideas need to be seen in the context of psychological behaviorism. Mead was quite impressed with this orientation and accepted many of its tenets. He adopted its focus on the actor and his behavior. He regarded as sensible the behaviorists' concern with the rewards and costs involved in the behaviors of the actors. What troubled Mead was that behaviorism did not seem to go far enough. That is, it excluded consciousness from serious considera-tion, arguing that it was not amenable to scientific study. Mead vehemently disagreed and sought to extend the principles of behaviorism to include an analysis of the "mind." In so doing, Mead enunciated a focus similar to that of Cooley. But while Cooley's position seemed unscientific, Mead promised a more scientific conception of consciousness by extending the highly scientific principles and methods of psycho-logical behaviorism.

Mead offered American sociology a social psychological theory that stood in stark contrast to the primarily societal theories offered by most of the major European theo-rists—Marx, Weber, Durkheim, Comte, and Spencer. The only exception here was Simmel. Thus symbolic interactionism was developed, in large part, out of Simmel's interest in action and interaction and Mead's interest in consciousness. However, such a focus led to a weakness in Mead's work, as well as in symbolic interactionism in general, at the societal and cultural levels.

THE WANING OF CHICAGO SOCIOLOGY

Chicago sociology reached its peak in the 1920s, but by the 1930s, with the death of Mead and the departure of Park, the department began to lose its position of central im-portance in American sociology. Fred Matthews (1977) pinpoints several reasons for the decline of Chicago sociology, two of which seem of utmost importance.

First, the discipline had grown increasingly preoccupied with being scientific—that is, using sophisticated methods and employing statistical analysis. However, the Chicago school emphasized descriptive, ethnographic studies, often focusing on their subjects' personal orientations (in Thomas's terms, their "definitions of the situation"). Park came progressively to despise statistics (he called it "parlor magic") because it seemed to prohibit the analysis of subjectivity, the idiosyncratic, and the peculiar.

Second, more and more individuals outside of Chicago grew increasingly resentful of Chicago's dominance of both the American Sociological Society and the *American Journal of Sociology*. In 1935 a revolt against Chicago led to a non-Chicago secretary of the association and the establishment of a new official journal, the *American Socio-logical Review* (Lengermann, 1979). This signaled the growth of other power centers, most notably Harvard and the Ivy League in general.

SOCIOLOGICAL THEORY TO MID-CENTURY

The Rise of Harvard, the Ivy League, and Structural Functionalism

We can trace the beginning of the rise of sociology at Harvard to the arrival of Pitirim Sorokin in 1930. When Sorokin arrived at Harvard, there was no sociology depart-ment, but by the end of his first year one had been organized, and he had been appointed its head. Although Sorokin was a sociological theorist, and he continued to publish into the 1960s, his work is surprisingly little cited today. His theorizing has not stood the test of time very well. Sorokin's long-term significance may well have been in the creation of the Harvard sociology department and the hiring of Talcott Parsons (who had been an instructor of economics at Harvard) for the position of instructor of sociol-ogy. It was Parsons who became *the* dominant figure in American sociology for his work introducing European theorists to an American audience, for his own sociological theories, and for his many students who themselves became major sociological theorists.

There was an interesting relationship between Sorokin, who was the senior member of the department, and Parsons, the young instructor of sociology. For one thing, despite his junior status, Parsons quickly surpassed Sorokin in significance in Ameri-can sociological theory. As a result, a considerable amount of hostility developed be-tween the two men. This was heightened by the extensive overlap between their theories. Despite the similarities, Parsons's work attracted a far wider and far more en-during audience than did Sorokin's. As the years went by, Sorokin developed a rather interesting attitude toward Parsons's work, which was reflected in several of his books. On the one hand, he was inclined to criticize Parsons for stealing many of his best ideas. On the other hand, he was severely critical of Parsonsian theory. Another ten-sion in their relationship was over graduate students. One of the great achievements of the early Harvard department was its ability to attract talented graduate students like Robert Merton. Although these students were influenced by the ideas of both men, Parsons's influence proved more enduring than Sorokin's.

PITIRIM SOROKIN (1889–1968)   In spite of his declining intellectual influence, we need to say at least a few words about Sorokin's theoretical orientation. Sorokin wrote an enormous amount and developed a theory that, if anything, surpassed Par-sons's in scope and complexity. The most complete statement of his theory is contained in the four-volume *Social and Cultural Dynamics* published between 1937 and 1941. In it, Sorokin drew on a wide range of empirical data to develop a general theory of social and cultural change. In contrast to those who sought to develop evolutionary theories of social change, Sorokin developed a cyclical theory. He saw societies as os-cillating between three different types of mentalities—sensate, ideational, and idealistic. Societies dominated by *sensatism* emphasize the role of the senses in comprehending reality, those dominated by a more transcendental and highly religious way of understanding reality are *ideational*, while *idealistic* societies are transitional types balancing sensatism and religiosity.

The motor of social change is to be found in the internal logic of each of these systems. That is, they are pressed internally to extend their mode of thinking to its logical extreme. Thus a sensate society ultimately becomes so sensual that it provides the groundwork for its own demise. As sensatism reaches its logical end point, people turn to ideational systems as a refuge from its excesses. But once such a system has gained ascendancy, it too is pushed to its end point, with the result that society becomes excessively religious. The stage is then set for the rise of an idealistic culture and, ultimately, for the cycle to repeat itself. Sorokin not only developed an elaborate theory of social change, but he also marshaled detailed evidence from art, philosophy, politics, and so forth to support his theory. It was clearly an impressive accomplishment.

There is much more to Sorokin's theorizing, but this introduction should give the reader a feeling for the breadth of his work. It is difficult to explain why Sorokin has fallen out of favor in sociological theory. Perhaps it is the result of one of the things that Sorokin loved to attack, and in fact wrote a book about, *Fads and Foibles in Modern Sociology and Related Sciences* (1956). It may be that Sorokin will be "rediscovered" by a future generation of sociological theorists. At the moment, his work remains outside the mainstream of modern sociological theorizing.

TALCOTT PARSONS (1902–1979) The pivotal year for Parsons and for American sociological theory was 1937, the year in which he published *The Structure of Social Action*. This book was of significance to sociological theory in America for four main reasons. First, it served to introduce grand-style European theorizing to a large American audience. The bulk of the book was devoted to Durkheim, Weber, and Pareto. His interpretations of these theorists shaped their images in American sociology for many years to come.

Second, Parsons devoted almost no attention to Marx, while he emphasized the work of Durkheim and Weber and even Pareto. As a result, Marxian theory was to continue to be largely excluded from legitimate sociology.

Third, *The Structure of Social Action* made the case for sociological theorizing as a legitimate and significant sociological activity. The theorizing that has taken place in the United States since then owes a deep debt to Parsons's work.

Finally, Parsons argued for specific sociological theories that were to have a profound influence on sociology. At first, Parsons was thought of, and thought of himself, as an action theorist (see Chapter Eight for a discussion of action theory). He seemed to focus on actors and their thoughts and actions. But by the close of his 1937 work, and increasingly in his later work, Parsons sounded more and more like a structural-functional theorist focusing on large-scale social and cultural systems (see Chapter Three for a discussion of this theory). Although Parsons argued that there was no contradiction between these theories, he became best known as a structural functionalist, and he was the primary exponent of this theory, which gained dominance within sociology and maintained that position until recent years. Parsons's theoretical strength, and that of structural functionalism, lay in delineating the relationships among large-scale social structures and institutions.

Parsons's major statements on his structural-functional theory came in the early 1950s in several works, most notably *The Social System* (1951). In that work and others, Parsons tended to concentrate on the structures of society and their relationship to each other. These structures were seen as mutually supportive and tending toward a dynamic equilibrium. The emphasis was on how order was maintained among the various elements of society. Change was seen as an orderly process and Parsons (1966; 1971) ultimately came to adopt a neoevolutionary view of social change. Parsons was concerned not only with the social system per se but also with its relationship to the other *action systems,* especially the cultural and personality systems. But his basic view on intersystemic relations was essentially the same as his view of intrasystemic relations, that is, that they were defined by cohesion, consensus, and order. In other words, the various *social structures* performed a variety of positive *functions* for each other.

It is clear, then, why Parsons came to be defined primarily as a *structural functionalist*. As his fame grew, so did the strength of structural-functional theory in the United States. His work lay at the core of this theory, but his students and disciples also concentrated on extending both the theory and its dominance in the United States.

Although Parsons played a number of important and positive roles in the history of sociological theory in the United States, his work also had a number of negative consequences. First, he offered interpretations of European theorists that seemed to reflect his own theoretical orientation more than theirs. Many American sociologists were intially exposed to erroneous interpretations of the European masters. Second, as was pointed out above, early in his career Parsons largely ignored Marx, with the result that Marx's ideas continued for many years on the periphery of sociology. Third, his own theory as it developed over the years had a number of serious weaknesses. However, Parsons's preeminence in American sociology served for many years to mute or overwhelm the critics. It was not until much later that the weaknesses of Parsons's theory, and more generally of structural functionalism, received a full airing.

But we are getting too far ahead of the story, and we need to return to the early 1930s and other aspects of the development of the Harvard school. We can gain a good deal of insight into the development of the Harvard department by looking at it through an account of its other major figure—George Homans.

GEORGE HOMANS (1910–   ) A wealthy Bostonian, George Homans received his bachelor's degree from Harvard in 1932 (Homans, 1962). As a result of the Great Depression, he was unemployed but certainly not penniless. In the fall of 1932, L. J. Henderson, a physiologist, was offering a course in the theories of Vilfredo Pareto, and Homans was invited to attend and accepted. (Parsons also attended the Pareto seminars.) Homans's description of why he was drawn to, and taken with, Pareto tells us much about why American sociological theory was so highly conservative, so anti-Marxist:

> I took to Pareto because he made clear to me what I was already prepared to believe. I do not know all the reasons why I was ready for him, but I can give one. Someone has said that much modern sociology is an effort to answer the arguments of the revolutionaries. As a Republican Bostonian who had not rejected his comparatively wealthy family, I felt during the thirties that

I was under personal attack, above all from the Marxists. I was ready to believe Pareto because he provided me with a defense.

(Homans, 1962:4)

Homans's exposure to Pareto led to a book, *An Introduction to Pareto* (coauthored with Charles Curtis), published in 1934. The publication of this book made Homans a sociologist even though Pareto's work was virtually the only sociology he had read up to that point.

In 1934 Homans was named a junior fellow at Harvard, a program started to avoid the problems associated with the Ph.D. program. In fact, Homans never did earn a Ph.D. even though he became one of the major sociological figures of his day. Homans was a junior fellow until 1939, and in those years he absorbed more and more sociology. In 1939 Homans was affiliated with the sociology department, but this connection was broken by the war.

By the time Homans had returned from the war, the department of social relations had been founded at Harvard, and he joined it. This new department had its roots, in part, in Parsons's split with Sorokin. Even though Parsons had been named chairman of the sociology department in 1944, the problem remained. Although personal differences were a factor, the main foundation of the new department was the commitment of Parsons and others at Harvard to multidisciplinary work. The new department of social relations was set up in 1946 through the combined efforts of Parsons, social psychologist Gordon Allport, anthropologist Clyde Kluckhohn, and others. Parsons was appointed chairman of the department, a position he held until 1956. Parsons's power was also growing in the field of sociology—he was elected president of the Eastern Sociological Society in 1942 and president of the American Sociological Society in 1949.

Although Homans respected some aspects of Parsons's work, he was highly critical of his style of theorizing. A long-run exchange began between the two men that later manifested itself publicly in the pages of many books and journals. Basically, Homans argued that Parsons's theory was not a theory at all but rather a vast system of intellectual categories into which most aspects of the social world fit. Further, Homans believed that theory should be built from the ground up on the basis of careful observations of the social world. Parsons's theory, however, started on the general theoretical level and worked its way down to the empirical level.

In his own work Homans amassed a large number of empirical observations over the years, but it was only in the 1950s that he hit upon a satisfactory theoretical approach with which to analyze these data. That theory was psychological behaviorism, as it was best expressed in the ideas of his colleague at Harvard, the psychologist B. F. Skinner. It is on the basis of this perspective that Homans developed his exchange theory. We will pick up the story of this theoretical development later in the chapter. The crucial point here is that Harvard, and its major theoretical product, structural functionalism, began to gain preeminence in sociology in the late 1930s, replacing the Chicago school and symbolic interactionism.

The Chicago School in Decline

We left the Chicago department in the early 1930s on the wane with the death of Mead and the departure of Park. But the Chicago school did not disappear. Into the early

1950s it continued to be an important, but declining, force in sociology. Important Ph.D.s were still produced there, such as Anselm Strauss and Arnold Rose. Major figures remained at Chicago, such as Everett Hughes (Faught, 1980), who was of central importance to the development of the sociology of occupations.

However, the central figure in the Chicago department in this era was Herbert Blumer (1900–   ). He was a major exponent of the theoretical approach developed at Chicago out of the work of Mead, Simmel, Park, Thomas, and others. In fact, it was Blumer who first coined the phrase "symbolic interactionism" in 1937. Blumer played a key role in keeping this tradition alive through his teaching at Chicago. He also wrote a number of essays that were instrumental in keeping symbolic interactionism vital into the 1950s. Blumer was also important because of the organizational positions he held in sociology. From 1930 to 1935 he was the secretary-treasurer of the American Sociological Society, and in 1956 he became its president. More important, he held institutional positions that affected the nature of what was published in sociology. Between 1941 and 1952 he was editor of the *American Journal of Sociology* and was instrumental in keeping it one of the major outlets for work in the Chicago tradition in general and symbolic interactionism in particular.

While the East Coast universities were coming under the sway of structural functionalism, the Midwest remained (and to this day remains) a stronghold of symbolic interactionism. In the 1940s major symbolic interactionists fanned out across the Midwest—Arnold Rose was at Minnesota, Robert Habenstein at Missouri, Gregory Stone at Michigan State, and, most important, Manford Kuhn (1911–1963) at Iowa.

There developed a split between Blumer at Chicago and Kuhn at Iowa; in fact, people began to talk of the differences between the Chicago and the Iowa schools of symbolic interactionism. Basically, the split occurred over the issue of science and methodology. Kuhn accepted the symbolic interactionist focus on actors and their thoughts and actions, but he argued that they should be studied more scientifically—for example, by using questionnaires. Blumer, on the other hand, was in favor of "softer" methods such as sympathetic introspection and participant observation.

Despite this flurry of activity, the Chicago school was in decline, especially given the movement of Blumer in 1952 from Chicago to the University of California at Berkeley. The University of Chicago continued to have a strong sociology department, of course, but it had less and less in common with the Chicago tradition that we have been discussing. Although the Chicago school was moribund, symbolic interactionism still had some life, with its major exponents being dispersed across the country.

Developments in Marxian Theory

From the early 1900s to the 1930s Marxian theory had continued to develop largely independently of mainstream sociological theory. At least partially, the exception to this was the emergence of the critical, or Frankfurt, school out of the earlier Hegelian Marxism.

The idea of a Frankfurt school for the development of Marxian theory was the product of Felix J. Weil. The Institute of Social Research was officially founded in Frankfurt, Germany, on February 3, 1923 (Jay, 1973). Over the years a number of the most famous thinkers in Marxian theory were associated with the critical school—Max Horkheimer, Theodor Adorno, Erich Fromm, Herbert Marcuse, and, more recently, Jurgen Habermas.

The institute functioned in Germany until 1934, but by then things were growing increasingly uncomfortable under the Nazi regime. The Nazis had little use for the Marxian ideas that dominated the institute, and their hostility was heightened because many of those associated with the institute were Jewish. In 1934 Horkheimer, as head of the institute, came to New York to discuss its status with the president of Columbia University. Much to Horkheimer's surprise, he was invited to affiliate the institute with the university, and he was even offered a building on campus. And so *a* center of Marxian theory moved to *the* center of the capitalist world. The institute stayed there until after the war, but with the end of the war pressure began to mount to return it to Germany. In 1949 Horkheimer did return to Germany, and he brought the institute with him. But while the institute itself moved to Germany, many of the figures associated with it took independent career directions.

We will discuss critical theory in Chapter Four, but at this point it would be useful to underscore a few of the most important aspects of this theoretical perspective. In its early years, those associated with the institute tended to be fairly traditional Marxists devoting a good portion of their attention to the economic domain. But around 1930 a major change took place as this group of thinkers began to shift its attention from the economy to the cultural system, which it came to see as the major force in modern capitalist society. This was consistent with, but an extension of, the position taken earlier by Hegelian Marxists like Georg Lukacs. To help them understand the cultural domain, the critical theorists were attracted to the work of Max Weber (Greisman and Ritzer, 1981). The effort to combine Marx with Weber gave the critical school some of its distinctive orientations and served to make it more legitimate in later years to sociologists who began to grow interested in Marxian theory.

A second major step taken by at least some members of the critical school was to employ the rigorous social scientific techniques developed by American sociologists to research issues of interest to Marxists. This, like the adoption of Weberian theory, made the critical school more acceptable to mainstream sociologists.

A third point to be mentioned is that critical theorists made an effort to integrate individually oriented Freudian theory with the societal- and cultural-level insights of Marx and Weber. This seemed to many sociologists to represent a more inclusive theory than that offered by either Marx or Weber alone. If nothing else, the effort to combine such disparate theories proved stimulating to sociologists and many other intellectuals.

The critical school has done much useful work since the 1920s, and a significant amount of it is of relevance to sociologists. However, the critical school had to await the late 1960s before it was "discovered" by large numbers of American theorists.

SOCIOLOGICAL THEORY FROM MID-CENTURY TO THE PRESENT

Structural Functionalism: Peak and Decline

The 1940s and 1950s were paradoxically the years of greatest dominance and the beginnings of the decline of structural functionalism. In these years Parsons produced his major statements that clearly reflected his shift from action theory to structural functionalism. Parsons's students had fanned out across the country and occupied dominant positions in many of the major sociology departments (for example, Columbia and Cornell). These students were producing works of their own that were widely recognized contributions to structural-functional theory. For example, in 1945 Kingsley Davis and Wilbert Moore published an essay analyzing social stratification from a structural-functional perspective. It was one of the clearest statements ever made of the structural-functional view. In it, they argued that stratification was a structure that was functionally necessary for the existence of society. In other words, in ideological terms they came down on the side of inequality.

In 1949 Merton (1949/1968) published an essay that became *the* program statement of structural functionalism. In it, Merton carefully sought to delineate the essential elements of the theory and to extend it in some new directions. He made it clear that structural functionalism should deal not only with positive functions but also with negative consequences (dysfunctions). Moreover, it should focus on the net balance of functions and dysfunctions, or whether a structure is overall more functional or more dysfunctional.

However, just as it was gaining theoretical hegemony, structural functionalism came under attack, and the attacks mounted until they reached a crescendo in the 1960s and 1970s. The Davis-Moore structural-functional theory of stratification was attacked from the start, and the criticisms persist to this day. Beyond that, a series of more general criticisms received even wider recognition in the discipline. There was an attack by C. Wright Mills on Parsons in 1959, and other major criticisms were mounted by David Lockwood (1956), Alvin Gouldner (1959/1967; 1970), and Irving Horowitz (1962/1967). In the 1950s these attacks were seen as little more than "guerrilla raids," but as sociology moved into the 1960s the dominance of structural functionalism was clearly in jeopardy.

Radical Sociology in America: C. Wright Mills

As we have seen, while Marxian theory was largely ignored or reviled by mainstream American sociologists, there were exceptions, the most notable of which is C. Wright Mills (1916–1962). Although Mills's own lasting theoretical contributions are few, he is notable for his almost single-handed effort to keep a Marxian tradition alive in sociological theory. Modern Marxian sociologists have far outstripped Mills in theoretical sophistication, but they owe him a deep debt nonetheless for his personal and professional activities that helped set the stage for their own work.

Mills received a master's degree in philosophy at the University of Texas in 1939 and moved on to the University of Wisconsin in sociology, largely because it offered him an assistantship while the philosophy department did not (Scimecca, 1977). He quickly came under the influence of Hans Gerth, a German who had fled Nazism, and it was Gerth who introduced Mills to European sociological theorists. Mills received his Ph.D. in 1942, and his work took a radical turn. However, Mills was not a Marxist, and he did not read Marx until the mid-1950s. Even then he was restricted to the few available English translations, since he could not read German. As Mills had published most of his major works by then, his work was not informed by a very sophisticated Marxian theory.

Mills published two major works that reflected his radical politics as well as his weaknesses in terms of Marxian theory. The first was *White Collar* (1951), an acid critique of the status of a growing occupational category, white-collar workers. The second was *The Power Elite* (1956), a book that sought to show how America was dominated by a small group of businessmen, politicians, and military leaders. Sandwiched in between was his most theoretically sophisticated work, *Character and Social Structure* (1953), coauthored with Hans Gerth. Ironically, considering Mills's major role in the history of Marxian sociological theory, this book was stronger in Weberian and Freudian theory than Marxian theory. Despite this, the book is a major theoretical contribution, though it is not widely read today—possibly because it did not seem to fit well with Mills's best-known radical works. In fact, it was heavily influenced by Hans Gerth, who had a keen interest in Weberian theory.

Mills's radicalism put him on the periphery of American sociology. He was the object of much criticism, and he, in turn, became a severe critic of sociology. The critical attitude culminated in *The Sociological Imagination* (1959). Of particular note is Mills's severe criticism of Talcott Parsons. In fact, many sociologists were more familiar with Mills's critique than they were with the details of Parsons's work.

Mills died in 1962, still an outcast in sociology. However, before the decade was out both radical sociology and Marxian theory were to begin to make important inroads into the discipline.

The Development of Conflict Theory

Another precursor to a true union of Marxism and sociological theory was the development of a conflict-theory alternative to structural functionalism. As we have just seen, structural functionalism had no sooner gained leadership in sociological theory than it came under increasing attack. The attack was multifaceted: structural functionalism was accused of such things as being politically conservative, unable to deal with social change because of its focus on static structures, and incapable of adequately analyzing social conflict.

One of the results of this criticism was an effort on the part of a number of sociologists to overcome the problems of structural functionalism by integrating a concern for structure with an interest in conflict. This work constituted the development of *conflict theory* as an alternative to structural-functional theory. Unfortunately, it often seemed little more than a mirror image of structural functionalism with little intellectual integrity of its own. (This subject will be dealt with in detail in Chapter Three.)

The first effort of note was Lewis Coser's (1956) book on the functions of social conflict. This work clearly tried to deal with social conflict from within the framework of a structural-functional view of the world. While it is useful to look at the functions of conflict, there is much more to the study of conflict than an analysis of its positive functions.

Other people sought to reconcile the differences between structural functionalism and conflict theory (van den Berghe, 1963; Himes, 1966; Coleman, 1971). While these efforts had some utility, the authors were generally guilty of papering over the major differences between the two theoretical alternatives (Frank, 1966).

The biggest problem with most of conflict theory was that it lacked what it needed most—a sound basis in Marxian theory. After all, Marxian theory was well developed outside of sociology and should have provided a base on which to develop a sophisticated sociological theory of conflict. The one exception here is the work of Ralf Dahrendorf (1929–   ).

Dahrendorf is a European scholar who is well versed in Marxian theory. He sought to embed his conflict theory in the Marxian tradition. However, in the end his conflict theory looked more like a mirror image of structural functionalism than a Marxian theory of conflict. Dahrendorf's major work, *Class and Class Conflict in Industrial Society* (1959), was the most influential piece in conflict theory, but that was largely because it sounded so much like structural functionalism that it was palatable to mainstream sociologists. That is, Dahrendorf operated at the same level of analysis as the structural functionalists (structures and institutions) and looked at many of the same issues. He recognized that while aspects of the social system could fit together rather neatly, there also could be considerable conflict and tension among them

In the end, conflict theory should be seen as little more than a transitional development in the history of sociological theory. It failed because it did not go far enough in the direction of Marxian theory. It was still too early in the 1950s and 1960s for American sociology to accept a full-fledged Marxian approach. But conflict theory was helpful in setting the stage for the beginning of that acceptance by the late 1960s.

We should note, in passing, a more recent contribution to conflict theory by Randall Collins (1975). On the one hand, Collins's effort suffers from the same weakness as the other works in the conflict tradition: it is relatively impoverished in terms of Marxian theory. However, Collins did point up another weakness in the conflict tradition, and he attempted to overcome it. The problem is that conflict theory generally focuses on social structures; it has little or nothing to say about actors and their thoughts and actions. Collins, schooled in the phenomenological-ethnomethodological tradition (see below), attempted to move conflict theory in this direction.

The Birth of Exchange Theory

Another important theoretical development begun in the 1950s was the rise of exchange theory. The major figure in this development is George Homans, a sociologist whom we left earlier just as he was being drawn to B. F. Skinner's psychological behaviorism. It is Skinner's behaviorism that is the major source of Homans's, and sociology's, exchange theory (see Chapter Seven).

Dissatisfied with Parsons's deductive strategy of developing theory, Homans was casting about for a workable alternative for handling sociological theory inductively. Further, Homans wanted to stay away from the cultural and structural foci of Parsonsian theory and wanted to concentrate instead on people and their behavior. With this in mind, Homans turned to the work of his colleague at Harvard, B. F. Skinner. At first, Homans did not see how Skinner's propositions, developed to help explain the behavior of pigeons, might be useful for understanding human social behavior. But as Homans looked further at data from sociological studies of small groups and anthropological studies of primitive societies, he began to see that Skinner's behaviorism was applicable and that it provided a theoretical alternative to Parsonsian-style structural functionalism. This led to an article entitled "Social Behavior as Exchange" in 1958 and in 1961 to a full-scale, book-length statement of Homans's theoretical position, *Social Behavior: Its Elementary Forms.* These works represented the birth of exchange theory as an important perspective in sociology. Since then exchange theory has attracted a good deal of attention, both positive and negative.

Homans's basic view was that the heart of sociology lies in the study of individual behavior and interaction. He was little interested in consciousness or in the various kinds of large-scale structures and institutions that were of concern to most sociologists. His main interest was rather in the reinforcement patterns, the history of rewards and costs, that lead people to do what they do. Basically, Homans argued that people will continue to do what they have found to be rewarding in the past. Conversely, they will cease doing what has proved to be costly in the past. In order to understand behavior we need to understand an individual's history of rewards and costs. Thus, the focus of sociology should not be on consciousness, or on social structures and institutions, but on patterns of reinforcement.

As its name suggests, exchange theory is concerned not only with individual behavior but also with interaction between people involving an exchange of rewards and costs. The basic premise is that interactions are likely to continue when there is an exchange of rewards. Conversely, interactions that are costly to one or both parties are much less likely to continue.

The other major statement in exchange theory is Peter Blau's *Exchange and Power in Social Life,* published in 1964. Blau basically adopted Homans's perspective, but there was an important difference. While Homans was content to deal mainly with elementary forms of social behavior, Blau wanted to integrate this with exchange at the structural and cultural levels, beginning with exchanges among actors, but quickly moving on to the larger structures that emerge out of this exchange. He ended by dealing with exchanges among large-scale structures. This is very different from the exchange theory envisioned by Homans. In some senses it represents a return to the kind of Parsonsian-style theorizing that Homans found so objectionable. Nevertheless, the effort to deal with both small- and large-scale exchange in an integrated way proved to be a useful theoretical step. Exchange theory has now developed into a significant strand of sociological theory, and it continues to attract new adherents and new criticisms.

Dramaturgical Analysis: The Work of Erving Goffman

Erving Goffman (1922–   ) is often thought of as the last major thinker associated with the original Chicago school. He received his Ph.D. from Chicago in 1953, one year after Herbert Blumer (who had been Goffman's teacher) had left Chicago for Berkeley. Soon after, Goffman joined Blumer at Berkeley, where they were able to develop something of a center of symbolic interactionism. However, it never became anything like Chicago had been. Blumer was past his organizational prime, and Goffman did not become a focus of graduate student work. After 1952 the fortunes of symbolic interactionism declined, although it continues to be a prominent sociological theory.

In spite of the decline of symbolic interactionism in general, Goffman has carved out a strong and distinctive place for himself in contemporary sociological theory. Between the 1950s and the 1970s Goffman published a series of books and essays that gave birth to dramaturgical analysis as a variant of symbolic interactionism. Although Goffman has shifted his attention in recent years, he remains best known for his *dramaturgical theory.* (We will discuss Goffman's work in Chapter Five.)

Goffman's best-known statement of dramaturgical theory, *Presentation of Self in Everyday Life*, was published in 1959. (Over the next fifteen years Goffman published several books and a number of essays that expanded upon his dramaturgical view of the world.) To put it simply, Goffman saw much in common between theatrical performances and the kinds of "acts" we all put on in our day-to-day actions and interactions. Interaction is seen as a very fragile setting that is maintained by social performances. Poor performances or disruptions are seen as great threats to social interaction just as they are to theatrical performances.

Goffman went quite far in his analogy between the stage and social interaction. In all social interaction there is a *front region,* which is the parallel of the stage front in a theatrical performance. Actors on the stage and in social life are both seen as being interested in appearances, wearing costumes, and using props. Furthermore, in both there is a *back region*, a place to which the actors can retire to prepare themselves for their performance. Backstage, or offstage in theater terms, the actors can shed their roles and be themselves.

Dramaturgical analysis is clearly consistent with its symbolic-interactionist roots. It has a focus on actors, action, and interaction. Working in the same arena as traditional symbolic interactionism, Goffman found a brilliant metaphor in the theater to shed new light on small-scale social processes.

Goffman's work is widely read today and acknowledged for its originality and its profusion of insights. Although he is viewed as an important contemporary theorist, Goffman remains on the periphery of sociological theory. There are several reasons for this. First, he is seen as being interested in rather esoteric topics rather than the truly essential aspects of social life. Second, he is a micro theorist in an era in which the great rewards have gone to macro theorists. Third, he attracted few students who were able to build upon his insights; indeed, some believe that it is impossible to build upon Goffman's work. It is seen as little more than a series of idiosyncratic bursts of brilliant insight. Finally, little work has been done by others in the dramaturgical tradition (with the exception of Lyman and Scott, 1970).

It is difficult to predict the future of dramaturgical analysis, although it has been dimmed because Goffman himself, as we will see later, has moved in new directions in his recent work.

The Development of the "Creative" Sociologies

The 1960s and 1970s witnessed a boom in several theoretical perspectives that Monica Morris (1977) lumped together under the heading of "creative" sociology. Included under this heading are phenomenological sociology, ethnomethodology, and existential sociology.

PHENOMENOLOGICAL SOCIOLOGY

The philosophy of phenomenology, with its focus on consciousness, has a long history, but the effort to develop a sociological variant of phenomenology can be traced to the publication of Alfred Schutz's *The Phenomenology of the Social World* in Germany in 1932. However, it was not translated into English until 1967, with the result that it has only recently had a dramatic effect on American sociological theory.

To orient the reader we need to say a few words about Schutzian *phenomenological sociology*. As we will see in Chapter Six, Schutzian theory and phenomenology in general are highly abstract, complicated, and sometimes internally inconsistent. Schutz offered both a theory of consciousness and action and a theory that focuses on the cultural constraints (that is, norms and values) on individual thought and action. The problem is that they are, at times, incompatible orientations. Thus at the individual level, Schutz discusses actors' consciousness—the way people construct social reality and its relationship to individual thought and action. We are left with the impression, at least at times, that actors are free to construct any reality they like. However, when Schutz focused on the cultural realm, we get a very different impression. That is, we feel that actors are constrained, sometimes even controlled, by the norms and values of society.

The mid-1960s were crucial in the development of phenomenological sociology. Not only was Alfred Schutz's major work translated and his collected essays published, but Peter Berger and Thomas Luckmann combined to publish a book, *The Social Construction of Reality* (1967), that became one of the most widely read theory books of the time. It made at least two important contributions. First, it constituted an introduction to Schutz's ideas that was written in such a way as to make it available to a large American audience. Second, it presented an effort to integrate Schutz's ideas with those of mainstream sociology. Since 1967 phenomenology has enjoyed a tremendous boom in interest; it is one of the "hot" theories in contemporary sociology.

ETHNOMETHODOLOGY

This theoretical perspective is, in the eyes of many people, indistinguishable from phenomenology (see Chapter Six). Indeed, the creator of this perspective, Harold Garfinkel, was a student of Alfred Schutz at the New School. Garfinkel had an interesting intellectual background. He was a student of Parsons in the late 1940s and fused his orientation with that of Schutz, whom he was exposed to a few years later. After he received his Ph.D. from Harvard in 1952, Garfinkel eventually wound up at the University of California at Los Angeles, and it was there that ethnomethodology was developed by Garfinkel and his students. Geographically, ethnomethodology was the first distinctive theoretical product of the West Coast, and it has remained centered there to this day. In part, this is a result of the desire of the ethnomethodologists to remain together, but it is at least equally the result of opposition to this perspective by most mainstream sociologists.

Garfinkel became the focal point for a group of students and faculty members at UCLA interested in his approach. A series of seminars was held at UCLA beginning in the early 1950s. A major figure in these seminars, and later in ethnomethodology, was Aaron Cicourel. He received his master's degree from UCLA, went off to Cornell for his Ph.D., and then returned to UCLA as a postdoctoral student. Over the years a number of major ethnomethodologists emerged from this milieu, including Egon Bittner, Troy Duster, and Peter McHugh.

Ethnomethodology began to receive a wide national audience with the publication in 1967 of Garfinkel's *Studies in Ethnomethodology.* Although written in a difficult and obscure style, the book elicited a lot of interest. Coming at the same time as the translation of Schutz's *The Phenomenology of the Social World* and the publication of Berger and Luckmann's *The Social Construction of Reality,* it seemed to indicate that "subjective" or "creative" sociology was coming of age. Basically, *ethnomethodology* focuses on the thoughts and the resulting actions of the actor. Writers in this tradition were heavily tilted in the direction of the individual level, although they also had a strong interest in large-scale subjective aspects of social life—norms, values, culture, and so forth. They stood in stark contrast to sociologists in the mainstream, especially to the latter's theoretical focus on such large-scale objective phenomena as bureaucracies, capitalism, the division of labor, and the social system. Although their works had links to earlier sociological perspectives such as symbolic interactionism and dramaturgical analysis, there was clearly something threatening here to the mainstream sociologists who were still in control of the discipline.

In fact, both phenomenology and, more important, ethnomethodology have been subjected to some brutal attacks by mainstream sociologists. Here are two examples. The first is from a review of Garfinkel's *Studies in Ethnomethodology* by James Coleman:

> Garfinkel simply fails to generate any insights at all from the approach. . . .   Perhaps the program would be more fertile in the hands of someone more carefully observant but it is strangely sterile here. . . .
>   . . . this chapter appears to be not only an ethnomethodological disaster in itself but also evidence of the more general inadequacies of ethnomethodology. . . .
>   . . . this chapter is another major disaster, combining the rigidities of the most mathematically enraptured technicians with the technical confusions and errors of the soft clinician and without the insights or the technical competence of the creative and trained sociologist.
>   Once again, Garfinkel elaborates very greatly points which are so commonplace that they would appear banal if stated in straightforward English. As it is, there is an extraordinarily high ratio of reading time to information transfer, so that the banality is not directly apparent upon a casual reading.
>
> (Coleman, 1968:126–130)

The second example is Lewis Coser's 1975 presidential address to the American Sociological Association. Coser saw few redeeming qualities in ethnomethodology and subjected it to a savage attack, engaging in a great deal of name-calling, labeling ethnomethodology "trivial," "a massive cop-out," "an orgy of subjectivism," and a "self-indulgent enterprise." The bitterness of these and other attacks is an indication of the success of both ethnomethodology and phenomenology and the degree to which they represent a threat to the establishment in sociology.

An interesting recent development is the effort by symbolic interactionism to bring both phenomenology and ethnomethodology within its domain. This can be seen as an effort (unlikely to succeed) by a declining theoretical perspective (symbolic interactionism) to gain control over newer theories and thereby enhance its future prospects. Ethnomethodologists and phenomenologists are not likely to want to tie their futures to symbolic interactionism.

EXISTENTIAL SOCIOLOGY

Of the three creative sociologies, existential sociology is the least important, at least at the moment (see Chapter Eight). It shares with the other approaches an interest in actors and their thoughts and actions. *Existential sociology* focuses on the complexities of individual life and the ways actors attempt to deal with those complexities. It has a particular interest in individual feelings, sentiments, and the self. Although it shares a number of intellectual roots with phenomenology and ethnomethodology, existential sociology also tries to separate itself from them (see Fontana, 1980). It sees itself as more involved in the real world than either of the other creative sociologies. It also has a number of distinctive sources, such as the work of Jean-Paul Sartre (Craib, 1976). Although existential sociology has made some headway in the discipline (for example, Tiryakian, 1965; Manning, 1973; Douglas and Johnson, 1977), it remains on the periphery. But when its influence is combined with that of ethnomethodology and phenomenology, we can see that the creative sociologies are making dramatic inroads in sociology despite substantial opposition from many sociologists.

The Rise and Fall of Systems Theory

One of the more interesting developments in sociology in the last twenty years was the meteoric rise and equally meteoric fall of systems theory. Systems theory more or less burst on the scene in the 1960s, culminating in the publication of Walter Buckley's *Sociology and Modern Systems Theory* in 1967. Systems theory is derived from the hard sciences, where both organic and mechanical entities are viewed in systems terms. *Systems theory* views society as a huge system composed of a number of interrelated parts. It is necessary to examine the relationship among the parts as well as the relationship between the system and other social systems. Concern is also focused on the inputs into the social system, the way the inputs are processed by society, and the outputs that are produced. There is much more to systems theory, of course, as will be seen in Chapter Eight.

Systems theory seemed quite attractive to sociologists in the 1960s. Structural functionalism was under attack, and systems theory seemed a likely successor. After all, Parsons had entitled his 1951 book *The Social System* and had talked in terms that were close to systems theory. Furthermore, systems theory, with its roots in the hard sciences, was very attractive to sociologists interested in furthering scientific sociology. But systems theory was a bright prospect that never blossomed. Little was done with it either theoretically or empirically. Only eleven years after Buckley's book was published, Robert Lilienfeld (1978) published a blistering attack on systems theory for its failures, its scientific pretensions, and its implicit conservative ideology. We will continue to hear of systems theory, but it now seems highly unlikely that systems theory will fulfill the promise it held for its supporters in the 1960s.

The Ascendancy of Marxian Sociology

The late 1960s were also the point at which Marxian theory finally began to make significant inroads into American sociological theory. There are a number of reasons for this. First, the dominant theory (structural functionalism) was under attack for a number of things, including being too conservative. Second, Mills's radical sociology and conflict theory, although not representing sophisticated Marxian theory, had laid the groundwork for an American theory that was true to the Marxian tradition. Third, the 1960s was the era of black protests, the reawakening of the women's movement, the student movement, and the anti–Vietnam War movement. Many of the young sociologists trained in this atmosphere were attracted to radical ideas. At first, this interest was manifest in what was called in those days "radical sociology" (Colfax and Roach, 1971). This was useful as far as it went, but like Mills's work, it was rather weak on the details of Marxian theory.

It is hard to single out one work as essential to the development of Marxian sociology in America, but one that did play an important role was Henri Lefebvre's *The Sociology of Marx* (1968). It was important for its essential argument, which was that although Marx was not a sociologist there was a sociology in Marx. Since that time an increasing number of sociologists have turned to Marx's original work, as well as that of many Marxists, for insights that would be useful in the development of a Marxian sociology. At first this simply meant that American theorists were finally reading Marx seriously, but we are now beginning to see the appearance of significant pieces of Marxian scholarship by American sociologists.

American theorists have been particularly attracted to the work of the critical school, especially because of its fusion of Marxian and Weberian theory. Many of the works have been translated into English, and a number of American sociologists have made careers for themselves by writing books about the critical school for an American audience (for example, Jay, 1973).

Along with an increase in interest has come institutional support for such an orientation. There are several journals that devote considerable attention to Marxian sociological theory, including *Theory and Society, Telos,* and *Marxist Studies.* Not only is the first generation of critical theorists now well known in America, but second-generation thinkers like Jurgen Habermas and Claus Offe have received wide recognition.

Of greatest importance is the development of significant pieces of American sociology done from a Marxian point of view. One very significant strand is a group of sociologists doing historical sociology from a Marxian perspective (for example, Wallerstein, 1974, 1980; Skocpol, 1979). Another is a group analyzing the economic realm from a sociological perspective (for example, Baran and Sweezy, 1966; Braverman, 1974). Still others are doing fairly traditional empirical sociology, but work that is informed by a strong sense of Marxian theory (Kohn, 1976, for example). There are many other trends and developments in this area, but the key point is that by the 1980s Marxian sociology had "arrived" in America.

Other Recent Developments

Both in number and range, sociological theories have been proliferating enormously in recent years. In a recent anthology (McNall, 1979), a number of theoretical perspec tives are singled out for treatment, including sociobiology, the sociology of emotions, environmental sociology, and even Buddhist sociology. Many of these are little more than brief bursts of theoretical activity that will pass in relatively short order. It would be useful to close this discussion with a brief mention of some very contemporary developments that show signs of being more than simply passing theoretical fads.

One such development that we have said nothing about up to this point is the increase in interest in *structuralism*. The problem is that structuralism in sociology is so undeveloped as yet that it is difficult to define it with any precision. The problem is exacerbated by structuralism's more or less simultaneous development in a number of fields; it is difficult to find one single coherent statement of structuralism. Indeed, there are significant differences among the various branches of structuralism.

Although we will deal with it in Chapter Eight, we can get a preliminary feeling for structuralism by delineating the basic differences that exist among those who support a structuralist perspective. There are those who focus on what they call the deep structures of the mind. It is their view that these unconscious structures lead people to think and act as they do. The work of the psychoanalyst Sigmund Freud might be seen as an example of this orientation. Then there are structuralists who focus on the invisible larger structures of society and see them as determinants of the actions of people as well as of society in general. Marx is sometimes thought of as someone who practiced such a brand of structuralism, with his focus on the unseen economic structure of capitalist society. Still another group sees structures as the models they construct of the social world. Finally, there are a number of structuralists who are concerned with the dialectical relationship between individual and social structures. They see a link between the structures of the mind and the structures of society. The anthropologist Claude Lévi-Strauss is most often associated with this view.

The problem with structural sociology at the moment is that it remains largely a mélange of ideas derived from various fields including linguistics (Saussure), anthropology (Lévi-Strauss), psychology (Freud), and Marxism (Althusser). Until these ideas are put together in a coherent fashion, structuralism will remain marginal to sociology. However, the developments in related fields have been so significant and so attractive to those in sociology that a structural theory in sociology is likely to attract more and more attention in coming years.

Another development worth noting in sociological theory is sociobiology (see Chapter Eight). Sociology has had a long, emotional, and cyclical relationship with biology. Many of the early grand theories in sociology were developed as analogies to biological theories; organicism was a significant force in the development of sociological theory. In fact, structural functionalism continues to have a number of strong similarities with biological organicism. Although such approaches waned in the 1930s, they are currently enjoying a significant rebirth, in large part as a result of the success and controversy surrounding the work of E. O. Wilson (1975). There are now a number of sociologists who are exploring the role of biological factors in social life.

It seems that much of *sociobiology* has two central interests—the proximate and the ultimate causes of human behavior (Greene, Morgan, and Barash, 1979). A proximate focus leads to concern with the role of immediate biological factors in individual behavior. For example, what is the role in individual aggression of chemical changes in the body? The more important focus of sociobiologists, on the ultimate causes of human behavior, leads to an interest in such issues as how the evolutionary process of natural selection has led people to behave altruistically, aggressively, or in virtually any other manner.

The future of sociobiology depends a great deal on how far its supporters are willing to press their claims. If sociobiologists are trying to argue that the complex social and cultural system of the United States can be explained by biological factors, then they are overstepping their bounds and will likely find only a small audience among sociologists. On the other hand, if they are simply arguing that biological factors play a role along with many other factors in shaping such a cultural system, then they are likely to acquire many more supporters in sociology. E. O. Wilson has enunciated the kind of conciliatory position that is likely to give sociobiologists a key role in the future of sociological theory:

> Human behavior is dominated by culture in the sense that the greater part, perhaps all, of the variation between societies is based on differences in cultural experience. But this is not to say that human beings are infinitely plastic. . . . Assisted by sociobiological analyses, a stronger social science might develop. An exciting collaboration between biologists and social scientists appears to have begun.
>
> (Wilson, 1978:xiv)

Sociobiologists can play a useful role in delineating both the proximate and the ultimate biological causes of social behavior. However, these factors, as Wilson suggests, only help describe the limits of social life. The actual development of a complex social world is defined by the many sociological variables that have been sketched throughout this chapter—in other words, that have been delineated throughout the history of sociology and, specifically, sociological theory.

Sociobiology, neo-Marxian theory, creative sociology, and structuralism are the "hottest" developments in sociological theory. In the coming years some may cool while others may come to the fore. It is likely that in the future some new sociological theories will be developed and some old ones resurrected. That is all to the good, and it is what makes sociological theory the exciting and vibrant field that it is and that it is likely to continue to be.

SUMMARY

This chapter picks up the story of the history of sociological theory at the end of the nineteenth century. We begin with the early history of American sociological theory, which was characterized by its liberalism, by its interest in Social Darwinism, and consequently by the influence of Herbert Spencer. In this context, the work of the two early sociological theorists Sumner and Ward are discussed. However, they did not leave a very lasting imprint on American sociological theory. In contrast, the Chicago school, as embodied in the work of people like Small, Park, Thomas, and, especially, Cooley and Mead, did leave a strong mark on sociological theory, especially on symbolic interactionism.

While the Chicago school was still predominant, a different form of sociological theory began to develop at Harvard. Pitirim Sorokin played a key role in the founding of sociology at Harvard, but it was Talcott Parsons who was to lead Harvard to a position of preeminence in American theory, replacing Chicago's symbolic interactionism. Parsons was important not only for legitimizing "grand theory" in the United States and for introducing European theorists to an American audience, but also for his role in the development of action theory and, more important, structural functionalism. In the 1940s and 1950s structural functionalism was aided by the disintegration of the Chicago school that began in the 1930s and was largely complete by the 1950s.

The major development in Marxian theory in the early years of the twentieth century was the creation of the Frankfurt, or critical, school. This was a Hegelianized form of Marxism that also showed the influence of sociologists like Weber and of the psychoanalyst Sigmund Freud. Marxism did not gain a widespread following among sociologists in the early part of the century.

Structural functionalism's dominance within American theory in mid-century was rather short-lived. Although traceable to a much earlier date, phenomenological sociology began to attract significant attention in the 1960s. Marxian theory was still largely excluded from American theory, but C. Wright Mills kept a radical tradition alive in America in the 1940s and 1950s. Mills was also one of the leaders of the attacks on structural functionalism, attacks that mounted in intensity in the 1950s and 1960s. In light of some of these attacks, a conflict theory alternative to structural functionalism emerged in this period. Although influenced by Marxian theory, conflict theory suffered from an inadequate integration of Marxism. Still another alternative born in the 1950s was exchange theory, and it continues to attract a small but steady number of followers. While symbolic interactionism was in eclipse, the work of Erving Goffman on dramaturgical analysis in this period kept it from being moribund.

Dramatic developments took place in the so-called creative sociologies in the 1960s and 1970s. Phenomenological sociology, ethnomethodology, and existential sociology continue to attract a great deal of attention in sociology. At the same time, Marxian sociology came into its own, and its several varieties continue to cause a great deal of excitement in sociological theory. While creative sociology and Marxian theory have been on the rise, systems theory gained popularity in the 1960s only to encounter a dramatic drop in popularity in the 1970s. The chapter closes with a discussion of two of the "hottest" developments in sociological theory—structuralism and sociobiology.

Chapters One and Two taken together provide the reader with the historical sketch needed to bring some order to the often bewildering array of theories discussed in the body of this book. Our focus is the major idea systems in sociology that deal with centrally important social issues and tend to be broad in range. In the ensuing chapters we are concerned with contemporary theories alone. Most of these have been in existence for some time and have demonstrated long-term and continuing significance. Others, of more recent vintage, are included because they show signs of being important for years to come. We will encounter detailed discussions of these theories as we proceed through the book.

PART TWO
THE MAJOR THEORIES

PART TWO
DETERMINATION OF SURROGATES

CHAPTER THREE
Structural Functionalism and the Emergence of a Conflict Theory Alternative

THE first part of this chapter will focus on structural functionalism, which was for years the dominant sociological theory. We will begin with a discussion of its basic principles and historical roots, especially in the work of Talcott Parsons. We will then discuss some examples of how structural functionalism has been used by more contemporary thinkers, as well as some of the basic criticisms of structural functionalism.

In the second part of the chapter we will discuss the emergence of conflict theory as an alternative to structural functionalism. We will deal with the criticisms of conflict theory, the most important of which is that it is not true to its Marxian roots. This, in turn, leads to Chapter Four, where we examine a variety of neo-Marxian theories.

STRUCTURAL FUNCTIONALISM

Many people have believed structural functionalism to be *the* dominant sociological theory. Robert Nisbet (cited in Turner and Maryanski, 1979:xi) argued that it was "without any doubt, the single most significant body of theory in the social sciences in the present century." Kingsley Davis (1959) took the position that structural functionalism was, for all intents and purposes, synonymous with sociology. More recently, Alvin Gouldner (1970) implicitly took a similar position when he attacked Western sociology largely through a critical analysis of the structural-functional theories of Talcott Parsons.

In fact, in the last decade, structural functionalism has declined in importance as a sociological theory. Even Wilbert Moore (1978:321), a man who is intimately associated with this theory, argued that it had almost "become an embarrassment in contemporary theoretical sociology." Two recent observers (Turner and Maryanski, 1979:141) even stated: "Thus, functionalism as an explanatory theory is, we feel, 'dead' and continued efforts to use functionalism as a theoretical explanation should be abandoned in favor of more promising theoretical perspectives."[1] Nicholas Demerath and Richard Peterson (1967) took a more positive view, arguing that structural functionalism is not a passing fad. However, they admitted that it is likely to evolve into another sociological theory, just as this theory itself evolved out of the earlier organicism. Whatever its status as a theory, structural functionalism is worth analyzing, if only because it dominated the field for such a long time.

Before undertaking this analysis, we need a definition of structural functionalism. Note that the terms "structural" and "functional" need not be used in conjunction, although this is typically done by practitioners. We could study the structures of society without being concerned with their functions (or consequences) for other structures.[2] Similarly, we could examine the functions of a variety of social processes that may not take a structural form. Still, the concern for both elements characterizes structural functionalism.

Mark Abrahamson (1978) argued that structural functionalism is not monolithic. He identified three varieties of structural functionalism. The first is *individualistic functionalism*. Here the focus is on the needs of actors and the various large-scale structures (for example, social institutions, cultural values) that emerge as functional responses to these needs. The anthropologist Bronislaw Malinowski was a major proponent of this perspective. The second is *interpersonal functionalism*, and the exemplar was again an anthropologist, A. B. Radcliffe-Brown. Here the focus is on social relationships, particularly the mechanisms to accommodate strains that exist in such relationships. The third variety, *societal functionalism*, is the dominant approach among sociological structural functionalists (Sztompka, 1974:48), and as such will be the focus of this chapter. The primary concern of societal functionalism is with the large-scale social structures and institutions of society, their interrelationships, and their constraining effects on actors.

Historical Roots

Three classic sociologists were the most important influences on contemporary structural functionalism (Turner and Maryanski, 1979): Auguste Comte, Herbert Spencer, and Emile Durkheim.

Comte had a normative conception of the "good" society, which led to an interest in what any given social phenomenon contributes to that society. He also had a sense of equilibrium within societies. However, his theory of *organicism*—the tendency to see

---

[1]Despite this statement, Jonathan Turner and Alexandra Maryanski (1979) are willing to argue that functionalism can continue to be useful as a method.
[2]This is, in effect, the course taken by macrostructural theory, which will be discussed in Chapter Eight.

analogies between societies and biological organisms—was his most influential concept. He viewed social systems as organic systems that functioned in much the same way as biological organisms. Thus, while biology was to study the individual organism, sociology was to study the social organism. Among the specific analogies that Comte saw between biological and social organisms were those of cells on the biological level to families in the social world, of tissues to social classes and castes, and of the organs of the body to cities and communities in the social world.

The English sociologist Herbert Spencer also adopted organicism, but in his sociology it coexisted uncomfortably with a utilitarian philosophy. Thus while his organicism led him to look at social wholes and the contributions of parts to the whole, his utilitarianism led him to focus on self-seeking actors. Despite the intellectual problems this presented, Spencer's organicism was influential in the development of structural functionalism.

Spencer saw various similarities between social and individual organisms. First, both social and individual organisms grow and develop, whereas inorganic matter does not. Second, in both, an increase in size tends to lead to increasing complexity and differentiation. Third, progressive differentiation of structures in both tends to be accompanied by progressive differentiation in function. Fourth, the parts of both organisms are mutually interdependent. Thus a change in one is likely to lead to changes in the other parts. Finally, each of the parts of both social and individual entities can be seen as an organism in itself.

Spencer had a number of other insights that were influential in the development of structural functionalism. His concern with the "needs" of the social organism was picked up by later structural functionalists, who, among other things, translated it into the idea that societies "need" various things in order to survive. Spencer also developed a law of social evolution, which influenced the development of later structural-functional theories of evolution, such as those associated with Durkheim and Parsons. Perhaps of greatest importance was Spencer's use of the terms "structure" and "function" as well as his differentiation between them. He tended to speak of the functions that various structures had for the society as a whole.

While both Comte and Spencer are important in their own right, their greatest impact on structural functionalism came through their effect on the thinking of Durkheim. Most generally, Durkheim's interest in social facts reflected an interest in the parts of the social organism and their interrelationships as well as their impact on the society as a whole. In terms of structural functionalism, Durkheim had much to say about structures, functions, and their relationship to the needs of society. Perhaps of greatest importance was his separation of the concepts of social cause and social function. The study of social causes is concerned with why a given structure exists as well as why it takes a certain form. In contrast, the study of social functions is concerned with the needs of the larger system met by a given structure.

Modern structural functionalism operates on the basis of several assumptions derived from the ideas of these three classic sociologists. Structural functionalists, especially the societal functionalists, are likely to take a macroscopic approach to the study of social phenomena. They focus on the social system as a whole as well as on the impact of the various parts (especially social structures and social institutions) on it.

They see the components of the system as contributing positively to its continued operation (Abrahamson, 1978). In addition, structural functionalism is concerned with the relationship of one part of the system to another (Davis, 1959). The parts of the system, as well as the system as a whole, are seen as existing in a state of equilibrium, so that changes in one part will lead to changes in other parts. Changes in parts may balance each other so that there is no change in the system as a whole; if they do not, the entire system will probably change. Thus while structural functionalism adopts an equilibrium perspective, it is not necessarily a static point of view. In this moving equilibrium of the social system, those changes that do occur are seen as doing so in an orderly, not a revolutionary, way.

Parsonsian Structural Functionalism

Over the course of his long career as America's premiere theorist, Talcott Parsons (1902–1979) made important contributions to a number of theoretical orientations,[3] but he is best known for his central role in the development of structural-functional theory. In addition to his own theoretical work, Parsons is also important because many of his students (as we will see throughout the first part of this chapter) became leading contributors to structural-functional theory. They include, among others, Robert Merton, Kingsley Davis, Wilbert Moore, Robin Williams, Marion Levy, and Neil Smelser. While our focus in this section is on Parsons's structural functionalism, the reader should keep in mind that Parsons's contributions extend far beyond a single sociological theory.

Although Parsons made contributions to individualistic functionalism and interpersonal functionalism, he is best known as a societal functionalist. The fact that his main concern was with large-scale social structures and culture, their interrelationships, and their constraining effects on actors is well-illustrated by what many consider to be the essence of Parsons's work—the action system. Figure 3.1 is a schematic outline of Parsons's action schema.

FIGURE 3.1   Parsons's Action Schema

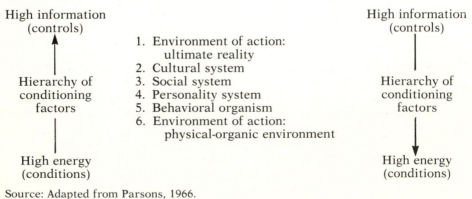

1. Environment of action:
     ultimate reality
2. Cultural system
3. Social system
4. Personality system
5. Behavioral organism
6. Environment of action:
     physical-organic environment

High information
(controls)

Hierarchy of
conditioning
factors

High energy
(conditions)

Source: Adapted from Parsons, 1966.

---

[3]See Chapter Eight for a discussion of Parsons's contributions to action theory. For a more detailed discussion of Parsons's work see the author's *Sociological Theory* (1983).

Parsons's societal functionalism is clear from this schema. The higher-order systems control the lower-order ones; the lower-order systems provide the conditions, or the energy, needed by the higher-order systems to exist. If we exclude for a moment the environment of action, we can see that the higher-order systems, the large-scale cultural and social systems, control the lower-order, smaller-scale personality and behavioral-organism systems. Like other societal functionalists, not only did Parsons consider the large-scale systems, especially the cultural system, as controlling, but his major contributions were to our understanding of the structure and functioning of these systems. Although he did have much to say about the personality system, he thought of personality as controlled by larger-scale systems. The behavioral organism is more of a residual category, and Parsons had relatively little to say about it.

Most of the remainder of our discussion of Parsons will be devoted to the four action systems (social, cultural, personality, and behavioral organism). First, however, a comment is necessary on the two environments of the action system. The lowest level, the physical and organic environment, involves the nonsymbolic aspects of the human body, its anatomy and physiology. The highest level, ultimate reality, has, as Jackson Toby (1977:3) suggests, "a metaphysical flavor," but Toby also argues that Parsons "is not referring to the supernatural so much as to the universal tendency for societies to address symbolically the uncertainties, concerns, and tragedies of human existence that challenge the meaningfulness of social organization."

THE FOUR ACTION SYSTEMS

The heart of Parsons's work is found in his four action systems. In the assumptions that Parsons made regarding his action systems we encounter the problem of order that was both his overwhelming concern and that of structural functionalism in general (Schwanenberg, 1971). The Hobbesian problem of order—what prevents a social war of all against all—was not answered to Parsons's (1937) satisfaction by the earlier philosophers. Parsons found his answer to the problem of order in structural functionalism, which operates in his theory with the following set of assumptions:

1. Systems have the property of order and interdependence of parts.
2. Systems tend toward self-maintaining order, or equilibrium.
3. The systems may be static or involved in an ordered process of change.
4. The nature of one part of the system has an impact on the form that the other parts could take.
5. Systems maintain boundaries with their environments.
6. Allocation and integration are two fundamental processes necessary for a given state of equilibrium of a system.
7. Systems tend toward self-maintenance involving the maintenance of boundaries and of the relationships of parts to the whole, control of environmental variations, and control of tendencies to change the system from within.

These assumptions led Parsons to make the analysis of the *ordered* structure of society his first priority. In so doing, he virtually ignored the issue of social change, at least until later in his career:

TALCOTT PARSONS: A Biographical Sketch

Long before his death in 1979, Talcott Parsons had become the most influential sociological theorist in the history of American sociology. Although he had published some essays previously, *The Structure of Social Action* (1937) launched Parsons toward the position of dean of American sociological theorists. Over the next forty years he wrote a prodigious number of books and essays on his developing theoretical orientation. In addition to his enormous influence as an author, Parsons was also a teacher at Harvard, where he influenced many who were later to become important American sociologists.

Throughout his career, Parsons was the center of considerable controversy. To some, he *was* American sociological theory. To others, his work had overwhelming weaknesses. He may not have been nearly as good as his supporters claimed or nearly as bad as his detractors contended. Whatever the ultimate judgment on the adequacy of his theory, Parsons dominated American sociological theory for over forty years.

Upon his death, a number of his former students, themselves sociologists of considerable note, reflected on Parsonsian theory as well as on the man behind the theory. In their musings, these sociologists offered some interesting insights into Parsons and his work. The few glimpses of Parsons reproduced here do not add up to a coherent picture, but they do offer some provocative glimpses of the man and his work.

Robert Merton was one of his students when Parsons was just beginning his teaching career at Harvard. Merton, who became a noted theorist in his own right, makes clear that graduate students did not come to Harvard in those years to study with Parsons, but rather with Pitirim Sorokin, the senior member of the department, who was to become Parsons's archenemy:

> Of the very first generation of graduate students coming to Harvard . . . precisely none came to study with Talcott. They could scarcely have done so for the simplest of reasons: in 1931, he had no public identity whatever as a sociologist.

> Although we students came to study with the renowned Sorokin, a subset of us stayed to work with the unknown Parsons.

> (Merton, 1980:69)

Merton's reflections on Parsons's first course in theory are interesting too, especially since the material provided the basis for one of the most influential theory books in history:

> Long before Talcott Parsons became one of the Grand Old Men of world sociology, he was for an early few of us its Grand Young Man. This began with his first course in theory. . . . [It] would provide him with the core of his masterwork, *The Structure of Social Action* which . . . did not appear in print until five years after its first oral publication.

> (Merton, 1980:69–70)

Most people think of Parsons as a ''grand theorist'' endeavoring to produce a theoretical system in sociology comparable to Newtonian theory in physics, yet Parsons never succeeded in producing such a theory. Instead, he created an elaborate conceptual scheme. In his obituary of Parsons, Robert Bellah makes some interesting points about such conceptual schemes as well as the possibility of grand theory in sociology:

> Talcott spoke of general theory and . . . the ideal of an abstract content-free theoretical science from which one could deduce the laws of social life. But those who took him at his word . . . were bitterly disappointed. His work remained . . . at the level of a conceptual scheme, the necessary phase, he said, before the construction of a tight theoretical system from which testable hypotheses could be deduced. And so the empiricists attacked him time and again on the ground that his ideas remained vague, untestable, incapable of empirical disconfirmation. What they did not know and what Talcott only gradually and obscurely discerned is that in the human studies there is not ever going to be a tight deductive theoretical system, that all we will ever have are analogies and metaphors that direct us to look in new ways at social reality.
>
> (Bellah, 1980:61)

One of the most often-made criticisms of Parsons was that he offered a static, consensual view of society in which actors were accorded progressively less voluntarism, a key characteristic of the actor in early Parsonsian theory. In his obituary of Parsons, Robin Williams deals with this criticism:

> Contrary to the interpretation by some critics, the fact is that Parsons repeatedly and emphatically called attention to strains and inconsistencies within and among the three analytically separable systems of society, culture, and personality. . . . Inherent in social action as he thus saw it are tendencies toward deviance and alienation of individuals, toward inconsistencies in cultural patterning, and toward secession, schism, and conflict in the relations of sub-units of social structure.
>
> Few sociologists of our time have been more subjected to stereotyping, to careless *ad hoc* readings, and to selectively distorted interpretations. Anything like a genuinely scholarly analysis will show how grossly misleading it is to imply that Parsons held any simplistic view of societal "consensus," that he had a "static theory," that he regarded human beings as oversocialized cultural robots, or that, indeed, there ever was any need to bring concrete living men or women "back into" his view of the social universe.
>
> (Williams, 1980:65–66)

Finally, those who have read Parsons's theoretical work have often found it difficult, dry, and dull. The assumption was made that the man who produced such a theory must resemble it in some ways. An anecdote reported by John Riley, Jr., belies this image and gives us the sense that Parsons was able to laugh at himself and his work:

> I recall an incident in which a paper about Parsonsian theory had been transcribed by a nonsociological typist. The author had been talking about Parsons's *pattern variables* and the typed script came out to read Parsons's *pet invariables*. Somehow the marvelous typo got to Talcott. He chuckled and said: "Do you suppose that they just might turn out to be invariable?"
>
> (Riley, 1980:68)

Although all would not share Merton's positive evaluation of Parsons, they would acknowledge the following:

> The death of Talcott Parsons marks the end of an era in sociology. When [a new era] does begin . . . it will surely be fortified by the great tradition of sociological thought which he has left to us.
>
> (Merton, 1980:71)

> We feel that it is uneconomical to describe changes in systems of variables before the variables themselves have been isolated and described; therefore, we have chosen to begin by studying particular combinations of variables and to move toward description of how these combinations change only when a firm foundation for such has been laid.
>
> (Parsons and Shils, 1951:6)

Parsons was so heavily criticized for his static orientation that he devoted more and more attention to change; in fact, as we will see, he eventually focused on the evolution of societies. However, in the view of most observers, even his work on social change tended to be highly static and structured.

SOCIAL SYSTEM   Parsons's conception of the social system begins at the micro level with interaction between ego and alter ego, defined as the most elementary form of the social system. He spent little time analyzing this level, although he did argue that features of this interaction system are present in the more complex forms taken by the social system. Parsons defined a social system thus:

> A social system consists in a plurality of individual actors *interacting* with each other in a situation which has at least a physical or environmental aspect, actors who are motivated in terms of a tendency to the "optimization of gratification" and whose relation to their situations, including each other, is defined and mediated in terms of a system of culturally structured and shared symbols.
>
> (Parsons, 1951:5–6)

Despite his commitment to viewing the social system as a system of interaction, Parsons did not take interaction as his fundamental unit in the study of the social system. Rather, he used the *status-role* complex as the basic unit of the system. This is not an aspect of interaction, but rather a *structural* component of the social system. *Status* refers to a structural position within the social system, and *role* is what the actor does in such a position seen in the context of its functional significance for the larger system. The actor is viewed (at least in terms of position in the social system) as nothing more than a bundle of statuses and roles.

In his analysis of the social system Parsons was interested primarily in its structural components. In addition to a concern with the status-role, Parsons was interested in such large-scale components of social systems as collectivities, norms, and values (Parsons, 1966:11). In his analysis of the social system, however, Parsons was not simply a structuralist but also a functionalist. He thus delineated a number of the functional prerequisites of a social system. First, social systems must be structured so that they operate compatibly with other systems. Second, in order to survive the social system must have the requisite support from other systems. Third, the system must meet a significant proportion of the needs of its actors. Fourth, the system must elicit adequate participation from its members. Fifth, it must have at least a minimum of control over potentially disruptive behavior. Sixth, if conflict becomes sufficiently disruptive, it must be controlled. Finally, a social system requires a language in order to survive.

In addition to the more specific discussion of the functional prerequisites of a social system, Parsons developed a more general schema that could be applied not only to the social system but to all action systems. He spoke of the four functional imperatives that he believed to be necessary for (characteristic of) all systems—(A) adaptation, (G) goal attainment, (I) integration, and (L) latency, or pattern maintenance (AGIL). In order to survive, a system must perform these four functions:

1. *Adaptation:* A system must cope with the situational exigencies facing it.
2. *Goal attainment*: A system must achieve its primary goal.
3. *Integration*: A system must regulate the interrelationship of the other three functional imperatives.
4. *Latency (pattern maintenance)*: A system must furnish, maintain, and renew both motivational and cultural patterns.

Parsons designed the AGIL scheme to be used at *all* levels in his theoretical system. As Chandler Morse noted:

> The four functional imperatives, or problems, operate at both a micro-analytic and a macro-analytic level in the Parsonsian model. At the micro-level they purport to specify the phases through which *individual actors* in a small action system and the action system as a whole must progress during an action cycle. At the macro-level the imperatives provide a means of (a) allocating roles analytically among four functional subsystems of any given system, and of(b) sorting out the input-output flows among those sub-systems.
>
> (Morse, 1961:116)

Although Parsons believed the four functional imperatives were operative at all levels, his focus was large-scale systems and their relationship to one another. Even when he talked about actors, it was from the point of view of the system. Also, the discussion reflected Parsons's concern with the maintenance of order within the social system.

However, Parsons did not completely lose sight of the issue of the relationship between actors and social structures in his discussion of the social system. In fact, he called the integration of the social and cultural systems and actors "the fundamental dynamic theorem of sociology" (Parsons, 1951:42). Given his central concern with the social system, of key importance in this integration are the processes of internalization and socialization. That is, Parsons was interested in the ways that the norms and values of a system are transferred to the actors within the system. In a successful socialization process these norms and values are internalized; that is, they become part of the actors' "consciences." As a result, in pursuing their own interests, the actors are in fact serving the interests of the system as a whole.

In general, Parsons assumed that actors are usually passive recipients in the socialization process.[4] Children learn not only how to act but also the norms and values, the morality, of society. Socialization is conceptualized as a conservative process in which needs (which are themselves largely molded by society) bind children to the social system, which provides the means by which the needs can be satisfied. There is little or no room for creativity; the need for gratification ties children to the system as it exists.

---

[4]This is a controversial interpretation of Parsons's work with which many disagree. François Bourricaud (1981:108), for example, talks of "the dialectics of socialization" in Parsons's work and not of passive recipients of socialization.

Parsons sees socialization as a lifelong experience. Because the norms and values inculcated in childhood tend to be very general, they do not prepare children for the various specific situations they will encounter in adulthood. Thus socialization must be supplemented throughout the life cycle with a series of more specific socializing experiences. Despite this need later in life, the norms and values learned in childhood tend to be stable and with a little gentle reinforcement tend to remain in force throughout life.

Despite the conformity induced by lifelong socialization, there is a wide range of individual variation in the system. The question is, why is this normally not a major problem for the social system, given its need for order? For one thing, a number of social control mechanisms can be employed to induce conformity. However, as far as Parsons was concerned, social control is strictly a second line of defense. A system runs best when social control is used only sparingly. For another thing, the system must be able to tolerate some variation, some deviance. A flexible social system is stronger than a brittle one that accepts no deviation. Finally, the social system should provide a wide range of role opportunities that allow different personalities to express themselves without threatening the integrity of the system.

Socialization and social control are the main mechanisms that allow the social system to maintain its equilibrium. Modest amounts of individuality and deviance are accommodated, but more extreme forms must be met by re-equilibrating mechanisms. Thus social order is built into the structure of Parsons's social system:

> Without deliberate planning on anyone's part there have developed in our type of social system, and correspondingly in others, mechanisms which, within limits, are capable of forestalling and reversing the deep-lying tendencies for deviance to get into the vicious circle phase which puts it beyond the control of ordinary approval-disapproval and reward-punishment sanctions.
>
> (Parsons, 1951:319)

Again, Parsons's main interest was the system as a whole rather than the actor in the system—how the system controls the actor, not how the actor creates and maintains the system. This reflects Parsons's commitment on this issue to a structural-functional orientation.

As important as the structures of the social system were to Parsons, the cultural system was of greater significance. In fact, as we saw earlier, the cultural system stood at the top of his action system and Parsons (1966) labeled himself a "cultural determinist."

CULTURAL SYSTEM   Parsons conceived of culture as the major force binding the various elements of the social world, or, in his terms, the action system. It mediates interaction among actors and integrates the personality and the social systems. Culture has the peculiar capacity to become, at least in part, a component of the other systems. Thus in the social system culture is embodied in norms and values, and in the personality system it is internalized by the actor. But the cultural system is not simply a part of other systems; it also has a separate existence in the form of the social stock of knowledge, symbols, and ideas. These aspects of the cultural system are available to the social and personality systems, but they do not become part of them (Parsons and Shils, 1951:6; Morse, 1961:105).

Parsons defined the cultural system, as he did his other systems, in terms of its relationship to the other action systems. Thus culture is seen as a patterned, ordered system of symbols that are objects of orientation to actors, internalized aspects of the personality system, and institutionalized patterns in the social system. Because it is largely symbolic and subjective, culture is readily transmitted from one system to another. This allows it to move from one social system to another through diffusion and from one personality system to another through learning and socialization. However, the symbolic (subjective) character of culture also gives it another characteristic, the ability to control Parsons's other action systems. Parsons came to the conclusion that moral standards (norms and values) are "the superordinate integrative techniques of a system of action" (Parsons and Shils, 1951:170). This conclusion reflects the crucial idea in Parsons's theory—that the cultural system is preeminent.

PERSONALITY SYSTEM   The personality system is controlled not only by the cultural system, but also by the social system. Although its subordinate position is clear, Parsons wanted to accord at least some independence to the personality system:

> My view will be that, while the main content of the structure of the personality is derived from social systems and culture through socialization, the personality becomes an independent system through its relations to its own organism and through the uniqueness of its own life experience; it is not a mere epiphenomenon.
>
> (Parsons, 1970:82)

We get the feeling here that Parsons is protesting too much. If the personality system is not an epiphenomenon, it is certainly reduced to secondary or dependent status in his theoretical system.

The *personality* is defined as the organized system of orientation and motivation of action of the individual actor. The basic component of the personality is the need-disposition. Parsons and Shils (1951:113) defined need-dispositions as the "most significant units of motivation of action." They differentiated need-dispositions from drives, which are innate tendencies—"physiological energy that makes action possible" (Parsons and Shils, 1951:111). In other words, drives are better seen as part of the biological organism. Need-dispositions are then defined as "these same tendencies when they are not innate but acquired through the process of action itself" (Parsons and Shils, 1951:111). In other words, need-dispositions are drives that are shaped by the social setting.

Need-dispositions impel actors to accept or reject objects presented in the environment or to seek out new objects if the ones that are available do not adequately satisfy need-dispositions. Parsons differentiated among three basic types of need-dispositions. The first type impels actors to seek love, approval, and so forth, from their social relationships. The second type includes internalized values that lead actors to observe various cultural standards. Finally, there are the role expectations that lead actors to give and get appropriate responses.

This gives a very passive image of actors. They seem to be either impelled by drives, dominated by the culture, or, more usually, shaped by a combination of drives and culture (that is, by need-dispositions). On various occasions, Parsons tried to endow the personality with some creativity. For example, he said: "We do not mean . . . to imply that a person's values are entirely 'internalized culture' or mere adherence to rules and laws. The person makes creative modifications as he internalizes culture; but the novel aspect is not the cultural aspect" (Parsons and Shils, 1951:72). Despite claims such as these, the dominant impression that emerges from Parsons's work is one of a passive personality system.

Parsons's emphasis on need-dispositions creates other problems. Because it leaves out so many other important aspects of personality, his system becomes a largely impoverished one. Alfred Baldwin, a psychologist, makes precisely this point:

> It seems fair to say that Parsons fails in his theory to provide the personality with a reasonable set of properties or mechanisms aside from need-dispositions, and gets himself into trouble by not endowing the personality with enough characteristics and enough different kinds of mechanisms for it to be able to function.
>
> (Baldwin, 1961:186)

Baldwin (1961:180) makes another telling point about Parsons's personality system, arguing that even when Parsons analyzed the personality system, he was really not focally interested in it: "Even when he is writing chapters on personality structure, Parsons spends many more pages talking about social systems than he does about personality." This is reflected in the various ways that Parsons linked the personality to the social system. First, actors must learn to see themselves in a way that fits with the place they occupy in society (Parsons and Shils, 1951:147). Second, role expectations are attached to each of the roles occupied by individual actors. Then there is the learning of self-discipline, internalization of value-orientations, identification, and so forth. All these forces point toward the integration of the personality system with the social system, which Parsons emphasized. However, he also pointed out the possible malintegration, which is a problem for the system that needs to be overcome.

Another aspect of Parsons's work reflects the passivity of the personality system. This is his interest in internalization as the personality system's side of the socialization process. Parsons (1970:2) derived this interest from Durkheim's work on internalization as well as from Freud's work, primarily that on the superego. In emphasizing internalization and the superego, Parsons once again manifested his conception of the personality system as passive and externally controlled.

BEHAVIORAL ORGANISM   Though he included the behavioral organism as one of the four action systems, Parsons had very little to say about it. It is included because it is the source of energy for the rest of the systems. Although it is based on genetic constitution, its organization is affected by the processes of conditioning and learning that occur during the individual's life. The biological organism is clearly a residual system in Parsons's work, but at the minimum Parsons is to be lauded for including it as a part of his sociology, if for no other reason than that he anticipated the current revival of interest in sociobiology in sociology.

EVOLUTIONARY THEORY

Parsons's work with conceptual tools such as the action systems and the functional imperatives led to the accusation that he offered a structural theory that was unable to deal with social change. Parsons had long been sensitive to this charge, arguing that although a study of change was necessary, it must be preceded by a study of structure. But by the 1960s he could resist the charges no longer and made a major shift in his work, turning to the study of social change, particularly the study of social evolution. By Parsons's (1977b:50) own testimony that interest was first stimulated by a seminar on social evolution held in 1963. Here, at least in outline, is Parsons's evolutionary theory.

Parsons's (1966) general orientation to the study of social change was shaped by biology. To deal with this process Parsons developed what he called ''a paradigm of evolutionary change.''

The first component of that paradigm is the process of *differentiation*. Parsons assumed that any society is composed of a series of subsystems that differ in terms of both their *structure* and their *functional* significance for the larger society. As society evolves, new subsystems are differentiated. This is not enough, however; they also must be more adaptive than earlier subsystems. This led Parsons to the essential aspect of his evolutionary paradigm, the idea of *adaptive upgrading*. Parsons described this process:

> If differentiation is to yield a balanced, more evolved system, each newly differentiated sub-structure . . . must have increased adaptive capacity for performing its *primary* function, as compared to the performance of *that* function in the previous, more diffuse structure. . . . We may call this process the *adaptive upgrading* aspect of the evolutionary change cycle.
> (Parsons, 1966:22)

This is a highly positive model of social change. It assumes that as society evolves it grows generally better able to cope with its problems. In contrast, in Marxian theory social change leads to the eventual destruction of capitalist society. For this reason, among others, Parsons is often thought of as a very conservative sociological theorist.

Next, Parsons argued that the process of differentiation leads to a new set of problems of *integration* for society. As subsystems proliferate, the society is confronted with new problems in coordinating the operations of these units.

A society undergoing evolution must move from a system of ascription to one of achievement. A wider array of skills and abilities is needed to handle the more diffuse subsystems. The generalized abilities of people must be freed from their ascriptive bonds so that they can be utilized by society. Most generally, this means that groups formerly excluded from contributing to the system must be freed for inclusion as full members of the society.

Finally, the *value* system of the society as a whole must undergo change as social structures and functions grow increasingly differentiated. However, since the new system is more diverse, it is harder for the value system to encompass it. Thus a more differentiated society requires a value system that is ''couched at a higher level of generality in order to legitimize the wider variety of goals and functions of its sub-units'' (Parsons, 1966:23). However, this process of generalization of values often does not proceed smoothly as it meets resistance from groups committed to their own narrow value systems.

Evolution proceeds through a variety of cycles, but no general process affects all societies equally. Some societies may foster evolution, whereas others may ''be so beset with internal conflicts or other handicaps'' that they impede the process of evolution, or they may even ''deteriorate'' (Parsons, 1966:23). What most interested Parsons were those societies in which developmental ''breakthroughs'' occur, since he believed that once they occur the process of evolution would follow his general evolutionary model.

Although Parsons (1966:26) conceived of evolution as occurring in stages, he was careful to avoid a unilinear evolutionary theory: ''We do not conceive societal evolution to be either a continuous or a simple linear process, but we can distinguish between broad levels of advancement without overlooking the considerable variability found in each.'' Making it clear that he was simplifying matters, Parsons distinguished three broad evolutionary stages—primitive, intermediate, and modern. Characteristically, he differentiated among these stages primarily on the basis of cultural dimensions. The crucial development in the transition from primitive to intermediate is the development of language, primarily written language. The key development in the shift from intermediate to modern is ''the institutionalized codes of normative order,'' or law (Parsons, 1966:26).

Parsons next proceeded to analyze a series of specific societies in the context of the evolution from primitive to modern society. One particular point is worth underscoring here: Parsons turned to evolutionary theory, at least in part, because he was accused of being unable to deal with social change. However, his analysis of evolution is *not* in terms of process; rather, it is an attempt to ''order structural types and relate them sequentially'' (Parsons, 1966:111). This is comparative *structural* analysis, not really a study of the processes of social change. Thus, even when he was supposed to be looking at change, Parsons remained committed to the study of structures and functions.

We have now spent several pages analyzing some of the major dimensions of Parsons's structural functionalism. Although there is much more to Parsons's work than structural functionalism, it is generally agreed that his most important contributions were to that theory. We turn now to some more specific examples of structural functional theory, many of which were produced by Parsons's students and disciples.

The Functional Theory of Stratification and Its Critics

The functional theory of stratification as articulated by two of Parsons's students, Kingsley Davis and Wilbert Moore (1945), is perhaps the best-known single piece of work in structural-functional theory. From the beginning, Davis and Moore made it clear that they regarded social stratification as both universal and necessary. They argued that no society is ever unstratified, or totally classless. Stratification is, in their view, a *functional* necessity. All societies need such a system, and it is this need that brings into existence a system of stratification.[5] They also viewed a stratification system as a structure, pointing out that stratification refers not to the individuals in the

---

[5]This is an example of a teleological argument. We will have occasion to discuss this issue later in the chapter, but for now we can define a *teleological argument* as one that sees the social world as having purposes, or goals, which bring needed structures or events into being. In this case society ''needs'' stratification, so it brings such a system into existence.

stratification system but rather to a system of *positions*. They focused on how certain positions come to carry with them different degrees of prestige and not on how individuals come to occupy certain positions.

Given this focus, the major functional issue is how a society motivates and places people in their "proper" positions in the stratification system. This is reducible to two problems. First, how does a society instill in the "proper" individuals the desire to fill certain positions? Second, once people are in the right positions, how does society then instill in them the desire to fulfill the requirements of those positions?

The problem of proper social placement in society arises for three basic reasons. First, some positions are more pleasant to occupy than others. Second, some positions are more important to the survival of society than others. Third, social positions require different abilities and talents.

While these issues apply to all social positions, Davis and Moore were concerned with the functionally more important positions in society. The positions that rank high within the stratification system are presumed to be those that are *less* pleasant to occupy but *more* important to the survival of society and that require the greatest ability and talent. In addition, society must attach sufficient rewards to these positions so that the individuals who occupy them will work diligently. The converse was implied by Davis and Moore but not discussed. That is, low-ranking positions in the stratification system are presumed to be *more* pleasant and *less* important and to require less ability and talent. Also, society has less need to be sure that individuals perform their duties in these positions with diligence.

Davis and Moore did not argue that a society consciously develops a stratification system in order to be sure that the high-level positions are filled, and filled adequately. Rather, they made it clear that stratification is an "unconsciously evolved device." However, it is a device that every society does, and *must*, develop if it is to survive.

In order to be sure that people occupy the higher-ranking positions, society must, in Davis and Moore's view, provide these individuals with various rewards, including great prestige, high salary, and sufficient leisure. For example, to ensure enough doctors for our society, we need to offer them these, and other, rewards. Davis and Moore implied that we could not expect people to undertake the "burdensome" and "expensive" process of medical education if we did not offer such rewards. The implication seems to be that people at the top must receive the rewards they do. If they did not, those positions would remain unfilled and society would crumble.

The structural-functional theory of stratification has been subject to much criticism since its publication in 1945 (see Tumin, 1953, for the first important criticism; Huaco, 1966, for a good summary of the main criticisms to that date).

One basic criticism is that the functional theory of stratification simply perpetuates the privileged position of those people already at the top who have power, prestige, and money. It does this by arguing that such people deserve their rewards; indeed they need to be offered such rewards for the good of society.

The functional theory also can be criticized for assuming that simply because a stratified social structure has existed in the past, it must continue to exist in the future. It is possible that future societies can be organized in other, nonstratified ways.

In addition, it has been argued that the idea of functional positions varying in their importance to society is difficult to support. Are garbage collectors really any less important to the survival of society than advertising executives? Despite the lower pay and prestige of the garbage collectors, they may actually be *more* important to the survival of the society. Even in cases where it could be said that one position serves a more important function for society, the greater rewards do not necessarily accrue to the more important position. The woman who is a nurse may be much more important to society than the movie actress, but she has far less power, prestige, and income than the actress.

Is there really a scarcity of people capable of filling high-level positions? In fact, many people are prevented from obtaining the training they need to achieve prestigious positions, even though they have the ability. In the medical profession, for example, there is a persistent effort to limit the number of practicing doctors. In general, many able people never get a chance to show that they can handle high-ranking positions even though there is a clear need for them and their contributions. The fact is that those in high-ranking positions have a vested interest in keeping their numbers small and their power and income high.

Finally, it can be argued that we do not have to offer people power, prestige, and income to get them to want to occupy high-level positions. People can be equally motivated by the satisfaction of doing a job well or by the opportunity to be of service to others.

The Functional Prerequisites of a Society

One of the major concerns of structural functionalists is an analysis of the things—the structures, and particularly the functions—that a social system needs in order to survive. Earlier we saw that Parsons discussed the four functional prerequisites of any social system—adaptation, goal attainment, integration, and pattern maintenance. Here we shall examine the major example of this kind of analysis by D. F. Aberle and his associates (1950/1967).

Aberle and his colleagues discuss the basic conditions that, were they to cease to exist, would cause the termination of society. The first factor deals with the population characteristics of the society. The extinction, or the dispersion, of its population would obviously threaten the existence of society. This would occur if society lost enough of its population to make its various structures inoperative. Second, an apathetic population would be a threat to society. Although this is a question of degree, since some segments of a society always manifest at least some apathy, at some point the population could become so apathetic that various components of society would cease to operate, and ultimately the entire society would disintegrate. Third, a war of "all against all" within the population would threaten society's existence. A high level of internal conflict within society would require the intervention of various social control agents who would use force to contain the conflict. Structural functionalists believe that a society cannot operate for any length of time on the basis of force. As Aberle and his colleagues (1950/1967:322) put it: "A society based solely on force is a contradiction in terms." To structural functionalists, society is held together by the consensus of its members; to them, a society held together by force is no society at all. Finally, a society could be terminated by absorption into another society through annexation, conquest, and so forth.

The reverse side of this discussion of functional prerequisites includes the characteristics a society must have in order to survive. For one thing, a society must have an adequate method of dealing with its environment. Of the two aspects of the environment that can be differentiated, the first is the ecology. A society must be able to extract what it needs to survive from the environment (food, fuel, raw materials, and so forth) without destroying the sources. We are all painfully aware of this problem in an era of environmental pollution, energy shortages, and starvation in many areas of the world. The second aspect of the environment is the other social systems with which a society must be able to cope. This involves, among other things, trade, cultural exchanges, adequate communication, and adequate military defense in the event of inter-societal hostilities.

A society must also have an adequate method for sexual recruitment. Heterosexual relationships have to be patterned in such a way that men and women have adequate opportunities to interact. Beyond that, both sexes must be endowed with the motivation needed for a rate of reproduction sufficient to maintain the society. This means that on the average a couple must produce something above two children. Furthermore, the society needs to be sure that there is a sufficient number of people and that they have enough diverse interests and skills to allow the society to function.

A society must also have sufficient differentiation of roles, as well as a way of assigning people to those roles. In all societies certain activities must be performed and roles must be constructed in order to allow them to be performed. The most important form of role differentiation is social stratification. As we have seen, one of the basic tenets of structural functionalism is that societies must be stratified in order to survive. Stratification is seen as performing various functions, such as ensuring that people are willing to take on the responsibilities of high-status positions, assuring the stability of the social system, and so forth.

An adequate communication system is also viewed as a functional requirement of any social system. Its elements include language and channels of communication. Clearly, society itself would be impossible if people were not able to interact and communicate. However, when structural functionalists discuss society's communication system, they also mean the shared symbolic systems that people learn during the socialization process and that make communication possible. Shared symbolic systems make possible a cultural value system. It is the cultural system that is crucial to the structural-functional view of society and how it is held together. The common value pattern is a major bulwark against the possibility of continual internal conflict in society.

Not only must there be a shared cultural system, but structural functionalists also talk of the need for a shared cognitive system of values at the individual level. What this means is that people must look at the world in essentially the same way. This allows them to predict, with a high degree of accuracy, what others will think and do. These mutual cognitive orientations perform various functions. Of perhaps greatest importance, they make social situations stable, meaningful, and predictable. In short, a stable society, which is of enormous importance to structural functionalists, is made possible by the fact that actors operate with shared orientations. Such shared orientations also allow people to account in similar ways for those things they cannot control or predict, which enables them to sustain their involvement in, and commitment to, social situations.

Structural functionalists also argue that society needs a shared, articulated set of goals. If people were pursuing many unrelated goals, the resulting chaos would make society impossible. Shared goals, such as marital happiness, the success of children, and occupational achievement, help to give a high level of cohesion to society.

Society requires some method of regulating the means to achieve these goals, and the normative system performs this function. Without the normative regulation of means, society would be afflicted by chaos, anomie, and apathy. If occupational success could be obtained by *any* means possible, there would be, according to the structural functionalists, societal disorder.

A society must also regulate affective expression, since unbridled emotions would be another source of chaos. Some emotions are clearly necessary; for example, "love" and family loyalty are necessary to ensure an adequate population. While it may be difficult for anyone to define precisely the line between necessary and dangerous levels of emotion, to the structural functionalists it is clear that at some level emotionalism is a threat to the social system.

Implied in many of the preceding points is the idea that society requires the socialization of new members in order to survive. People must learn many things, including their "place" in the stratification system, the common value system, shared cognitive orientations, acceptable goals, norms defining proper means to these goals, and regulations on affective states. If actors have not learned and internalized such things, society is viewed as impossible by the structural functionalist.

Finally, society requires effective control over disruptive forms of behavior. Ideally, if the socialization process has led actors to internalize all the proper values, then they will conform of their own volition. To the structural functionalists, society runs best when there is no need for external control of actors. However, when external control proves necessary, various social control agents are brought to bear, ranging from the raised eyebrow of a friend to the billy club of the police officer, or even, in extreme cases, to the bayonet of the soldier.

This completes a brief summary of the functional prerequisites of society. A critical evaluation will be deferred until later, when we discuss the general criticisms of structural functionalism.

Robert Merton's Model of Structural Functionalism

Merton's essay, "Toward the Codification of Functional Analysis in Sociology" (1949/1968), is *the* most important statement on structural functionalism in sociology. In this essay Merton criticized some of the more extreme and indefensible aspects of structural functionalism. But equally important, his new conceptual insights helped to give structural functionalism a continuing usefulness.

Merton criticized what he saw as the three basic postulates of functional analysis. The first is the postulate of the functional unity of society. This postulate holds that all standardized social and cultural beliefs and practices are functional for society as a whole as well as for individuals in society. This view implies that the various parts of a social system must show a high level of integration. However, Merton maintained that while it may be true of small, primitive societies, the generalization cannot be extended to larger, more complex societies.

Universal functionalism is the second postulate. That is, it is argued that *all* standardized social and cultural forms and structures have positive functions. Merton argued that this contradicts what we find in the real world. It is clear that not every structure, custom, idea, belief, and so forth has positive functions. For example, rabid nationalism can be highly dysfunctional in a world of rapidly proliferating nuclear arms.

Third is the postulate of indispensability. The argument here is that all standardized aspects of society not only have positive functions but also represent indispensable parts of the working whole. This postulate leads to the idea that all structures and functions are functionally necessary for society. No other structures and functions could work quite as well as those that are currently found within society. Merton's criticism was that we must at least be willing to admit that there are various structural and functional alternatives to be found within society.

Merton's position was that all of these functional postulates rely on nonempirical assertions based on abstract, theoretical systems. At a minimum, it is the responsibility of the sociologist to examine each empirically. His belief that empirical tests, not theoretical assertions, are crucial to functional analysis led Merton to develop his "paradigm" of functional analysis as a guide to the integration of theory and research.

Merton made it clear from the outset that structural-functional analysis focuses on groups, organizations, societies, and cultures. He stated that any object that can be subjected to structural-functional analysis must "represent a standardized (that is, patterned and repetitive) item" (Merton, 1949/1968:104). He had in mind such things as "social roles, institutional patterns, social processes, cultural patterns, culturally patterned emotions, social norms, group organization, social structure, devices for social control, etc." (Merton, 1949/1968:104).

Early structural functionalists tended to focus almost entirely on the *functions* of one social structure or institution for another. However, in Merton's view, early analysts tended to confuse the subjective motives of individuals with the functions of structures or institutions. The focus of the structural functionalist should be on social functions rather than on individual motives. Functions, according to Merton (1949/1968:105), are defined as "those observed consequences which make for the adaptation or adjustment of a given system." However, there is a clear ideological bias when one focuses only on adaptation or adjustment, for they are always positive consequences. It is important to note that one social fact can have negative consequences for another social fact. To rectify this serious omission in early structural functionalism, Merton developed the idea of a *dysfunction*. Just as structures or institutions could contribute to the maintenance of other parts of the social system, they could also have negative consequences for them. Slavery in the southern United States, for example, clearly had positive consequences for white southerners, such as supplying cheap labor, support for the cotton economy, and social status. It also had dysfunctions, such as making southerners overly dependent on an agrarian economy and therefore unprepared for industrialization. The lingering disparity between the North and the South in terms of industrialization can be traced, at least in part, to the dysfunctions of the institution of slavery in the South.

Merton also posited the idea of *nonfunctions,* which he defined as consequences that are simply irrelevant to the system under consideration. Included here might be social forms that are "survivals" from earlier historical times. While they may have had positive or negative consequences in the past, they have no significant effect on contemporary society. One example, although a few might disagree, is the Women's Christian Temperance Movement.

To help answer the question of whether positive functions outweigh dysfunctions, or vice versa, Merton developed the concept of *net balance*. However, we can never simply add up positive functions and dysfunctions and objectively determine which outweighs the other, because the issues are so complex and based on so much subjective judgment that they cannot easily be calculated and weighed. The usefulness of

---

ROBERT K. MERTON: An Autobiographical Sketch*

It is easy enough to identify the principal teachers, both close at hand and at a distance, who taught me most. During my graduate studies, they were: P. A. Sorokin, who oriented me more widely to European social thought and with whom, unlike some other students of the time, I never broke although I could not follow him in the directions of inquiry he began to pursue in the late 1930s; the then quite young Talcott Parsons, engaged in thinking through the ideas which first culminated in his magisterial *Structure of Social Action*; the biochemist and sometime sociologist L. J. Henderson, who taught me something about the disciplined investigation of what is first entertained as an interesting idea; the economic historian E. F. Gay, who taught me about the workings of economic development as reconstructible from archival sources; and, quite consequentially, the then dean of the history of science, George Sarton, who allowed me to work under his guidance for several years in his famed (not to say, hallowed) workshop in the Widener Library of Harvard. Beyond these teachers with whom I studied directly, I learned most from two sociologists: Emile Durkheim, above all others, and Georg Simmel, who could teach me only through the powerful works they left behind, and from that sociologically sensitive humanist, Gilbert Murray. During the latter period of my life, I learned most from my colleague, Paul F. Lazarsfeld, who probably had no idea of how much he taught me during our uncountable conversations and collaborations during more than a third of a century.

Looking back over my work through the years, I find more of a pattern in it than I had supposed was there. For almost from the beginning of my own work, after those apprenticeship years as a graduate student, I was determined to follow my intellectual interests as they evolved rather than pursue a predetermined lifelong plan. I chose to adopt the practice of my master-at-a-distance, Durkheim, rather than the practice of my master-at-close-range, Sarton. Durkheim repeatedly changed the subjects he chose to investigate. Starting with his study of the social division of labor, he examined methods of sociological inquiry and then turned successively to the seemingly unrelated subjects of suicide, religion, moral education and socialism, all the while developing a theoretical orientation which, to his mind, could be effectively developed by attending to such varied aspects of life in society. Sarton had proceeded quite the other way: in his earliest years as a scholar, he had worked out a program of research in the history of science that was to culminate in his monumental five-volume *Introduction [sic] to the History of Science* (which carried the story through to the close of the 14th century!).

Merton's concept comes from the way it orients the sociologist to the question of relative significance. To return to the example of slavery, the question becomes whether, on balance, slavery was more functional or dysfunctional to the South. Still, this question is too broad and obscures a number of issues (for example, that slavery was functional for groups like white slaveholders).

To cope with problems like these Merton added the idea that there must be *levels of functional analysis*. Functionalists had generally restricted themselves to analysis of the society as a whole, but Merton made it clear that analysis could also be done on an organization, institution, or group. Returning to the issue of the functions of slavery for

---

The first of these patterns seemed more suitable for me. I wanted and still want to advance sociological theories of social structure and cultural change that will help us understand how social institutions and the character of life in society come to be as they are. That concern with theoretical sociology has led me to avoid the kind of subject specialization that has become (and, in my opinion, has for the most part rightly become) the order of the day in sociology, as in other evolving disciplines. For my purposes, study of a variety of sociological subjects was essential.

In that variety, only one special field—the sociology of science—has persistently engaged my interest. During the 1930s, I devoted myself almost entirely to the social contexts of science and technology, especially in 17th-century England, and focused on the unanticipated consequences of purposive social action. As my theoretical interests broadened, I turned, during the 1940s and afterward, to studies of the social sources of nonconforming and deviant behavior, of the workings of bureaucracy, mass persuasion and communication in modern complex society, and to the role of the intellectual, both within bureaucracies and outside them. In the 1950s, I centered on developing a sociological theory of basic units of social structure: the role-set and status-set and the role models people select not only for emulation but also as a source of values adopted as a basis for self-appraisal (this latter being "the theory of reference groups"). I also undertook, with George Reader and Patricia Kendall, the first large-scale sociological study of medical education, aiming to find out how, all apart from explicit plan, different kinds of physicians are socialized in the same schools of medicine, this being linked with the distinctive character of professions as a type of occupational activity. In the 1960s and 1970s, I returned to an intensive study of the social structure of science and its interaction with cognitive structure, these two decades being the time in which the sociology of science finally came of age, with what's past being only prologue. Throughout these studies, my primary orientation was toward the connections between sociological theory, methods of inquiry, and substantive empirical research.

I group these developing interests by decades only for convenience. Of course, they did not neatly come and go in accord with such conventional divisions of the calendar. Nor did all of them go, after the first period of intensive work on them. I am at work on a volume centered on the unanticipated consequences of purposive social action, thus following up a paper first published almost half a century ago and intermittently developed since. Another volume in the stocks, entitled *The Self-Fulfilling Prophecy*, follows out in a half-dozen spheres of social life the workings of this pattern as first noted in my paper by the same title, a mere third of a century ago. And should time, patience, and capacity allow, there remains the summation of work on the analysis of social structure, with special reference to status-sets, role-sets, and structural contexts on the structural side, and manifest and latent functions, dysfunctions, functional alternatives, and social mechanisms on the functional side.

Mortality being the rule and painfully slow composition being my practice, there seems small point in looking beyond this series of works-in-progress.

the South, it would be necessary to differentiate several levels of analysis and ask about the functions and dysfunctions of slavery for black families, white families, black political organizations, white political organizations, and so forth. In terms of net balance, slavery was probably more functional for certain social units and more dysfunctional for other social units. Addressing the issue at these more specific levels helps to analyze the functionality of slavery for the South as a whole.

Merton also introduced the concepts of manifest and latent functions. These two terms have also been important additions to functional analysis.[6] In simple terms, *manifest functions* are those that are intended, while *latent functions* are unintended. The manifest function of slavery, for example, was to increase the economic productivity of the South, but it had the latent function of providing a vast underclass that served to increase the social status of southern whites, both rich and poor. This idea is related to another of Merton's concepts—*unanticipated consequences*. Actions have both intended and unintended consequences. While everyone is aware of the intended consequences, it requires sociological analysis to uncover the unintended consequences; indeed, to some this is the very essence of sociology. Peter Berger (1963) has called this "debunking," or looking beyond stated intentions to real effects.

Merton made it clear that unanticipated consequences and latent functions are not the same. A latent function is one type of unanticipated consequence, one that is functional for the designated system. But there are two other types of unanticipated consequences: "those that are dysfunctional for a designated system, and these comprise the latent dysfunctions," and "those which are irrelevant to the system which they affect neither functionally or dysfunctionally . . . non-functional consequences" (Merton, 1949/1968:105).

As further clarification of functional theory, Merton pointed out that a structure may be dysfunctional for the system as a whole and yet may continue to exist. One might make a good case that discrimination against blacks, females, and other minority groups is dysfunctional for American society, yet it continues to exist because it is functional for a part of the social system; for example, discrimination against females is generally functional for males. However, these forms of discrimination are not without some dysfunctions, even for the group for which they are functional. Males do suffer from their discrimination against females; similarly, whites are hurt by their discriminatory behavior toward blacks. One could argue that these forms of discrimination adversely affect those who discriminate by keeping vast numbers of people underproductive and by increasing the likelihood of social conflict.

Merton contended that not all structures are indispensable to the workings of the social system. Some parts of our social system *can* be eliminated. This helps functional theory overcome another of its conservative biases. By recognizing that some structures are expendable, functionalism opens the way for meaningful social change. Our

---

[6]Recently, Colin Campbell (1982) has criticized Merton's distinction between manifest and latent functions. Among other things, he points out that Merton is vague about these terms and uses them in various ways (for example, as intended versus actual consequences and as surface meanings versus underlying realities). More important, he feels that Merton never adequately integrated action theory (see Chapter Eight) and structural functionalism. The result is that we have an uncomfortable mixture of the intentionality ("manifest") of action theory and the structural consequences ("functions") of structural functionalism. It is because of these and other confusions that Campbell believes Merton's distinction between manifest and latent function is so little used in contemporary sociology.

society, for example, could continue to exist (and even be improved) by the elimination of discrimination against various minority groups.

Merton's clarifications are of great utility to modern sociologists who wish to perform structural-functional analyses. His modifications of the older versions of the theory were so substantial that those who follow his ideas may be called neo-functionalists. Let us now turn to the work of Herbert Gans, as an example of how structural-functional analysis should be done using Merton's neo-functionalist model.

A Structural-Functional Analysis of Poverty

It has been said that Gans's 1972 essay "The Positive Functions of Poverty" was written, as least in part, as a parody of structural-functional analysis. It may have been written to show how ludicrous this type of analysis was, by taking an obviously serious social problem, poverty, and focusing attention on its positive functions. Whatever his motivations, Gans produced an excellent illustration of how structural functionalism can be used.

Gans's thesis was that although poverty obviously has all sorts of dysfunctions, it has not been exposed to a systematic functional analysis that seeks to uncover its positive functions. In conducting such an analysis, Gans was not being an apologist for poverty, nor was he saying that because poverty has functions for various segments of society it should or must persist. What he was arguing, following Merton, was that functional analysis is (when used correctly) ideologically neutral. The results of a functional analysis can be used either to help or to hurt the poor, but the analysis itself can and should be as value-neutral as possible. Gans even noted that his effort to point out the positive functions of poverty can be used by those who are inclined to improve the lot of the poor by providing alternate sources of rewards to those who gain from the existence of poverty. This, in Merton's terms, exemplifies the existence of functional alternatives. We will examine some of these functional alternatives as well as the implications of Gans's work, but first let us turn to the essence of his thesis—the many functions he saw poverty performing. These functions can be subdivided into four categories: economic, social, cultural, and political.

ECONOMIC FUNCTIONS

Gans thought that poverty could be seen as serving four economic functions:

1. The existence of poverty provides society with a group of people, the poor, who are willing, or unable to be unwilling, to perform the "dirty work" in society. Gans (1972:278) defined such work as that which is "physically dirty or dangerous, temporary, dead-end, and underpaid, undignified, and menial." Perhaps most important, these occupations command low pay. Furthermore, certain sorts of enterprises, such as hospitals, restaurants, and industrial agriculture, often depend for their very existence on the availability of poor people to fill the jobs they offer.
2. That the poor receive so little money is a kind of subsidy to the rich, allowing them to use the money they save to further their own ends or, through saving and investment, the ends of the entire capitalistic economy. This subsidy function can also take a variety of noneconomic forms. For example, poor people who work as

domestics free wealthy women for other activities; the poor who serve as paid volunteers in medical experiments pave the way for the wealthy, who can afford the treatments when and if they are proven safe and useful.

3. A whole series of occupations exist because there are poor people. If poverty were to disappear, many middle- and upper-class people would be out of work. In Gans's opinion, examples of occupations dependent on the poor are policeman, penologist, numbers runner, Pentecostal minister, loan shark, and heroin pusher. In addition, the peacetime army exists mainly because the poor are willing to serve in it.

4. Poor people also purchase goods and use services that otherwise would go unused. Day-old bread and quack doctors find a market in depressed areas.

SOCIAL FUNCTIONS

In addition to economic functions, the poor serve certain social functions:

1. The existence of the poor validates dominant societal norms. Although the poor probably do not deviate more, they can be more easily labeled as deviant. For example, if a middle-class and a poor youth commit the same deviant act, the poor youth is far more likely to be labeled a juvenile delinquent than the middle-class adolescent. Norms such as hard work, honesty, and monogamy need some violators so that they can be reaffirmed and thereby retain their potency. The poor perform the very valuable function of enabling society to keep its norms powerful.

2. A subgroup among the poor is defined as deserving. These people may be poor because they are suffering disabilities or have experienced bad luck. Whatever the cause, this group provides upper classes with psychic gratification by providing an outlet for their altruism, pity, and charity.

3. More affluent people can also live vicariously by imagining that the poor engage in, and enjoy more, "uninhibited sexual, alcoholic, and narcotic behavior."

4. Since social status is so important in our society, the poor provide a measuring rod for other classes. The poor enable the working class to know where it is and, more important, that it stands above some group in the social hierarchy.

5. Poor people also aid other groups in ascending the stratification ladder. "By being denied educational opportunities or being stereo-typed as stupid or unteachable, the poor thus enable others to obtain better jobs" (Gans, 1972:281). Furthermore, the poor provide those who are rising in the stratification system some of the things they need (cheap maid service, for example) to make it to the next rung on the ladder.

6. While the deserving poor provide a source of psychic gratification to those above them in the stratification system, the poor in general provide them with things to do. For example, members of the aristocracy can serve the poor through various charitable agencies. Similarly, the middle classes can derive a great deal of satisfaction from doing volunteer work for the needy.

CULTURAL FUNCTIONS

The poor can be thought of as serving two cultural functions:

1. They have provided the physical labor needed to construct our more impressive cultural monuments and their exploitation provides the basis of the funds that support various types of intellectuals and artists.

2. An aspect of the culture of the poor (for example, jazz) is frequently adopted by those above them in the stratification system, and some members of the poor (for example, the hobo, the prostitute) become heroes and subjects of study by other members of society.

POLITICAL FUNCTIONS

Finally, the poor may be thought of as serving important political functions:

1. They serve as the rallying point or enemy of various political groups. The political left rallies around the poor while the political right attacks the poor with such epithets as "welfare chiselers."
2. The burden for change and growth in American society can be placed on the shoulders of the poor. Gans gave the following examples:

> During the 19th century, they did the backbreaking work that built the cities; today, they are pushed out of their neighborhoods to make room for "progress." . . . The major costs of the industrialization of agriculture in America have been borne by the poor, who are pushed off the land without recompense, just as in earlier centuries in Europe, they bore the brunt of the transformation of agrarian societies into industrial ones. The poor have also paid a large share of the human cost of the growth of American power overseas, for they have provided many of the foot soldiers for Vietnam and other wars.
> (Gans, 1972:283)

3. Since the poor vote less and participate less in the political process, they have been a less potent force in the political system than their number would indicate. In Gans's view this has made American politics more "centrist" than it would otherwise have been, and it has made the political system more stable.

FUNCTIONAL ALTERNATIVES

To repeat: Gans is *not* in favor of poverty; rather, one of the implications of his work is that if we really want to do away with poverty, we must find alternatives to a variety of the functions that the poor now perform. As an alternative to the first function, he suggested that automation do some of society's dirty work and that the rest could be performed at higher wages. Similarly, he suggested that instead of the third economic function, professionals could perform other useful chores than those dependent on the poor. Social workers could help the ulcer-ridden business executive instead of the skid-row bum. For the social functions he suggested that we reserve our pity and charity for the disabled and leave the poor alone. Overall, this type of analysis makes the point that when we examine poverty functionally, we see that there are alternative ways of performing some of the functions the poor now perform. Those who "profit" from the existence of poor people would be more likely to accept changes among the poor if they knew their own gains would continue, although from other sources and in other ways.

Despite the existence of alternatives for some functions, Gans found no suitable alternatives for others—namely, the political functions. Furthermore, in many cases he found that the alternative would be more costly, particularly to more affluent members of society. In summary, poverty persists for three basic reasons:

1. It is functional to a variety of units in society. Entrepreneurs, executives, welfare workers, and many others profit from poverty.
2. There are no alternatives to some of the functions performed by the poor.
3. Where there are alternatives, they are costlier to the affluent than retaining the poor.

Gans concluded that social phenomena such as poverty persist when they are functional for the affluent and dysfunctional for the poor. This led him to the further conclusion that poverty can be eliminated in either of two ways: first, if it becomes sufficiently dysfunctional for the affluent, or second, if the poor achieve enough power to change the dominant system of social stratification. Gans regarded these conclusions as very similar to a radical sociologist's, even though he arrived at them using what is considered the most conservative sociological orientation—structural functionalism.

We now turn to a discussion of the criticisms of contemporary functionalism, one of which is its supposed conservative orientation.

The Major Criticisms

No single sociological theory in the history of the discipline has been the focus of as much interest as structural functionalism. From the late 1930s to the early 1960s it was virtually unchallenged as the dominant sociological theory in the United States. In recent years, however, criticism of the theory has increased rapidly and now is far more prevalent than praise. Abrahamson (1978:37) depicts this situation quite vividly: "Thus, metaphorically, functionalism has ambled along like a giant elephant, ignoring the stings of gnats, even as the swarm of attackers takes its toll."

Let us look at some of these major criticisms. First, we will deal with the major *substantive* criticisms of structural functionalism and then focus on the *logical and methodological* problems associated with the theory.

SUBSTANTIVE CRITICISMS

One major criticism is that structural functionalism does not deal adequately with history—that it is inherently ahistorical. In fact, structural functionalism was developed, at least in part, in reaction to the historical evolutionary approach of certain anthropologists. Many of the early anthropologists were seen as describing the various stages in the evolution of a given society, or society in general. Frequently, depictions of the early stages were highly speculative. Furthermore, the later stages were often little more than idealizations of the society in which the anthropologist lived. Early structural functionalists were seeking to overcome the speculative character and ethnocentric biases of these works. In its early years in particular, structural functionalism went too far in its criticism of evolutionary theory and came to focus on either contemporary or abstract societies. However, structural functionalism need not be ahistorical (Turner and Maryanski, 1979). Although practitioners have tended to operate as if it were ahistorical, nothing in the theory prevents them from dealing with historical issues. In fact, Parsons's (1966, 1971) work on social change, as we have seen, reflects the ability of structural functionalists to deal with change if they so wish.

Structural functionalists are also attacked for being unable to deal effectively with the *process* of social change (Mills, 1959; P. Cohen, 1968; Abrahamson, 1978;

Turner and Maryanski, 1979). While the preceding criticism deals with the seeming inability of structural functionalism to deal with the past, this one is concerned with the parallel incapacity of the approach to deal with the contemporary process of social change. Structural functionalism is far more likely to deal with static structures than with change processes. Percy Cohen (1968) sees the problem as lying in structural functional theory, in which all of the elements of a society are seen as reinforcing one another, as well as the system as a whole. This makes it difficult to see how these elements can also contribute to change. While Cohen sees the problem as inherent in the theory, Turner and Maryanski believe again that the problem lies with the practitioners and not the theory.

In the view of Turner and Maryanski, structural functionalists frequently do not address the issue of change and, even when they do, it is in developmental rather than revolutionary terms. However, according to them, there is no reason why structural functionalists could not deal with social change. Whether the problem lies in the theory or in the theorists, the fact remains that the main contributions of structural functionalists lie in the study of static, not changing, social structures.

Perhaps the most often-voiced criticism of structural functionalism is that it is unable to deal effectively with conflict (Mills, 1959; Horowitz, 1962/1967; Cohen, 1968; Gouldner, 1970; Abrahamson, 1978; Turner and Maryanski, 1979). This criticism takes a variety of forms. Gouldner argues that Parsons, as the main representative of structural functionalism, tended to overemphasize harmonious relationships. Irving Louis Horowitz contends that structural functionalists tend to see conflict as necessarily destructive and as occurring outside the framework of society. Most generally, Abrahamson argues that structural functionalism exaggerates societal consensus, stability, and integration and, conversely, tends to disregard conflict, disorder, and change. The issue once again is whether this is inherent in the theory or in the way practitioners have interpreted and used it (Cohen, 1968; Turner and Maryanski, 1979). Whatever one's position, it is clear that structural functionalism has had little to offer on the issue of social conflict.

The overall criticisms that structural functionalism is unable to deal with history, change, and conflict have led many (for example, Cohen, 1968; Gouldner, 1970) to argue that structural functionalism has a conservative bias. As Gouldner (1970:290) vividly puts it in his criticism of Parsons's structural functionalism: "Parsons persistently sees the partly filled glass of water as half-*full* rather than half-*empty*." One who sees a glass as half-full is emphasizing the positive aspects of a situation, while one who sees it as half-empty is focusing on the negative side. To put this in social terms, a conservative structural functionalist would emphasize the economic advantages of living in our society rather than its disadvantages.

It may indeed be true that there is a conservative bias in structural functionalism that is attributable not only to what it ignores (change, history, conflict) but also to what it chooses to focus on. For one thing, structural functionalists have tended to focus on culture, norms, and values (Lockwood, 1956; Mills, 1959; Cohen, 1968). David Lockwood (1956), for example, is critical of Parsons for his preoccupation with the normative order of society. More generally, Cohen (1968) argues that structural functionalists focus on normative elements, although this is not inherent in the theory. Crucial to structural functionalism's focus on cultural and societal factors, and what leads to the theory's conservative orientation, is a passive sense of the individual actor. People are seen as constrained by cultural and social forces. Structural functionalists lack a dynamic, creative sense of the actor. As Gouldner (1970:220) says, to emphasize his criticism of structural functionalism: "Human beings are as much engaged in using social systems as in being used by them."

Related to their cultural focus is the tendency of structural functionalists to mistake the legitimizations employed by elites in society for social reality (Mills, 1959; Horowitz, 1962/1967; Gouldner, 1970). The normative system is interpreted as reflective of the society as a whole, when it may in fact by better viewed as an ideological system promulgated by, and existing for, the elite members of society. Horowitz (1962/1967: 270) enunciates this position quite explicitly: "Consensus theory . . . tends to become a metaphysical representation of the dominant ideological matrix."

These substantive criticisms point in two basic directions. First, it seems clear that structural functionalism has a rather narrow focus that prevents it from addressing a number of important issues and aspects of the social world. Second, its focus tends to give it a very conservative flavor; as it was often practiced and still is, to some degree, structural functionalism operates in support of the status quo and dominant elites.

METHODOLOGICAL AND LOGICAL CRITICISMS

Before discussing two overarching criticisms of structural functionalism, we shall dispense with several of the minor methodological and logical criticisms of this theory.

One of the often-expressed criticisms (see, for example, Mills, 1959; Abrahamson, 1978) is that structural functionalism is basically vague, unclear, and ambiguous. For example: What exactly is a structure? A function? A social system? How are parts of social systems related to each other as well as to the larger social system? Part of the ambiguity is traceable to the level on which structural functionalists choose to work. They deal with abstract social systems instead of real societies. In much of Parsons's work no "real" society is discussed. Similarly, the discussion of functional prerequisites by Parsons (AGIL) and by Aberle and his colleagues (1950/1967) are not concretely tied to a real society but occur at a very high level of abstraction.

A related criticism is that, although no one grand scheme can ever be used to analyze all societies throughout history (Mills, 1959), structural functionalists have been motivated by the belief that there is a single theory, or at least a set of conceptual categories, that could be used to do this. The belief in the existence of such a grand theory lies at the basis of much of Parsons's work, the functional prerequisites of Aberle and his colleagues (1950/1967), and the Davis-Moore (1945) theory of stratification. Many critics regard this grand theory as an illusion, believing that the best sociology can hope for are more historically specific, "middle-range" (Merton, 1968) theories.

Among the other specific methodological criticisms is the issue of whether there exist adequate methods to study the questions of concern to structural functionalists. Cohen (1968), for instance, wonders what tools can be used to study the contribution of one part of a system to the system as a whole. Another methodological criticism is that structural functionalism makes comparative analysis difficult. If the assumption is that part of a system only makes sense in the context of the social system in which it exists, how can we compare it with a similar part in another system? Cohen asks, for example: If the English family makes sense only in the context of English society, how can we compare it to the French family?

TELEOLOGY AND TAUTOLOGY   Cohen (1968) and Turner and Maryanski (1979) see teleology and tautology as the two most important logical problems confronting structural functionalism. Some tend to see teleology as an inherent problem (Cohen, 1968; Abrahamson, 1978), but the author believes that Turner and Maryanski (1979) are correct when they argue that the problem with structural functionalism is not teleology per se, but *illegitimate* teleology. In this context *teleology* is defined as the view that society (or other social structures) has purposes or goals. In order to achieve these ends, society creates, or causes to be created, specific social structures and social institutions. Turner and Maryanski do not see this view as necessarily illegitimate; in fact, they argue that social theory *should* take into account the teleological relationship between society and its component parts.

The problem, to Turner and Maryanski, is the extension of teleology to unacceptable lengths. An illegitimate teleology is one that implies "that purpose or end states guide human affairs when such is not the case" (Turner and Maryanski, 1979:118). For example, it is illegitimate to assume that because society needs procreation and socialization it will create the family institution. A variety of alternative structures could meet these needs; society does not "need" to create the family. The structural functionalist must define and document the various ways in which the goals do, in fact, lead to the creation of specific substructures. It would also be useful to be able to show why other substructures could not meet the same needs. A legitimate teleology would be able to define and demonstrate *empirically* and *theoretically* the links between society's goals and the various substructures that exist within society. An illegitimate teleology would be satisfied with a blind assertion that a link between a societal end and a specific substructure must exist. Turner and Maryanski (1979:124) admit that functionalism is often guilty of presenting illegitimate teleologies: "We can conclude that functional explanations often become illegitimate teleologies—a fact which seriously hampers functionalism's utility for understanding patterns of human organization."

The other major criticism of the logic of structural functionalism is that it is tautological. A tautological argument is one in which the conclusion merely makes explicit what is implicit in the premise, or is simply a restatement of the premise. In structural functionalism, this circular reasoning often takes the form of defining the whole in terms of its parts and then defining the parts in terms of the whole. Thus, it would be argued that a social system is defined by the relationship among its component parts and the component parts of the system are defined by their place in the larger social system. Since each is defined in terms of the other, neither the social system nor its parts are in fact defined at all. We really learn nothing about either the system or its parts. Structural functionalism has been particularly prone to tautologies, although there is some question about whether this propensity is inherent in the theory, or simply characteristic of the way most structural functionalists have used, or misused, the theory.

THE EMERGENCE OF A THEORETICAL ALTERNATIVE: CONFLICT THEORY

A basic premise of this chapter is that conflict theory can be seen as a development that took place, at least in part, in reaction to structural functionalism and as a result of many of the criticisms we have just discussed. However, it should be noted that conflict theory has various other roots, such as Marxian theory and Simmel's work on social conflict. In the 1950s and 1960s conflict theory provided an alternative to structural functionalism, but it has been superseded in recent years by a variety of neo-Marxian theories (see Chapter Four). Indeed, one of the major contributions of conflict theory was the way it laid the groundwork for theories more faithful to Marx's work, theories that came to attract a wide audience in sociology. The basic problem with conflict theory is that it never succeeded in divorcing itself sufficiently from its structural-functional roots. It was more a kind of structural functionalism turned on its head than a truly critical theory of society.

The Work of Ralf Dahrendorf

Conflict theorists, like functionalists, are oriented toward the study of social structures and institutions. In the main, this theory is little more than a series of contentions that are often the direct opposites of functionalist positions. This is best exemplified by the work of Ralf Dahrendorf (1958; 1959), in which the basic tenets of conflict and functional theory are juxtaposed. To the functionalists society is static or, at best, in a state of moving equilibrium, but to Dahrendorf and the conflict theorists every society at every point is subject to processes of change. Where functionalism emphasizes the orderliness of society, conflict theorists see dissension and conflict at every point in the social system. Functionalists (or at least early functionalists) argue that every element in society contributes to stability, while the exponents of conflict theory see many societal elements contributing to disintegration and change.

Functionalists tend to see society as being held together informally by norms, values, and a common morality. Conflict theorists see whatever order there is in society as stemming from the coercion of some members by those at the top. Where functionalists focus on the cohesion created by shared societal values, conflict theorists emphasize the role of power in maintaining order in society.

Dahrendorf (1959; 1968) is the major exponent of the position that society has two faces (conflict and consensus) and that sociological theory should therefore be divided into two parts, conflict theory and consensus theory. Consensus theorists should examine value integration in society, and conflict theorists should examine conflicts of interest and the coercion that holds society together in the face of these stresses. He recognized that society could not exist without both conflict and consensus, which are prerequisites for each other. Thus, we cannot have conflict unless there is some prior consensus. For example, French housewives are highly unlikely to conflict with Chilean chess players since there is no contact between them, no prior integration to serve as a basis for a conflict. Conversely, conflict can lead to consensus and integration. An example is the alliance between the United States and Japan that has developed since World War II.

Despite the interrelationship between the processes of consensus and conflict, Dahrendorf (1959:164) was not optimistic about developing a single sociological theory encompassing both processes: "It seems at least conceivable that unification of theory is not feasible at a point which has puzzled thinkers ever since the beginning of Western philosophy." Eschewing a singular theory, Dahrendorf set out to construct a conflict theory of society.[7]

Dahrendorf began with, and was heavily influenced by, structural functionalism. He noted that to the functionalist the social system is held together by voluntary cooperation or general consensus or both. However, to the conflict (or coercion) theorist, society is held together by "enforced constraint." This means that some positions in society are delegated power and authority over others. This fact of social life led Dahrendorf (1959:165) to his central thesis that the differential distribution of authority "invariably becomes the determining factor of systematic social conflicts."

AUTHORITY

Dahrendorf concentrated on larger social structures.[8] Central to his thesis is the idea that various positions within society have different amounts of authority. Authority does not reside in individuals but in positions. Dahrendorf (1959:165) was interested not only in the structure of these positions, but also in the conflict among them: "The *structural* origin of such conflicts must be sought in the arrangement of social roles endowed with expectations of domination or subjection" (italics added). The first task of conflict analysis, to Dahrendorf, was to identify various authority roles within society. In addition to making the case for the study of large-scale structures like authority roles, Dahrendorf was opposed to those who focus on the individual level. For example, he was critical of those who focus on the psychological or behavioral characteristics of the individuals who occupy such positions. He went so far as to say that those who adopted such an approach were not sociologists.

The authority attached to positions is the key element in Dahrendorf's analysis. Authority always implies both superordination and subordination. Those who occupy positions of authority are expected to control subordinates; that is, they dominate because of the expectations of those who surround them, not because of their own psychological characteristics. These expectations, like authority, are attached to positions, not people. Authority is not a generalized social phenomenon; those who are subject to control, as well as permissible spheres of control, are specified in society. Finally, because authority is legitimate, sanctions can be brought to bear against those who do not comply.

Authority is not a constant as far as Dahrendorf was concerned. This is traceable to the fact that authority resides in positions and not persons. Thus, a person in authority in one setting does not necessarily hold a position of authority in another setting. Similarly, a person in a subordinate position in one group may be in a superordinate position in another. This follows from Dahrendorf's argument that society is composed of a number of units he called *imperatively coordinated associations*. These may be

---

[7]Dahrendorf (1959:164) called conflict and coercion "the ugly face of society." We can ponder whether a man who regards them as "ugly" can develop an adequate theory of conflict and coercion.

[8]In his other work, Dahrendorf (1968) continued to focus on social facts (for example, positions and roles), but he also manifested a concern for the dangers of reification endemic to such an approach.

seen as associations of people controlled by a hierarchy of authority positions. Since society contains many such associations, an individual can occupy a position of authority in one and a subordinate position in another.

Authority within each association is dichotomous; thus two, and only two, conflict groups can be formed within any association. Those in positions of authority and those in positions of subordination hold certain interests that are "contradictory in substance and direction." Here we encounter another key term in Dahrendorf's theory of conflict —*interests*. Groups on top and at the botton are defined by common interests. Dahrendorf continued to be firm in his thinking that even these interests, which sound so psychological, are basically large-scale phenomena:

> For purposes of the sociological analysis of conflict groups and group conflicts, it is necessary to assume certain *structurally generated* orientations of the actions of incumbents of defined *positions*. By analogy to conscious ("subjective") orientations of action, it appears justifiable to describe these as interests. . . . The assumption of "objective" interests associated with social positions has *no psychological implications* or ramifications; it belongs to the level of sociological analysis proper.
>
> (Dahrendorf, 1959:175; italics added)

Within every association those in dominant positions seek to maintain the status quo while those in subordinate positions seek change. A conflict of interests within any association is at least latent at all times, which means that the legitimacy of authority is *always* precarious. This conflict of interest need not be conscious in order for superordinates or subordinates to act. The interests of superordinates and subordinates are objective in the sense that they are reflected in the expectations (roles) attached to positions. Individuals do not have to internalize these expectations or even be conscious of them in order to act in accord with them. If they occupy given positions, then they will behave in the expected manner. Individuals are "adjusted" or "adapted" to their roles when they contribute to conflict between superordinates and subordinates. Dahrendorf called these unconscious role expectations *latent interests*. *Manifest interests* are latent interests that have become conscious. Dahrendorf saw the analysis of the connection between latent and manifest interests as a major task of conflict theory. Nevertheless, actors need not be conscious of their interests in order to act in accord with them.

Next Dahrendorf distinguished three broad types of groups. The first is the *quasi-group*, or "aggregates of incumbents of positions with identical role interests" (Dahrendorf, 1959:180). These are the recruiting grounds for the second type of group—the *interest group*. Dahrendorf described the two groups:

> Common modes of behavior are characteristic of *interest groups* recruited from larger quasi-groups. Interest groups are groups in the strict sense of the sociological term; and they are the real agents of group conflict. They have a structure, a form of organization, a program or goal, and a personnel of members.
>
> (Dahrendorf, 1959:180)

Out of all of the many interest groups emerge *conflict groups,* or those that actually engage in group conflict.

Dahrendorf felt that the concepts of latent and manifest interests, of quasi-groups, interest groups, and conflict groups, were basic to an explanation of social conflict. Under *ideal* conditions no other variables would be needed. However, since conditions are never ideal, many different factors do intervene in the process. Dahrendorf mentioned technical conditions such as adequate personnel, political conditions such as the overall political climate, and social conditions such as the existence of communication links. The way people are recruited into the quasi-group is another social condition important to Dahrendorf. He felt that if the recruitment is random and determined by chance, then an interest group, and ultimately a conflict group, is unlikely to emerge. In contrast to Marx, Dahrendorf did not feel that the *lumpenproletariat*[9] would ultimately form a conflict group, since people are recruited to it by chance. However, when recruitment to quasi-groups is structurally determined, these groups provide fertile recruiting grounds for interest groups and, in some cases, conflict groups.

The final aspect of Dahrendorf's conflict theory is the relationship of conflict to change. Here Dahrendorf recognized the importance of Lewis Coser's work, which, as we will see, focused on the functions of conflict in maintaining the status quo. Dahrendorf felt, however, that the positive function of conflict is only one part of social reality; conflict also leads to change and development.

Briefly, Dahrendorf argued that once conflict groups emerge, they engage in actions that lead to changes in social structure. When the conflict is intense, the changes that occur are radical. When it is accompanied by violence, structural change will be sudden. Whatever the nature of conflict, sociologists must be attuned to the relationship between conflict and change as well as that between conflict and the status quo.

Dahrendorf's conflict theory can be criticized for ignoring order and stability, whereas functionalism has been criticized for being oblivious to conflict and change. Conflict theory has also been criticized for being ideologically radical, whereas functionalism was criticized for its conservative orientation.

In comparison, conflict theory is far less developed than functional theory. It is not nearly so sophisticated, perhaps because it is not truly an innovative perspective. Furthermore, many of the best sociologists, at least in the United States, have, until recently, devoted their attention to functional theory, and relatively few have worked toward developing conflict theory.

Dahrendorf's conflict theory has been subjected to a number of critical analyses (for example, Weingart, 1969; Hazelrigg, 1972; J. Turner, 1973), including some critical reflections by Dahrendorf (1968) himself. First, Dahrendorf's model is not as clear a reflection of Marxian ideas as he claimed. In fact, it constitutes an inadequate translation of Marxian theory into sociology. Second, as has been noted, conflict theory has more in common with structural functionalism than with Marxian theory. Dahrendorf's emphasis on such things as systems (imperatively coordinated associations), positions, and roles links him directly to structural functionalism. As a result, his theory suffers from many of the same inadequacies as structural functionalism. For example, conflict seems to emerge mysteriously from legitimate systems (just as it does in structural functionalism). Further, conflict theory seems to suffer from many of the same concep-

---

[9]This is Marx's term for the mass of people at the bottom of the economic system, standing below even the proletariat.

tual and logical problems (for example, vague concepts, tautologies) as structural functionalism. Finally, like structural functionalism, it is almost wholly a macroscopic theory
and as a result has little to offer to our understanding of individual thought and action.

Both functionalism and Dahrendorf's conflict theory are inadequate, because each
is itself useful for explaining only a *portion* of social life. Obviously, sociology must
be able to explain order as well as conflict, structure as well as change. This last fact
has motivated several efforts to reconcile conflict and functional theory. Although none
has been totally satisfactory, these efforts suggest at least some agreement among
sociologists that what is needed is a theory explaining *both* consensus and dissension.
Still, not all theorists seek to reconcile these conflicting perspectives. Dahrendorf, for
example, saw them as alternative perspectives to be used situationally. According to
Dahrendorf, when we are interested in conflict we should use conflict theory; when we
wish to examine order, we should take a functional perspective. This seems an unsatisfactory position, since there is a strong need for a theoretical perspective that
enables us to deal with conflict and order *simultaneously.*

Recently, Jonathan Turner (1975; 1982) has sought to reformulate conflict theory.
Turner pointed to three major problems in conflict theories like that of Dahrendorf.
First, there is a lack of a clear definition of conflict, delimiting both what it is and what
it is not. Second, conflict theory remains vague, largely because there is a failure to
specify the level of analysis on which one is working: "Typically, just what units are in
conflict is left vague—whether they be individuals, groups, organizations, classes, nations, communities, and the like" (J. Turner, 1982:178). Third, there is the implicit
functionalism in conflict theory, which leads it away from its Marxian roots.

Turner (1982:183) focused on "conflict as a process of events leading to overt interaction of varying degrees of violence among at least two parties." He developed a
nine-stage process leading to overt conflict. Although it appears at first glance to be a
one-way causal model, Turner was careful to specify a number of feedback loops, or
dialectical relations, among the stages. The nine-stage process looks like this:

1. The social system is composed of a number of interdependent units.
2. There is an unequal distribution of scarce and valued resources among these units.
3. Those units not receiving a proportionate share of the resources begin to question
    the legitimacy of the system. Turner noted that this questioning is most likely to
    take place when people feel their aspirations for upward mobility are blocked,
    when there are insufficient channels for redressing grievances, and when people
    are deprived of rewards in a variety of sectors.
4. This is followed by an initial awareness of the fact that it is in the interests of
    deprived people to alter the system of resource allocation.
5. Those who are deprived become emotionally aroused.
6. There are periodic, albeit often disorganized, outbursts of frustration.
7. Those involved in the conflict grow increasingly intense about it and more emo-
    tionally involved in it.
8. Increased efforts are made to organize the deprived groups involved in the conflict.
9. Finally, open conflict of varying degrees of violence breaks out between the
    deprived and the privileged. The degree of violence is affected by such things as the
    ability of the conflict parties to define their true interests and the degree to which
    the system has mechanisms for handling, regularizing, and controlling conflict.

Turner has done a useful job of filling in conflict theory, especially in beginning to delineate some of the conflict relations between actors and social structures. However, Turner's work, like that of many other conflict theorists, remains embedded within the structural-functional tradition. As a result, he has failed to reflect the many insights into the nature of social conflict found within the various branches of neo-Marxian theory.

Efforts to Reconcile Structural Functionalism and Conflict Theory

To date, Pierre van den Berghe (1963) has made the major effort to reconcile structural functionalism and conflict theory. He noted several points that the two approaches have in common. First, both perspectives are *holistic*; that is, they look at societies as inter-related parts with a concern for the interrelationship among the parts. Second, the theorists focus on the variables in their own theory while ignoring variables of concern to the other perspective. They should recognize, however, that conflict can contribute to integration and, conversely, that integration can be a cause of conflict. Third, van den Berghe noted that the two theories share an evolutionary view of social change—the view that society is moving forward and upward. A conflict theorist is likely to see society as advancing irrevocably toward a utopian society. A functionalist such as Parsons sees it as becoming increasingly differentiated and ever better able to cope with its environment. Finally, van den Berghe saw both as basically equilibrium theories. Functional theory emphasizes societal equilibrium. In conflict theory relational processes lead inevitably to a new state of equilibrium in some future stage. Van den Berghe's work demonstrates points in common between the two theories but does not reconcile them; many outstanding differences remain.

The work of Lewis Coser (1956) and Joseph Himes (1966) focused on the functions of social conflict. These basically functional treatments of conflict do move toward integrating conflict and structural-functional theory. While their concern was the equilibrating effect of conflict, what is needed is parallel work discussing the disequilibrating effects of order. Certain kinds of order, or too much order, can lead to disequilibrium in the social system; for example, totalitarian rulers, despite their emphasis on order, can destroy the stability of society. However, since little work has been done on the way order produces change, we focus below on the functions of social conflict.

The early seminal work on the functions of social conflict was done by Georg Simmel, but it has been expanded more recently by Coser, who argued that conflict may serve to solidify a loosely structured group. In a society that seems to be disintegrating, conflict with another society might restore the integrative core. Thus the heating up of the Cold War with the Soviet Union in the early 1980s might help to reintegrate the United States, which was wracked in the 1970s by the disintegrative effects of the Vietnam War. The cohesiveness of Israeli society might be attributed, at least in part, to the long-standing conflict with the Arab nations in the Middle East. The end of the conflict might well cause underlying strains in Israeli society to become more prominent. Conflict as an agent for solidifying a society is an idea that has long been recognized by propagandists, who may construct an enemy where none exists or seek to fan antagonisms toward an inactive opponent.

Conflict with one group may serve to produce cohesion by leading to a series of alliances with other groups. For example, conflict with the Soviet Union has led to American membership in such groups as NATO. Lessening of the Soviet-American conflict in the 1970s seemed to have weakened the bonds that held groups like NATO together.

Within a society, conflict can bring some ordinarily isolated individuals into an active role. The protests over the Vietnam War motivated many young people to take vigorous roles in American political life for the first time. With the end of that conflict a more apathetic spirit seems to have emerged again among American youth.

Conflict also serves a communication function. Prior to conflict, groups may be unsure of their adversary's position, but as a result of conflict, positions and boundaries between groups often become clarified. Individuals are therefore better able to decide on a proper course of action in relation to their adversary. Conflict also allows the parties to get a better idea of their relative strengths and may well increase the possibility of rapprochement, or peaceful accommodation.

From a theoretical perspective it is possible to wed functional and conflict theory by looking at the functions of social conflict. Still, it must be recognized that conflict also has dysfunctions.

Himes (1966), like Coser, was interested in the functions of conflict, although he focused specifically on the functions of racial conflict. Himes discussed what he considered to be *rational* group action by American blacks. He was concerned with deliberate collective behavior designed to achieve predetermined social goals. Such behavior involves a conscious attack on overtly defined social abuses. Examples include legal redress (to achieve voting rights, educational opportunities, and public accommodations), political action (such as voting and lobbying), and nonviolent mass action. The kind of conflict with which Himes was concerned involves peaceful work within the system: his analysis excludes acts of violence, such as riots and lynchings.

Although Himes ignored violent collective conflict, we could just as easily perform a functional analysis of these forms as of peaceful conflict. The riots of the late 1960s clearly had functions for American blacks, demonstrating their power and the weakness of the white power structure, although they certainly had dysfunctions (in the form of white backlash).

As Himes saw it, racial conflict has structural, communications, solidarity, and identity functions. *Structurally*, conflict can change the power balance between blacks and the dominant white majority, increasing the power of blacks so that whites will meet with them to discuss issues of mutual importance. Racial conflict can perform such *communications* functions as increasing attention to racial matters, increasing coverage of racial matters by the mass media, allowing uninformed people to get new information, and changing the content of interracial communication. Racial conflict will put an end to the old "etiquette of race relations," bringing a greater likelihood of open dialogue over substantive issues. Racial conflict may increase *solidarity*, because it may help unify blacks and establish a relationship between the races. Even if this relationship is one based only on conflict, it ultimately may form the basis for a more peaceful and long-lasting relationship. The *identity* functions of racial conflict include giving blacks a greater sense of who they are and clarifying group boundaries. Perhaps the most important identity function is the sense black participants can get of their identity as Americans fighting for the basic principle of freedom.

James Coleman's (1971) work on conflict is somewhat different from that of Coser and Himes. While Coser and Himes looked at the functions of conflict, Coleman examined the sources of both integration *and* conflict within a local community. Coleman looked *simultaneously* at integrative and disintegrative processes. The ultimate reconciliation of functional and conflict theory, if it is to occur, is most likely to lie in this direction.

Coleman stated that dissimilar activities leading to different attitudes, values, and beliefs can be a source of disintegration within the community. Conversely, similar activities carrying with them similar attitudes, values, and beliefs can aid in community integration. Integration is also likely to be aided by common problems requiring joint action and be adversely affected by idiosyncratic problems and solutions. Yet, Coleman argued, dissimilar activities can often result in integration. His view here is similar to Durkheim's concept of organic solidarity, in which a community is held together because each person performing specialized tasks needs many others with their specialties in order to survive. The butcher needs the tailor, who needs the grocer, who needs the truck driver, and so forth. A community can be held together by the very force of its differences.

Each of these conflict theories is concerned with integrating, or at least relating, structural functionalism and conflict theory. Virtually all the efforts have remained at the large-scale, societal level. We turn now to a more recent form of conflict theory, one that tries to relate large-scale and small-scale concerns under the heading of conflict theory.

Toward a More Integrated Conflict Theory: The Work of Randall Collins

Randall Collins (1975) made it clear from the beginning that his focus on conflict would not be ideological—that is, he did not begin with a political view that conflict is either good or bad. Rather, he claimed, he chose conflict as a focus on the realistic ground that conflict is a—perhaps *the*—central process in social life.

Unlike the others who started, and stayed, at the societal level, Collins approached conflict from an individual point of view. He made it clear that his theoretical roots lie in phenomenology and ethnomethodology. Despite his preference for the individual level and small-scale theories, Collins (1975:11) was aware that "sociology cannot be successful on the microlevel alone." In his view, sociology cannot do without the societal level of analysis. However, whereas most of the theorists we have encountered in this chapter believed that social structures are external to, and coercive of, the actor, Collins saw social structures as inseparable from the actors who construct them and whose interaction patterns are their essence. Collins was inclined to see social structures as interaction patterns rather than external and coercive entities. In addition, while most of the theorists discussed above saw the actor as constrained by external forces, Collins viewed the actor as constantly creating and re-creating social organization.

Collins saw Marxian theory as the "starting point" for conflict theory, but it is, in his view, laden with problems. For one thing, he saw it (like structural functionalism) as heavily ideological, which he wanted to avoid. For another, he tended to see Marx's orientation as reducible to an analysis of the economic domain, although this is an unwarranted criticism of Marx's theory. Actually, although Collins invoked Marx frequently, his conflict theory shows relatively little Marxian influence. It is far more influenced by Weber, Durkheim, and above all phenomenology and ethnomethodology.

Collins chose to focus on social stratification because it is an institution that touches so many features of life, including "wealth, politics, careers, families, clubs, communities, lifestyles" (Collins, 1975:49). In Collins's view, the great theories of stratification are "failures." In this category he placed both the Marxian and the structural-functional theories. He criticized Marxian theory, for example, as "a monocausal explanation for a multicausal world" (Collins, 1975:49). He viewed Weber's theory as little more than an "antisystem" with which to view the features of the two great theories. Weber's work was of some use to Collins, but "the efforts of phenomenological sociology to ground all concepts in the observables of every life" (Collins, 1975:53) were the most important to him because his major focus in the study of social stratification was small-scale, not large-scale. In his view, social stratification, like all other social structures, is reducible to people in everyday life encountering each other in patterned ways.

Despite his ultimate commitment to a microsociology of stratification, Collins began (even though he had some reservations about them) with the large-scale theories of Marx and Weber as underpinnings for his own work. He started with Marxian principles, arguing that they, "with certain modifications, provide the basis for a conflict theory of stratification" (Collins, 1975:58).

First, Collins contended that it was Marx's view that the material conditions involved in earning a living in modern society are the major determinants of a person's life style. The basis of earning a living for Marx is a person's relationship to private property. Those who own, or control, property are able to earn their livings in a much more satisfactory way than those who do not and who must sell their labor-time to gain access to the means of production.

Second, from a Marxian perspective, material conditions affect not only how individuals earn a living but also the nature of social groups in the different social classes. The dominant social class is better able to develop more coherent social groups, tied together by intricate communication networks, than is the subordinate social class.

Finally, Collins argued that Marx also pointed out the vast differences among the social classes in their access to, and control over, the cultural system. That is, the upper social classes are able to develop highly articulated symbol and ideological systems, systems they are often able to impose on the lower social classes. The lower social classes have less developed symbol systems, many of which are likely to have been imposed on them by those in power.

Collins viewed Weber as working within and developing further Marx's theory of stratification. For one thing, Weber was said to have recognized the existence of different forms of conflict that lead to a multifaceted stratification system (for example, class, status, and power). For another, Weber developed the theory of organizations to a high degree, which Collins saw as still another arena of conflict of interest. Weber was also important to Collins for his emphasis on the state as the agency that controls the means of violence, which shifted attention from conflict over the economy (means of production) to conflict over the state. Finally, Weber was recognized by Collins for his understanding of the social arena of emotional products, in particular religion. Conflict can clearly occur in this arena, and these emotional products, like other products, can be used as weapons in social conflict.

With this background, Collins turned to his own conflict approach to stratification, which has more in common with phenomenological and ethnomethodological theories than with Marxian or Weberian theory. Collins opened with several assumptions. People are seen as inherently sociable but also as particularly conflict-prone in their social relations. Conflict is likely to occur in social relations because "violent coercion" can always be used by one person or many people in an interaction setting. Collins believed that people seek to maximize their "subjective status," and their ability to do this depends on their resources as well as the resources of those with whom they are dealing. He saw people as self-interested; thus, clashes are possible since sets of interests may be inherently antagonistic.

This conflict approach to stratification can be reduced to three basic principles. First, Collins believed that people live in self-constructed subjective worlds. Second, other people may have the power to affect, or even control, an individual's subjective experience. Third, other people will frequently try to control the individual, who will oppose them. The result is likely to be interpersonal conflict.

On the basis of this, Collins developed five principles of conflict analysis that he applied to social stratification, although he believed that they could be applied to any area of social life.

First, Collins believed that conflict theory must focus on real life rather than abstract formulations. This seems to reflect a preference for a Marxian-style material analysis over the abstraction of structural functionalism. Collins urged us to think of people as animals whose actions, motivated by self-interest, can be seen as maneuvers to obtain various advantages so that they can achieve satisfaction and avoid dissatisfaction. However, unlike exchange theorists (see Chapter Seven), Collins did not see people as wholly rational. He recognized that they are vulnerable to emotional appeals in their efforts to find satisfaction.

Second, Collins believed that a conflict theory of stratification must examine the material arrangements that affect interaction. Although the actors are likely to be affected by such material factors as "the physical places, the modes of communication, the supply of weapons, devices for staging one's public impression, tools, goods" (Collins, 1975:60), not all actors are affected in the same way. A major variable is the resources that the different actors possess. Actors with considerable material resources can resist, or even modify, these material constraints, whereas those with fewer resources are more likely to have their thoughts and actions determined by their material setting.

Third, Collins argued that in a situation of inequality those groups that control resources are likely to try to exploit those that lack resources. He was careful to point out that this need not involve conscious calculation on the part of those who gain from the situation; rather, they are merely pursuing what they perceive to be their best interests. In the process they may be taking advantage of those who lack resources.

Fourth, Collins wanted the conflict theorist to look at such cultural phenomena as beliefs and ideals from the point of view of interests, resources, and power. It is likely that those groups with resources and that thus have power will be able to impose their idea systems on the entire society; those without resources will have an idea system imposed on them.

Finally, Collins made a firm commitment to the scientific study of stratification and every other aspect of the social world. This led him to prescribe several things. Sociologists should not simply theorize about stratification but should study it empirically, if possible in a comparative way. Hypotheses should be formulated and tested empirically through comparative studies. Last, the sociologist should look for the causes of social phenomena, particularly the multiple causes of any form of social behavior.

This kind of scientific commitment led Collins to develop a wide array of propositions about the relationship between conflict and various specific aspects of social life. We can present only a few here, but they should allow readers to get a feel for Collins's type of conflict sociology.

> 1.0   Experiences of giving and taking orders are the main determinants of individual outlooks and behaviors.
> 1.1   The more one gives orders, the more he is proud, self-assured, formal, and identifies with organizational ideals in whose name he justifies the orders.
> 1.2   The more one takes orders, the more he is subservient, fatalistic, alienated from organizational ideals, externally conforming, distrustful of others, concerned with extrinsic rewards, and amoral.
>
> (Collins, 1975:73–74)

Among other things, these propositions all reflect Collins's commitment to the *scientific study* of the small-scale social manifestations of social conflicts.

Collins was not content to deal with conflict within the stratification system but sought to extend it to various other social domains. For example, he extended his analysis of stratification to relationships between the sexes as well as among age groups. He took the view that the family is an arena of sexual conflict, in which males have been the victors, with the result that women are dominated by men and subject to various kinds of unequal treatment. Similarly, he saw the relationship between age groups—in particular, between young and old—as one of conflict. This contrasts with the view of structural functionalists, who saw harmonious socialization and internalization in this relationship. Collins looked at the resources possessed by the various age groups. Adults have a variety of resources they can use, including experience, size, strength, and the ability to satisfy the physical needs of the young. In contrast, one of the few resources young children have is physical attractiveness. This means that young children are likely to be dominated by adults. However, as children mature they acquire more resources and are better able to resist, resulting in increasing social conflict between the generations.

Collins also looked at formal organizations from a conflict perspective. He saw them as networks of interpersonal influences and also as the arenas in which conflicting interests are played out. In short, "organizations are arenas for struggle" (Collins, 1975:295). Collins again couched his argument in propositional form. For example, he argued that "coercion leads to strong efforts to avoid being coerced" (Collins, 1975:298). On the other hand, he felt that the offering of rewards is a preferable strategy: "Control by material rewards leads to compliance to the extent that rewards are directly linked to the desired behavior" (Collins, 1975:299). These propositions and others all point to Collins's commitment to a scientific, largely micro-oriented study of conflict.

In sum, Collins is, like Dahrendorf, not a true exponent of Marxian conflict theory, although for different reasons. Although he used Marx as a starting point, Weber, Durkheim, and particularly ethnomethodology were much more important influences on his work. Collins's small-scale orientation is helpful; however, despite his stated intentions of integrating large- and small-scale theory, he did not accomplish the task.

Toward a More Marxian Conflict Theory

As a transition to the next chapter on Marxian theories, we now offer André Gunder Frank's (1966/1974) criticisms of van den Berghe's efforts to reconcile conflict theory and structural functionalism. Of greatest importance is Frank's contention that conflict theory is an inadequate Marxian theory. Thus, while van den Berghe may be able to reconcile conflict theory as it stands with structural functionalism, he would find it much more difficult to reconcile the two if conflict theory were true to Marxian theory.

Frank refuted, point by point, van den Berghe's argument on the reconciliation of conflict and structural-functional theory. Van den Berghe's first point was that both theories take a holistic approach to the social world. Frank admitted that there is at least some correspondence here. He also noted a number of crucial differences. For one thing, Frank argued that true Marxists do tend to focus on the whole, while structural functionalists, despite a supposedly similar focus, spend most of their time on parts of social systems. Frank was correct here, but at least some varieties of truer neo-Marxian theory have also tended to focus on one component (for example, the economy, the culture) of the social whole. Frank's second refutation of van den Berghe's first point was more telling. He argued that Marxian thinkers, given their commitment to materialism, look at real social wholes, while structural functionalists (and some conflict theorists) tend to look at abstract wholes. Parsons's concept of a social system is an excellent example of the latter point.

Still on the issue of holism, Frank argued that structural functionalists and true Marxian thinkers ask very different questions when they study social totalities. For one thing, the former tend to take the existing social system for granted and do not question its legitimacy. Marxian scholars, however, question existing society (whether it be capitalist, socialist, or communist) and subject it to intense scrutiny and criticism. They are oriented toward the development of some future society, not a deification of the contemporary one. In addition, there is a substantive difference here between the two approaches. True Marxists focus on the social totality and view knowledge of it as helpful in understanding its various parts. On the other hand, even when structural functionalism focuses on the whole of society, its ultimate goal is to understand the parts, especially specific social institutions.

Finally, since structural functionalists work on abstract systems, they can focus on any totality they wish. Since Marxian thinkers are committed to naturalism, the totality they choose to study is constrained by the real social world. The world, not an abstract theoretical system, determines what they study. Furthermore, the dialectician is oriented to changing the social whole, not just studying it, as is the case with structural functionalists.

Van den Berghe's second point was that each school ignores the variables of concern to the other. Thus structural functionalists are urged by van den Berghe to learn about conflict from conflict theorists and, conversely, conflict theorists can learn about consensus from structural functionalists. Frank criticized this position in several ways. First, he argued that it slights both perspectives, since both Marxian theory and structural functionalism have had things to say about *both* conflict and consensus. Second, Frank contended that when the structural functionalists do try to integrate Marxian ideas, they distort them beyond all recognition. Third, even when structural functionalists are interested in conflict, it is only a very limited concern. For instance, they might be willing to look at the functions of social conflict, but not to examine such issues as social disintegration and social revolution.

According to Frank, structural functionalism has a limited ability to integrate the issues of conflict and consensus. However, he felt that these issues could be integrated with Marxian theory. Marxian theory can cover a wide range of kinds and degrees of conflict, including disintegrative conflict. More important, given its commitment to the dialectic, Marxian theory is particularly well suited to deal with the integration of cohesion and conflict.

Van den Berghe's third point was that the two theories share an interest in evolutionary change, but Frank noted three important differences. First, structural functionalists are likely to look solely at change within the system, whereas dialecticians are more likely to be interested in the change of the entire system and its social structure. Second, the two schools have different priorities in their study of change. To structural functionalists, structure is the source of change; to dialecticians, change is the source of structure. Finally, for the functionalist change is an abstract process, whereas for Marxists it is a dialectical process within real societies.

Finally, van den Berghe argued that both approaches were basically equilibrium theories. This is clearly true of structural functionalism, but it does not adequately describe Marxian theory. It ignores, above all, the Marxian sense of disequilibrium, of negations, within the society. To the Marxist, society contains within it the seeds of its own transformation and revolution. Marxists may have a sense of equilibrium, but they have an even stronger image of disequilibrium and change.

In sum, Frank argued that van den Berghe was not true to Marxian theory in his delineation of conflict theory and its integration with structural functionalism. Although conflict theory has some Marxian elements, it is not a true heir of Marx's original theory. In the next chapter we turn to those theories that are more legitimate heirs.

SUMMARY

Not too many years ago, structural functionalism was *the* dominant theory in sociology. Conflict theory was its major challenger and was the likely alternative to replace it in that position. However, dramatic changes have taken place in these two theories in recent years. They have both been the subject of intense criticism, whereas a series of alternative theories (to be discussed throughout the rest of this book) have attracted ever greater interest and ever larger followings. Today structural functionalism and conflict theory are certainly still significant, but they must take their place alongside a number of important theories in sociology.

Although several varieties of structural functionalism exist, our focus here is on societal functionalism and its large-scale focus, its concern with the interrelationships at the societal level and with the constraining effects of social structures and institutions on actors. Societal structural functionalism has its roots in the work of Comte, Spencer, and Durkheim and their interest in organicism, societal needs, and more pointedly, structures and functions. Based on this work, structural functionalists developed a series of large-scale concerns in social systems, subsystems, relationships among subsystems and systems, equilibrium, and orderly change.

Much of the first part of this chapter is devoted to a discussion of the work of Talcott Parsons. Parsons's work went through a series of theoretical changes over the course of his career, but he is best known as a structural functionalist.

The heart of Parsons's theory lies in his sense of the major structures (and functions) of social reality, especially the four action systems. Parsons is more often associated with his work on the social system, but the most important system in his theory is the cultural system. It stands at the pinnacle of the four action systems (the others are the social, personality, and behavioral organism systems) and exercises control over them. Although the other systems are not completely controlled by the cultural system, Parsons described himself as a ''cultural determinist.'' Parsons tended to see the personality system and the behavioral organism as determined by the systems that stand above them, the social system and, particularly, the cultural system.

Because of criticisms that his action systems could not account for change, Parsons turned later in his career to evolutionary theory. But even when looking at change, he concentrated on structures and functions, not the process of change itself.

Parsons influenced many leading contributors to structural-functional theory. We examine four works by structural functionalists to illustrate both traditional structural functionalism (Davis and Moore; Aberle et al.) and more sophisticated, contemporary versions (Merton and Gans). Davis and Moore, in one of the best-known and most criticized pieces in the history of sociology, examined social stratification as a social system and the various positive functions it performs. In a more general essay, Aberle and his colleagues (like Parsons in his AGIL schema) were concerned with the various structures and functions that they believed a society must have in order to survive. Among others, a society must have sufficient population, means to deal with its environment, methods of sexual recruitment, role differentiation and the means to assign people to different roles, communications systems, shared cognitive orientations, shared goals, methods of regulating means to those goals, methods of regulating affectivity, adequate socialization, and effective social control.

Merton's effort to develop a ''paradigm'' for functional analysis is the most important piece in modern structural functionalism. Merton began by criticizing some of the more naive positions of structural functionalism, a number of which are to be found in the work mentioned above. He then sought to develop a more adequate model of structural-functional analysis. On one point Merton agreed with his predecessors—the need to focus on large-scale social phenomena. But, Merton argued, in addition to focusing on positive functions, structural functionalism should also be concerned with dysfunctions and even nonfunctions. Given these additions, Merton urged that analysts concern themselves with the net balance of functions and dysfunctions. Further, he argued, in performing structural-functional analysis, we must move away from global analyses and specify the *levels* on which we are working. Merton also added the idea that structural functionalists should be concerned not only with manifest (intended) but also with latent (unintended) functions.

Gans's work can be seen as at least a partial application of Merton's model to the issue of poverty. He argued that although it is obvious that poverty has dysfunctions, it also has a series of positive functions (especially for societal elites) at the economic, social, cultural, and political levels. Gans believed that it will be possible to eliminate poverty only when we recognize its positive functions and seek alternatives to them.

The first part of the chapter closes with the discussion of the numerous criticisms of structural functionalism that have succeeded in damaging its credibility and popularity. We discuss the criticisms that structural functionalism is ahistorical, unable to deal with conflict and change, highly conservative, preoccupied with societal constraints on actors, accepting of elite legitimations, teleological, and tautological.

The second part of this chapter is devoted to the major alternative to structural functionalism in the 1950s and 1960s—conflict theory. The best-known work in this tradition is by Ralf Dahrendorf, who, although he consciously tried to follow the Marxian tradition, is best seen as having inverted structural functionalism. Dahrendorf looked at change rather than equilibrium; conflict rather than order; how the parts of society contribute to change rather than stability; and conflict and coercion rather than normative constraint. Dahrendorf offered a large-scale theory of conflict that parallels the structural functionalist's large-scale theory of order. His focus on authority, positions, imperatively coordinated associations, interests, quasi-groups, interest groups, and conflict groups reflects this orientation. Dahrendorf's theory suffers from some of the same problems as structural functionalism; in addition, it represents a rather impoverished effort to incorporate Marxian theory. Dahrendorf can also be criticized for being satisfied with alternative theories of order and conflict rather than seeking a theoretical integration of the two.

This last criticism leads us to several pieces of work aimed at reconciling conflict theory and structural functionalism. Van den Berghe discussed several general points the two theories have in common, and Coser and Himes analyzed the functions of social conflict. Coleman's effort to deal with sources of integration and conflict within a community setting was useful. Although all these efforts offer some insights, they have serious weaknesses, especially in the tendency to concentrate almost exclusively on large-scale phenomena. Collins sought to overcome this by integrating the large-scale theories of conflict with an ethnomethodological approach, but he did not do enough with the large-scale phenomena.

We close this chapter with Frank's criticism of van den Berghe's effort to integrate conflict and structural-functional theory. Frank's central point is that conflict theory is an inadequate reflection of insights from Marxian theory. With this in mind, we turn in Chapter Four to a discussion of a number of the efforts to develop a more adequate Marxian sociological theory.

CHAPTER FOUR
Varieties of Neo-Marxian Sociological Theory

IN Chapter Three we discussed the emergence of conflict theory as a reaction to some of the problems of structural functionalism. A central point made in that chapter was that although conflict theory purported to be within the Marxian tradition, it was actually a rather poor version of Marxian theory. In this chapter we will deal with a variety of sociological theories that are better reflections of Marx's ideas. As we will note, Marx's influence has been far from uniform. Because Marx's theory is so encyclopedic, a variety of different theorists can all claim to be working within the guidelines set down in his original work. In fact, although each claims to be the "true" inheritor of Marx's theory, there are many irreconcilable differences among them.

It is interesting to note that, in spite of the great attention devoted to neo-Marxian theories in recent years in sociology, textbooks in sociological theory usually devote little or no attention to it. For example, in a recent edition of *The Structure of Sociological Theory*, Jonathan Turner (1982:417) devoted a few pages to critical theory but was forced to add in a footnote: "I am not terribly sympathetic to this school of thought." It is important that textbooks in the field deal sympathetically with important recent developments in sociological theory—in this case, the rise of various branches of neo-Marxian theory.

In this book, care has been exercised to focus on the sociological elements of the Marxian theories we discuss. To paraphrase Henri Lefebvre's (1968) comment about Marx, there is a sociological theory in neo-Marxism, but not all neo-Marxism is sociological theory.

This chapter will generally follow the outline used by Ben Agger (1978) in his book on modern Marxism. Our goal is to survey the wide variety of work being done in neo-Marxian sociological theory. First, we will provide a brief statement on the economic determinists. Their work is not directly related to sociology, but it does represent the position that many neo-Marxian sociologists reacted against in developing their own orientation. Second, we will deal with some early Hegelian Marxists, in particular Georg Lukács and Antonio Gramsci. Their significance lies in their effort to integrate subjective concerns with traditional Marxian interests in objective, material structures. Third, we will discuss the critical, or Frankfurt, school, which turned these early Hegelian criticisms into a full-scale revision of Marxian theory. In connection with this, we will comment on those who sought to extend traditional Marxian interests to individual-level phenomena. Fourth, we will discuss structural Marxism, which constitutes a reaction against the Hegelian revisionists and a return to what these theorists call Marx's "real" concern with unconscious structures. Fifth, we will discuss some of the work in institutional neo-Marxian economics that is relevant to sociology (for example, Baran and Sweezy, 1966; Braverman, 1974). Sixth, we will touch on some of the work being done in historically oriented Marxism (for example, Wallerstein, 1974, 1980). As we proceed we offer a variety of critiques of these Marxian theories.

ECONOMIC DETERMINISM

In a number of places in his work Marx sounded like an economic determinist; that is, he seemed to see the economic system as of paramount importance and to argue that it determined all other sectors of society—politics, religion, idea systems, and so forth. Although Marx did see the economic sector as preeminent, at least in capitalist society, as a dialectician he could not have taken a deterministic position because the dialectic is characterized by the notion that there is continual feedback and mutual interaction among the various sectors of society. Politics, religion, and so on cannot be reduced to epiphenomena determined by the economy, since they affect the economy just as they are affected by it. Despite the nature of the dialectic, Marx is still being interpreted as an economic determinist. Although there are some aspects of Marx's work that would lead to this conclusion, adopting it means ignoring the overall dialectical thrust of his theory.

Ben Agger (1978) argued that economic determinism reached its peak as an interpretation of Marxian theory during the period of the Second Communist International, between 1889 and 1914. This historical period is often seen as the apex of early market capitalism, and its booms and busts led to many predictions about its imminent demise. Those Marxists who believed in economic determinism saw the breakdown of capitalism as inevitable. In their view Marxism was capable of producing a scientific theory of this breakdown (as well as other aspects of capitalist society) with the predictive reliability of the physical and natural sciences. All an analyst had to do was examine the structures of capitalism, especially the economic structures. Built into these structures was a series of processes that would inevitably bring down capitalism, so it was up to the economic determinist to discover how these processes worked.

Friedrich Engels, Marx's collaborator and benefactor, led the way in this interpretation of Marxian theory, as did such people as Karl Kautsky and Eduard Bernstein. Kautsky, for example, discussed the inevitable decline of capitalism as:

> unavoidable in the sense that the inventors improve technic and the capitalists in their desire for profit revolutionize the whole economic life, as it is also inevitable that the workers aim for shorter hours of labor and higher wages, that they organize themselves, that they fight the capitalist class and its state, as it is inevitable that they aim for the conquest of political power and the overthrow of capitalist rule. Socialism is inevitable because the class struggle and the victory of the proletariat is inevitable.
>
> (Kautsky, cited in Agger, 1978:94)

The imagery here is of actors impelled by the structures of capitalism into a series of actions.

It was this imagery that led to the major criticism of scientifically oriented economic determinism—that is was untrue to the dialectical thrust of Marx's theory. Specifically, the theory seemed to short-circuit the dialectic by making individual thought and action insignificant. The economic structures of capitalism that determined individual thought and action were the crucial element. This interpretation also led to political quietism and therefore was inconsistent with Marx's thinking. Why should individuals act if the capitalist system was going to crumble under its own structural contradictions? Clearly, given Marx's desire to integrate theory and practice, a perspective that omits action and even reduces it to insignificance would not be in the tradition of his thinking.

HEGELIAN MARXISM

As a result of the criticisms discussed above, economic determinism began to fade in importance and a number of theorists developed other varieties of Marxian theory. One group of Marxists returned to the Hegelian roots of Marx's theory in search of a subjective orientation to complement the strength of the early Marxists at the objective, material level. The early Hegelian Marxists sought to restore the dialectic between the subjective and the objective aspects of social life. Their interest in subjective factors laid the basis for the later development of critical theory, which came to focus almost exclusively on subjective factors. A number of thinkers could be taken as illustrative of Hegelian Marxism, but we will focus on the work of one who has gained great prominence: Georg Lukács. We will also give brief attention to the ideas of Antonio Gramsci.

Georg Lukács

The attention of Marxian scholars of the early twentieth century was limited mainly to Marx's later, largely economic works, such as *Capital* (1867/1967). The early work, especially *The Economic and Philosophic Manuscripts of 1844* (1932/1964), which was more heavily influenced by Hegelian subjectivism, was largely unknown to Marxian thinkers. The rediscovery of the *Manuscripts* and their publication in 1932 was a major turning point. However, by the 1920s Lukács already had written his major work, in which he emphasized the subjective side of Marxian theory.

Lukács's major contribution to Marxian theory lies in his work on two major ideas—reification and class consciousness. Lukács made it clear from the beginning that he was not totally rejecting the work of the economic Marxists on reification, but simply seeking to broaden and extend their ideas. Lukács (1922/1968:83) commenced with the Marxian concept of commodities, which he characterized as "the central, structural problem of capitalist society." A *commodity* is at base a relation among people that, they come to believe, takes on the character of a thing and develops an objective form. People in their interaction with nature in capitalist society produce various products, or commodities (for example, bread, automobiles, motion pictures). However, people tend to lose sight of the fact that they produce these commodities and give them their value. Value comes to be seen as produced by a market that is independent of the actors. The *fetishism of commodities* is the process by which commodities and the market for them are granted independent objective existence by the actors in capitalist society. Marx's concept of the fetishism of commodities was the basis for Lukács's concept of reification.

The crucial difference between the fetishism of commodities and reification is in the extensiveness of the two concepts. Whereas the former is restricted to the economic institution, the latter is applied by Lukács to all of society—the state, the law, *and* the economic sector. The same dynamic applies in all sectors of capitalist society: people come to believe that social structures have a life of their own, and as a result they do come to have an objective character. Lukács delineated this process:

> Man in capitalist society confronts a reality "made" by himself (as a class) which appears to him to be a natural phenomenon alien to himself; he is wholly at the mercy of its "laws," his activity is confined to the exploitation of the inexorable fulfillment of certain individual laws for his own (egoistic) interests. But even while "acting" he remains, in the nature of the case, the object and not the subject of events.
>
> (Lukács, 1922/1968:135)

The second major contribution of Lukács was his work on *class consciousness*, which refers to the belief systems shared by those who occupy the same class position within society. Lukács made it clear that class consciousness is neither the sum nor the average of individual consciousnesses; rather, it is a property of a group of people who share a similar place in the productive system. This view leads to a focus on the class consciousness of the bourgeoisie and especially of the proletariat. In Lukács's work there is a clear link between objective economic position, class consciousness, and the "real, psychological thoughts of men about their lives" (Lukács, 1922/1968:51).

The concept of class consciousness necessarily implies, at least in capitalism, the prior state of *false consciousness*. That is, classes in capitalism generally do not have a clear sense of their true class interests. For example, until the revolutionary stage, members of the proletariat do not fully realize the nature and extent of their exploitation in capitalism. The falsity of class consciousness is derived from the class's position within the economic structure of society: "Class consciousness implies a class-conditioned *unconsciousness* of one's own socio-historical and economic condition. . . . The 'falseness,' the illusion implicit in this situation, is in no sense arbitrary" (Lukács, 1922/1968:52). Most social classes throughout history have been unable to overcome false consciousness, and thereby achieve class consciousness. The structural position of the proletariat within capitalism, however, gives it the peculiar ability to achieve class consciousness.

The ability to achieve class consciousness is a characteristic peculiar to capitalist societies. In precapitalist societies a variety of factors prevented the development of class consciousness. For one thing, the state, independent of the economy, affected social strata; for another, status (prestige) consciousness tended to mask class (economic) consciousness. As a result, Lukács (1922/1968:57) concluded: "There is therefore no possible position within such a society from which the economic basis of all social relations could be made conscious." In contrast, the economic base of capitalism is clearer and simpler. People may not be conscious of its effects, but they are at least unconsciously aware of them. As a result, "class consciousness arrived at the point where *it could become conscious*" (Lukács, 1922/1968:59). At this stage society turns into an ideological battleground in which those who seek to conceal the class character of society are pitted against those who seek to expose it.

Lukács compared the various classes in capitalism on the issue of class consciousness. He argued that the petty bourgeoisie and the peasants cannot develop class consciousness because of the ambiguity of their structural position within capitalism. Because these two classes represent vestiges of society in the feudal era, they are not able to develop a clear sense of the nature of capitalism. The bourgeoisie can develop class consciousness, but at best it understands the development of capitalism as something external, subject to objective laws, that it can experience only passively.

The proletariat has the capacity to develop true class consciousness, and as it does the bourgeoisie is thrown on the defensive. Lukács refused to see the proletariat as simply driven by external forces but viewed it instead as an active creator of its own fate. In the confrontation between the bourgeoisie and the proletariat, the former class has all the intellectual and organizational weapons, whereas all the latter has, at least at first, is the ability to see society for what it is. As the battle proceeds, the proletariat moves from being a "class in itself," that is, a structurally created entity, to a "class for itself," a class conscious of its position and its mission. In other words, "the class struggle must be raised from the level of economic necessity to the level of conscious aim and effective class consciousness" (Lukács, 1922/1968:76). When the struggle reaches this point, the proletariat is capable of the action that can overthrow the capitalist system.

Lukács had a rich sociological theory, although it is embedded in Marxian terms. He was concerned with the dialectical relationship among the structures (primarily economic) of capitalism, the idea systems (especially class consciousness), individual thought, and, ultimately, individual action. His theoretical perspective provides an important bridge between the economic determinists and more modern Marxists.

Antonio Gramsci

The Italian Marxist Antonio Gramsci, although offering a less rich theoretical perspective than Lukács, also played a key role in the transition from economic determinism to more modern Marxian positions. Gramsci (1971:336) was critical of Marxists who are "deterministic, fatalistic and mechanistic." In his view such a perspective reduces social classes to "things." Although he recognized the importance of structural forces, especially economics, Gramsci focused on idea systems, and particularly on the role of intellectuals in the creation of revolutionary ideology. He had a rather elitist conception, in which ideas are produced from "above" by intellectuals and then extended to the masses. In his view the masses cannot become self-conscious alone; they need the help of social elites. However, once the masses have been influenced by these ideas, they put them into action in creating a social revolution. Gramsci, like Lukács, focused on collective ideas rather than on social structures, and both operated within traditional Marxian theory. We turn now to critical theory, which has moved even further from the traditional Marxian roots of economic determinism.

CRITICAL THEORY

Critical theory is the product of a group of German neo-Marxists who were dissatisfied with the state of Marxian theory, particularly its tendency toward economic determinism. The school was officially founded in Frankfurt, Germany, on February 23, 1923, although a number of its members had been active prior to that time. With the coming to power of the Nazis in the 1930s many of the major figures emigrated to the United States and continued their work at an institute affiliated with Columbia University in New York City. Following World War II some of the critical theorists returned to Germany, while others remained in the United States (Jay, 1973; Slater, 1977; Held, 1980). Today critical theory has spread beyond the confines of the Frankfurt school, but the most important work is being done by a group of second-generation critical thinkers based in Germany. Critical theory was, and is today, largely a European orientation, although its influence in American sociology is growing (van den Berg, 1980).

The Major Critiques

Critical theory is composed largely of criticisms of various aspects of social and intellectual life. It takes its inspiration from Marx's work, which was first shaped by a critical analysis of philosophical ideas and later by analysis of the nature of the capitalist system. The critical school constitutes a critique both of society and of various systems of knowledge (Farganis, 1975). Much of the work is in the form of critiques, but its ultimate goal is to reveal more accurately the nature of society (Bleich, 1977). First we will focus on the major critiques offered by the school, all of which manifest a preference for oppositional thinking and for unveiling and debunking various aspects of social reality (Connerton, 1976).

CRITICISMS OF MARXIAN THEORY

Critical theory constitutes a variant of Marxian theory that takes as its starting point a critique of Marxian theories. The critical theorists are most disturbed by the economic determinists, the mechanistic, or mechanical, Marxists (Schroyer, 1973; Sewart, 1978;

Antonio, 1981). Some (for example, Habermas, 1968) criticize the determinism implicit in parts of Marx's original work, but most focus their criticisms on the neo-Marxists, primarily because they had interpreted Marx's work too mechanistically. The critical theorists do not say that economic determinists were wrong in focusing on the economic realm but that they should have been concerned with other aspects of social life as well. As we will see, the critical school seeks to rectify this imbalance by focusing its attention on the cultural realm (Schroyer, 1973:33).

CRITICISMS OF POSITIVISM

Critical theorists also focus their attention on the philosophical underpinnings of scientific inquiry, a philosophy often labeled positivism. The criticism of positivism is related, at least in part, to the criticism of economic determinism, because some of those who were determinists accepted part or all of the positivistic theory of knowledge. Positivism is depicted as standing for various things (Schroyer, 1970; Sewart, 1978). Positivism accepts the idea that a single scientific method is applicable to all fields of study. It takes the physical sciences as the standard of certainty and exactness for all disciplines. Positivists believe that knowledge is inherently neutral. This means that they feel they can keep human values out of their work. This, in turn, leads to the view that science is not in the position of advocating any specific form of social action.

Positivism is opposed by the critical school on various grounds (Sewart, 1978). For one thing, positivism tends to reify the social world and see it as a natural process. The critical theorists prefer to focus on human activity as well as on the ways in which such activity affects larger social structures. In short, positivism loses sight of the actors, reducing them to passive entities determined by ''natural forces.'' Given their belief in the distinctiveness of the actor, the critical theorists would not accept the idea that the general laws of science can be applied without question to human action. Positivism is assailed for being content to judge the adequacy of means toward given ends and for not making a similar judgment about ends. This leads to the view that positivism is inherently conservative, incapable of challenging the existing system. As Martin Jay (1973:62) says of it, ''The result was the absolutizing of 'facts' and the reification of the existing order.'' Positivism leads the actor and the social scientist to passivity. Few Marxists of any type would support a perspective that does not relate theory and practice. Despite these criticisms of positivism, some Marxists (for example, some structuralists) espouse positivism, and Marx himself was often guilty of being overly positivistic (Habermas, 1968).

CRITICISMS OF SOCIOLOGY

The critical school has also taken on sociology as a target (Frankfurt Institute for Social Research, 1973). It is attacked for its ''scientism,'' that is, for making the scientific method an end in itself. In addition, sociology is accused of accepting the status quo. The critical school maintains that sociology does not seriously criticize society, nor does it seek to transcend the contemporary social structure. Sociology, the critical school contends, has surrendered its obligation to help people oppressed by contemporary society.

In addition to such political criticisms, the critical school also has a related substantive criticism. That is, it is critical of sociologists' tendency to reduce everything human to social variables. When sociologists focus on society as a whole rather than on individuals in society, they ignore the interaction of the individual and society. While most sociological perspectives are *not* guilty of ignoring this interaction, this view is a cornerstone of the critical school's attacks on sociologists. Because they ignore the individual, sociologists are seen as being unable to say anything meaningful about political changes that could lead to a "just and humane society" (Frankfurt Institute for Social Research, 1973:46). As Zoltan Tar (1977:x) put it, sociology becomes "an integral part of the existing society instead of being a means of critique and a ferment of renewal."

CRITIQUE OF MODERN SOCIETY

Most of the critical school's work is aimed at a critique of modern society and a variety of its components. Whereas much of early Marxian theory aimed specifically at the economy, the critical school has shifted its orientation to the cultural level in light of what it considers the realities of modern capitalist society. That is, the locus of domination in the modern world had shifted from the economy to the cultural realm. Still, the critical school retains its interest in domination,[1] although in the modern world it is likely to be domination by cultural rather than economic elements. The critical school thus seeks to focus on the cultural repression of the individual in modern society.

The critical thinkers have been shaped not only by Marxian theory but also by Weberian theory, as reflected in their focus on rationality as the dominant development within the modern world. As Trent Schroyer (1970) made clear, the view of the critical school is that in modern society the repression produced by rationality has replaced economic exploitation as the dominant social problem. The critical school clearly has adopted Weber's differentiation between *zweckrationality* (instrumental rationality) and *wertrationality*, or what the critical theorists think of as *reason*. To the critical theorists, instrumental rationality is concerned unreflectively with the question of the most effective means for achieving any given purpose (Tar, 1977). This is viewed as "technocratic thinking," in which the objective is to serve the forces of domination, not to emancipate people from domination. The goal is simply to find the most efficient means to whatever ends are defined as important by those in power. Technocratic thinking is contrasted to reason, which is, in the minds of critical theorists, the hope for society. Reason involves the assessment of means in terms of the ultimate human goals of justice, peace, and happiness.

Despite the seeming rationality of modern life, the critical school views the modern world as rife with irrationality. This can be labeled the "irrationality of rationality," or more specifically the irrationality of *zweckrationality*. As Herbert Marcuse (1964:ix; see also Farganis, 1975) saw it, although it appears to be the embodiment of rationality, "this society is irrational as a whole." It is irrational that the rational world is destructive of individuals and their needs and abilities; that peace is maintained

---

[1]This is made abundantly clear by Trent Schroyer (1973), who entitles his book on the critical school *The Critique of Domination*.

through a constant threat of war; and that despite the existence of sufficient means people remain impoverished, repressed, exploited, and unable to fulfill themselves.

The critical school focuses its attention primarily on one form of instrumental rationality—modern technology. Marcuse (1964), for example, was a severe critic of modern technology. He saw technology in modern society as leading to totalitarianism. In fact, he viewed it as leading to new, more effective, and even more "pleasant" methods of external control over individuals. The prime example is the use of television to socialize and pacify the population (other examples are mass sports and sex). He rejected the idea that technology is neutral in the modern world and saw it instead as a means to dominate people. It is effective because it is made to seem neutral when it is in fact enslaving. It serves to suppress individuality. The actor's inner freedom has been "invaded and whittled down" by modern technology. The result is what Marcuse called "one-dimensional society" in which individuals lose the ability to think critically and negatively about society. Marcuse did not see technology per se as the enemy, but rather technology as it is employed in modern capitalist society: "Technology, no matter how 'pure,' sustains and streamlines the continuum of domination. This fatal link can be cut only by a revolution which makes technology and technique subservient to the needs and goals of free men" (Marcuse, 1969:56). Marcuse retained Marx's original view that technology is not inherently a problem and that it can be used to develop a "better" society.

Here we encounter a split among critical theorists that is manifest in the work of its foremost modern exponent, Jurgen Habermas (1970). Habermas accepted Weber's views on the progressive rationalization and disenchantment of the modern world. Habermas focused on technology and science as the most important manifestations of instrumental rationality. These manifestations of rationality are used in the modern world to control the mass of people. They also obscure and conceal domination by wrapping it in a cloak of value-neutrality. Although Habermas accepted much of Marcuse's position here, he seemed to reject the idea that instrumental rationality can be used for the betterment of humankind. Rather, he accepted the original Weberian position that rationality is an inherent problem, whether it occurs in capitalism or socialism. To Habermas, the answer is to be found in creating a society in which "true" human interaction is possible. Habermas called this true human interaction "symbolic interaction," or what he defined as interaction and communication without compulsion (Habermas, 1970:88). He sought a society in which symbolic interaction is the norm rather than pure purposive-rational action. Whereas in modern society the norm is to work, to engage in instrumentally rational action, Habermas favored a society in which symbolic interaction is normative. Habermas sought to remove restrictions on communication so that the distortions characteristic of modern society could be replaced by symbolic interaction.

CRITIQUE OF CULTURE

The critical theorists level significant criticisms at what they called the "culture industry." Interest in the culture industry reflects their concern with the Marxian concept of "superstructure" rather than with the economic base. The culture industry, or what is conventionally called "mass culture," is defined as the "administered . . . nonspontaneous, reified, phony culture rather than the real thing" (Jay, 1973:216). Two things worry the critical thinkers most about this industry. First, they are concerned about its falseness. They think of it as a prepackaged set of ideas mass-produced and disseminated to the masses by the media. Second, the critical theorists are disturbed by its pacifying and stupefying effect on people (Tar, 1977:83).

The critical school is also interested in and critical of what they call the "knowledge industry," which refers to entities concerned with knowledge production (for example, universities and research institutes) that have become autonomous structures in our society. Their autonomy has allowed them to extend themselves beyond their original mandate (Schroyer, 1970). They have become oppressive structures interested in expanding their influence throughout society.

Marx's critical analysis of capitalism led him to have hope for the future, but the critical theorists have come to a position of despair and hopelessness. They see the problems of the modern world not as specific to capitalism, but as endemic to a rationalized world, including socialist societies. They see the future, in Weberian terms, as an "iron cage" of increasingly rational structures from which hope for escape lessens all the time.

Much of critical theory (like the bulk of Marx's original formulation) is in the form of critical analyses. Even though the critical theorists also have a number of positive interests, one of the basic criticisms made of critical theory is that it offers more criticisms than it does positive contributions. This incessant negativity galls many, and for this reason it is felt by many that critical theory has little to offer to sociological theory.

The Major Contributions

SUBJECTIVITY

The great contribution of the critical school has been its effort to reorient Marxian theory in a subjective direction. While this constitutes a critique of Marx's materialism and his dogged focus on economic structures, it also represents a strong contribution to our understanding of the subjective elements of social life. The subjective contributions of the critical school are at both the individual and the cultural levels.

The Hegelian roots of Marxian theory are the major source of interest in subjectivity. Many of the critical thinkers see themselves as returning to those roots, as expressed in Marx's early works, especially *The Economic and Philosophic Manuscripts of 1844* (1932/1964). In this, they are following up on the work of the early-twentieth-century Marxian revisionists, such as Karl Korsch and Georg Lukács, who sought not to focus on subjectivity but simply to integrate such an interest with the traditional Marxian concern with objective structures (Agger, 1978:119). Korsch and Lukács did not seek a fundamental restructuring of Marxian theory, although the later critical theorists do have this broader and more ambitious objective.

We begin with the critical school's interest in culture. Reversing the traditional Marxian focus, the critical school has shifted to a concern with the "superstructure" rather than with the economic "base." One factor motivating this shift is that the critical school feels that Marxists have overemphasized economic structures and that this has served to overwhelm their interest in the other aspects of social reality, especially the culture. In addition to this factor, a series of external changes in the society point to such a shift (Agger, 1978). In particular, the prosperity of the post–World War II period *seems* to have led to a disappearance of internal economic contradictions in general, and class conflict in particular. False consciousness *seems* to be nearly universal as all social classes, including the working class, appear to be beneficiaries and ardent supporters of the capitalist system. To this might be added the growing realization that the Soviet Union, despite its socialist economy, is at least as oppressive as capitalist society. Since the two societies have different economies, the critical thinkers have had to look elsewhere for the major source of oppression. What they looked toward initially was the culture.

To the previously discussed aspects of the Frankfurt school's concerns—rationality, the culture industry, and the knowledge industry—can be added an additional set of concerns, the most notable of which is an interest in ideology. By ideology they mean the idea systems, often false and obfuscating, produced by societal elites. All of these specific aspects of the superstructure, and the critical school's orientation to them, can be subsumed under the heading of a "critique of domination" (Schroyer, 1973; Agger, 1978). This interest in domination was at first stimulated by fascism in the 1930s and 1940s, but it has shifted to a concern with domination in capitalist society. The modern world has reached a stage of unsurpassed domination of individuals. In fact, the control is so complete that it no longer requires deliberate actions on the part of the leaders. The control pervades all aspects of the cultural world and, more important, is internalized in the actor. In effect, actors have come to dominate themselves in the name of the larger social structure. Domination has reached such a complete stage that it no longer appears to be domination at all. Since domination is no longer perceived as personally damaging and alienating, it often seems as if the world is the way it is supposed to be. It is no longer clear to actors what the world *ought* to be like. This buttresses the pessimism of the critical thinkers, who can no longer see how rational analysis can help alter the situation.

One of the critical school's concerns at the cultural level is with what Habermas (1975) called *legitimations*. These can be defined as systems of ideas generated by the political system, and theoretically by any other system, to support the existence of the system. They are designed to "mystify" the political system, to make it unclear exactly what is happening. Above all, these systems of ideas legitimate the status quo. However, people are having increasing difficulty in accepting these legitimations, with the result that modern political systems, like the one in the United States, are undergoing a "legitimation crisis." Ralph Miliband (1974), for example, wondered how long people can be expected to believe in democracy in the light of increasingly centralized state capitalism. Habermas (1975) asked if people will continue to believe in the idea of a better life in the future in view of problems such as accelerating inflation and recurrent recession. Accepting the idea that the United States has a free-enterprise market system becomes increasingly hard in light of the public bailouts of such corporate giants as Lockheed and Chrysler. The result is rising public cynicism that threatens many of our legitimations.

In addition to such cultural interests, the critical school is also concerned with actors and their consciousness, and what happens to them in the modern world. Unfortunately, the critical theorists, like most Marxists and most sociologists, often fail to differentiate clearly between individual consciousness and culture, nor do they specify the many links between them. In much of their work they move freely back and forth between consciousness and culture with little or no sense that they are changing levels.

Of great importance here is the effort by critical theorists, most notably Marcuse (1969), to integrate Freud's insights at the level of consciousness (and unconsciousness) into the critical theorists' interpretation of the culture. One of the benefits of this interest in individual consciousness is that it offers a useful corrective to the pessimism of the critical school and its focus on cultural constraints. Although people are controlled, imbued with false needs, and anesthetized, in Freudian terms they are also endowed with a libido (broadly conceived as sexual energy), which provides the basic source of energy for creative action oriented toward the overthrow of the major forms of domination.

DIALECTICS

The second main positive focus of critical theory is an interest in dialectics in general, as well as in a variety of its specific manifestations. At the most general level, a dialectical approach means a focus on the social *totality*. Paul Connerton (1976:12) gave a good sense of the critical approach to the social totality: "No partial aspect of social life and no isolated phenomenon may be comprehended unless it is related to the historical whole, to the social structure conceived as a global entity." This involves a rejection of a focus on any *specific* aspect of social life, especially the economic system, outside of its broader context. This approach also means a concern with the interrelation of the various levels of social reality—most important, individual consciousness, the cultural superstructure, and the economic structure. Dialectics also carries with it a methodological prescription: one component of social life cannot be studied in isolation from the rest.

This idea has both diachronic and synchronic components. A *diachronic* view leads us to be concerned with the interrelationship of components of society within a contemporary totality. A *synchronic* view carries with it a concern for the historical roots of today's society as well as for where it might be going in the future (Bauman, 1976:81). The domination of people by social and cultural structures—the "one-dimensional" society, to use Marcuse's phrase—is the result of a specific historical development and is not a universal characteristic of humankind. This historical perspective counteracts the commonsense view that emerges in capitalism that the system is a natural and inevitable phenomenon. In the view of the critical theorists (and other Marxists), people have come to see society as "second nature"; it is "perceived by commonsensical wisdom as an alien, uncompromising, demanding and high-handed power—exactly like non-human nature. To abide by the rules of reason, to behave rationally, to achieve success, to be free man now had to accommodate himself to the 'second nature'" (Bauman, 1976:6).

The critical theorists are also oriented to thinking about the future, but following Marx's original lead, they refuse to be utopian; rather, they focus on criticizing and changing contemporary society. However, instead of directing their attention to society's economic structure as Marx had done, they concentrated on its cultural superstructure. Their dialectical approach commits them to work in the real world. On one level, this means that they are not satisfied with seeking truth in scientific laboratories. The ultimate test of their ideas is the degree to which they are accepted and utilized in practice. This process they call *authentication*, which occurs when the people who have been the victims of distorted communication take up the ideas of critical theory and use them to free themselves from that system (Bauman, 1976:104). This leads to another aspect of the concerns of the critical thinkers—the *liberation* of humankind (Marcuse, 1964:222).

In more abstract terms, critical thinkers can be said to be preoccupied with the interplay and relationship between theory and practice. The view of the Frankfurt school was that the two have been severed in capitalist society (Schroyer, 1973:28). That is, theorizing is done by one group, which is delegated, or more likely takes, that right, whereas practice is relegated to another, less powerful group. In many cases, the theorist's work is uninformed by what went on in the real world, leading to an impoverished and largely irrelevant body of Marxian and sociological theory. The point is to unify theory and practice so as to restore the relationship between them. Theory would thus be informed by practice while practice would be shaped by theory. In the process, both theory and practice would be enriched.

Despite this avowed goal, most of critical theory has failed abysmally to integrate theory and practice. In fact, one of the most often-voiced criticisms of critical theory is that it is written in such a way as to be totally inaccessible to the mass of people. Furthermore, in its commitment to study culture and superstructure it addresses a number of very esoteric topics and has little to say about the pragmatic, day-to-day concerns of most people.

One of the best-known dialectical concerns of the critical school is that of Jurgen Habermas (1968; 1970). His interest in the relationship between knowledge and human interests is an example of a broader dialectical concern with the relationship between subjective and objective factors. But he has been careful to point out that subjective and objective factors cannot be dealt with in isolation from one another. To Habermas, knowledge exists at the objective level while human interests are a more subjective phenomena.

Habermas differentiated between three knowledge systems and their corresponding interests. The interests that lie behind each system of knowledge are generally unknown to laypeople, and it is the task of the critical theorists to uncover them. The first type of knowledge is *analytic science*, or *classical positivistic scientific systems*. In Habermas's view, the underlying interest of such a knowledge system is technical control, which can be applied to the environment, other societies, or people within society. In Habermas's view, analytic science lends itself quite easily to enhancing oppressive control. The second type of knowledge system is *humanistic knowledge*, and its interest is in *understanding* the world. It operates from the general view that understanding our past generally helps us to understand what is transpiring today. It is also seen as an aid in mutual understanding. It is not oppressive, nor is it liberating; it has little or no relevance to practice either in contemporary life or in the future. The third type is *critical knowledge*, which Habermas, and the Frankfurt school in general, espoused. The interest attached to this type of knowledge is *human emancipation*. It was hoped that the critical knowledge generated by Habermas and others would raise the self-consciousness of the masses (through mechanisms articulated by the Freudians) and lead to a social movement that would result in the hoped-for emancipation.

STRUCTURAL MARXISM

Structural Marxism is usually associated with a group of French thinkers (for example, Louis Althusser, Nicos Poulantzas, and Maurice Godelier) and thus is sometimes called French structuralism. However, since this approach has many followers outside of France, we refer to this school as structural Marxism.

As the name suggests, *structural Marxism* represents the fusion of two schools— Marxism and structuralism. Structuralism is devoted to the analysis of the hidden, underlying structures of social life. Later we will see that structuralism encompasses a wide array of complicated ideas. In the last chapter of this book, in addition to a detailed discussion of structuralism, we will include a discussion of the relationship between structuralism in general and structural Marxism in particular. We will see that although the two orientations have a number of things in common, there are important differences between them. Our concern here will be with the kind of Marxism that structural Marxism represents; later we will deal with it as a kind of structuralism.

Structuralist Criticisms of Other Marxian Theories

A good way to approach structural Marxism is to discuss its criticisms of other Marxian theories. In general, structural Marxists see themselves as being truest to Marx's work, especially his later work. In addition to questioning the purity of other Marxian theorists, structural Marxists make a number of more specific attacks (Burris, 1979).

First, structural Marxists criticize the tendency of many Marxists to emphasize empirical data in their analyses. In the view of such structural Marxists as Godelier (1972a:xviii–xix), the truly important realities of capitalist life are to be found in the underlying structure and not in the observable facts that often obscure the true nature of that structure.

Second, structural Marxists reject the tendency of many Marxists toward historical research, because historicism is also seen as focusing on empirical data and neglecting the underlying structure. In addition, they reject historicism because of their belief that the primary task of Marxism is the study of contemporary structure. Only after we understand the basic structure of the contemporary world can we begin to grasp historical processes. Interestingly, this is reminiscent of the position taken by a major critic of Marxian theory, Talcott Parsons, who also argued that a study of structure was a prerequisite to a theory of history and social change.

Third, structural Marxists criticize sharply the reductionistic economic determinism that is characteristic of some Marxian theories. While the structural Marxists see the importance of the economy, and even see it as determinant "in the last instance," they also accord significance to other sectors of the social world, especially the political and ideological structures. Poulantzas, for example, rejected the idea that the state merely reflects the economy; it can be seen as possessing "relative autonomy." More specifically, he took issue with those determinists who argue that economic development would follow whatever type of state exists. In other words, he criticized those who argued that it makes no difference whether we have fascism or democracy. Poulantzas (1976:21) concluded: "Here, as elsewhere, the forms that bourgeois domination assumes are far from a matter of indifference."

Poulantzas singled out for criticism the passive position of those Marxian theorists who argued that fascism would somehow crumble as a result of its own internal economic contradictions and that thus there was no need to take any action against fascist societies. Poulantzas also criticized those who argued that imperialism is simply an economic phenomenon. To him, it is a much more complex process involving political, ideological, and economic aspects. Although Poulantzas (and other structural Marxists) recognized the importance of the economy, they also contended that at any given moment other social structures may come to occupy a dominant position.

Finally, the structural Marxists criticize the tendency of a large number of other Marxists (especially critical theorists) to subjectivize and humanize the field. To the structuralists, the focus should be on the objective structures of society—economy, polity, ideology—and not the human actors within those structures. Thus the structuralists reject a humanistic interpretation of Marx's theory; the effort to resurrect Marx's historical concerns; a focus on Marx's more humanistic works (for example, the *1844 Manuscripts*); the emphasis on the Hegelian roots of Marxian theory; and a focus on voluntaristic actors, feelings, interpersonal relations, or even conscious efforts at self-organization (Appelbaum, 1979). For example, instead of seeing social classes as composed of voluntaristic actors, structuralists see them as "objectively antagonistic relations" (Burris, 1979:14). Althusser depicted the emphasis on structures and the fact that actors are determined by those structures:

> The structure of the relations of production determines the *places* and *functions* occupied and adopted by the agents of production, who are never anything more than the occupants of these places, insofar as they are the "supports" . . . of the functions. The true "subjects" (in the sense of constitutive subjects of the process) are therefore not these occupants or functionaries . . . but the *relations* of *production* (and political and ideological social relations).
>
> (Althusser, cited in Burris, 1979:8)

In sum, in rejecting humanistic Marxism, the structuralists have clearly enunciated an interest in the structures of capitalist society. Let us now state the premises of structural Marxism in more positive terms.

Basic Tenets of Structural Marxists

Structural Marxists are oriented to the study of the hidden underlying structures of capitalist society. Although their basic concern is not "real" structures, they do believe that there are real structures in the world that constrain or determine what actors think and do. Structural Marxists accept the importance of the economy but also look at various other structures, especially political and ideological structures. Furthermore, although they accept the idea of the economy as determinant in the last instance, they do not simply reduce other structures to reflections of it. In fact, not only do structural Marxists accept the importance of the polity and ideology, they also see them as possessing "relative autonomy." These structures may follow rather independent paths of development and may at any given time come to be the dominant forces in society.

Whatever structures they focus on, to structural Marxists actors simply fill positions in those structures; that is, they are seen as largely constrained by those structures. Despite the passive implications of such a viewpoint, as practicing Marxists the structuralists are disinclined to conclude that people should simply sit and wait for the ultimate breakdown of the structural system. As Poulantzas (1976:133) said: "If we confine ourselves to waiting, we will not get the 'great day' at all, but rather the tanks in the small hours of the morning."

The idea of a breakdown of the structures of society implies another major concern of structural Marxists—the contradictions within the system. Their tendency is to focus on contradictions among structures rather than on the contradictions that confront the actor.

Structural Marxists emphasize the importance of theoretical rather than empirical research. Obviously, since the structures are invisible, the presumption is that they can only be ascertained theoretically; thus no amount of empirical research can uncover them.

In part for the same reason, structural Marxists focus on *contemporary* society. They put little credence in historical data or research. They believe that the priority should be the study of static structures rather than historical processes; history can only be known when we have a good grasp of contemporary structure.

Reanalyzing Marx: The Work of Louis Althusser

The work of Louis Althusser is defined largely by the nature of his focus on Marx's work. Althusser's view was that most Marxists had not interpreted Marx's work properly; indeed, he felt that they had done great violence to it. He sought to deal with this problem by developing what he believed to be a "correct" reading of Marx's work. Althusser's work is best examined in the context of the debate surrounding Marx's work.

One issue in the debate is whether Marx took a consistent intellectual position throughout his life (Veltmeyer, 1978). This is related to the issue of whether Marx is a structural and deterministic, or a humanistic and dialectical, thinker. Those Marxists who see Marx as a structuralist focus on his later works, particularly *Capital* (1867/1967). Others point to what they see as a more humanistic perspective in the essential continuity between *Capital* and *The Economic and Philosophic Manuscripts of 1844* (1932/1964). In fact, there is ample evidence in Marx's work to support either interpretation.

One of the most convincing pieces of evidence for those who see Marx as a structural or economic determinist, or both, is the preface to the *Critique of Political Economy*:

In the social production of their existence, men inevitably enter into definite relations, which are independent of their will, namely relations of production appropriate to a given stage in the development of their material forces of production. The totality of these relations of production constitutes the economic structure of society, the real foundation, on which arises a legal and political superstructure and to which correspond definite forms of social consciousness. The mode of production of material life conditions the general process of social, political and intellectual life. It is not the consciousness of men that determines their existence, but their social existence that determines their consciousness. At a certain stage of development, the material productive forces of society come into conflict with the existing relations of production or—this merely expresses the same thing in legal terms—with the property relations within the framework of which they have operated hitherto. From forms of development of the

LOUIS ALTHUSSER: A Biographical Sketch

On November 16, 1980, Louis Althusser, a renowned French structural Marxist, ran clad in his pajamas into the courtyard of the school where he had taught for many years, the Ecole Normale Superieure, shouting that he had just killed his wife. Those who went to his quarters found that his wife Heléne, a noted scholar-sociologist in her own right, had been strangled. Althusser, who had suffered from increasingly serious bouts of depression, had been hospitalized for four months not long before the murder took place. Instead of being taken to jail, Althusser was whisked off to a hospital. A judge who went to the hospital to tell him that he was to be charged with the murder found him too seriously depressed to understand the information or to be questioned about the event.

Althusser is not only a well-known scholar but a renowned public figure in France. He is best known as an active member, and severe critic, of the French Communist party. He believed that Marx had developed a new and highly rigorous science in his later economic works and that the members and leaders of the French Communist party had strayed too far from these basic ideas.

Althusser was born in Algeria on October 16, 1918, and spent five years as a prisoner of war during World War II. Prior to the war Althusser had been politically conservative and active in Catholicism, but after the war he turned to the ideas and the practice of communism. Since the end of the war, Althusser has made his mark as both a political figure and as a major interpreter of the ideas of Karl Marx. In his best-known works, *For Marx* and *Reading Capital*, he established the view that there is a major discontinuity in Marx's work. While the early Marx was humanistic and philosophical, the later Marx was much more rigorously scientific and important, Althusser maintained.

productive forces these relations turn into their fetters. Then begins an era of social revolution. The changes in the economic foundation lead sooner or later to the whole immense superstructure.

(Marx, 1859/1970:21)

The earliest and most general response to this theme was to consider Marx an *economic* determinist, a view that persists in many quarters to this day. However, the most recent interpretations by critical theorists and others deny that Marx was, or even could have been, an economic determinist. First, it can be argued that even though Marx devoted the bulk of his attention to the economic dimension in capitalism, that does not mean that the same factor would predominate in other types of social systems. That is, it can be argued that Marx's focus on economics is peculiar to capitalism because of the exaggerated significance that sector acquires in that particular social system.

Second, it is doubtful that Marx devoted as much attention to the economic dimension as many think. When Marx spoke about productive activity, he was not restricting himself to work or economic production (Mészáros, 1970:115). Rather, productive activity can include not only the production of cars but also the production of religious ideas, the development of the Constitution, and the composition of music.

Third, the whole notion of economic determinism contradicts the dialectical method that stands at the base of Marx's thinking. As István Mészáros (1970:118) argued: "The Marxian system . . . is organized in terms of an inherently historical— 'open'—teleology which cannot admit 'fixity' at any stage whatsoever."

Fourth, Bertell Ollman (1976) argued that because Marx wrote in dialectical fashion, we cannot always assume that he meant the same thing by his words as we do by ours. It is virtually impossible to write dialectically. Thus Marx's deterministic statements must be reinterpreted as simply partial statements of causality that exist within a broader dialectical system. Vernon Venable (1945:95) summed up the now dominant interpretation of Marx on this issue: "No, no monism, technological or other, can be made out of the Marxian theory of production." Specifically addressing himself to the quotation above from the *Critique of Political Economy*, Ollman (1976:8–9) stated that when Marx says, "The mode of production of material life conditions the general process of social, political, and intellectual life," we must understand this claim "in a way that allows the latter group of factors to vitally affect the mode of production, and in a way that removes the automatic dependence of the social superstructure on the economic base. We must do this, because this is how Marx used his theories in practice."

It is ironic that the belief in Marx as an economic determinist persists even though Engels confronted the issue directly and gave an eminently reasonable explanation for Marx's focus on economics as well as his simultaneous rejection of a one-sided determinism:

> Marx and I are ourselves partly to blame for the fact that younger writers sometimes lay more stress on the economic side than is due it. We had to emphasize this main principle in opposition to our adversaries, who denied it, and we had not always the time, the place or the opportunity to allow the other elements involved in the interaction to come into their rights.
>
> (Engels, 1890/1972:642)

Althusser represents a somewhat different but equally deterministic perspective on Marx's work. This is clear from his position in the debate about the "two Marxes," or "What distinguishes the object of *Capital* . . . from the object . . . of the *1844 Manuscripts*" (Althusser and Balibar, 1970:14). To Althusser the *1844 Manuscripts* were written while Marx was still heavily influenced by Hegel, philosophy, humanism, and a concern for the devastating effect of the alienating conditions of capitalism on the individual. As far as Althusser was concerned, such concerns were unscientific and needed to be overcome in order to develop scientific materialism (Anderson, 1976:71). The philosophical, humanistic, and historical bases of Marx's early work led him to center on an active, creative, and free actor. Such imagery was, in Perry Anderson's view, anathema to Althusser: "The archetypical delusion was men's belief that they were in any way free in their volition, when in fact they were permanently governed by *laws* of which they were *unconscious*" (Anderson, 1976:65; italics added). Althusser believed that the heart of Marxian theory lies in the structure of society and the laws that govern the operation of these structures rather than with free actors. In his view, in *Capital* this focus emerges most clearly. As Althusser (1977:168) said: "If we take seriously what Marx tells us about the real dialectic of history, it is not 'men' who make history, although its dialectic is realized in them and in their practice, but the masses in the relations of class struggle.''

Althusser argued that there is a clear "epistemological break" in the history of Marx's work and that Marx shifted, rather dramatically, from philosophical subjectivity (an ideological position) to abstract theory (a scientific position). Although he detailed a number of substages, Althusser basically divided Marx's work into the pre- and the post-1845 works. Prior to 1845 Marx was largely a philosophical humanist. This was his ideological period. After 1845 he moved toward a more scientific orientation, his scientific period. Althusser (1969:13) argued that in 1845 Marx made "a scientific discovery without historical precedent, in its nature and effects. . . . Marx established a new *science*: the science of the history of 'social formations.' ''

In Althusser's (1969:227) view, in 1845 "Marx broke radically with every theory that based history and politics on an essence of man." He saw three main elements involved in this dramatic change. First, Marx developed a whole new set of concepts, replacing ideas like alienation, species-being, and other humanistic concepts with a new set of scientific structural concepts such as social formations, superstructure, relations of production, and forces of production. Second, Marx engaged in a theoretical critique of all varieties of philosophical humanism. Third, Marx defined humanism as a form of ideology—an elitist and distorted idea system. Althusser (1969:227) concluded: "This rupture with every *philosophical* . . . humanism is no secondary detail; it is Marx's scientific discovery."

Althusser's position constitutes something of a throwback to the economistic and mechanistic thinking that dominated communist theorists prior to the 1917 Russian Revolution. This position was dominant earlier in part because *Capital*, which was easily interpreted mechanistically, was available to Marxian scholars, whereas the *1844 Manuscripts* were lost and not published until 1932. As we saw earlier in this chapter, however, even before these more humanistic works were available, there were critics of mechanical Marxism. Gramsci (1971:336) argued that "the deterministic, fatalistic and mechanistic element has been a direct ideological 'aroma' . . . rather like religion or drugs (in their stupefying effect).'' He (1971:353–354) maintained that instead we must deal with the relationship between the structure of society and the actor, "the consciousness of the individual man who knows, wishes, admires, creates." Gramsci's humanistic image of Marxism was anathema to Althusser and was seen by him as characteristic of the early Marx.

This debate has been radically affected by the belated publication of seven notebooks drafted by Marx in the winter of 1857–1858 and now known as the *Grundrisse* (Marx, 1857–1858/1974). Although published in two parts in 1939 and 1941 in the Soviet Union, the German original was not published until 1953, and the English version did not appear until 1974. Many observers (for example, McLellan, 1971:69–70; Ollman, 1976; Mészáros, 1970:221; Struik, 1964:55; Nicolaus, 1974) believe that the *Grundrisse* tends to support Gramsci's interpretation of Marx rather than Althusser's. Ollman (1976:xv) was quite clear on this point: "The *Grundrisse* . . . which served as Marx's first draft for *Capital*, contains many pages which could have been lifted bodily from the *1844 Manuscripts*. Even in the published version of *Capital*, there is much more of Marx's 'earlier' ideas and concepts than is generally recognized.'' Ollman was arguing, not that Marx's ideas were always the same, but rather that there was an evolution of ideas already present in the early works. This view has been accepted by a significant number of Marxian scholars, but some, like Althusser, still see Marx as a structural determinist.

In addition to endeavoring to develop a structural interpretation of Marx's work, Althusser tried to derive a structural analysis of capitalist society from it. To begin with, Althusser adopted the position that the economy is the determinant ''in the last instance.'' This is certainly a weaker position than that taken by the economic determinists. But despite the basic importance of the economy, other structural components of capitalist society are of great, if not paramount, importance.

As mentioned above, Althusser conceived of capitalist society as a *social formation*, a concrete, complex totality at a specific point in historical development. This is a static, ahistorical conception of capitalist society.

Althusser also examined the major components of the social formation. In this, he rejected the simple dichotomization of base and superstructure. To Althusser, the superstructures of capitalist society do not merely reflect the economic base; rather, they have *relative autonomy* and may even come to predominate at any given time. In the end, of course, the economy will be dominant. In Althusser's view a social formation is composed of three basic elements—the economy, polity, and ideology. The mutual interaction of these structural components make up the social whole at any given time.

As a Marxist, Althusser was attuned to the contradictions among these structural entities. This concern for contradictions led Althusser to develop the concept of overdetermination, derived from the work of Lenin and Mao. *Overdetermination* means that any given contradiction within a social formation cannot work itself out simply on its own, since other contradictions within society affect it. This interpenetration of contradictions led Althusser to the idea that societies cannot evolve uniformly; there is always *uneven development*. The idea of uneven development within the different components of the social formation allowed Althusser to go beyond a totally deterministic position. Actors are determined by structures, but because of uneven development, social formations are not totally determined. Contradictions within the social formation give Althusser's formations their dynamic quality. The result is that the development of societies cannot be explained by a single determinant. This allowed Althusser to be critical of the economic determinists.

> It is ''*economism*'' (mechanism) and not the true Marxist tradition that sets up the hierarchy of instances once and for all, assigns each its essence and role and defines the universal meaning of their relations; it is economism that identifies roles and actors eternally, not realizing that the necessity of the process lies in an exchange of roles ''according to circumstances.''
> (Althusser, 1969:213)

Althusser went on to criticize economic determinists for defining economic factors as always occupying the principal position and other factors, such as politics and ideology, as always occupying the role of secondary factors. In Althusser's view it is possible for social institutions other than the economy (for example, the polity) to occupy a position of preeminence, at least for a time. Furthermore, we must be attuned to the relationships among various social institutions. Thus, although Althusser had a deterministic view of actors, he did not have a similar view of structures; there is a dialectic among structures.

Maurice Godelier:
Economic Rationality and Irrationality

Maurice Godelier, an interesting figure in the field of structural Marxism, shared a number of concerns with Althusser, including a critique of Marx's work and a focus on the structures of capitalism and society in general. Godelier also had distinctive characteristics. He combined a background in Marxian theory with training in anthropology, particularly Lévi-Strauss's structural anthropology—a combination that had a profound effect on his thinking. In his best-known work (Godelier, 1972a) he was more focused than his structural Marxian peers. He was especially interested in the issue of rationality, in particular economic rationality.

Godelier began, like many other structural Marxists, by examining Marx's early work, particularly the *1844 Manuscripts*. Because of his orientation toward scientific Marxism, he criticized the speculative and ideological orientation adopted by Marx in the *Manuscripts*. Godelier argued that in the *Manuscripts* Marx adopted an a priori, speculative, ideological, and philosophical definition of rationality. Marx equated rationality with human potential (species-being), particularly in a future society that would permit the full development and expression of human potential. To Godelier, this was a teleological argument, in that it posited a final cause that precedes and transcends contemporary societies. Godelier argued that such ideological and philosophical explanations must be replaced by a scientific orientation whose central concern is the social and economic structure of society. Specifically, Godelier (1972a:vii; italics added) sought a fully developed comparative economic science that aims at discovering "the rationality of economic systems that appear and disappear throughout history —in other words, what is their *hidden logic* and the *underlying necessity* for them to exist, or to have existed: *and* what are the conditions needed for a *rational understanding* of these systems."

Much to his credit, Godelier (1972a) differentiated between the rationality of agents and the rationality of social and cultural systems. On the issue of the rationality of agents, he argued that the issue is how, in a given economic system, economic agents must behave in order to secure the objectives they set for themselves. On rationality at the societal level, the issue is what the rationality of the economic system itself is and whether it can be compared with that of other systems. On both levels, Godelier argued that the focus should not be on the inevitably ideological issue of the rationality of goals, but rather on the more scientifically ascertainable question of the rationality of means to those ends. As a structural Marxist Godelier focused on large-scale systems, but his distinction between societal and individual levels is useful nonetheless.

Despite the utility of the differentiation between agents and systems, Godelier confused this distinction by hopelessly intertwining it with another, that between *intentionality* and *unintentionality*. To him, the rationality of agents "aims at making explicit a rationality of *intention* that is adhered to by individuals" while the rationality of systems involves "*unintended* rationality—the capacity, for example, possessed by a number of systems to ensure growth of the means of production, improvement of the standard of living, and so on'' (Godelier, 1972a:11; italics added). The problem here from our point of view is that there is no obvious reason that levels and intentionality are linked in the way Godelier suggested. It seems at least possible that actors can be unintentionally rational while systems (at least through their representatives) can be intentionally rational. However, this problem is mitigated somewhat by Godelier's determination not to focus on individual action, either intentional or unintentional. Rather his concern was with the ''real'' structures of capitalist society. He was interested in actors only as they were affected by larger systems.

On the issue of rationality, particularly economic rationality, Godelier argued that two basic views are extant in the economic literature, both of which he found wanting. The first is that rationality is a universal fact of life, ''a constant feature of human nature, an everyday and commonplace fact of experience derived from some non-historical or trans-historical 'a priori''' (Godelier, 1972a:15). This view is associated with the work of the classical economists in general and Adam Smith in particular. Godelier rejected it because it is ideological, a priori, and unscientific.

The second view is that rationality is a product of history, particularly the development of capitalism. This view is, as we have seen, often associated with Max Weber. Godelier rejected it for two reasons. First, he saw it as an apology for the capitalist system. Second, he argued that it holds an implicit and untenable view of the irrationality of precapitalist society in its

> claim that all the technical progress accomplished by mankind before the rise of capitalism was *not* the result of the activity consciously striving to discover and adapt means for attaining ends. Mankind, according to this view, waited for the coming of capitalism before learning to economize effort and get the best out of the means of its disposal.
>
> (Godelier, 1972a:21)

Here Godelier's (1972a:21) anthropological training came into play and led him to the very different position that ''everything that we know of ethnology and history shows that, in all societies, individuals and groups have tried to maximize [that is, rationalize] certain objectives.'' Thus rationality is not in his view a distinctively modern capitalist invention.

Godelier sought to develop a science of rationality that focused on social structures, not individuals; that is, a rational economics, and more generally a rational social science, that would enable us to understand the workings of a rational economic system. He saw two alternative theories—traditional (or marginal) economics or Marxism—and had two concerns about them: first, which theory would best enable us to understand the economic rationality of capitalism; second, which theory would offer a general theory of the economy and be able to deal with the comparative rationality of capitalism and socialism?

Godelier concluded that Marxism, especially the theory developed in *Capital*, was the better theoretical alternative; however, he thought that even Marxian theory was not yet sufficiently developed to deal with these issues adequately. In order to become a satisfactory theory, Marxism would have to satisfy two conditions. First, it would have to be able to encompass the knowledge produced by traditional marginal economic theory and to develop it still further. Second, it would have to be able to deal with the issue of the comparative rationality of capitalism and socialism. In other words, "to become a general theory, it must offer a scientific explanation of the rise and evolution of economic systems" (Godelier, 1972a:30). Marxism would have to develop beyond the point at which Marx stopped in *Capital* and "deal with the forms of competition characteristic of private or state monopolies, the new forms of management of enterprises and of state intervention in the economy, the world market, and so on" (Godelier, 1972a:76). Further, it would have to go beyond an analysis of capitalism and also be able to provide the theoretical tools needed for an analysis of socialism.

With this as background, Godelier then analyzed the various actors in capitalism— the entrepreneur, the worker, and the consumer—and identified what it means for each of them to behave in a rational manner. Although the details do not concern us, Godelier's (1972a:44) ultimate structural explanation of the behavior of actors does: "It is thus the nature and the role played by the various *social structures* [italics added] in a particular society that explain the way individuals behave, and not *vice versa*, and it is this nature and role of the social structure that science has to explain." He made clear here, as elsewhere, that one must be concerned not simply with economic rationality but with the wider notion and various forms of social rationality. He wanted to look at "the overall rationalization of the system," and "this means no longer considering individuals, even as embodiments of functions, but instead considering the objective properties of social structures" (Godelier, 1972a:47–48).

Ultimately, Godelier concluded that Marxian theory as first expressed in *Capital* provides a scientific basis for the conclusion that socialism is at this point in history "superior" to any other form of social and economic organization. This superiority has nothing to do with people's happiness, human freedom, and so forth. Rather, in Marx's theory it is based on the need for a correspondence between the economic structure of society and the social relations within it (Godelier, 1972a:84). Marx had concluded that capitalism was more rational than feudalism, but less rational than socialism. Although Marx was on the right track here, Godelier argued that we must go beyond economic rationality to the rationality of various societal structures. He thus extended Marxian theory to an analysis of the "laws of necessary correspondence between the different structures of social life" and of the contradictions between them (Godelier, 1972a:102). In other words, Godelier was interested in a general theory of the various structures of all societies, and he saw the roots of such a theory in the late work of Marx.

Nicos Poulantzas: Economics, Politics, and Ideology

Nicos Poulantzas is another major contemporary structural Marxist, and he has much in common with Althusser, Godelier, and other French structural Marxists. However, while Althusser, and Godelier to a lesser extent, are best known for their critiques of Marx's texts, Poulantzas concentrated more on an analysis of the real world and such issues as social class, fascism, and dictatorship. In the process, Poulantzas developed a critique not only of economism (economic determinism) but also of the structuralism of Althusser and his colleagues. He thus saw himself as set apart, at least in some ways, from others in the school of French structural Marxism. For instance, Poulantzas

(1975:10) tried resolutely to make his theorizing concrete. Also, Poulantzas (1975:9) did not try to develop a general theory, because he saw himself and other theorists as incapable of this.

Poulantzas does, however, share with other structural Marxists a number of orientations. For example, he too rejected the economism of earlier Marxists:

> How . . . is the neglect of theoretical study of the State . . . to be explained? . . . The absence of a study of the State derived from the fact that the dominant conception . . . was a deviation, *economism*, which is generally accompanied by an absence of revolutionary strategy. . . . In effect, economism considers the other levels of social reality, including the State, as epiphenomena reducible to the economic "base." . . . Economism considers that every change in the social system happens first of all in the economy and that political action should have the economy as its principal objective.
>
> (Poulantzas, 1972:239)

Poulantzas (1973:39; 1975:16) rejected not only economistic Marxism but also Hegelian Marxism (for example, the work of Lukács) and the critical school, both of which emphasize subjective factors. Poulantzas especially opposed a focus on individual actors:

> This is a problematic of *social actors*, of individuals as the origin of *social action*: sociological research thus leads finally, not to the study of objective co-ordinates that determine the distribution of agents into social classes and the contradictions between these classes, but to the search for *finalist* explanations founded on the *motivations of conduct* of the individual actors. This is notoriously one of the aspects of the problematic both of Weber and of contemporary functionalism. To transpose this problematic of the subject into Marxism is in the end to admit the epistemological principles of the adversary and to risk vitiating one's own analyses.
>
> (Poulantzas, 1972:242–243)

Poulantzas also rejected a focus on the motivations of actors:

> Thus the characterization of the existing social system as capitalist in no way depends on the motivations of the conduct of managers. Furthermore: to characterize the class position of managers, one need not refer to the motivations of their conduct, but only to their place in production and their relationship to the ownership of the means of production.
>
> (Poulantzas, 1972:243–244)

The heart of Poulantzas's work, and that of structural Marxism in general, is the view that modern capitalism is composed of three major components—the state, ideology, and the economy. Poulantzas adopted a realist view of these structures and, unlike other structural Marxists, analyzed them in great empirical detail in his works. However, his major contribution goes beyond empirical detail and is found in the theoretical analysis that is needed to uncover the hidden structures of capitalist society. One of his key theoretical ideas, again shared with other structural Marxists, is *relative autonomy*, or the idea that the various structures of capitalist society are relatively independent of each other. Poulantzas applied this idea more broadly than most other thinkers. He argued that the capitalist state is characterized by "the relative separation of the economic from the political, and the relative autonomy of the state from the dominant classes'' (Poulantzas, 1974:313). The same point can be made about the economy and ideology. Poulantzas's extension of the idea of relative autonomy to other areas of society is distinctive. He discussed, for example, the relative autonomy of various components of a social class, such as "various cliques, factions, and clans" (Poulantzas, 1976:112). Poulantzas saw all the structural components of capitalist society as interrelated, although he also emphasized that each is relatively autonomous.

This leads to another distinctive aspect of Poulantzas's work—his discussion of the various components of many of the structures that he analyzed. He was disinclined to think of structures as unified totalities but saw them rather as composed of a number of substructures. His best-known idea here is that of *fractions* of social classes (Poulantzas, 1975:23). In other words, a social class is not a unified totality, but is rather composed of various subunits (Poulantzas, 1976:92). Similarly, within political and ideological structures he spoke of subunits, this time called *categories* and "defined principally by their place in the political and ideological relations. Examples of categories include the state bureaucracy, defined by its relation to the state apparatuses, and the intellectuals, defined by their role in elaborating and deploying ideology" (Poulantzas, 1975:23). He also differentiated among the various subunits within the state (*apparatuses*), whose main function is maintaining social cohesion politically and ideologically. These apparatuses include

> on the one hand, the repressive state apparatus in the strict sense and its branches: army, police, prisons, judiciary, civil service; on the other hand, the ideological state apparatuses: the educational apparatus, the religious apparatus (the churches), the information apparatus (radio, television, press), the cultural apparatus (cinema, theatre, publishing), the trade-union apparatus of class collaboration and the bourgeois and petty-bourgeois political parties, etc., as well as in a certain respect, at least in the capitalist mode of production, the family.
> (Poulantzas, 1975:24–25)

Thus Poulantzas had a much more complicated image of the structures of capitalism and its numerous substructures than did many of his peers.

Poulantzas took great care in these structural differentiations, because he saw each of the substructures as having relatively autonomous social consequences. Furthermore, each has at least the potential to play a central role in society (Poulantzas, 1975:23; 1973:255–321).

Poulantzas's thinking on contradictions was shaped by his pluralistic image of the structures of capitalist society. Like other structural Marxists, Poulantzas did not restrict himself to the analysis of economic contradictions but was interested in, among other things, the contradictions among the economy, the polity, and ideology. Poulantzas, however, went much further and examined the contradictions among the various fractions, categories, and apparatuses within each of the three basic structural units. For example, Poulantzas (1976:103–104) argued "that every bourgeois state is riven by contradictions between its various apparatuses and branches (and not just between political parties), as the organizational bases of one or other fraction and component of the power bloc.''

Poulantzas's main theoretical focus, and that of most structural Marxists, was on the interrelationship of the three major components of capitalist society. For example, he linked the state and ideology by arguing that the *state* can never exercise its function of domination, in the long run, by repression alone; this must always be accompanied by *ideological* domination (Poulantzas, 1976:83).

Poulantzas also linked ideology to the economy. The most important role of ideology, expressed through the socialization process, is training people to occupy various positions and occupations within the economic sector. Although he saw socialization as important, he was careful to point out that a capitalist society must not only produce (socialize) people to fill positions, it must also continually produce the positions for these people to fill. To underscore his structuralist orientation, Poulantzas stated clearly that the primary significance lies with structural positions and not with actors and their socialization:

> While it is true that the agents themselves must be reproduced—"trained" and "subjected"— in order to occupy certain places, it is equally true that the distribution of agents does not depend on their own choices or aspirations but on the reproduction of these places themselves. This is because the principal aspect of class determination is that of their places, and not that of the agents that occupy these places.
>
> (Poulantzas, 1975:29)

Although he recognized the importance of socialization, Poulantzas carefully differentiated his position from that taken by many sociologists, in which ideological factors are given much greater significance than he thought due them:

> However, in order to break with the misunderstandings of the "functionalist-institutionalist" tradition, which has always spoken of . . . the "socialization process," it is necessary to go further. On the one hand, . . . it is because there is extended reproduction of places, and to the extent that this is so, that there is this or that reproduction and distribution of agents between places. On the other hand, we should not forget that the determining role, as far as the distribution of agents in the social formation as a whole is concerned, falls to the labour market, as the expression of the extended reproduction of the relations of production.
>
> (Poulantzas, 1975:34)

In terms of links between the state and the economy, Poulantzas argued that in the stage of monopoly capitalism the state acquires decisive importance. This follows logically from his more general position that "there was *never* a stage in capitalism in which the state did not play an important economic role" (Poulantzas, 1974:220; italics added).

At the most general level, Poulantzas was likely to look at the interrelationship of *all three* of the basic structures of capitalism. For example, he noted that imperialism "is not a phenomenon which can be reduced to economic developments alone. . . . Imperialism is a phenomenon with economic, political and ideological implications" (Poulantzas, 1974:22). This is another way of saying that Poulantzas rejected the simplistic economic determinism of many Marxists. To Poulantzas (1974:41) the superstructure that is made of "juridico-political and ideological forms . . . intervenes decisively in the production process." Such a pluralistic notion led Poulantzas, like

Althusser, to the notion of the uneven development of the capitalist system. This, in turn, gave Poulantzas's work a dialectic at the structural level that kept it, like the work of Althusser, from being totally deterministic.

We conclude this discussion of Poulantzas's orientation with mention of his work on social classes. As a structuralist, Poulantzas argued, according to Andor Skotnes (1979:35), that "social classes are *structurally determined*; they exist objectively, independent of the will and 'consciousness' of class members." However, classes are not determined totally by economic structures (Poulantzas, 1974:14) but also by political and ideological factors. Poulantzas made a great effort to avoid that perpetual problem of structuralists, a static view of social classes. He argued that social classes are determined only in the continuing process of class struggle, which is itself broken down into economic, political, and ideological struggles. Classes are formed out of the confluence of these ongoing struggles.

Poulantzas was careful to differentiate between such a general analysis of social classes and class positions at any given historical juncture. At any particular point in history, classes or fractions of classes may take up positions not in accord with their general structural position. A labor aristocracy, for example, may identify with the bourgeoisie, or members of the middle class may take positions aligned with those of the proletariat. But these are temporary historical developments not in line with the general structure of class struggle. Thus deviations are possible within the broad sweep of history. This is another area of flexibility and dialectical process within Poulantzas's structural Marxism.

Critical Reactions to Structural Marxism

Structural Marxism has come under attack by other Marxists. First, it has been attacked for being ahistorical. The famous Marxist historian E. P. Thompson (1978) correctly viewed Althusser (whom he singled out for discussion) as unleashing an attack on precisely what Thompson is best known for—empirically oriented, historical Marxian research. Thompson argued that Althusser's position is that history is scientifically and politically valueless:

> Not only does it turn out that men have never "made their own history" at all (being only . . . vectors of ulterior structural determinations) but it is also revealed that the enterprise has been misbegotten from the start, since "real" history is unknowable and cannot be said to exist.
> (E. P. Thompson, 1978:194)

Thompson regarded Althusser's position as ludicrous. He argued that structuralists do not understand historical categories and are therefore unable to deal with contradiction, class struggle, and social change. Thompson (1978:197) argued that the structuralists have not even accomplished their goal of being true to Marx: "Althusser's structuralism is a structuralism of *stasis*, departing from Marx's own historical method." In the end, Thompson regarded Althusser as a dangerous intellectual who had become the darling of bourgeois intellectuals who do not really understand what he is saying. They are attracted to his work because of its pseudosophistication and because it does not require them to sully themselves in the real world of class struggle.

Similarly, Val Burris (1979) argued that structural Marxists have lost sight of the fact that to Marx the analysis of structures is specific to a given historical epoch. Thus they misrepresented historically specific structures as "universal principles of social organization" (Burris, 1979:16).

Second, structural Marxists have been attacked for their blind support of scientism. "At a time when science is one of the principal legitimating props of the social order, an uncritical belief in science is urged upon us . . . [and] dogmatic authority is reasserted on all fronts" (Appelbaum, 1979:26).

Third, there is the view that structuralism leads to an elitist orientation:

Structuralism is dogmatism—a "learned and sophisticated variety," to be sure—but dogmatism nonetheless. The Party scientists and bureaucrats alone possess truth—they alone have symptomatically read the works of Marx, Engels, Lenin, and Gramsci—and they alone understand history: they reveal the hidden facts and the underlying laws, the masses submit.

(Appelbaum, 1979:25)

Fourth, structuralism has been attacked for losing sight of the actor and consciousness. As Appelbaum (1979:25) put it: "Here structuralism has at last arrived at its ultimate objective: it has achieved 'scientificity' by obliterating the conscious individual."

Fifth, structuralists have been criticized for giving inadequate attention to empirical research. This position was taken by Ralph Miliband in a response to Poulantzas's attack on his work:

After all, it was none other than Marx who stressed the importance of empirical validation (or invalidation) and who spent many years of his life in precisely such an undertaking: and while I do not suggest for a moment that Poulantzas is unaware of this fact, I do think that he, and the point also goes for Louis Althusser and his collaborators, may tend to give it rather less attention than it deserves.

(Miliband, 1972:256)

Sixth, structuralism has been attacked for its determinism. Miliband stated:

But his [Poulantzas's] own analysis seems to me to lead straight towards a kind of structural determinism, or rather a structural super-determinism, which makes impossible a truly realistic consideration of the dialectical relationship between the state and "the system." . . . The political danger of structural super-determinism would seem to me to be obvious. For if the state elite is as totally imprisoned in objective structures as is suggested, it follows that there is *really* no difference between a state ruled, say, by bourgeois constitutionalists, whether conservative or social-democrat and one ruled by, say, fascists.

(Miliband, 1972:259)

Interestingly, structuralism has come to be associated in the minds of some critics with sociological theories that most Marxists find anathema—structural functionalism and conflict theory:

What remains when Hegel has been excised appears to be little more than a pluralist functionalism recast in Marxian categories. . . . Thus stated, Althusser's formulation is itself a formal inversion of structural-functionalism, perhaps not so distant from what is sometimes termed "conflict theory."

(Appelbaum, 1979:27–28)

Along these same lines, Nancy DiTomaso (1982) has seen strong similarities in the work of Althusser and Parsons.

Structural Marxism is one of the most controversial developments in neo-Marxian theory. It involves pointed criticism of other varieties of Marxian theory and is itself subject to much criticism by Marxists of other theoretical persuasions.

NEO-MARXIAN ECONOMIC SOCIOLOGY

As we have seen throughout this chapter, many neo-Marxists (for example, critical theorists, structural Marxists) have made relatively few comments on the economic institution, at least in part as a reaction against the excesses of the economic determinists. However, these reactions have themselves set in motion a series of counterreactions. In this section we will deal with the work of those Marxists who have returned to a focus on the economic realm. Their work does not simply repeat early Marxian theory; rather, it constitutes an effort to adapt Marxian theory to the realities of modern capitalist society.

There is, of course, a vast literature dealing with economic issues from a Marxian point of view. Much of this is relevant only to the field of economics, but some of it has also been influential in sociology. In this section we will focus on two works that have been particularly influential in sociology—Paul Baran and Paul M. Sweezy's *Monopoly Capital* (1966) and Harry Braverman's *Labor and Monopoly Capital* (1974).

Monopoly Capital

Marx's original insights into economic structures and processes were based on his analysis of the capitalism of his time—what we can think of as competitive capitalism. Capitalist industries were comparatively small, with the result that no one industry, or small group of industries, could gain complete and uncontested control over a market. Much of Marx's economic work was based on the premise, accurate for his time, that capitalism was a competitive system. To be sure, Marx foresaw the possibility of future monopolies, but he commented only briefly on them. Many later Marxian theorists continued to operate as if capitalism remained much as it had been in Marx's time.

It is in this context that we must examine the work of Baran and Sweezy (1966). They began with a criticism of Marxian social science for repeating familiar formulations and for failing to explain important recent developments in capitalistic society. They accused Marxian theory of stagnating because it continued to rest on the assumption of a competitive economy. A modern Marxian theory must, in their view, recognize that competitive capitalism has been largely replaced by monopoly capitalism.

A central issue for Baran and Sweezy (1966) was a delineation of the nature of monopoly capitalism. Monopoly capitalism means that one, or a few, capitalists control a given sector of the economy. Clearly, there is far less competition in monopoly capitalism than in competitive capitalism. In competitive capitalism organizations competed on a price basis; that is, capitalists tried to sell more goods by offering lower prices. In monopolistic capitalism firms no longer have to compete in this way since one firm, or a few firms, control a market; competition shifts to the sales domain. Advertising, packaging, and other methods of appealing to potential consumers are the main areas of competition.

The movement from price to sales competition is part of another process characteristic of monopoly capitalism—*progressive rationalization*. Price competition comes to be seen as highly irrational. That is, from the monopoly capitalist's point of view, offering lower and lower prices can lead only to chaos in the marketplace, to say nothing of lower profits and perhaps even bankruptcy. Sales competition, on the other hand, is not a cutthroat system; in fact, it even provides work for the advertising industry. Furthermore, prices can be kept high, with the costs of the sales and promotion simply added to the price. Thus sales competition is also far less risky than price competition.

Another crucial aspect of monopoly capitalism is the rise of the giant corporation, with a few large corporations controlling most sectors of the economy. In competitive capitalism the organization was controlled almost single-handedly by an entrepreneur. The modern corporation is owned by a large number of stockholders, but a few large stockholders own most of the stock. Although stockholders "own" the corporation, managers exercise the actual day-to-day control. The managers are crucial in monopoly capitalism, whereas the entrepreneurs were central in competitive capitalism. Managers have considerable power, which they seek to maintain. They even seek financial independence for their firms by trying, as much as possible, to generate whatever funds they need internally rather than relying on external sources of funding.

Baran and Sweezy commented extensively on the central position of the corporate manager in modern capitalist society. Managers are viewed as a highly rational group oriented to maximizing the profits of the organization. Because of this goal they are not inclined to take the risks that were characteristic of the early entrepreneurs. They have a longer time perspective than the entrepreneur. Whereas the early capitalist was interested in maximizing profits in the short run, modern managers are aware that such efforts may well lead to chaotic price competition that might adversely affect the long-term profitability of the firm. The manager will thus forgo *some* profits in the short run in order to maximize long-term profitability.

The central issue in monopoly capitalism is the ability of the system to generate and utilize economic surplus. *Economic surplus* is defined as the difference between the value of what a society produces and the costs of producing it. Because of their concern with the surplus issue, Baran and Sweezy moved away from Marx's interest in the exploitation of labor and stressed instead the links between the economy and other social institutions, in particular in the absorption of economic surplus by these other institutions.

Modern capitalistic managers are victims of their own success. On the one hand, they are able to set prices arbitrarily because of their monopolistic position in the economy. On the other hand, they seek to maximize cost cutting within the organization, particularly in terms of the costs associated with blue-collar work. The ability to set high prices and to cut costs leads to the rising level of economic surplus.

The issue that then confronts the capitalist is what to do with the surplus. One possibility is to consume it—to pay managers huge salaries and stockholders huge dividends that are turned into yachts, Rolls-Royces, jewelry, and caviar. This *is* done to some extent, but the surplus is so huge that elites could never consume even a small part of it. In any case, conspicuous consumption was more characteristic of the early entrepreneurs than it is of the modern manager and stockholder.

A second alternative is to invest the surplus in such things as improved technology and foreign ventures. This seemingly reasonable action, which is taken by managers to some extent, has the major drawback that such investments, if made wisely, will generate even more surplus. This only exacerbates the problem of using economic surplus.

Increasing the sales effort might also serve to absorb some of the surplus. Modern capitalists can stimulate the demand for their products by advertising; by creating and expanding the markets for their products; and by such devices as model changes, planned obsolescence, and readily available consumer credit. However, this alternative also has problems. First, it cannot absorb enough surplus. Second, it is likely to stimulate even further expansion of the corporation, which, in turn, will lead to still greater levels of surplus.

According to Baran and Sweezy, the only choice remaining is *waste*. The surplus needs to be squandered, and there are two ways of so doing. The first is nonmilitary government spending through keeping millions of workers in government jobs and supporting myriad government programs. The second is military spending, including the military's vast payroll and its budget of billions of dollars for expensive hardware that rapidly becomes obsolete.

Baran and Sweezy's position has several weaknesses. For one thing, it seems as if there is really *no good way* of getting rid of surplus, and perhaps that is the view Baran and Sweezy wish communicated. It leaves us with the clear impression that this is an irresolvable contradiction within capitalism. Virtually all of the capitalists' expenditures lead to greater demand and ultimately to greater surpluses. Government and military employees spend their money on more goods; as some military equipment is consumed, there is a demand for new and better equipment.

Another criticism that can be leveled at Baran and Sweezy is that they overemphasize the rationality of managers. Herbert Simon (1957), for example, would argue that managers are more interested in finding (and are only able to find) minimally satisfactory solutions than they are in finding the most rational and most profitable solutions. Another issue is whether managers are, in fact, the pivotal figures in modern capitalism. Many would argue that the large stockholders really control the capitalistic system.

In sum, Baran and Sweezy accepted the traditional economic focus of Marxian theory, then moved it in a new and important direction. In particular, they shifted the focus from the labor process to economic structures of modern capitalistic society. We turn now to Braverman, who was influenced by the work of Baran and Sweezy but sought to return to the traditional Marxian interest in the labor process.

Labor and Monopoly Capital

Harry Braverman (1974) considered the labor process and the exploitation of the worker to be the heart of Marxian theory. Although his emphasis is different from that of Baran and Sweezy, he saw his work as tied closely to theirs (Braverman, 1974:253). The main title of his book, *Labor and Monopoly Capital*, reflects his main focus, while its subtitle, *The Degradation of Work in the Twentieth Century*, shows his interest in adapting Marx's perspective to the realities of work in the twentieth century.

Braverman intended not only to update Marx's interest in manual workers but also to examine what has happened to white-collar and service workers. Marx paid little attention to these two groups, but since his time they have become major occupational categories that need to be subjected to serious scrutiny. In relation to Baran and Sweezy's work, it could be said that one of the major developments in monopoly capitalism has been the relative decline in blue-collar workers and the simultaneous increase in white-collar and service workers to staff the large organizations characteristic of monopoly capitalism.

Braverman's analysis begins with a point reminiscent of Marx's orientation. Braverman made it quite clear that his criticisms of the contemporary work world do not reflect a yearning for an era now past. He said he was not romanticizing the old-time crafts and "the outworn conditions of now archaic modes of labor" (Braverman, 1974:6). Also like Marx, Braverman was a critic not of science and technology per se but simply of the way they are used in capitalism "as weapons of domination in the creation, perpetuation and deepening of a gulf between classes in society" (Braverman, 1974:6). In the employ of the capitalist, science and technology have been used systematically to rob work of its craft heritage without providing anything to take its place. Braverman believed that in different (that is, socialist) hands, science and technology could be used differently to produce

> an age that has not yet come into being, in which, for the worker, the craft satisfaction that arises from conscious and purposeful mastery of the labor process will be combined with the marvel of science and the ingenuity of engineering, an age in which everyone will be able to benefit, in some degree, from this combination.
>
> (Braverman, 1974:7)

Toward the goal of extending Marx's analysis of blue-collar workers to white-collar and service workers, Braverman argued that the concept "working class" does not describe a specific group of people or occupations but is rather an expression of a process of buying and selling labor power. In terms of that process, Braverman argued that in modern capitalism virtually no one owns the means of production; therefore the many, including most white-collar and service workers, are forced to sell their labor power to the few who do. In his view capitalist control and exploitation, as well as the derivative processes of mechanization and rationalization, are being extended to white-collar and service occupations, although their impact is not yet as great as it has been on blue-collar occupations.

Braverman based his analysis on Marx's anthropology, specifically his concept of human potential (species-being). Braverman argued that all forms of life need to sustain themselves in their natural environment; that is, they need to appropriate nature for their own use. Work is the process by which nature is altered in order to enhance its usefulness. In that sense animals work too, but what is distinctive about humans is their consciousness. People have a set of mental capacities that other animals lack. Human work is thus characterized by a unity of conception (thought) and execution (action). This unity can be dissolved, and capitalism is a crucial stage in the destruction of the unity of thought and execution in the working world.

A key ingredient in this breakdown in capitalism is the sale and purchase of labor power. Capitalists can purchase certain kinds of labor power and not others. For instance, they can purchase manual labor and insist that mental labor be kept out of the process. Although the opposite can also occur, it is less likely. As a result, capitalism is characterized by an increasing number of manual workers and fewer and fewer mental workers. This seems to contradict the statistics, which reflect a massive growth in white-collar, presumably mental, occupations. However, as we will see, Braverman believed that many white-collar occupations are being *proletarianized*, made indistinguishable in many ways from manual work.

MANAGERIAL CONTROL

Braverman recognized economic exploitation, which was Marx's focus, but concentrated on the issue of *control*. He asked the question: How do the capitalists control the labor power that they employ? One answer is that they exercise such control through managers. In fact, Braverman (1974:267) defined management as *"a labor process conducted for the purpose of control within the corporation."*

Braverman concentrated on the more impersonal means employed by managers to control workers. One of his central concerns was the utilization of specialization to control workers. Here he carefully differentiated between the division of labor in society as a whole and specialization of work within the organization. All known societies have had a division of labor (for example, between men and women, farmers and artisans, and so forth), but the specialization of work within the organization is a special development of capitalism, although it appears in existing socialist societies as well. Braverman (1974:73) believed that the division of labor at the societal level may enhance the individual, whereas specialization in the workplace has the disastrous effect of subdividing human capabilities: "The subdivision of the individual, when carried on without regard to human capabilities and needs, is a crime against the person and against humanity."

Specialization in the workplace involves the continual division and subdivision of tasks or operations into minute and highly specialized activities, each of which is then likely to be assigned to a *different* worker. This constitutes the creation of what Braverman calls "detail workers." Out of the range of abilities any individual possesses, capitalists select a small number that the worker is to use on the job. As Braverman (1974:78) put it, the capitalist first breaks down the work process and then "dismembers the worker as well" by requiring him to utilize only a small proportion of his skills and abilities. In Braverman's (1974:78) terms, the worker "never voluntarily converts himself into a lifelong detail worker. This is the contribution of the capitalist."

Why does the capitalist do this? First, it increases the control of management. It is easier to control a worker doing a specified task than it is one employing a wide range of skills. Second, it increases productivity. That is, a group of workers performing highly specialized tasks can produce more than the same number of craftspeople, each of whom has all the skills and performs all the production activities. For instance, workers on an automobile assembly line produce more cars than would a corresponding number of skilled craftspeople, each of whom produces his own car. Third, specialization allows the capitalist to pay the least for the labor power needed. Instead of highly paid skilled craftspeople, the capitalist can employ lower-paid unskilled workers. Following the logic of capitalism, employers seek progressively to cheapen the labor of workers, which results in a virtually undifferentiated mass of what Braverman called "simple labor."

Specialization is not a sufficient means of control for capitalists and the managers in their employ. Another important means is scientific technique, including such efforts as scientific management, which is an attempt to apply science to the control of labor on the behalf of management. To Braverman (1974:90), scientific management is the science of "how best to control alienated labor." Scientific management is found in a series of stages aimed at the control of labor—gathering many workers in one workshop, dictating the length of the workday, supervising workers directly to ensure diligence, enforcing rules against distractions (for example, talking), and setting minimum acceptable production levels. Overall scientific management contributed to control by *"the dictation to the worker of the precise manner in which work is to be performed"* (Braverman, 1974:90). For example, Braverman discussed F. W. Taylor's early work on the shoveling of coal, which led him to develop rules about the kind of shovel to use, the way to stand, the angle at which the shovel should enter the coal pile, and how much coal to pick up in each motion. In other words, Taylor developed methods that assured almost total control over the labor process. Workers were to be left with as little independent decision making as possible; thus, a separation of the mental and manual was accomplished. Management used its monopoly over work-related knowledge to control each step of the labor process. In the end, the work itself was left without any meaningful skill, content, or knowledge. Craftsmanship was utterly destroyed.

Braverman also saw machinery as a means of control over workers. Modern machinery comes into existence "when the tool and/or the work are given a fixed motion path by the structure of the machine itself" (Braverman, 1974:188). The skill is built into the machine rather than left for the worker to acquire. Instead of controlling the work process, workers come to be controlled by the machine. Furthermore, it is far easier for management to control machines than workers.

Braverman argued that through such mechanisms as the specialization of work, scientific management, and machines, management has been able to extend its control over its manual workers. Although this is a useful insight, especially the emphasis on control, Braverman's distinctive contribution has been his effort to extend this kind of analysis to sectors of the labor force that were not analyzed in Marx's original analysis of the labor process. Braverman argued that white-collar and service workers are now being subjected to the same processes of control that were used on manual workers in the last century.

One of Braverman's examples is white-collar clerical workers. At one time such workers were considered to be a group distinguished from manual workers by such things as their dress, skills, training, and career prospects (Lockwood, 1956). However, today both groups are being subjected to the same means of control. Thus it has become more difficult to differentiate between the factory and the modern factorylike office, as the workers in the latter are progressively proletarianized. For one thing, the work of the clerical worker has grown more and more specialized. This means, among other things, that the mental and manual aspects of office work have been separated. Office managers, engineers, and technicans now perform the mental work while the "line" clerical workers do little more than manual tasks such as typing, filing, and keypunching. As a result, the level of skills needed for these jobs has been lowered, and the jobs require little or no special training.

Scientific management is also now seen as invading the office. Clerical tasks have been scientifically studied, and as a result of that research, they have been simplified, routinized, and standardized. Finally, mechanization is beginning to make significant inroads into the office, primarily through the computer and computer-related equipment.

By applying these mechanisms to clerical work, managers find it much easier to control such workers. It is unlikely that such control mechanisms are as strong and effective in the office as in the factory; still, the trend is toward the development of the white-collar ''factory.''[2]

Several obvious criticisms can be leveled at Braverman. For one thing, he has probably overestimated the degree of similarity between manual and clerical work. For another, his preoccupation with control has led him to devote relatively little attention to the dynamics of economic exploitation in capitalism. Nonetheless, he has enriched our understanding of the labor process in modern capitalist society.

In sum, the works of Baran and Sweezy and Braverman represent a return to the traditional Marxian focus on the economic sector. At a theoretical level they are valuable for reinstilling interest in the economic factor as well as refining and making more contemporary our understanding of this dimension. In addition, they have been important sources of sociological thinking and research into various aspects of work and industry. Thus, although these works are not overtly sociological, they are important both theoretically and empirically.

HISTORICALLY ORIENTED MARXISM

Structural Marxism makes the case *for* ahistorical and *against* historical analyses, but there are many Marxists who are oriented toward historical research. In adopting this orientation they argue that they are being true to the Marxian concern for historicity. The most notable of Marx's historical researches was his study of precapitalist economic formations (Marx, 1857–1858/1964). There is a good deal of subsequent historical work from a Marxian perspective (for example, Dobb, 1964; Hobsbawm, 1965; Amin, 1977). In this section we will deal with two pieces of work reflecting a historical orientation—Immanuel Wallerstein's *The Modern World-System* (1974) and Theda Skocpol's *States and Social Revolutions* (1979). Although these are not typical of Marxian historical research in all respects, they are among the most influential in contemporary sociology.

The Modern World-System

Wallerstein chose a unit of analysis unlike those used by most Marxian thinkers. He did not look at workers, classes, or even states, since he found most of these too nar-

---

[2]It is important to note that Braverman's book was written before the boom in computer technology in the office, especially the now-widespread use of the word processor. It may be that such technology, requiring greater skill and training than older office technologies, will serve to increase worker autonomy.

row for his purposes. Instead, he looked at a broad economic entity with a division of labor that is not circumscribed by political or cultural boundaries. He found that unit in his concept of the *world-system*, which is a largely self-contained social system with a set of boundaries and a definable life span; that is, it does not last forever. It is composed internally of a variety of social structures and member groups. However, Wallerstein was not inclined to define the system in terms of a consensus that holds it together. Rather, he saw the system as held together by a variety of forces that are in inherent tension. These forces always have the potential for tearing the system apart.

The world-system is a very abstract concept, and in fact Wallerstein offered it only at the end of his book, after he had discussed all the historical detail needed for its for-

IMMANUEL WALLERSTEIN: A Biographical Sketch

Although he achieved recognition in the 1960s as an expert on Africa, Immanuel Wallerstein's most important contribution to sociology is his 1974 book, *The Modern World-System*. That book was an instant success. It has received world-wide recognition and has been translated into nine languages and Braille.

Born on September 28, 1930, Wallerstein received all of his degrees from Columbia University, culminating with a doctorate in 1959. He next assumed a position on the faculty at Columbia; after many years there, and a five-year stint at McGill University in Montreal, Wallerstein became, in 1976, Distinguished Professor of Sociology at the State University of New York at Binghamton.

Wallerstein was awarded the prestigious Sorokin Award for *The Modern World-System* in 1975. Since that time he has continued to work on the topic and has produced a number of articles as well as a second volume, in which he takes his analysis of the world-system up to the year 1750. We can anticipate more work from Wallerstein on this issue in the coming years. He is in the process of producing a body of work that will attract attention for years to come.

In fact, in many ways the attention it has already attracted, and will continue to attract, is more important than the body of work itself. The concept world-system has become the focus of a recognized area of thought and research in sociology, an accomplishment few scholars can lay claim to. Many of the sociologists now doing research and theorizing about the world-system are critical of Wallerstein in one way or another, but they all clearly recognize the important role he played in the genesis of their ideas.

While the concept of the world-system is an important contribution, at least as significant has been the role Wallerstein played in the revival of theoretically informed historical research. The most important work in the early years of sociology, by people like Marx, Weber, Durkheim, and Spencer, was largely of this type. But in more recent years most sociologists have turned away from this kind of research and in the direction of utilizing such ahistorical methods as questionnaires and interviews. These methods are quicker and easier to use than historical methods, and the data produced are easier to analyze with a computer. Use of such methods tends to require a narrow range of technical knowledge rather than a wide range of historically oriented knowledge. Furthermore, theory plays a comparatively minor role in research utilizing questionnaires and interviews. Wallerstein has been in the forefront of those involved in a revival of interest in historical research with a strong theoretical base.

mulation. Wallerstein argued that thus far we have had only two types of world-systems. One was the world empire, of which ancient Rome is an example. The other is the modern world-capitalist economy. A world empire is based on political (and military) domination, while a world-system relies on economic domination. A world-system is seen as more stable than a world empire for several reasons. For one thing, it has a broader base, since it encompasses many states. For another, it has a built-in process of economic stabilization. The separate political entities within the world-system absorb whatever losses occur, while economic gain is distributed to private hands. Wallerstein foresaw the *possibility* of still a third world-system, a *socialist world government* . Whereas the capitalist world-system separates the political from the economic sector, a socialist world-system would reintegrate them.

To orient the reader for the historical discussion to follow, we now introduce the concepts developed by Wallerstein that describe the geographical international division of labor in the modern world-system—the core, the periphery, and the semiperiphery. In general, the *core* geographical area dominates the world economy and exploits the rest of the system. The *periphery* consists of those areas that provide raw materials to the core and are heavily exploited by it. The *semiperiphery* is a residual category that encompasses a set of regions somewhere between the exploiting and the exploited. The key point here is that to Wallerstein the international division of exploitation is defined not by state borders but rather by the economic division of labor in the world.

Although Wallerstein had a broader, long-term interest, in *The Modern World-System* (1974) he dealt with the origin of the world system roughly between the years 1450 and 1640. The significance of this development was the shift from political (and thus military) to economic dominance. Wallerstein saw economics as a far more efficient and less primitive means of domination than politics. Political structures are very cumbersome, whereas economic exploitation "makes it possible to increase the flow of the surplus from the lower strata to the upper strata, from the periphery to the center, from the majority to the minority" (Wallerstein, 1974:15). In the modern era, capitalism had provided a basis for the growth and development of a world economy; this has been accomplished without the aid of a unified political structure. Capitalism can be seen as an economic alternative to political domination. It is better able to produce economic surpluses than the more primitive techniques employed in political exploitation.

Wallerstein argued that three things were necessary for the rise of the capitalist world economy out of the "ruins" of feudalism: geographical expansion through exploration and colonization; development of different methods of labor control for zones (for example, core, periphery) of the world economy; and development of strong states that were to become the core states of the emerging capitalist world economy. Let us look at each of these in turn.

GEOGRAPHICAL EXPANSION

Wallerstein argued that geographical expansion by nations is a prerequisite for the other two stages. Portugal took the lead in overseas exploration and other European nations followed. Wallerstein was wary of talking about specific countries, or Europe, in general terms. He preferred to see overseas expansion as caused by a group of people acting in terms of their immediate interests. Elite groups, such as nobles, needed overseas expansion for various reasons. For one thing, they were confronted with a nascent class war brought on by the crumbling of the feudal economy. The slave trade provided them with a tractable labor force on which to build the capitalist economy. The expansion also provided them with various commodities needed to develop it—gold bullion, food, and raw materials of various types.

A WORLD-WIDE DIVISION OF LABOR

Once the world had undergone geographical expansion it was prepared for the next stage, the development of a world-wide division of labor. In the sixteenth century capitalism replaced statism as the major mode of dominating the world, but capitalism did not develop uniformly around the world. In fact, Wallerstein argued, the solidarity of the capitalist system was ultimately based on its unequal development. Given his Marxian orientation, Wallerstein did not think of this as a consensual equilibrium, but rather as one that was laden with conflict from the beginning. Different parts of the capitalist world-system came to specialize in specific functions—breeding labor power, growing food, providing raw materials, and organizing industry. Furthermore, different areas came to specialize in producing particular types of workers. For example, Africa produced slaves; western and southern Europe had many peasant tenant-farmers; western Europe was also the center of wage workers, the ruling classes, and other skilled and supervisory personnel.

More generally, each of the three parts of the international division of labor tended to differ in terms of mode of labor control. The core had free labor; the periphery was characterized by forced labor; and the semiperiphery was the heart of sharecropping. In fact, Wallerstein argued the key to capitalism lies in a core dominated by a free labor market for skilled workers and a coercive labor market for less-skilled workers in peripheral areas. Such a combination is the essence of capitalism. If a free labor market should develop throughout the world, we would have socialism.

Some regions of the world begin with small initial advantages, which are used as the basis for developing greater advantages later on. The core area in the sixteenth century, primarily western Europe, rapidly extended its advantages as towns flourished, industries developed, and merchants became important. It also moved to extend its domain by developing a wider variety of activities. At the same time, each of its activities became more specialized in order to produce more efficiently. In contrast, the periphery stagnated and moved more toward what Wallerstein called a "monoculture," or an undifferentiated, single-focus society.

DEVELOPMENT OF CORE STATES

The third stage of the development of the world-system involves the political sector and how various economic groups used state structures to protect and advance their interests. Absolute monarchies arose in western Europe at about the same time as capitalism developed. From the sixteenth to the eighteenth centuries the states were the central economic actors in Europe, although the center later shifted to economic enterprises. The strong states in the core areas played a key role in the development of capitalism and ultimately provided the economic base for their own demise. The European states strengthened themselves in the sixteenth century by, among other things, developing and enlarging bureaucratic systems and creating a monopoly of force in society, primarily by developing armies and legitimizing their activities so that they were assured of internal stability. While the states of the core zone developed strong political systems, the periphery developed correspondingly weak states.

In addition to this general perspective, Wallerstein offered considerable historical detail on the various European states and their roles in the development of the world economy. In fact, Wallerstein would probably say that his theoretical system emerged from his historical data, since this would be in line with the orientation of historical Marxian sociologists, who do not want to separate empirical historical research from theory. Thus Wallerstein described the rise and fall of Spain and the Netherlands as centers of the world economy, and then described the more pervasive influence of England. This historical detail was important to the development of Wallerstein's conceptual system.

In a later work Wallerstein (1980) picked up the story of the consolidation of the world economy between 1600 and 1750. This was not a period of a significant expansion of the European world economy, but there were a number of significant changes within that system. For example, Wallerstein discussed the rise and subsequent decline in the core of the Netherlands. Later, he analyzed the conflict between two core states, England and France, as well as the ultimate victory of England. In the periphery, Wallerstein detailed, among other things, the cyclical fortunes of Hispanic America. In the semiperiphery we witness, among other things, the decline of Spain and the rise of Sweden. Wallerstein continued his historical analysis, from a Marxian viewpoint, of the various roles played by different societies within the division of labor of the world economy. Although Wallerstein paid close attention to political and social factors, his main focus remained the role of economic factors in world history.

States and Social Revolutions

Another example of Marxian-influenced historical research is Theda Skocpol's *States and Social Revolutions* (1979). Although she shared some common intellectual roots with Wallerstein, she had a much different orientation. Skocpol recognized the importance of Wallerstein's work, and of the world-system, but she argued that it is not necessary to "accept arguments that national economic developments are actually determined by the overall structure and market dynamics of a 'world capitalist system'" (1979:70). In fact, she accused Wallerstein of being "economically reductionistic." Similarly, Skocpol (1979:292) accorded Marx the central position in her theoretical roots, even though she was also critical of him: "Marxism failed to foresee or adequately explain the autonomous power, for good or ill, of states as administrative and coercive machineries embedded in a militarized international states system." Skocpol thus made it clear that although she was working within the Marxian tradition, she intended to stress political rather than economic factors.

In a historical-comparative study that focused on social revolutions in France (1787–1800), Russia (1917–1921), and China (1911–1949), Skocpol concentrated on the similarities between these revolutions. However, she was also attuned to crucial differences. Her objective was to develop explanations of social revolutions that were both historically grounded and generalizable. For comparative purposes, Skocpol also looked at nations (Japan, Prussia, England) where revolutions did not take place.

The focus of Skocpol's research was social revolutions, which she defined as "rapid, basic transformations of a society's state and class structures; and they are accompanied and in part carried through by class-based revolts from above" (Skocpol, 1979:4). Despite this objective, she returned over and over again to economic (class-based) considerations.

As our focus is on theory, the general principles that stand behind her work are our concern here. First, she intended to adopt what she called a "structural, nonvoluntaristic perspective." Second, she considered it important to single out the international and world-historical contexts for particular examination. Third, her objective was to focus on the *state* as at least a potentially autonomous unit. We shall consider each of these principles separately.

A STRUCTURAL, NONVOLUNTARISTIC APPROACH

Skocpol (1979:14) began by setting her approach apart from what she called "voluntaristic images" of how revolutions occur. Most observers, in her view, see revolutions as deliberate efforts by leaders, followers, or both. She saw this tendency in Marx's work itself, but it was exaggerated by those who followed in his tradition. This is manifest in the Marxian focus on such factors as class consciousness and the party organization. However, Skocpol (1979:17) rejected this position outright: "No successful social revolution has ever been 'made' by a mass-mobilizing, avowedly revolutionary movement."

In rejecting a voluntaristic image of social revolutions, Skocpol rejected a focus on both the thoughts and motives of actors and the large-scale idea systems, such as ideology and class consciousness. Skocpol's focus on the structural level *may* be right, but that does not mean that the other levels are insignificant.

In Skocpol's view revolutions are not made; they happen. This includes both causes and outcomes of revolutions. We need to focus on the structural factors that cause revolutions. As she pointedly put it: "A structural perspective . . . is essential for the analysis of social revolutions" (Skocpol, 1979:18).

INTERNATIONAL AND WORLD-HISTORICAL CONTEXTS

Skocpol (1979:18) recognized the importance of intranational factors, but she underscored the importance of transnational, or international, factors: "Transnational relations have contributed to the emergence of all social revolutionary crises and have invariably helped to shape revolutionary struggles and outcomes." However, she set herself apart from Wallerstein, who had adopted a similar perspective. He focused on international *economic* relations, whereas her intention was to focus on international *political* factors. While not denying the importance of international economic variables, Skocpol looked to what she called the "international system of competing states." However, she did recognize the interplay between the two factors: "Throughout modern history, it [the international states system] represents an analytically autonomous level of transnational realism—interdependent in its structure and dynamics with world capitalism, but not reducible to it'' (Skocpol, 1979:2).

Skocpol differentiated between two aspects of transnational relations along a time dimension—the structural relationships between states in the contemporary period, and relationships between states over time. For example, actors in a later revolution are affected by the successes and failures of actors in an earlier revolution. Or breakthroughs such as the Industrial Revolution create a series of new opportunities and necessities between one social revolution and the other.

POTENTIAL AUTONOMY OF THE STATE

Within the structural realm, Skocpol singled out the state for special attention. She said that the state is ''a structure with a logic and interests of its own not necessarily equivalent to, or fused with, the interests of the dominant class in society or the full set of member groups in the polity'' (Skocpol, 1979:27). She argued that there is a need for an explanation of social revolutions that is more state-centered than economic-centered. Political factors are not epiphenomena but rather have direct effects on social revolutions. Skocpol adopted here the structural Marxian position on the potential autonomy of the state. However, she was careful to point out that the degree to which the state is autonomous, free from class control, varies from one setting to another.

Skocpol closed her theoretical introduction with a clear statement of her perspective:

> We shall analyze the causes and processes of social revolutions from a nonvoluntarist, structural perspective, attending to international and world-historical, as well as intranational structures and processes. And an important theoretical concomitant will be to move states—understood as potentially autonomous organizations located at the interface of class structures and international situations—to the very center of attention.
>
> (Skocpol, 1979:33)

FINDINGS

We now highlight some of Skocpol's major conclusions. She found the roots of the French, Russian, and Chinese revolutions in the political crises that existed in what she termed their ''old-regime states.'' Crises developed when those states were unable to meet the challenges of evolving international relations. The states faced not only international problems but intranational conflicts among social classes, especially between the landed aristocracy and the peasantry. Unable to cope with these pressures, the old-regime autocratic states broke down.

These crises made the situation ripe for revolution, but a revolution would not have occurred unless the sociopolitical structures were conducive to it. Since these were primarily agrarian societies, the peasantry rather than the urban workers were crucial to the revolution. Skocpol (1979:112–113) said: ''Peasant revolts have been the crucial insurrectionary ingredient in virtually all (that is, successful) social revolutions to date.''

In this explanation of peasant revolts, Skocpol rejected extant theories that focus on ideology as well as theories focusing on relative deprivation of actors. Instead, her view was that the key factors in peasant rebellions are structural and situational. One such factor is the degree of solidarity of the peasant communities. Another is the degree of freedom of the peasants from the direct day-to-day supervision and control of landlords and their agents. Finally, the relaxation of the state's coercive sanctions against peasants is likely to be conducive to revolutionary activity. The susceptibility of the old-regime states to international pressures and the existence of such structures in the agrarian sector were, in Skocpol's view, the "sufficient" causes of the revolutions in France in 1789, Russia in 1917, and China in 1911.

Such structural factors were significant not only in the genesis of social revolutions but also in their outcomes. That is, the outcomes of these revolutions were "fundamental and enduring structural transformations" in the societies in question (Skocpol, 1979:161). There are important variations in the cases she studied, but there are also these important similarities. First, the agrarian class relationships were dramatically transformed. Second, the autocratic and proto-bureaucratic regimes of the old states were replaced by bureaucratic, professionalized states able to manage masses of people. Third, the prerevolutionary landed upper classes lost exclusive privileges.

In her discussion of structural outcomes of revolutions, Skocpol attacked those who emphasize ideological factors. She refused to see the leaders of social revolutions as merely the representatives of social classes and their actions as simple reflections of the ideologies of those classes. Rather, she wanted to focus on what revolutionary leaders *do*—struggle for state power. She took their activities more seriously than the ideological pressures on them. Furthermore, the results of their activities are determined not by ideologies but by structural exigencies: "Revolutionary crises are *not* total breakpoints in history that suddenly make anything at all possible if only it is envisaged by willful revolutionaries" (Skocpol, 1979:171). We need to look at real structural forces and constraints and not people's ideas about them.

In this section we have looked briefly at two examples of historical-comparative research from a Marxian perspective. They are not necessarily representative of all Marxian work of this variety, but they are offered as illustrations.

SUMMARY

In this chapter we examine a wide range of approaches that can be categorized as neo-Marxian sociological theories. All of them take Marx's work as their point of departure, but they often go in very different directions. Although these diverse developments give neo-Marxian theory considerable vitality, they also create at least some unnecessary and largely dysfunctional differentiation and controversy. Thus one task for the modern Marxian sociological theorist is to integrate this broad array of theories while recognizing the value of various specific pieces of work.

The first neo-Marxian theory historically, but the least important at present, especially to the sociologically oriented thinker, is economic determinism. It was against this limited view of Marxian theory that other varieties developed. Hegelian Marxism, especially in the work of Georg Lukács, was one such reaction. This approach sought to overcome the limitations in economic determinism by returning to the subjective, Hegelian roots of Marxian theory. Hegelian Marxism is also of little contemporary relevance; its significance lies largely in its impact on later neo-Marxian theories.

The critical school, which was the inheritor of the tradition of Hegelian Marxism, *is* of contemporary importance to sociology. The great contributions of the critical theorists (Marcuse, Habermas, and so forth) are the insights offered into culture, consciousness, and their interrelationships. These theorists have enhanced our understanding of such cultural phenomena as instrumental rationality, the ''culture industry,'' the ''knowledge industry,'' domination, and legitimations. To this they add a concern with consciousness, primarily in the form of an integration of Freudian theory in their work. However, critical theory has gone too far in its efforts to compensate for the limitations of economic determinism; it needs to reintegrate a concern for economics, indeed, for large-scale social forces in general.

Another very vibrant neo-Marxian approach is structural Marxism. While the critical school emphasizes subjective factors, the structural Marxists focus primarily on structural factors. Structural Marxists like Althusser, Poulantzas, and Godelier also take economic determinism as their starting point. This leads them toward such structures as the state and ideology, which are seen as having ''relative autonomy'' vis-à-vis the economy. Nevertheless, the economy is still seen as *the* most important structural factor. The structural Marxists not only reject the limitations of economic determinism at the structural level but are also highly critical of the subjectivity of the critical school and Hegelian Marxism. They regard these developments as dangerous, antiscientific trends in Marxian theory. While the structural Marxists are highly critical of other branches of Marxian theory, they themselves have been the subject of a series of strong attacks from both within and without Marxian theory.

The chapter ends with two other major examples of neo-Marxian theory. The first, represented by the work of Baran and Sweezy and of Braverman, is an effort to return to the traditional economic focus of Marxian theory. This work is significant for its effort to update Marxian economics by taking into account the realities of modern capitalist society. Second, there are two examples of Marxian historical scholarship: Wallerstein, who analyzed economics and world-systems; and Skocpol, who focused on politics and social revolution.

In sum, modern Marxian sociological theory is lively, controversial, sometimes confused, and likely to continue to attract the attention of large numbers of sociologists.

CHAPTER FIVE
Symbolic Interactionism

LIKE other major sociological theories, symbolic interactionism presents an extremely broad perspective. The theories of George Herbert Mead and, to a lesser extent, Charles Horton Cooley and W. I. Thomas provided its initial cohesive core, but it has become a group of clearly differentiated perspectives in recent years. Traditional symbolic interactionism is represented by the ideas of Herbert Blumer; other varieties include Manford Kuhn's more "scientific" approach, Erving Goffman's dramaturgical approach, and perhaps even ethnomethodology and phenomenology.[1] The last two theories are conceived of as separate orientations and will be dealt with in Chapter Six. Here we will discuss the core of symbolic interaction theory, as represented primarily in the works of Mead and Blumer, although some of the other approaches will also receive some attention.

THE MAJOR HISTORICAL ROOTS

We begin our discussion of symbolic interactionism with Mead, who actually taught philosophy, not sociology, at the University of Chicago from 1894 to 1931 (Faris,

---

[1]This was manifest in the plenary session of the 1979 meetings at the Society of Symbolic Interaction, at which the theme was varieties of symbolic interaction. Two of the speakers were George Psathas (a phenomenologist) and Don Zimmerman (an ethnomethodologist).

1970). However, many graduate students in sociology took his courses. Those students were later instrumental in turning Mead's "oral tradition" of symbolic interactionism (Kuhn, 1964) into a written one, using their notes from Mead's classes as the basis for his seminal work, *Mind, Self and Society: From the Standpoint of a Social Behaviorist* (Mead, 1934/1962). The two most significant intellectual roots of Mead's work in particular, and of symbolic interactionism in general, are the philosophy of pragmatism and psychological behaviorism.

Pragmatism is a wide-ranging philosophical position, but we can identify several aspects of it that influenced Mead's developing sociological orientation (Charon, 1979). First, to pragmatists truth, or reality, does not exist "out there" in the real world; it exists only when people intervene in the world and interpret what is occurring there. Second, people remember, and base their knowledge of the world on, what has proven useful to them. They are likely to alter that which no longer "works." Third, people define the social and physical "objects" they encounter in the world according to their use for them. Finally, if we want to understand actors, we must base that understanding on what they actually do in the world. Three points are critical for symbolic interactionism: (1) a focus on the interaction between the actor and the world; (2) a view of both the actor and the world as dynamic processes and not static structures; and (3) the great importance attributed to the actor's ability to interpret the social world.

The last point is most pronounced in the work of the philosophical pragmatist John Dewey. Dewey did not conceive of the mind as a thing or a structure, but rather as a thinking process that involves a series of stages. These stages include defining objects in the social world, outlining possible modes of conduct, imagining the consequences of alternative courses of action, eliminating unlikely possibilities, and finally selecting the optimal mode of action (Stryker, 1980). This focus on the thinking process was enormously influential in the development of symbolic interactionism.

Had philosophical pragmatism been the only influence on Mead, he probably would have philosophized about the relationship between actors and society. However, psychological behaviorism also influenced him and led him in a more empirical direction. In fact, Mead called his basic concern "social behaviorism" in order to differentiate it from the "radical behaviorism" of John B. Watson.

Radical behaviorists of Watson's persuasion were concerned with the *observable* behaviors of individuals. Their focus was on the stimuli that elicited the responses, or behaviors, in question. They either denied, or were disinclined to attribute much importance to, the covert mental process that occurred between the time that a stimulus was applied and a response emitted. Mead recognized the importance of observable behavior, but he also felt that there were *covert* aspects of behavior the radical behaviorists had ignored. But since he accepted the empiricism that was basic to behaviorism, Mead did not simply want to philosophize about these covert phenomena. Rather, he sought to extend the empirical science of behaviorism to them—that is, to what goes on between stimulus and response. Bernard Meltzer summarized Mead's position:

> For Mead, the unit of study is "the act," which comprises both overt and covert aspects of human action. Within the act, all the separated categories of the traditional, orthodox psychologies find a place. Attention, perception, imagination, reasoning, emotion, and so forth, are seen as parts of the act . . . the act, then encompasses the total process involved in human activity.
>
> (Meltzer, 1964/1978:23)

Mead and the radical behaviorists also differed in their views on the relationship between human and animal behavior. While radical behaviorists tended to see no difference between humans and animals, Mead argued that there was a significant qualitative difference. The key to this difference was seen as the human possession of mental capacities that allowed people to use language between stimulus and response in order to decide how to respond.

The confluence of pragmatism and behaviorism shaped Mead's orientation, which was transmitted to many graduate students at the University of Chicago, primarily in the 1920s. These students, among them Herbert Blumer, established symbolic interactionism. There were, of course, other important theorists who influenced these students, the most important of whom was Georg Simmel. Robert E. Park, the leading figure in the sociology department at Chicago in the 1920s, had earlier been a student of Simmel's in Europe, and he was instrumental in conveying Simmel's ideas to Chicago students as well as to the general sociological audience. Simmel's interest in forms of action and interaction was both compatible with, and an extension of, Meadian theory. There were, of course, many other influences on the development of symbolic interaction, but pragmatism, radical behaviorism, and Simmelian theory are far and away the most important.

Mead simultaneously demonstrated his debt to Watsonian behaviorism and dissociated himself from it. Mead (1934/1962:2) made this clear when he said that on the one hand, "we shall approach this latter field [social psychology] from a behavioristic point of view." On the other hand, Mead (1934/1962:2) criticized Watson's position when he said: "The behaviorism which we shall make use of is *more adequate* than that of which Watson makes use" (italics added).

Charles Morris (1934/1962), in his introduction to *Mind, Self and Society*, enumerated three basic differences between Mead and Watson. First, Mead considered Watson's exclusive focus on behavior too simplistic. In effect, he accused Watson of wrenching behavior out of its broader social context. Mead wanted to deal with behavior as a small part of the broader social world.

Second, Mead accused Watson of an unwillingness to extend behaviorism into mental processes. Watson had no sense of the actor's consciousness and mental processes, as Mead (1934/1962:2-3) made vividly clear: "John B. Watson's attitude was that of the Queen in *Alice in Wonderland*—'Off with their heads!'—there were no such things. There was no . . . consciousness." Mead (1934/1962:8) contrasted his perspective with Watson's: "It is behavioristic, but unlike Watsonian behaviorism it recognizes the parts of the act which do not come to external observation." More concretely, Mead saw his mission as extending the principles of Watsonian behaviorism to include mental processes.

Finally, because Watson rejected the mind, Mead saw him as having a passive image of the actor as puppet. Mead, on the other hand, subscribed to a much more dynamic and creative image of the actor, and it was this that made him attractive to later symbolic interactionists.

Although Mead set forth some of its basic principles, symbolic interactionism as such did not exist in Mead's time. But by the time Blumer became one of its leaders in the 1930s it had become institutionalized. Blumer not only coined the term "symbolic interactionism" in 1937 but wrote several essays that were instrumental in its development. Whereas Mead sought to differentiate the nascent symbolic interactionism from behaviorism, Blumer saw symbolic interactionism as embattled on two fronts. First was the reductionist behaviorism that had worried Mead. To this was added the serious threat from more large-scale sociological theories, especially structural functionalism. To Blumer, behaviorism and structural functionalism both tended to focus on factors (for example, external stimuli and norms) that cause human behavior. As far as Blumer was concerned, both ignored the crucial process by which actors endow the forces acting upon them, as well as their own behaviors, with meaning.

To Blumer, behaviorists, with their emphasis on the impact of external stimuli on individual behavior, were clearly psychological reductionists. In addition to behaviorism, several other types of psychological reductionism troubled Blumer. For example, he criticized those who seek to explain human action by relying on conventional notions of the concept of ''attitude'' (Blumer, 1955/1969:94). In his view, most of those who use the concept think of an attitude as an ''already organized tendency'' within the actor; they tend to think of actions as being impelled by attitudes. In Blumer's view, this is very mechanistic thinking; what is important is not the attitude as an internalized tendency, ''but the defining process through which the actor comes to forge his act'' (Blumer, 1955/1969:97). Blumer also singled out for criticism those who focus on conscious and unconscious motives. He was particularly irked by their view that actors are impelled by independent, mentalistic impulses over which they are supposed to have no control. Freudian theory, which sees actors as impelled by such forces as the id or libido, is an example of the kind of psychological theory to which Blumer was opposed. In short, Blumer was opposed to any psychological theory that ignores the process by which actors construct meaning—the fact that actors have selves and relate to themselves. Blumer's general criticisms were similar to Mead's, but he extended them beyond behaviorism to include other forms of psychological reductionism as well.

Blumer was also opposed to sociologistic theories that view individual behavior as determined by large-scale external forces. In this category Blumer included those theories that focus on such social structural and cultural factors as '' 'social system,' 'social structure,' 'culture,' 'status position,' 'social role,' 'custom,' 'institution,' 'collective representation,' 'social situation,' 'social norm,' and 'values' '' (Blumer, 1962/1969:83). Both sociologistic theories and psychological theories ignore the importance of meaning and the social construction of reality. Blumer summarized his criticisms of both psychological and sociologistic theories in this way:

> In both such typical psychological and sociological explanations the meanings of things for the human beings who are acting are either bypassed or swallowed up in the factors used to account for their behavior. If one declares that the given kinds of behavior are the result of the particular factors regarded as producing them, there is no need to concern oneself with the meaning of the things towards which human beings act.
>
> (Blumer, 1969b:3)

With this background of symbolic interactionism, we are ready to discuss the basic principles of its contemporary manifestations. First, however, we will examine the ideas of George H. Mead, the most important thinker in the founding of symbolic interactionism, and his most important work, *Mind, Self and Society.*

MEAD: MIND, SELF AND SOCIETY

In *Mind, Self and Society*, Mead started with the radical Watsonian behaviorist assumption that social psychology begins with observable activity—that is, social action and interaction. However, unlike Watson and more traditional behaviorists, Mead extended behaviorism in two directions, into the mind and into society. Thus, we are dealing with two types of behaviorism here. The first, associated with Watson, is traditional, psychological, reductionistic or "radical" behaviorism. The second is the *social* behaviorism that Mead sought to develop in order to overcome the problems of the Watsonian perspective. Mead argued that psychological behaviorism, with its roots in animal psychology, ignored both the internal (mental) and the external (societal) dimensions. Animal psychologists cannot really "understand" the mind of a rat, but sociologists can understand human mental processes. Similarly, Mead doubted that animals are capable of creating a society in the same sense that people are. Mead was not content simply to postulate a society; he was also anxious to accord it causal primacy in his system: "We attempt, that is, to explain the conduct of the individual in terms of the organized conduct of the social group, rather than to account for the organized conduct of the social group in terms of the conduct of the separate individuals belonging to it" (Mead, 1934/1962:7). Given Mead's association with symbolic interactionism, this statement seems to be startling. However, as we will soon see, Mead promised more on large-scale social structures than he actually delivered.

GEORGE HERBERT MEAD: A Biographical Sketch

Many of the thinkers discussed in this book were important teachers, but they achieved their greatest recognition through their books and articles. Mead, however, was far more important for what he said than for what he wrote. Mead himself had great difficulty in writing, and as a result relatively few of his ideas were published. As one of his students said, "Conversation was his best medium; writing was a poor second best" (T. V. Smith, 1931:369).

Born in Massachusetts on February 27, 1865, Mead was trained mainly in philosophy and its application to social psychology. After a brief teaching stint at the University of Michigan, Mead moved to the new University of Chicago in 1893, where he remained until his death on April 26, 1931. It was among the graduate students in sociology at Chicago that Mead found his most important audience. They took his courses and found that they meshed well with the social psychological ideas being taught in the sociology department. It was in the interaction between Mead's philosophical social psychology and sociological social psychology that the school known as symbolic interactionism was born.

In this development, it was Mead's spoken words that played a crucial role. It was only after his death that his students edited their class notes and produced a major volume under Mead's name, *Mind, Self and Society*. Despite its unusual origin, this book continues to be widely read today.

Mead's argument progressed through three main components—mind, self, and society. Although he did not discuss behavior at length in *Mind, Self and Society*, it is clear that he had a strong conception of it. He obviously felt that he was building his own theory on the well-known basis of behaviorism.

Mind

Mead did not conceive of the human mind as a thing, an entity. Rather, he viewed it as a social process. In Mead's view the human mind is qualitatively different from the minds of lower animals. To illustrate the latter, he described a dog fight as merely a *conversation of gestures*. That is, one dog's actions elicit another dog's reactions. No mental deliberation intervenes between the two. Although some human behavior occurs in this way, most action involves the intervention of deliberative mental processes between stimulus and response. In a human fight the raised fist of an opponent becomes not simply a gesture, but a *significant symbol*. It has for all of us a set of meanings. Because the same symbol can have a multitude of meanings, depending on the context, we need our mental capacities to interpret the meaning. In a dark alley a raised fist may well mean an impending struggle, but on a busy street corner it may simply constitute an effort to flag a cab. Significant symbols may take the form of such physical symbols or a linguistic form. This capability of creating, storing, and utilizing language ultimately sets humans apart from other animals. Language enables us to respond not only to physical symbols but also to words. The words "ice cream" can then stimulate much the same reaction in people as the actual physical presence of the dessert. The human possession of language accounts for the enormous qualitative difference between the human mind and those of lower animals.

In fact, the existence of language, which is a *social* product, ultimately allows the mind to exist. The mind can be defined as an internal conversation with one's self through the use of significant symbols. What was pivotal for Mead in this deliberative process is the ability to take the role of the other in the interaction process. By putting ourselves in the place of the other we can better understand the meaning of what that person says or does. In the example of the fight, we are able to understand the meaning of the raised fist by placing ourselves in the position of the actor taking that action in a dark alley or busy street. The internal conversation we have with ourselves over the meaning of that gesture is, in Mead's view, the essence of the mind.

It is important for the existence of social life that actors have shared significant symbols. The processes of thinking, and ultimately of acting and interacting, are facilitated by the fact that significant symbols have basically the same meaning for all and arouse the same reaction in the people using them as in the people reacting to them. Mead also placed great importance on the flexibility of the mind. Beyond a base of shared meanings of symbols, this flexibility allows interaction to occur even in situations where a given stimulus does not have an identical meaning for all involved. People do have the mental ability to adapt constantly to each other and to the situation, and thus figure out the meaning of a particular symbol.

The verbal significant symbol was particularly important to Mead, because we can almost always hear ourselves, although we may not always be able to see our physical gestures. What we say affects us as well as those with whom we are communicating.

Thus, as we are speaking, and before the other person has a chance to react, we can decide whether what we are saying is likely to elicit the desired reaction. If we decide that it is not going to elicit the response we want, we can quickly clarify our meaning to elicit what we desire.

The concept of meaning was important to Mead. Conduct is meaningful when we can use our minds to put ourselves in the place of others in order to interpret their thoughts and actions. Yet here, as elsewhere, Mead argued that meaning comes originally not from the mind but from the social situation. It is present in the social act before the emergence of consciousness of it. An act is meaningful if a gesture indicates to one actor the resultant behavior of another actor. Meaning need not be conscious. Before people created significant symbols, meaning was not conscious. However, now that we have such symbols, meaning has the potential of becoming a conscious phenomenon. Still, not all of our actions are consciously meaningful to us. Unconsciously motivated actions—that is, stimulus-response reflexes involving nonsignificant symbols—fall into this category.

Mead's ideas on the thinking process are deeply embedded in his behavioristic orientation. From this point of view, what is critical about the thinking process is the ability to inhibit action temporarily. That is, when a stimulus is presented people do not inevitably emit the desired response. They decide what they want to do by trying out mentally a set of alternatives before acting in that situation. This set of alternatives "makes possible the exercise of intelligent or reflective choice in the acceptance of that one among these possible alternative responses" (Mead, 1934/1962:98). This gives the human being unparalleled ability to organize and control action. In contrast, lower animals are capable only of trial and error. It is far more costly to try and to fail than to mentally reject courses of action that one feels have a high probability of failure. Lower animals can only react immediately, but humans can delay their reactions and "delayed reaction is necessary to intelligent conduct" (Mead, 1934/1962:99). Intelligence, for Mead, includes a number of abilities, including remembering, foreseeing, delaying, organizing, and selecting.

Although Mead placed great importance on the mind, he rejected as "hopeless" the use of introspection as a methodological tool to study it (Mead, 1934/1962:105). For Mead, "consciousness is functional, not substantive" (Mead, 1934/1962:112). In other words, the process of thinking is part of the social world, not something occurring solely in the head. Mead believed, for that reason, that mental processes should be studied in the social world and not as things that are simply in the actor's head. In this way, the mind can be seen as a relationship between actor and situation mediated by a set of symbols.

In rejecting the ideas of introspection and of a separable consciousness, Mead fell into a dangerous trap (the same trap, as we will see, that Alfred Schutz fell into; see Chapter Six). That is, Mead, schooled as a behaviorist, did not see introspection as a scientific method nor did he see the mind as an entity that can be studied scientifically. This orientation leaves much to be desired, since it eliminates an important part of social life from serious scientific consideration.

Self

To Mead, reflexiveness, or the ability to respond to one's self as one does to others, "is the essential condition, within the social process, for the development of mind"

(Mead, 1934/1962:134). In this sense, the self, like the mind, is not an object but a conscious process that involves several dimensions:

1.   The ability to respond to one's self as others respond to it
2.   The ability to respond to one's self as the collectivity, the *generalized other*, responds to it
3.   The ability to take part in one's own conversation with others
4.   The ability to be aware of what one is saying and to use that awareness to determine what one is going to do next

This process is not purely mental, and the abilities needed to engage in it are socially acquired. Of central importance is language, by means of which we use and interpret verbal significant symbols.

Mead's general theory of the stages of socialization is important here, for people need to learn more than simply language in order to acquire a self. In the *play stage* the child learns to take the roles of specific significant people, such as father, mother, sister, or brother. This important stage in the life cycle gives children a discrete sense of social reality. Since children are taking a series of discrete roles, they develop a very discrete sense of their selves. They can see themselves in different ways, as a number of different people might see them. However, they lack a coherent or integrated sense of the self.

To acquire a more coherent sense of the self children must move on to the *game stage*, in which they develop the ability to take a more generalized view of the situation and of the self. In Mead's terms, they learn to take the role of the "generalized other." To illustrate this idea, Mead used the example of a baseball game. In the play stage the child was able to take the role, alternately, of manager, fan, catcher, pitcher, batter, and so on. However, these discrete images did not give the child a coherent sense of what the game of baseball was all about. In the game stage the child begins to acquire such an overall perspective, not only as it relates to baseball but to the social world in general. This perspective leads to a more coherent sense of the self. Once again, Mead gave priority to social causes. For the self to arise, the group must already exist.

Mead's two basic components of the self are the "I" and the "me." Once again, remember that these are not things, but processes within the self. The "me" is that part of the self of which the actor is aware, the internalization of the organized attitude of others, of the generalized other. It represents the forces of conformity and of social control. The "I" is that part of the self of which the actor is unaware; we are only aware of it after an act is completed. It is the immediate response of the actor that both calls out and responds to the "me." The self is the product of the relationship between the "I" and the "me." "The 'I' is the response of the individual to the organized attitude of the community as this appears in his own experience. Its response to that organized attitude in turn changes it" (Mead, 1934/1962:196).

The existence of the "I" gives Mead's social psychology much dynamism. Mead does have, at least to some degree, a creative dynamic sense of consciousness. Mead (1934/1962:177) said, for example, "the 'I' gives the sense of freedom, of initiative." He also maintained that "the 'I' is something that is never entirely calculable" (Mead, 1934/1962:178). Or later, "the attitudes involved are gathered from the group, but the individual in whom they are organized has the opportunity of giving them an expression which perhaps has never taken place before'' (Mead, 1934/1962:198). Although Mead was willing to discuss what takes place internally, he saw it as simply the internal phase of a broader, naturalistic social process. This applies to both the self and the mind.

Society

In the discussions of mind and self, we have seen the outlines of Mead's very sophisticated treatment of consciousness, at least from the naturalistic perspective of a behaviorist. However, the rest of Mead's sociology is weak, especially his conception of society. When Mead discussed society he had little or no sense of the kind of large-scale structures that so interested structural functionalists and conflict theorists. To Mead, society was little more than the social organization in which mind and self arise, a residual category. Also, he conceived of society largely as patterns of interaction: ''The society in which we belong represents an organized set of responses to certain situations in which the individual is involved'' (Mead, 1934/1962:270). Similarly, he viewed an institution as nothing more than a set of common responses. Thus, despite the title of his main work, Mead did not offer a large-scale sociology to complement his very strong insights into individual action and consciousness.

CONTEMPORARY SYMBOLIC INTERACTIONISM

The heart of this chapter is our discussion of the basic principles of contemporary symbolic interaction theory. Although we will try to characterize the theory in general terms, there are significant differences within symbolic interactionism, some of which will be discussed as we proceed. We will also address a number of the criticisms of symbolic interactionism. Finally, we will discuss the recent work of Sheldon Stryker (1980), which can be seen as an effort to cope with at least some of the most important of these criticisms.

Capacity for Thought

A number of symbolic interactionists (Rose, 1962; Blumer, 1969a; Manis and Meltzer, 1978) have tried to enumerate the basic principles of the theory. These principles include the following:

1. Human beings, unlike lower animals, are endowed with the capacity for thought.
2. The capacity for thought is shaped by social interaction.
3. In social interaction people learn the meanings and the symbols that allow them to exercise their distinctively human capacity for thought.
4. Meanings and symbols allow people to carry on distinctively human action and interaction.
5. People are able to modify or alter the meanings and symbols they use in action and interaction on the basis of their interpretation of the situation.
6. People are able to make these modifications and alterations because, in part, of their ability to interact with themselves, which allows them to examine possible

courses of action, assess their relative advantages and disadvantages, and then choose one.

7. The intertwined patterns of action and interaction make up groups and societies.

The crucial assumption that human beings possess the ability to think differentiates symbolic interactionism from its behaviorist roots. This assumption also provides the basis for the entire theoretical orientation of symbolic interactionism. Bernard Meltzer, James Petras, and Larry Reynolds (1975:42) stated that the assumption of the human capacity for thought is one of the major contributions of early symbolic interactionists, such as James, Dewey, Thomas, Cooley, and of course Mead: "Individuals in human society were not seen as units that are motivated by external or internal forces beyond their control, or within the confines of a more or less fixed structure. Rather, they were viewed as reflective or interacting units which comprise the societal entity." The ability to think enables people to act reflectively rather than just behave unreflectively. People must often construct and guide what they do, rather than just release it.

The ability to think is embedded in the mind, but the symbolic interactionists have a somewhat unusual conception of the mind. They distinguish it from the physiological brain. People must have brains in order to develop minds, but a brain does not inevitably produce a mind, as is clear in the case of lower animals (Troyer, 1946). Also, symbolic interactionists do not conceive of the mind as a thing, a physical structure, but rather as a continuing process. It is a process that is itself part of the larger process of stimulus and response. The mind is related to virtually every other aspect of symbolic interactionism, including socialization, meanings, symbols, the self, interaction, and even society.

Thinking and Interaction

People possess only a general capacity for thought. This capacity must be shaped and refined in the process of social interaction. Such a view leads the symbolic interactionist to focus on a specific form of social interaction—*socialization*. The human ability to think is developed early in childhood socialization and is refined later during adult socialization. Symbolic interactionists have a view of the socialization process that is different from that of most other sociologists. To symbolic interactionists, conventional sociologists are likely to see socialization as simply a process by which people learn the things they need to survive in society (for instance, culture, role expectations). To the symbolic interactionists, socialization is a more dynamic process that allows people to develop the ability to think, to develop in distinctively human ways. Furthermore, socialization is not simply a one-way process in which the actor receives information, but rather is a dynamic process in which the actor shapes and adapts the information to his or her own needs (Manis and Meltzer, 1978:6).

Symbolic interactionists are, of course, interested not simply in socialization but in interaction in general, which is of "vital importance in its own right" (Blumer, 1969b:8). Interaction is the process in which the ability to think is both developed and expressed. All types of interaction, not just interaction during socialization, refine our ability to think. Beyond that, thinking shapes the interaction process. In most interaction, actors must take account of others and decide if and how to fit their activities to others. However, not all interaction involves thinking. The differentiation made by Blumer (following Mead) between two basic forms of social interaction is relevant here. The first, nonsymbolic interaction—Mead's conversation of gestures—does not involve thinking. The second, symbolic interaction, does require mental processes.

The importance of thinking to symbolic interactionists is reflected in their views on *objects*. Blumer differentiates among three types of objects: *physical objects*, such as a chair or a tree; *social objects*, such as a student or a mother; and *abstract objects*, such as an idea or a moral principle. Objects are seen simply as things "out there" in the real world: what is of greatest significance is the way they are defined by actors. This leads to the relativistic view that different objects have different meanings for different individuals: "A tree will be a different object to a botanist, a lumberman, a poet, and a home gardener" (Blumer, 1969b:11).

Individuals learn the meanings of objects in the socialization process. Most of us learn a common set of meanings, but in many cases, as with the tree mentioned above, we have different definitions of the same objects. Although this can be taken to an extreme, symbolic interactionists need not deny the existence of objects in the real world. All they need do is point out the crucial nature of the definition of those objects as well as the possibility that actors may have different definitions of the same object. As Herbert Blumer (1969b:11) said: "The nature of an object . . . consists of the meaning that it has for the person for whom it is an object."

Learning Meanings and Symbols

Symbolic interactionists, following Mead, tend to accord causal significance to social interaction. Thus, meaning does not stem from mental processes, but rather from the process of interaction. This focus derives from Mead's pragmatism: he focused on human action and interaction, not isolated mental processes. Symbolic interactionists have in general continued in this direction. Among other things, this means that the central concern is not how people mentally create meanings and symbols, but rather how they learn them during interaction in general, and socialization in particular.

People learn symbols as well as meanings in social interaction. While people respond to signs unthinkingly, they respond to symbols in a thoughtful manner. Signs stand for themselves (for example, the gestures of angry dogs, or water to a person dying of thirst). Symbols are special types of social objects that "are *used to represent* or stand for whatever it is that people agree they should stand for" (Charon, 1979:39–40). Not all social objects stand for other things, but those that do are symbols. Words, physical artifacts, and physical actions (for example, the world "boat," a cross or a Star of David, and a clenched fist) can all be symbols. People often use symbols to communicate something about themselves: they drive Rolls-Royces, for instance, to communicate a certain style of life.

Symbolic interactionists conceive of language as a vast system of symbols. Words are symbols, since they are used to stand for things. Words make all other symbols possible. Acts, objects, and other words exist and have meaning for us only because they have been and can be described through the use of words.

Symbols are crucial in allowing people to act in distinctively human ways. Because of the symbol, the human being "does not respond passively to a reality that imposes itself but actively creates and re-creates the world acted in" (Charon, 1979:62). In addition to this general utility, symbols in general, and language in particular, have a number of specific functions for the actor (Charon, 1979).

First, symbols allow people to deal with the material and social world by allowing them to name, categorize, and remember the objects they encounter there. In this way people are able to order a world that otherwise would be confusing. Language allows people to name, categorize, and especially remember much more efficiently than they could with other kinds of symbols, such as pictorial images.

Second, symbols improve people's ability to perceive the environment. Instead of being flooded by a mass of indistinguishable stimuli, the actor can be alerted to some parts of the environment rather than others.

Third, symbols improve the ability to think. While a set of pictorial symbols would allow a limited ability to think, language greatly expands this ability. Thinking, in these terms, can be conceived of as symbolic interaction with one's self.

Fourth, symbols greatly increase the ability to solve various problems. Lower animals must use trial and error, but human beings can think through symbolically a variety of alternative actions before actually taking one. This reduces the chance of making costly mistakes.

Fifth, the use of symbols allows actors to transcend time, space, and even their own persons. Through the use of symbols actors can imagine what it was like to live in the past or might be like to live in the future. In addition, actors can transcend their own persons symbolically and imagine what the world is like from another person's point of view. This is the well-known symbolic interactionist concept of *taking the role of the other*.

Sixth, symbols allow us to imagine a metaphysical reality, such as heaven or hell. Seventh, and most generally, the use of symbols allows people to avoid being enslaved by their environment. They can be active rather than passive—that is, self-directed in terms of what they do.

Action and Interaction

Symbolic interactionists' primary concern is with the impact of meanings and symbols on human action and interaction. Here it is useful to employ Mead's differentiation between covert and overt behavior. *Covert behavior* is the thinking process, involving symbols and meanings. *Overt behavior* is the actual behavior performed by an actor. Some overt behavior does not involve covert behavior (habitual behavior or mindless responses to external stimuli). However, most human action involves both kinds. Covert behavior is of greatest concern to symbolic interactionists, whereas overt behavior is of greater concern to exchange theorists or to traditional behaviorists in general.

Meanings and symbols give human social action (which involves a single actor) and social interaction (which involves two or more actors engaged in mutual social action) some distinctive characteristics. Social action is that in which the individuals are "acting with others in mind" (Charon, 1979:127). In other words, in undertaking an action people are simultaneously trying to gauge its impact on the other actors involved. Although they often engage in mindless, habitual behavior, people have the capacity to engage in social action.

In the process of social interaction, people are symbolically communicating meanings to the others involved. The others are interpreting those symbols and orienting their responding action on the basis of their interpretation. In other words, in social interaction, actors are engaged in a process of mutual influence.

Making Choices

Partly because of the ability to handle meanings and symbols, people, unlike lower animals, can make choices in terms of the actions in which they engage. People need not accept the meanings and symbols that are imposed on them from without. On the basis of their own interpretation of the situation, "humans are capable of forming new meanings and new lines of meaning" (Manis and Meltzer, 1978:7).

W. I. Thomas was instrumental in underscoring this creative capacity in his concept of *definition of the situation*: "If men define situations as real, they are real in their consequences" (Thomas and Thomas, 1928:572). Thomas knew that most of our definitions of situations have been provided for us by society. In fact, he emphasized this, pointing especially to the family and the community as sources of our social definitions. However, Thomas's position is distinctive for his emphasis on the possibility of "spontaneous" individual definitions of situations, which allow people to alter and modify meanings and symbols.

The Self

The self is a concept of enormous importance to symbolic interactionists. In attempting to understand this concept beyond its initial Meadian formulation we must first understand the idea of the *looking-glass self* developed by Charles Horton Cooley. Cooley defined this concept as:

> a somewhat definite imagination of how one's self—that is, any idea he appropriates—appears in a particular mind, and the kind of self-feeling one has is determined by the attitude toward this attributed to that other mind . . . So in imagination we perceive in another's mind some thought of our appearance, manners, aims, deeds, character, friends, and so on, and are variously affected by it.
>
> (Cooley, 1902/1964:169)

By the looking-glass self Cooley meant the capacity to see ourselves as we see any other social object. The idea of a looking-glass self can be broken down into three components. First, we imagine how we appear to others. Second, we imagine what their judgment of that appearance must be. Third, we develop some self-feeling, such as pride or mortification, as a result of our imagining others' judgments.

Cooley's concept of the looking-glass self and Mead's concept of the self were important in the development of the modern symbolic interactionist conception of the self. Blumer (1969b:12) defined the self in extremely simple terms: "Nothing esoteric is meant by this expression [self]. It means merely that a human being can be an object of his own action . . . he acts toward himself and guides himself in his actions toward others on the basis of the kind of object he is to himself." The self is a process, not a thing. As Blumer made clear, the self helps allow human beings to act rather than simply respond to external stimuli:

The process [interpretation] has two distinct steps. First, the actor indicates to himself the things toward which he is acting; he has to point out in himself the things that have meaning. . . . This interaction with himself is something other than an interplay of psychological elements; it is an instance of the person engaging in a process of communicating with himself. . . . Second, by virtue of this process of communicating with himself, interpretation becomes a matter of handling meanings. The actor selects, checks, suspends, regroups, and transforms the meanings in the light of the situation in which he is placed and the direction of his action.

(Blumer, 1969b:5)

Although this underscores the part played by the self in the process of choosing how to act, Blumer has really not gone very far beyond the early formulations of Cooley and Mead. However, other modern thinkers and researchers have refined the concept of the self.

THE WORK OF MORRIS ROSENBERG

Although mainstream symbolic interactionists have made important contributions to our understanding of the self (for example, Ralph Turner, 1968), the best-known recent work on this topic has been done by a sociologist not usually associated with this theory, Morris Rosenberg (1979). Although not a symbolic interactionist, Rosenberg has been heavily influenced by people like Mead and Cooley. His thoughts on the self are generally compatible with, and constitute an extension of, the symbolic interactionist orientation to this concept.

Rosenberg began by making it clear that his main interest was in the self-concept and not the self. The self is a more general concept, being both a subject and an object. The self-concept is the self as an object. What this means is clarified by Rosenberg's (1979:7) definition of the self-concept: *"the totality of the individual's thoughts and feelings having reference to himself as an object."* Thus the self-concept is only a part of the self, and an even smaller part of the total personality, but it is endowed with unusual significance, since it "is an important object to everyone, usually the most important object in the world" (Rosenberg, 1979:24). In addition to their importance, beliefs about the self are distinctive in a number of other ways. For example, they are the only attitudes that are reflexive—that is, the individual is both subject and object. The self-concept is the result of certain incommunicable information; it reflects the individual's unique body of information and point of view about himself. Although attitudes toward the self have much in common with other attitudes, there are unique attitudes toward the self, especially pride and shame. Accuracy and verifiability are much more important in attitudes toward the self than in attitudes toward bowling or tuna fish. In spite of its importance, the accuracy of self-attitudes "is difficult to ascertain because of low verifiability" (Rosenberg, 1979:33).

Rosenberg differentiated among the content, the structure, the dimensions, and the boundaries of the self-concept. In terms of *content*, Rosenberg distinguished social identities from dispositions. *Social identities* are the "groups, statuses or categories" to which an individual "is socially recognized as belonging" (Rosenberg, 1979:10). Examples include being recognized as a Democrat, middle-aged, black, or male. An individual not only sees himself in terms of such categories, but also comes to see himself as possessing certain tendencies to respond, certain *dispositions*. A person who sees himself as brave or introverted or liberal is likely to have his actions affected by such dispositions. In addition to the content of the self-concept, Rosenberg also discussed its structure. The *structure* of the self is the relationship among an individual's various social identities and dispositions. *Dimensions* refers to the attitudes and feelings one has about one's self. Self-attitudes, like all other attitudes, vary on a variety of dimensions, including "content, direction, intensity, salience, consistency, stability, clarity, accuracy and verifiability" (Rosenberg, 1979:23). Finally, Rosenberg discussed the *boundaries* of the self-concept, especially the ego-extensions to which it is applied. These are objects outside the actor that lead him to feel pride and shame: "pride in my shiny new automobile, shame at my unfashionable clothes, pride in an honor bestowed, shame or embarrassment at the defeat of my school team" (Rosenberg, 1979:35).

Rosenberg also distinguished among the extant self, the desired self, and the presenting self. The *extant self* is our picture of what we are like; the *desired self* is a picture of what we would like to be like; and the *presenting self* is the way we present ourselves in a given situation.

Rosenberg underscored the point that the self-concept involves a set of motivations, a set of desired goals for the actors. Two motives stand out above all of the others. First is *self-esteem*, or "the wish to think well of one's self" (Rosenberg, 1979:53). Second is *self-consistency*, or "the wish to protect the self-concept against change or to maintain one's self-picture" (Rosenberg, 1979:53). Rosenberg has done extensive empirical research on self-esteem and is widely recognized for this research. However, his conceptual analysis of the self-concept is an important contribution to the key idea of symbolic interactionism.

THE WORK OF ERVING GOFFMAN

Another important work on the self is *Presentation of Self in Everyday Life* (1959) by Erving Goffman, one of the most exciting modern symbolic interactionists. Goffman's conception of the self is deeply indebted to Mead's ideas, in particular his discussion of the tension between *I*, the spontaneous self, and *me*, social constraints within the self. This is mirrored in Goffman's (1959:56) work in what he called the "crucial discrepancy between our all-too-human selves and our socialized selves." The tension is due to the difference between what people expect us to do and what we may want to do spontaneously. We are confronted with the demand to do what is expected of us; moreover, we are not supposed to waver. As Goffman (1959:56) put it, "We must not be subject to ups and downs." In order to maintain a stable self-image, people perform for their social audiences. As a result of this interest in performance, Goffman focused on *dramaturgy*, or a view of social life as a series of dramatic performances akin to those performed on the stage.

DRAMATURGY   Goffman's sense of the self is shaped by his dramaturgical approach. To Goffman (as to Mead and most other symbolic interactionists), the self is:

> not an organic thing that has a specific location. . . . In analyzing the self then we are drawn
> from its possessor, from the person who will profit or lose most by it, for he and his body

merely provide the peg on which something of collaborative manufacture will be hung for a time. . . . The means for producing and maintaining selves do not reside inside the peg.

(Goffman, 1959:252–253)

He perceived the self not as a possession of the actor but rather as the product of the dramatic interaction between actor and audience. The self "is a dramatic effect arising . . . from a scene that is presented" (Goffman, 1959:253). Since the self is a product of dramatic interaction, it is vulnerable to disruption during the performance. Goffman's dramaturgy is concerned with the processes by which such disturbances are prevented or dealt with. Although the bulk of his discussion focuses on these dramaturgical contingencies, Goffman pointed out that most performances are successful. The result is that in ordinary circumstances a firm self is accorded to performers, and it "appears" to emanate from the performer.

Goffman assumed that when individuals interact they want to present a certain sense of self that will be accepted by others. However, even as they present that self, actors are aware that members of the audience can disturb their performance. For that reason actors are attuned to the need to control the audience, especially those elements of it that might be disruptive. The actors hope that the sense of self they present to the audience will be strong enough for the audience to define the actors as the actors want. The actors also hope that this will cause the audience to act voluntarily the way the actors want them to. Goffman characterized this central interest as "impression management." It involves techniques actors use to maintain certain impressions, problems they are likely to encounter, and methods they use to cope with these problems.

Following his theatrical analogy, Goffman spoke of a front stage. The *front* is that part of the performance that generally functions in rather fixed and general ways to define the situation for those who observe the performance. Within the front stage, Goffman further differentiated between the setting and the personal front. The *setting* refers to the physical scene that ordinarily must be there if the actors are to perform. Without it, the actors will usually not be able to perform. For example, a surgeon generally requires an operating room, a taxi driver a cab, and an ice skater a frozen surface. The *personal front* consists of those items of expressive equipment that the audience identifies with the performers and expects them to carry with them into the setting. A surgeon, for instance, is expected to dress in a medical gown, have certain instruments, and so on.

Goffman then subdivided the personal front into appearance and manner. *Appearance* includes those items that tell us the performer's social status (for instance, the surgeon's medical gown). *Manner* tells the audience what sort of role the performer expects to play in the situation (for example, the use of physical mannerisms, demeanor). A brusque manner and a meek manner indicate quite different kinds of performances. In general, we expect appearance and manner to be consistent.

Although Goffman approached the front and other aspects of his system as a symbolic interactionist, he did discuss their structural character. For example, he argued that fronts tend to become institutionalized so that "collective representations" arise about what is to go on in a certain front. Very often when actors take on established roles they find particular fronts already established for such performances. The result, Goffman argued, is that fronts tend to be selected, not created. This conveys a much more structural image than we would receive from most symbolic interactionists.

Despite such a structural view, Goffman's most interesting insights lie in the domain of interaction. He argued that since people generally endeavor to present an idealized picture of themselves in their front stage performances, inevitably they feel they must hide things in their performances. First, actors may want to conceal secret pleasures (for instance, drinking alcohol) engaged in prior to the performance or, more generally, past lives (for instance, as a drug addict) that are incompatible with their performance. Second, actors may want to conceal errors that have been made in the preparation of the performance, as well as steps that have been taken to correct these errors. For example, a taxi driver may seek to hide the fact that he started in the wrong direction. Third, actors may find it necessary to show only end products and to conceal the process involved in producing them. For example, professors may spend several hours preparing a lecture, but they may want to act as if they have always known the material. Fourth, it may be necessary for actors to conceal from the audience that "dirty work" was involved in the making of the end products. Dirty work may include tasks that "were physically unclean, semi-legal, cruel, and degrading in other ways" (Goffman, 1959:44). Fifth, in giving a certain performance actors may have to let other standards slide. Finally, actors will probably find it necessary to hide any insults or humiliations suffered, or deals made, that were necessary in order to put on the performance. Generally, actors have a vested interest in hiding all such facts from their audience.

Another aspect of dramaturgy in the front stage is that actors often try to convey the impression that they are closer to the audience than they actually are. For example, actors may try to foster the impression that the performance in which they are engaged at the moment is their only performance, or at least their most important one. In order to do this actors have to be sure that their audiences are segregated from one another so that the falsity of the performance is not discovered. Even if it is discovered, Goffman argued, the audiences themselves may try to cope with the falsity, so as not to shatter their idealized image of the actor. This reveals the interactional character of performances. A successful performance depends on the involvement of all of the parties. Another example of this kind of impression management is an actor's attempt to convey the idea that there is something unique about this performance as well as his or her relationship to the audience. The audience, too, wants to feel that it is the recipient of a unique performance.

Actors try to make sure that all the parts of any performance blend together. In some cases a single discordant aspect can disrupt a performance. However, performances vary in the amount of consistency required. A slip by a priest on a sacred occasion would be terribly disruptive, but if a taxi driver made one wrong turn it would not be likely to damage the overall performance greatly.

Another technique employed by performers is *mystification*. Actors often tend to mystify their performance by restricting the contact between themselves and the audience. By generating "social distance" between themselves and the audience, they try to create a sense of awe in the audience. This, in turn, keeps the audience from questioning the performance. Again Goffman pointed out that the audience is involved in this process and will often itself seek to maintain the credibility of the performance by keeping its distance from the performer.

This leads us to Goffman's interest in teams. To Goffman, as a symbolic interactionist, a focus on individual actors obscured important facts about interaction. Goffman's basic unit of analysis was thus not the individual but the team. A *team* is any set of individuals who cooperate in staging a single routine. Thus the preceding discussion of the relationship between the performer and audience is really about teams.[2] Each member is reliant on the others, since all can disrupt the performance and all are aware that they are putting on an act. Goffman concluded that a team is a kind of "secret society."

Goffman also discussed a *back stage* where facts suppressed in the front, or various kinds of informal actions, may appear. A back stage is usually adjacent to the front stage, but it is also cut off from it. Performers can reliably expect no members of their front audience to appear in the back. Furthermore, they will engage in various types of impression management to make sure of this. A performance is likely to become difficult when actors are unable to prevent the audience from entering the back stage. There is also a third, residual domain, the *outside*, which is neither front nor back.

No area is *always* one of these three domains. Also, a given area can occupy all three domains at different times. A professor's office is front stage when a student visits, back stage when the student leaves, and outside when the professor is at a university basketball game.

IMPRESSION MANAGEMENT Goffman closed *Presentation of Self in Everyday Life* with some additional thoughts on the art of impression management. In general, impression management is oriented to guarding against a series of unexpected actions, such as unintended gestures, inopportune intrusions, and faux pas, as well as intended actions, such as making a scene. Goffman was interested in the various methods of dealing with such problems. First, there is a set of methods involving actions aimed at producing dramaturgical loyalty by, for example, fostering high ingroup loyalty, preventing team members from identifying with the audience, and changing audiences periodically so that they do not become too knowledgeable about the performers. Second, Goffman suggested various forms of dramaturgical discipline, such as having the presence of mind to avoid slips, maintaining self-control, and managing the facial expressions and verbal tone of one's performance. Third, he identified various types of dramaturgical circumspection, such as determining in advance how a performance should go, planning for emergencies, selecting loyal teammates, selecting good audiences, being involved in small teams where dissension is less likely, making only brief appearances, preventing audience access to private information, and settling on a complete agenda to prevent unforeseen occurrences.

The audience also has a stake in successful impression management by the actor or team of actors. The audience often acts to save the show through such devices as giving great interest and attention to it, avoiding emotional outbursts, not noticing slips, and giving special consideration to a neophyte performer.

Goffman followed up on his work in *Presentation of Self in Everyday Life* with a series of fascinating and important books and essays (for instance, Goffman, 1961, 1963a, 1963b, 1967, 1971, 1972, 1974, 1976). We close this discussion with just a few illustrations of his distinctive mode of thought.

---

[2] A performer and the audience are one kind of team, but Goffman also talked of a group of performers as one team and the audience as another. Interestingly, Goffman argued that a team can also be a single individual. His logic, following classic symbolic interactionism, was that an individual can be his or her own audience—can *imagine* an audience to be present.

In "Role Distance" (1961) Goffman was interested in the degree to which an individual embraces a given role. In his view, because of the large number of roles, few people get completely involved in any given role. Role distance deals with the degree to which individuals separate themselves from the roles they are in. For example, if older children ride on a merry-go-round, they are likely to be aware that they are really too old to enjoy such an experience. One way of coping with this is to demonstrate distance from the role by doing it in a careless, lackadaisical way or performing seemingly dangerous acts while on the merry-go-round. In performing such acts the older children are really explaining to the audience that they are not as immersed in the activity as small children might be, or if they are, it is because of the special things they are doing.

One of Goffman's key insights is that role distance is a function of one's social status. High-status people often manifest role distance for reasons other than do those in low-status positions. For example, a high-status surgeon may manifest role distance in the operating room to relieve the tension of the operating team. People in low-status positions usually manifest more defensiveness in exhibiting role distance. For instance, people who clean toilets may do so in a lackadaisical and disinterested manner. They may be trying to tell their audience that they are too good for such work.

One of Goffman's most interesting books is *Stigma* (1963b). Goffman was interested in the gap between what a person ought to be, "*virtual social identity*," and what a person actually is, "*actual social identity*." Anyone who has a gap between these two identities is stigmatized. The book focuses on the dramaturgical interaction between stigmatized people and normals. The nature of that interaction depends on which of the two types of stigma an individual is troubled by. In the case of *discredited* stigma, the actor assumes that the differences are known by the audience members or are evident to them (for example, a paraplegic or someone who has lost a limb). A *discreditable* stigma is one in which the differences are neither known by audience members nor perceivable by them (for example, a person who has had a colostomy or a homosexual "passing" as straight). For someone with a discredited stigma, the basic dramaturgical problem is managing the tension produced by the fact that people know of the problem. For someone with a discreditable stigma, the dramaturgical problem is managing information so that the problem remains unknown to the audience.

Most of the text of *Stigma* is devoted to people with obvious, often grotesque stigmas (for instance, the loss of a nose). However, as the book unfolds the reader realizes that Goffman is really saying that we are all stigmatized at some time or other, or in one setting or other. His examples include the Jew "passing" in a predominantly Christian community, the fat person in a group of people of normal weight, and the individual who has lied about his past and must be constantly sure that the audience does not learn of this.

At this point mention of the more recent directions and changes in Goffman's mode of thinking is called for. In *Frame Analysis* (1974), Goffman moved away from his classic symbolic interactionist roots and toward the study of the small-scale structures of social life. Although he still felt that people define situations in the sense meant by W. I. Thomas, he now thought that such definitions were less important: "Defining situations as real certainly has consequences, but these may contribute very marginally to the events in progress" (Goffman, 1974:1). Furthermore, even when people define situations, they do not ordinarily create those definitions. Action is defined more by mechanical adherence to rules than through an active, creative, and negotiated process. Goffman (1974:10) enunciated his goal: "to try to isolate some of the basic frameworks of understanding available in our society for making sense out of events and to analyze the special vulnerabilities to which these frames of reference are subject."

Goffman's primary interest has become the small-scale structures that govern the thoughts and actions of actors. This constitutes a shift in emphasis and a movement away from classic symbolic interactionism. In fact, George Gonos (1977:855) said that "Goffman's work stands opposed to the central tenets and most basic assumptions of symbolic interactionism." Gonos argued that Goffman's work, especially *Frame Analysis*, is better seen as structuralism than symbolic interactionism. (Discussion of this issue will be deferred until we address structuralism in Chapter Eight.)

Groups and Societies

Much of what has been said up to this point about symbolic interactionism has concerned the interrelationships of individual thought and action. This constitutes the clear focus of symbolic interactionism, which has a distinctive perspective on society's large-scale structures.

BLUMER ON LARGE-SCALE SOCIAL STRUCTURES

Symbolic interactionists generally are highly critical of the tendency of other sociologists to focus on macro structures. Blumer (1962/1969:84) is in the forefront of those who are critical of this "sociological determinism [in which] the social action of people is treated as an outward flow or expression of forces playing on them rather than as acts which are built up by people through their interpretation of the situations in which they are placed." This focus on the constraining effects of large-scale social structures leads traditional sociologists to a set of assumptions about the actor and action different from those held by symbolic interactionists. Instead of seeing actors as those who actively define their situations, traditional sociologists tend to reduce actors to "mindless robots on the societal or aggregate level" (Manis and Meltzer, 1978:7). In an effort to stay away from determinism and a robotlike view of actors, symbolic interactionists take a very different view of large-scale social structures, a view that is ably presented by Blumer.

To Blumer, society is not made up of macro structures. The essence of society is to be found in actors and action: "Human society is to be seen as consisting of acting people, and the life of the society is to be seen as consisting of their actions" (Blumer, 1962/1969:85). Human society is action; group life is a "complex of ongoing activity." However, society is not made up of an array of isolated acts. There is collective action as well, which involves "individuals fitting their lines of action to one another . . . participants making indications to one another, not merely each to himself" (Blumer, 1969b:16). This gives rise to what Mead called the "social act" and Blumer labeled "joint action."

Blumer accepted the idea of emergence, that large-scale structures emerge from micro processes. For Blumer, joint action is the largest-scale concern. A joint action is not simply the sum total of its individual acts—it comes to have a distinctive character of its own. A joint action is thus not external to, nor coercive of, actors and their actions; rather, it is created by actors and their actions. The study of joint action is, in Blumer's view, the domain of the sociologist.

From this discussion one gets the sense that the joint act is of almost total flexibility —that is, that society can become almost anything the actors want it to be. However, Blumer was not prepared to go that far. He argued that each instance of joint action must be formed anew, but he did recognize that joint action is likely to have a "well-established and repetitive form" (Blumer, 1969b:17). Not only does most joint action recur in patterns, but Blumer was also willing to admit that such action is guided by systems of pre-established meanings, such as culture and social order.

It would appear that Blumer admitted that there are large-scale structures and that they are important. Here Blumer followed Mead (1934/1962:75), who admitted that such structures are very important. Despite this, such structures have an extremely limited role in symbolic interactionism. For one thing, Blumer most often argued that large-scale structures are little more than "frameworks" within which the really important aspects of social life, action and interaction, take place (Blumer, 1962/1969: 87). Large-scale structures do set the conditions and set limitations on human action, but they do not determine it. In his view, people do not act within the context of such structures as society; rather, they act in situations. Large-scale structures are important in that they shape the situations in which individuals act and supply to actors the fixed set of symbols that enable them to act.

Even when Blumer discussed such pre-established patterns, he hastened to make it clear that "areas of unprescribed conduct are just as natural, indigenous, and recurrent in human group life as those areas covered by pre-established and faithfully followed prescriptions of joint action" (Blumer, 1969b:18). Not only are there many unprescribed areas, but even in prescribed areas joint action has to be consistently created and re-created. Actors are guided by generally accepted meanings in this creation and re-creation, but they are not determined by them. They may accept them as is, but they also can make minor and even major alterations in them. In Blumer's (1969b:19) words: "It is the social process in group life that creates and upholds the rules, not the rules that create and uphold group life."

Clearly, Blumer was not inclined to accord culture independent and coercive status in his theoretical system. Nor was he about to accord this status to the extended connections of group life, or what is generally called "social structure," for example the division of labor. "A network or an institution does not function automatically because of some inner dynamics or system requirements; it functions because people at different points do something, and what they do is a result of how they define the situation in which they are called on to act" (Blumer, 1969b:19).

METHODOLOGICAL PRINCIPLES

In addition to its theoretical principles, symbolic interactionism also encompasses a set of methodological postulates. A review of a few of these methodological principles will provide a better basis for understanding the theoretical orientation of symbolic interactionism.

Blumer on Methods

Blumer had great respect for the difficulties involved in studying the action and interaction that take place in the real world. He often spoke of the "obdurate character" of the real world. Sociologists must engage in constant efforts to develop ways of studying it. Scientific models are to be developed and tested in and against the real world, and are only useful if they help us understand that world.

Blumer was a severe critic of what he considered the tendency toward mindless scientism in sociology. He did not reject the use of quantitative methods, though he clearly saw them as far less valuable than most conventional sociologists consider them. There are many methods that may prove useful in understanding the real world. Similarly, Blumer (1956/1969) was critical of the tendency to reduce the complexity of social life to scientific variables. The simplistic correlation of variables tends to ignore the interpretive process that is so central to social life. Blumer (1954/1969:141) criticized abstract theoretical schema for much the same reason: "primarily an interpretation which orders the world into its mold, not a studious cultivation of empirical facts to see if the theory fits."

Blumer was also critical of most sociological concepts that serve as prescriptions for what sociologists should see in the real world. Such concepts do enormous violence to the reality of that world. Instead of traditional concepts, Blumer (1954/1969:148) supported the use of "sensitizing concepts," which simply suggest what to look for and where to look, and which do less violence to the real world. Finally, Blumer urged the use of *sympathetic introspection* in order to study social life. In other words, in their research symbolic interactionists must put themselves in the places of the actors they are studying in order to understand the situation from their point of view. This leads to a preference for "soft" rather than "hard" methods in symbolic interactionism. However, Blumer did not believe that this preference reflects the scientific immaturity of sociology; rather, it indicates the distinctive subject matter of the field.

Blumer was not the only spokesperson for symbolic interactionism on methodological issues (or any other issue, for that matter). We can get a sense of at least one of the schisms in symbolic interactionism by discussing the methodological differences between Blumer, a leading spokesperson for the Chicago school, and Manford Kuhn, the major representative of the Iowa school of symbolic interactionism.

BLUMER VERSUS KUHN ON METHODS

The most basic differences between Blumer and Kuhn are methodological (Meltzer, Petras, and Reynolds, 1975). Blumer, as we have seen, argued for a distinctive methodology for studying human behavior, a methodology that is nongeneralizing. Kuhn (1964), on the other hand, stressed the unity of the scientific method; all scientific fields, including sociology, should aim toward generalization and laws. Although Blumer and Kuhn agreed on at least one essential subject matter of symbolic interactionism—"what goes on 'inside the heads' of humans" (Meltzer, Petras, and Reynolds, 1975:57)—they disagreed on how it should be studied.

Blumer was inclined to use sympathetic introspection in order to get inside the actors' world and view it as they do. Sociologists should use their intuition in order to take the point of view of the actors they are studying, even going so far as using the same categories as they do. Kuhn was interested in the same empirical phenomena, but he urged sociologists to reject nonscientific techniques and instead use overt behavioral indices of what goes on in actors' heads. For instance, the answers of respondents to a series of questions should be the data for the symbolic interactionist to work with, not the "unreliable" and "unscientific" intuition of the sociologist.

In addition, Blumer accepted less formal sensitizing concepts and rejected the use of more scientific operational concepts to define the real world. Kuhn, on the other hand, preferred the traditional scientific methods of using researchable variables and operational definitions. For example, Kuhn operationalized the concept of the self, which can be so elusive in traditional symbolic interactionism, as the answer to the question "Who am I?" The responses that people give to this simple question were viewed as the empirical manifestations of the self. Also, Blumer was inclined to attack sociological variables as mechanistic tools, but Kuhn accepted and used them. While Blumer saw large elements of unpredictability in human action, Kuhn held that action was socially determined and hence could be studied scientifically in the search for antecedent causes of action. Finally, Blumer was inclined to think in terms of continuing processes, while Kuhn was inclined to think in more static terms, which are also more amenable to scientific study.

BLUMER'S INTERPRETATION OF MEAD

The debate between supporters of Blumer and supporters of Kuhn continues, but Blumer's orientation is still the dominant position within symbolic interactionism. However, questions have recently been raised about whether Blumer was being as true to his Meadian roots as he claimed. Clark McPhail and Cynthia Rexroat (1979) argued that there are marked differences between the methodological orientations of Mead and Blumer. Because of the influence of behaviorism, Mead was much more oriented to "hard" science than was Blumer and may, in fact, have been closer to Kuhn than Blumer. As McPhail and Rexroat (1979:449) expressed their position, "Mead's emphasis on systematic observation and experimental investigation is quite different from Blumer's naturalistic methodology. . . . Naturalistic inquiry neither compliments [sic] nor extends Mead's methodological perspective, nor is Blumer's framework suited to the investigation and development of Mead's theoretical ideas."

Blumer (1980) responded heatedly to the charges made by McPhail and Rexroat. He argued that they "seriously misrepresented" his views on social reality and naturalistic study, as well as Mead's views on social behavior and scientific method. McPhail and Rexroat (1980) responded that Blumer in his reply failed to specify his criteria for arguing that they misinterpreted him, and that he failed to utilize systematic evidence in support of his position. Blumer was accused of often failing to cite the relevant passages in Mead's work in his counterargument. McPhail and Rexroat (1980:420) argued that in many cases Blumer "simply asserts that *his* interpretation of Mead is *the* correct one." In the end, we have Blumer proclaiming his interpretation of Mead to be the correct one and McPhail and Rexroat taking the opposite position. Although this debate is of current interest, the historical fact is that it was Blumer's interpretation of Mead's position, not Mead's methodological position itself, that became the dominant orientation in symbolic interactionism.

The key issue in the debate between Blumer and McPhail and Rexroat was the "hard" versus "soft" science issue. In Blumer's view, McPhail and Rexroat are interested in fostering a "hard" science image of Meadian theory:

> I discern underneath the McPhail-Rexroat discussion what they really have in mind in alleging ontological and methodological differences between Mead and me. Their fundamental intention is to justify and promote a special mode of scientific inquiry that relies on controlled experiments. But they also regard themselves as followers of George Herbert Mead. They are, thus, forced to interpret Mead in such a way as to support their methodological orientation. They seek to do this in two ways. First, they try to interpret Mead's thought on "scientific method" in such a way as to uphold their methodological preference. Second, they endeavor to depict Mead's "social behaviorism" in such a manner as to fit their experimental or near-experimental commitment.
>
> (Blumer, 1980:414–415)

In McPhail and Rexroat's response to Blumer, they argued that Mead favored *both* experimental and nonexperimental methods. Whether or not Mead did, McPhail and Rexroat clearly favored a more "hard" science, experimental approach to symbolic interaction than did Blumer. The issue here is whether complex forms of social behavior are amenable to experimental study. Blumer felt that they are not, whereas McPhail and Rexroat felt that they are. What we have here, at least in part, is a more recent version of the debate between Blumer and Kuhn.

CRITICISMS

Having analyzed the ideas of symbolic interactionism, particularly those of the Chicago school of Mead, Blumer, and Goffman, we will now enumerate some of the major criticisms of this perspective.

The first criticism is that the mainstream of symbolic interactionism has too readily given up on conventional scientific techniques. Eugene Weinstein and Judith Tanur (1976:105) expressed this point well: "Just because the contents of consciousness are qualitative, does not mean that their exterior expression cannot be coded, classified even counted." Science and subjectivism are *not* mutually exclusive.

Second, Manford Kuhn (1964), William Kolb (1944), Bernard Meltzer, James Petras, and Larry Reynolds (1975), and many others have criticized the vagueness of essential Meadian concepts such as mind, self, I, and me. Most generally, Kuhn (1964) spoke of the ambiguities and contradictions in Mead's theory. Beyond Meadian theory, they have criticized many of the basic symbolic interactionist concepts for being confused and imprecise and therefore incapable of providing a firm basis for theory and research. Because these concepts are imprecise, it is difficult, if not impossible, to operationalize them; the result is that testable propositions cannot be generated (Stryker, 1980).

The third criticism of symbolic interactionism is that larger structures are ignored. Somewhat less predictable is the fourth criticism, that symbolic interactionism is not sufficiently microscopic, that it ignores the importance of such factors as the unconscious and emotions (Stryker, 1980; Meltzer, Petras, and Reynolds, 1975). Similarly, symbolic interactionism has been criticized for ignoring such psychological factors as needs, motives, intentions, and aspirations. In their effort to deny that there are immutable forces impelling the actor to act, symbolic interactionists have focused instead on meanings, symbols, action, and interaction. They ignore psychological factors that might be impelling the actor, which parallels their neglect of the larger societal constraints on the actor. In both cases, symbolic interactionists are accused of making a "fetish" out of everyday life (Meltzer, Petras, and Reynolds, 1975:85). This, in turn, leads to a marked overemphasis on the immediate situation and an "obsessive concern with the transient, episodic and fleeting" (Meltzer, Petras, and Reynolds, 1975:85).

The major criticism of symbolic interactionism has been of its tendency to ignore large-scale social structures. This has been expressed in various ways. For example, Weinstein and Tanur (1976:106) argued that symbolic interactionism ignores the connectedness of outcomes to each other: *"It is the aggregated outcomes that form the linkages among episodes of interaction that are the concern of sociology qua sociology. . . .* The concept of social structure is necessary to deal with the incredible density and complexity of relations through which episodes of interaction are interconnected." Sheldon Stryker (1980:146) argued that the micro focus of symbolic interactionism serves "to minimize or deny the facts of social structure and the impact of the macro-organizational features of society on behavior." Meltzer, Petras, and Reynolds were inclined to see this weakness at the structural level as one of the two main problems with symbolic interactionism:

> Of all the presumed difficulties of the symbolic interactionist paradigm, then, two stand forth as the most crucial: (1) limited consideration of human emotions, and (2) unconcern with social structure. In effect, the first of these shortcomings implies that symbolic interaction is not psychological enough, while the second implies that symbolic interaction is not sociological enough.
>
> (Meltzer, Petras, and Reynolds, 1975:120)

TOWARD A MORE ADEQUATE SYMBOLIC INTERACTIONISM

To become a more adequate sociological theory symbolic interactionism must focus on both smaller-scale and larger-scale phenomena. The latter seems to be the more important task. We close this chapter with a discussion of the recent work of Sheldon Stryker (1980) and his effort to develop a more macroscopically oriented symbolic interactionism. We agree with David R. Maines (1977), who argued that symbolic interactionism has not competely ignored large-scale social structures, although it has not paid as much attention to them as structural functionalism and conflict theory. However, Maines (1977:235) is also right in arguing that "there is nothing inherent in the perspective that precludes the analysis of social organizations and social structure"— and this is what Stryker's work demonstrates.

Stryker (1980:53) enunciated an integrative goal for symbolic interactionism: "A satisfactory theoretical framework must bridge social structure and person, must be able to move from the level of the person to that of large-scale social structure and back again. . . . There must exist a conceptual framework facilitating movement across the levels of organization and person." Stryker embedded his orientation in Meadian symbolic interactionism but sought to extend it to the societal level, primarily through the utilization of role theory:

> This version begins with Mead, but goes beyond Mead to introduce role theoretic concepts and principles, in order to adequately deal with the reciprocal impact of social person and social structure. The nexus in this reciprocal impact is interaction. It is in the context of the social process—the ongoing patterns of interaction joining individual actors—that social structure operates to constrain the conceptions of self, the definitions of the situation, and the behavioral opportunities and repertoires that bound and guide the interaction that takes place.
> (Stryker, 1980:52)

Stryker developed his orientation in terms of eight general principles:

1. Human action is dependent on a named and classified world in which the names and classifications have meaning for actors. People learn through interaction with others how to classify the world as well as how one is expected to behave toward it.
2. Among the most important things that people learn are the symbols used to designate social *positions*. A critical point here is that Stryker conceived of positions in structural terms: "the relatively stable, morphological components of social structure" (Stryker, 1980:54). Stryker also accorded *roles* central importance, conceiving of them as shared behavioral expectations attached to social positions.
3. Stryker also recognized the importance of larger social structures, although he was inclined, like other symbolic interactionists, to conceive of them in terms of organized patterns of behavior. In addition, his discussion treated social structure as simply the "framework" within which people act. Within these structures people name one another, that is, recognize one another as occupants of positions. In so doing people evoke reciprocal expectations of what each is expected to do.
4. Furthermore, in acting in this context people not only name each other, but they name themselves; that is, they apply positional designations to themselves. These self-designations become part of the self, internalized expectations with regard to their own behavior.
5. When interacting, people define the situation by applying names to it, to other participants, to themselves, and to particular features of the situation. These definitions are then used by the actors to organize their behavior.
6. Social behavior is not determined by social meanings, although it is constrained by them. Stryker is a strong believer in the idea of *role making*. People do not simply take roles; rather, they take an active, creative orientation to their roles.
7. Social structures also serve to limit the degree to which roles are "made" rather than just "taken." Some structures permit more creativity than others.
8. The possibilities of role making make various social changes possible. Changes can occur in social definitions—in names, symbols, and classifications, and in the possibilities for interaction. The cumulative effect of these changes can be alterations in the larger social structures.

Although Stryker offered a useful beginning toward a more adequate symbolic interactionism, his work has a number of limitations. The most notable is that he said little about larger social structures per se. Stryker saw the need to integrate these larger structures in his work, but he recognized that a "full-fledged development of how such incorporation could proceed is beyond the scope of the present work" (Stryker, 1980:69). Stryker saw only a limited future role for large-scale structural variables in symbolic interactionism. He hoped ultimately to incorporate such structural factors as class, status, and power as variables constraining interaction, but he was disinclined to see symbolic interactionism deal with the interrelationships among these structural variables (Stryker, 1980:151). Presumably, this kind of issue is to be left to other theories that focus more on large-scale social phenomena.

SUMMARY

Symbolic interactionism, like structural functionalism, was for many years a dominant force in American sociological theory. Recently, however, it too has receded somewhat in importance. Nevertheless, it has historical and contemporary significance.

This chapter begins with a brief discussion of the roots of symbolic interactionism in philosophical pragmatism (the work of John Dewey) and psychological behaviorism (the work of John B. Watson). Out of the confluence of pragmatism, behaviorism, and other influences, such as Simmelian sociology, symbolic interactionism developed at the University of Chicago in the 1920s.

The symbolic interactionism that developed stood in contrast to the psychological reductionism of behaviorism and the structural determinism of more macro-oriented sociological theories, such as structural functionalism. Its distinctive orientation was toward the mental capacities of actors and their relationship to action and interaction. All of this was conceived in terms of process; there was a disinclination to see the actor impelled by either internal psychological states or large-scale structural forces.

The single most important work in symbolic interactionism is Mead's *Mind, Self and Society*. Basically, Mead sought to extend the principles of psychological behaviorism to one of the basic concerns of pragmatists—mental processes. Mead's great concern was the relationship between mental processes, action, and interaction. In analyzing this relationship, he defined many of the basic interests of symbolic interactionists: gestures, symbols, language, meanings, self, "I" and "me," and socialization. Although Mead told us much about mind and self, his work was relatively impoverished in terms of its analysis of society, of large-scale structures and institutions in general.

The current state of symbolic interactionism may be summarized by the following basic principles:

1. Human beings, unlike lower animals, are endowed with a capacity for thought.
2. The capacity for thought is shaped by social interaction.
3. In social interaction people learn the meanings and the symbols that allow them to exercise their distinctively human capacity for thought.
4. Meanings and symbols allow people to carry on distinctively human action and interaction.
5. People are able to modify or alter the meanings and symbols they use in action and interaction on the basis of their interpretation of the situation.

6. People are able to make these modifications and alterations because, in part, of their ability to interact with themselves, which allows them to examine possible courses of action, assess their relative advantages and disadvantages, and then choose one.
7. The intertwined patterns of action and interaction make up groups and societies.

In the context of these general principles, we seek to clarify the nature of the work of several important thinkers in the symbolic interactionist tradition, including Charles Horton Cooley, Herbert Blumer, Morris Rosenberg, and most important, Erving Goffman. We present in detail Goffman's dramaturgical analysis of the self and his related works on "role distance" and stigma. However, we also note that Goffman's recent work has exaggerated a tendency in his earlier work and moved further in the direction of a structuralist analysis.

Although we are not interested in methodology per se in this book, several of the methodological principles of symbolic interactionism are discussed, since they help us gain a greater understanding of this theoretical orientation. Especially important here is the debate between Blumer, representing the "soft," intuition-guided Chicago school orientation to symbolic interactionism, and Manford Kuhn, representing the more "hard science" approach characteristic of the Iowa school. Although this debate continues, the Chicago approach has predominated within symbolic interactionism.

We close with a discussion of a number of the criticisms of symbolic interactionism, in particular its weakness at the level of large-scale phenomena. In this context we discuss Stryker's recent effort to move symbolic interactionism toward a structural level.

CHAPTER SIX
Phenomenological Sociology and Ethnomethodology

TWO of the most frequently discussed and debated theories in contemporary sociological theory are phenomenological sociology and ethnomethodology. Along with the various neo-Marxian theories discussed in Chapter Four, ethnomethodology and phenomenology are today's "hottest" theories. The two theories are often discussed together. George Ritzer (1975a) sees them as two theoretical components of the social definition paradigm; Monica Morris (1977) sees them as two varieties of what she calls "creative sociology"; and Jack Douglas (1980) includes them under the heading of the "sociologies of everyday life." [1] However, there are persuasive reasons why the two theories should not be discussed together. Thus, after a brief analysis of their similarities and differences, we will analyze the two theories separately. We will first deal with phenomenological sociology because it is the older of the two theories and provided some of the roots for the development of ethnomethodology. Later we will discuss some of the main aspects of ethnomethodology as a sociological theory.

SIMILARITIES AND DIFFERENCES

Contemporary practitioners of both phenomenological sociology and ethnomethodology trace their intellectual roots to a common heritage in the philosophical work of

---

[1] These are not the only theories discussed under these headings. Symbolic interactionism, which we have already discussed at length in Chapter Five, and existential sociology, to be discussed in Chapter Eight, are also often included under these rubrics. However, phenomenological sociology and ethnomethodology are the two theories of this kind that are receiving the most attention.

Edmund Husserl (1859–1938). Many of his ideas are the inspiration for a number of contemporary aspects of phenomenological sociology. More important, they were the major inspiration for the work of Alfred Schutz. Schutz took Husserl's philosophy and transformed it into a sociology, and it is that orientation that lies at the base of both phenomenological sociology and ethnomethodology. Contemporary phenomenological sociology is traceable directly to the work of Schutz. In ethnomethodology, Husserl's influence is less direct. That is, Harold Garfinkel, the founder of ethnomethodology, studied with Schutz, and it is Garfinkel's (and his supporters') adaptation of Schutz's ideas that is a major basis of ethnomethodology.

The two theories have a similar set of interests in the social world. Both theories focus on social definitions—how actors come to define social situations and to act on the basis of those definitions (Ritzer, 1975a). Both are creative sociologies, that is, actors are not seen as passive receptacles, but rather as active creators of the social scene (Morris, 1977). In addition, phenomenology and ethnomethodology both have a micro focus on the sociology of everyday life, that is, on highly commonplace thoughts and actions (Douglas, 1980). Social definitions, creativity, and a micro focus are not the only substantive elements the two theories have in common, but they illustrate their overlapping concerns.

Some followers of both theories do similar kinds of work, especially conceptual pieces. In reading such a work (for instance, Heap and Roth, 1973), it is sometimes difficult to know exactly which theory the author accepts. Despite similarities in conceptual pieces, there are important differences in the realm of empirical research.

Sometimes sociologists identified with one of the theories do work within the other theory. For example, in 1973 George Psathas, edited an anthology of phenomenological essays, *Phenomenological Sociology: Issues and Applications*. Appearing in that book is an essay he coauthored with Frances G. Waksler, which is an excellent example of phenomenological sociology. In 1979 Psathas edited a book on ethnomethodology, *Everyday Language: Studies in Ethnomethodology*. Psathas again included an essay of his own, this time an ethnomethodological analysis. Although Psathas is a rather extreme example, his work is evidence that people can move rather easily from one theory to the other.

In spite of these and other similarities, many adherents of both theories seem to agree that there are differences between the two theories and that it is best to keep them separate. For example, James Heap and Phillip Roth (1973) argued that ethnomethodology involves a combination of phenomenology and elements of sociology that has produced a unique and independent domain of study. Similarly, Don Zimmerman (1978:8) contended that despite their common intellectual heritage, the two theories are not equivalent: "Strictly speaking, the term 'phenomenological' is inappropriate as a blanket characterization of the working tools, methods and problems of ethnomethodology, if for no other reason than that it blurs the distinction between heritage and intellectual content." While phenomenology, both philosophical and sociological, has influenced ethnomethodology, ethnomethodology has also been shaped by linguistics, anthropology, and even mainstream sociology. Ethnomethodology has blended phenomenology with these other sources to produce a theoretical orientation that is not reducible to phenomenology.

One of the key areas of difference between the two theories is the methodology each employs. In general, those who practice phenomenological sociology tend to remain

true to their philosophical roots and to write conceptual pieces and do thought experiments (Freeman, 1980). Phenomenological sociology has spawned comparatively little empirical research in the sense that the term is used in contemporary sociology—that
is, few experiments, surveys, or observational studies. Some see this as inherent in
phenomenological sociology, but others see it as a stage in the development of the
theory. Psathas (1973a:1), for example, said that because of the "current stage" of the
development of phenomenological sociology practitioners focus on their "theoretical
and philosophical underpinnings." Psathas believed that in the future phenomenological sociologists would be doing much more empirical research.

Ethnomethodology, however, has been highly empirical and has produced many
more empirical works than theoretical or philosophical treatises. Examples include
studies of sentence structure, telephone conversations, maps, newspaper reports,
courtroom procedures, and even walking. In these studies ethnomethodologists have
generally used methods not too different from those used in mainstream sociological
research. However, they have also developed some distinctive methodologies. One of
the best known is the so-called *breaching experiments* developed by Garfinkel as a way
of demonstrating basic ethnomethodological principles. The basic procedure is for the
researcher to enter a social setting, violate (or breach) the rules that govern it, and then
study how people deal with the breach. Among other things, what the ethnomethodologist hopes to study is the way people construct, or reconstruct, social reality.
Another rather distinctive methodology is detailed analysis of audio and video tapes.
Ethnomethodologists are very interested in conversational analysis, and they have used
audio tapes to good advantage. Video tapes have proven useful in the analysis of such
behaviors as walking, face-to-face communication, and interaction in various settings.

Robert Freeman (1980) saw these methodological differences as derived from more
fundamental differences in the substantive focuses of the two theories. Phenomenological sociologists have a great concern for consciousness. Ethnomethodologists, following in the phenomenological tradition, accept the fundamental importance of consciousness in social life. However, given their roots in traditional sociology, they tend
to focus on more empirically observable social activities.

One of the most difficult problems in the history of all of sociology has been how to
study consciousness empirically. Like other theorists, phenomenologists have not been
able to solve this problem adequately. As a result their best work lies in their efforts to
philosophize, theorize, or reflect on the operation of consciousness and meaning construction. However, since ethnomethodologists focus on more observable activities
stemming from conscious processes, they can rely more on traditional sociological
research methods.

Finally, Freeman (1980) offered another useful contrast between the two theories
by pointing out that they tend to pick up two different, and in some ways conflicting,
strands in the work of Alfred Schutz. As we will see, Schutz offered a highly complicated and in some ways self-contradictory phenomenological theory. Hence it is entirely
possible for two theoretical schools, both claiming Schutz as their inspiration, to go in
very different directions.

Schutz was interested in consciousness, but as it is constrained by the larger culture
with its language, typifications, and recipes. This orientation most influenced those
phenomenological sociologists who tend to emphasize the constraining effects of cul-

tural phenomena on consciousness. Although they recognize that actors are creative, they emphasize the forces that shape and constrain that creativity. Ethnomethodology tends to focus less on cultural constraints, which means that many of its practitioners have an image of the actor as more creative. The actors are thus seen as sustaining society, not vice versa. Freeman's (1980:134) point was that this image of the actor as more creative is also found in Schutz's work: "Society is regarded as originating in the *sense of social structure* members sustain through their interpretive procedures" (italics added). The emphasis is on the "sense of structure" and how it is constructed and maintained, not on the structure per se.

This is a very gross differentiation between the two schools, and adherents of the two theories cross from one to the other frequently. Also, this characterization of ethnomethodology as concerned with the creative actor does some injustice to at least some contemporary ethnomethodologists, who focus on the constraints on actors; however, they tend to be different constraints than those examined by phenomenological sociologists.

PHENOMENOLOGICAL SOCIOLOGY

The major thinker associated with phenomenological sociology, as we have said, is Alfred Schutz, but we will begin with a brief discussion of the ideas of Edmund Husserl, who was a major influence on the thinking of Alfred Schutz and is also important for his more direct influence on post-Schutzian phenomenological sociologists.

The Ideas of Edmund Husserl

Husserl's highly complicated philosophy is not easily translated into sociological concepts and, indeed, a good portion of it is not directly relevant to sociology. We will discuss here a few of his main ideas as they have proven useful to sociological phenomenologists.

Joseph Kockelmans (1967b:24) noted the essence of the problem in dealing with Husserl's phenomenology, indeed with philosophical phenomenology in general: "Anyone familiar with the situation knows that as soon as he uses the term 'phenomenology' he enters a sphere of ambiguity." This ambiguity is one of the main reasons Husserl's phenomenology is so difficult to translate into usable sociological concepts.

Husserl's general orientation to the social world can be used as a starting point (Freeman, 1980). In general, people view the world in a highly ordered way. Actors are always engaged in the active, and highly complex, process of ordering the world. However, they are most often unaware that they are ordering the social world; hence they do not question it. To Husserl, this is the general thesis of the "natural standpoint." To actors, the social world is naturally ordered, not ordered by them. However, phenomenologists are acutely aware that ordering is being done, and it becomes for them an important subject of phenomenological investigation.

The natural standpoint, or "natural attitude," was conceived by Husserl as an obstacle to the discovery of phenomenological processes. These basic components are hidden to actors and remain hidden to phenomenologists if they are unable to overcome their own natural attitude to the world. Philosophers must be able to set aside ("bracket") the natural attitude so that they will be able to get to the most basic aspects of consciousness. The natural attitude is, to Husserl, a source of bias and distortion for the phenomenologist. In Freeman's (1980) view, this is one of the crucial points on which Schutz differed from Husserl. Whereas the natural attitude was a barrier to Husserl, to Schutz, as we will see, it was a basic subject of phenomenological investigation. One way of interpreting a good portion of Schutz's work is to say that he was engaged in an effort to explain the natural attitude in order to uncover the basic structure of people's commonsense experiences.

One of the key orientations of Husserl's work was the *scientific* study of the basic structures of consciousness. As Husserl put it, he wanted to develop "philosophy as a rigorous science" (cited in Kockelmans, 1967b:26). However, to Husserl science did not mean empiricism and statistics. In fact, he feared that such a science would reject consciousness as an object of scientific scrutiny and that it would either be found too metaphysical or be turned into something physical.[2]

What Husserl did mean by science was a philosophy that was rigorous, systematic, and critical. In utilizing science in this way, phenomenologists could ultimately arrive at absolutely valid knowledge of the basic structures of consciousness. This orientation to science has had two effects on contemporary phenomenologists. First, most modern phenomenological sociologists continue to eschew the tools of modern social science research—elaborate methods, high-powered statistics, and computerized results. They prefer, as did Husserl, a serious and systematic reflection on the nature and constitution of consciousness. Second, modern phenomenologists do not favor vague, "soft" intuitionism. Philosophizing about consciousness is a rigorous and systematic enterprise.

Husserl's phenomenology involves a commitment to penetrate the various layers constructed by actors in the real world in order to get to the essential structure of consciousness. To do this, the phenomenologist must "disconnect" the natural attitude (Freeman, 1980), a very difficult task. Once the natural attitude is set aside, or is "bracketed," the phenomenologist can begin to examine the invariant properties of consciousness that govern all people. The phenomenologist must also set aside the incidental experiences of life that tend to dominate consciousness. Husserl's ultimate objective was to look beyond all the layers in order to see the basic properties of the "transcendental ego" in all its purity.

The idea of the transcendental ego reflects Husserl's interest in the basic and invariant properties of human consciousness. Although he is often misinterpreted on this point, he did not have a mentalistic, metaphysical conception of consciousness. For him, it was not a thing or a place, but rather a process. Consciousness was found not in the head of the actor but in the relationship between the actor and the objects in the world. Husserl expressed this in his notion of *intentionality*. For him, consciousness is always consciousness of something, some object. Consciousness is found in this relationship: consciousness is not interior to the actor, it is relational. Furthermore, mean-

---

[2]These same fears animated the work of the father of symbolic interactionism, George Herbert Mead. Behaviorism, as it was practiced in Mead's day, and even today, either rejects the idea of consciousness or turns it into physical phenomena.

ing does not inhere in the objects but in the relationship of actors to those objects. This conception of consciousness as a process that gives meaning to objects is at the heart of contemporary phenomenological sociology.

INTERPRETING HUSSERL'S IDEAS

Heap and Roth (1973) pointed out that many contemporary phenomenological sociologists who operate within the Husserlian tradition have done grave damage to his original orientation. An overriding problem from their point of view is that sociologists have used Husserl's terminology as it is understood in everyday conversation rather than as it was meant by Husserl or used by rigorous phenomenologists. Let us look at a few examples.

Heap and Roth (1973:355) argued that Husserl's concept of *intention* is "greatly misunderstood and misinterpreted." For example, sociologists have interpreted intention as relaxed when things are running smoothly for the actors, but called into play when problems arise in the social world. However, for Husserl, intentionality is not operant at some times and inoperant at others. Rather, consciousness always involves intentionality and an object. What some sociologists are thinking of here is the ability of actors to attend to objects, which actors may or may not do. However, whether or not actors pay attention to the world, take note of it, and try to manipulate it, their consciousness involves intentionality for, according to Heap and Roth (1973:355), "intention is an essential feature of consciousness *prior to* the operation of attention" (italics added). Or, to put it another way, "Consciousness is not 'intentionally' directed—consciousness *is* intentional" (Heap and Roth, 1973:355).

Another Husserlian concept that has been misinterpreted by some sociologists is the idea of *reduction*, or *bracketing*. To some sociologists this often means reducing one aspect of the real world to another aspect of that world. In this sense of the word, Marx might be said to be reducing ideological manifestations to their material or economic roots. However, this is not what phenomenologists mean by reduction. Instead of reduction within the empirical world, the phenomenologist brackets all of the empirical world in order to get at the essence of consciousness. (Again, to bracket is to set aside the idea that the real world is naturally ordered.) Thus, the phenomenologist, unlike Marx, would bracket not only ideological factors but material factors as well. No sociologists, not even ethnomethodologists, bracket the real world, since their primary concerns lie in that realm.

Heap and Roth offered a further example of a sociological distortion of a phenomenological concept. That is the idea of *phenomenon*, clearly implied as a basic concern of phenomenology. Husserl urged that phenomenologists return to the things in themselves, phenomena devoid of reality attributed to them by actors in the real world. Thus those sociologists are wrong who argue that Durkheim's dictum that social facts are to be studied as things is the equivalent of Husserl's idea that we should return to the things themselves. Durkheim's social facts are still theoretical constructs, whereas Husserl's phenomena are devoid of *all* theorizing.

Finally, we come to the Husserlian concept of *essence*. To Husserl, essences are the invariant properties of consciousness that do not exist in the real world (Heap and

Roth, 1973:358). When sociologists invoke Husserl's concept of essence, they are most often referring to what they consider to be the essential aspect of the world. It is probably important to look for such essential structures, but it is important to recognize that one is not looking for essences in the sense used by Husserl.

The basic problem, in Heap and Roth's view, is that sociologists interested in phenomenology have used the terminology of phenomenology but have fundamentally misunderstood the original meanings. In fact, to be absolutely faithful to phenomenology, sociology would have to be fundamentally reconstituted, a dramatic alteration not envisioned by many sociologists attracted to Husserlian theory: "Any attempt to graft phenomenological concepts onto a sociology that has not been fundamentally reconstituted can only lead to a distortion, if not perversion, of both phenomenology and sociology" (Heap and Roth, 1973:359). In sum, "the possibility of a phenomenological sociology in the sense envisioned by Husserl is highly questionable" (Heap and Roth, 1973:361).

The Ideas of Alfred Schutz[3]

The major inheritor and interpreter of Husserl's ideas in sociology is Alfred Schutz. Schutz produced a complex body of work that has been subjected to many interpretations. We can divide interpretations of Schutz's work into three camps. First, some phenomenologists (and ethnomethodologists) saw in Schutz the source of their interest in the way actors create or construct social reality. Among the ethnomethodologists, for example, Hugh Mehan and Houston Wood (1975:115) argued that the focus of their approach was on the way actors "create situations and rules, and so at once create themselves and their social realities." They went on to say that "ethnomethodologists adopted this research program from Schutz" (Mehan and Wood, 1975:115). Monica Morris (1977:15), in her book on creative sociology, came to a similar conclusion: "For Schutz, the subject matter of sociology is the manner in which human beings constitute, or create, the world of everyday life." These commentators, as well as many others, have generally seen Schutz as focusing on the way actors create social reality, and they have lauded him for this micro orientation.

Other commentators have taken a similar view of the substance of his work but have come to very different conclusions about it. A good example is Robert Bierstedt, who criticized Schutz for his focus on the way actors construct social reality and his corresponding lack of concern with the reality of the larger structures of society:

> The phenomenological reduction . . . has consequences of a . . . rather serious kind for sociology. . . . Society itself, as an objective phenomenon, tends to disappear in the realm of the intersubjective. That is, society itself . . . comes to be a creation of the mind in intersubjectivity and something that is wholly exhausted in the common-place affairs of daily living.
> (Bierstedt, 1963:91)

Thus Bierstedt criticized Schutz for precisely the same thing for which Mehan and Wood, Morris, and others praised him.

---

[3]This section was coauthored with Roger Reitman.

ALFRED SCHUTZ: A Biographical Sketch

Alfred Schutz was not widely known during his lifetime, and it is only in recent years that his work has attracted the attention of large numbers of sociologists. Although his obscurity was in part a result of his intellectual orientation—his then highly unusual interest in phenomenology—a more important cause was his very unusual career as a sociologist.

Born in Vienna, Austria, in 1899 Schutz received his academic training at the University of Vienna. In 1932 he published what was to become an important book in sociology, *The Phenomenology of the Social World*. It was not translated into English until 1967, so that a wide appreciation of Schutz's work in the United States was delayed thirty-five years. As World War II approached Schutz emigrated to the United States, where for many years he divided his time between serving as legal counsel to a number of banks and writing about and teaching phenomenological sociology. Simultaneously with his work in banking, Schutz taught courses at the New School for Social Research in New York City. As Richard Grathoff (1978:112) points out, the result was that "the social theorist for whom scientific thought and everyday life defined two rather distinct and separate realms of experience upheld a similar division in his personal life." Not until 1953 did Schutz give up his dual career and concentrate entirely on teaching and writing phenomenological sociology. It was because of his interest in phenomenology, his dual career, and his teaching at the then avant-garde New School that Schutz remained on the periphery of sociology during his lifetime. Nevertheless, Schutz's work and his influence on students (for example, Peter Berger, Thomas Luckmann, Harold Garfinkel) moved him to the center of sociological theory.

Another factor in Schutz's marginal position in sociological theory was that his theory seemed highly abstract and irrelevant to the mundane social world. Although Schutz did separate theory from reality, he did not feel that his work was irrelevant to the world in which he lived. To put it in terms of his phenomenology, he saw a relationship between the everyday construction of reality and the pre-given historical and cultural world. To think otherwise is to think that the man who fled National Socialism (Nazism) regarded his academic work as irrelevant. The following quotation from one of his letters indicates that while Schutz was not optimistic, he was not prepared to accept the irrelevance of his theorizing and, more generally, the social construction of reality to the world as a whole:

> You are still optimist enough to believe that phenomenology may save itself among the ruins of this world—as the *philosophica aera perennis*? I do not believe so. More likely the African natives must prepare themselves for the ideas of national socialism. This shall not prevent us from dying the way we have lived; and we must try, therefore, to build . . . order into *our* world, which we must find lacking in—our *world*. The whole conflict is hidden in this shift of emphasis.
>
> (Grathoff, 1978:130)

In short, although the ability of people to affect the larger society is restricted by such phenomena as Nazism, they must continue to strive to build a social and cultural reality that is *not* beyond their reach and control.

Although these two camps came to very different conclusions about Schutz's work, they did at least agree on its focus. A third school of thought, however, views Schutz in an almost diametrically opposite way, as a cultural determinist. For example, Robert Gorman (1975a, 1975b, 1977) suggested that, contrary to the interpretations of the ethnomethodological and sociological establishments, Schutz emphasized the constraints imposed on the actor by society. Actors do not freely choose beliefs or courses of action, nor do they freely construct a sense of social reality. Rather, as members of society, they are free only to obey.

> Socially determined action patterns are adhered to by free actors. Each actor bases his action on his stock of knowledge at hand, and this knowledge consists of these socially determined action patterns. Each of us chooses, for himself, to act as these patterns prescribe, even though they have been imposed from outside.
>
> (Gorman, 1975a:11)

Gorman (1977:71) concluded that for Schutz "social behavior is apparently caused by factors independent of the subject [actor]."

As we discuss Schutz's ideas in some detail and clarify them, we hope also to shed some light on the debate implied by the three contrasting views of his work. Much of the debate arises because of the difference between those things Schutz was willing to philosophize about and those that he considered amenable to scientific analysis.

SCIENCE AND THE SOCIAL WORLD

Schutz tried to provide both a philosophical base for sociology and the basic premises of a science of sociology. He philosophized a great deal about what we may term "consciousness" as well as the actions that emanate from conscious processes. He recognized that people have minds, that they engage in the social construction of reality, and that their constructions set the limits for their activity. It is social actors who construct the social world through their conscious activity. The constructions, in turn, constrain further creative activity. Schutz provided us with a dialectical image of social reality in which, on the one hand, people are constrained by social forces and, on the other, people are able and are sometimes forced to overcome these constraints.

Although the social world is in actuality peopled by social actors who have minds and who engage in creative activity, and although Schutz discussed this world at length and offered rich insights into it, he concluded that it is not amenable to scientific analysis. As we shall see, what Schutz called "we relations" and the world of directly experienced reality (*umwelt*) are difficult if not impossible to analyze scientifically. Consciousness and the social construction of reality are far too ephemeral and idiosyncratic to be subject to the rigorous demands of an objective science. Schutz argued that a science of sociology must focus on social forces in abstraction. These forces have been constructed, negotiated, and modified in social interaction, but as ongoing processes, they cannot be studied scientifically.

Schutz found himself in the paradoxical position of attempting to develop a subjective sociology in the tradition of Max Weber while also meeting, like Husserl, the demands of a rigorous conception of science. As Schutz (1962:35) put it: "How is it,

then, possible to grasp by a system of objective knowledge subjective meaning structures?'' As we will see in the rest of this section, the bulk of Schutz's work was
devoted to answering this question.

REALMS OF THE SOCIAL WORLD

Schutz identified four distinct realms of social reality. Each is an abstraction of the
social world and is distinguished by its degree of immediacy (the degree to which
situations are within reach of the actor) and determinability (the degree to which they
can be controlled by the actor). The four realms are: *umwelt*, the realm of directly experienced social reality; *mitwelt*, the realm of indirectly experienced social reality;
folgewelt, the realm of successors; and *vorwelt*, the realm of predecessors. The realms
of successors and predecessors (*folgewelt* and *vorwelt*) were of peripheral interest to
Schutz. However, we shall deal with them briefly because the contrast between them
illustrates some of the characteristics of Schutz's major focus—the *umwelt* and the
mitwelt.

FOLGEWELT AND VORWELT   The future (*folgewelt*) is a purely residual
category in Schutz's work (in contrast to Marx's, where it plays a crucial role in his
dialectic). It is a totally free and completely indeterminate world that is not dominated
by any scientific laws. It can only be anticipated by the social scientist in a very general
way and cannot be pictured in any detail. Given its indeterminate quality, it falls outside the bounds of Schutz's scientific work.

The past (*vorwelt*), on the other hand, is partially amenable to scientific analysis.
The action of those who lived in the past is totally determined; there is no element of
freedom, since the causes of their actions, the actions themselves, and their outcomes
have already occurred. Despite its determinacy, the study of predecessors presents difficulties for a subjective sociology. It is difficult to interpret the actions of people who
lived in an earlier time because we would probably have to utilize contemporary categories of thought in the historical glance back rather than the categories that prevailed
at the time. The interpretation of contemporaries is likely to be more accurate because
sociologists will share interpretive categories with those whose action they seek to
understand. Thus, although a subjective sociology of the past is possible, the probability of misinterpretation is great.

The essential point here is that the objective for Schutz was to develop a sociology
based on the interpretations of the social world made by the actors being studied. It is
difficult to know the interpretations of predecessors and impossible to understand those
of successors. However, it is possible to understand contemporaries (*mitwelt*) and even
more possible to understand the interpretations of those with whom we are in immediate face-to-face contact (*umwelt*).

UMWELT   The realms of directly experienced social reality (*umwelt*) and indirectly
experienced social reality (*mitwelt*) are more central to Schutz's work. Within the
realm of immediate experience the social construction of reality takes place and the
scientist has a good chance of understanding it. An analysis of the actor's experience
within immediate social reality would necessarily deal with both the actor's con-

sciousness and face-to-face interaction. Within this realm the actor, in Schutz's view, has a considerable amount of freedom and creativity. But Schutz asserted that the free, conscious, and therefore unpredictable actor is outside the realm of scientific sociology. Although Schutz recognized the creative potential of mental processes and offered many philosophical insights into their operation, he eliminated them from scientific consideration. Schutz (1932/1967:190) went so far as to say that we can ignore "the ultimate roots of the action in the person's consciousness."

Schutz was disinclined to deal with face-to-face interaction in the *umwelt* for much the same reason. All people have minds and are therefore unpredictable, especially in their face-to-face interaction with other people. After all, in the process of relating to other people individuals can, and very often do, change their actions based on what other people do, or even on what they think other people have in mind. As with mental processes, Schutz was inclined to eliminate face-to-face interaction from scientific sociology. In Schutz's terms, the *umwelt*, the world composed of directly experienced fellow interactants, cannot be part of a science of sociology. What, then, is the appropriate subject matter of scientific sociology? Instead of looking at the *umwelt*, Schutz focused on the *mitwelt*, or the realm of contemporaries whom sociologists do not encounter as actual individuals but merely as types.

MITWELT   The *mitwelt* is that aspect of the social world in which people ordinarily deal with types of people, or with larger social structures, rather than with actual actors. People do fill these types and these structures, but in the world of contemporaries, these people are rarely experienced directly. Since actors are dealing with types rather than with actual people, their knowledge of people is not subject to constant revision on the basis of face-to-face interaction. This relatively constant knowledge of general types of subjective experience can be studied scientifically and can help shed light on the general process by which people deal with the social world.

The *mitwelt* is a stratified world involving a number of different levels arranged in terms of degree of anonymity. The more anonymous the level, the more people's relationships are amenable to scientific study. Some of the major levels within the *mitwelt*, beginning with the least anonymous, are:

1.   Those whom actors encountered on a face-to-face basis in the past and could meet once again. Actors are likely to have fairly current knowledge of them since they have been met before and could be met again. Although there is a relatively low level of anonymity here, such a relationship does not involve ongoing face-to-face interaction. If these people were to be met personally at a later date, this relationship would become part of the *umwelt* and no longer be part of the *mitwelt*.
2.   Those once encountered not by us but by people with whom we deal. Since this level is based on second-hand knowledge of others, it involves more anonymity than the level of relationships with people we have encountered in the past. If we were ever to meet people at this level, the relationship would become part of the *umwelt*.
3.   Those whom we are on the way to meet. As long as we have not yet met them, we relate to them as types, but once we actually meet them, the situation again becomes part of the *umwelt*.
4.   Those whom we know not as concrete individuals but simply as positions and roles. For example, we know that there are people who sort our mail or process

our checks, but, although we have attitudes about them as types, we never encounter them personally.

5. Collectivities whose function we may know without knowing any of the individuals who exist within them. For example, we know about the Senate, but
few people actually know any of the individuals in it, although we do have the
possibility of meeting those people.

6. Collectivities that are so anonymous that we have little chance of ever encountering people in them. For most people, the Mafia would be an example of such a
collectivity.

7. Objective structures of meaning that have been created by contemporaries with
whom actors do not have, and have not had, face-to-face interaction. The rules of
English grammar would be an example of such a structure of meaning.

8. Physical artifacts that have been produced by a person we have not met and
whom we are not likely to meet. For example, people would have a highly anonymous relationship with a museum painting.

As we move further into the *mitwelt* relationships, they become more impersonal
and anonymous. People do not have face-to-face interaction with others and thus cannot know what goes on in others' minds. Their knowledge is therefore restricted to
"general types of subjective experience" (Schutz, 1932/1967:181).

Typifications can be defined as *recipes* for action that exist in the culture as a whole.
As people are socialized, they learn these recipes, these typical actions for typical
situations, and use them in situations they have learned are appropriate for them. In any
given situation an action is determined "by means of a type constituted in earlier experiences" (Schutz and Luckmann, 1973:229). These typifications are part of the
social stock of knowledge, but we also carry many of them around in our heads as a
result of socialization. Knowledge of contemporaries is not of a specific person, but of
a *type* of person. For example, it is not necessary to know the particular person who
sorts and distributes the mail; it is enough to have knowledge of the type of person who
does that and the type of actions that person undertakes. Within the realm of indirect
experience, knowledge is "homogeneous and repeatable" and shared by people, with
the result that it is amenable to scientific study.

Although cultural typifications of contemporaries are constant, we often encounter
unusual situations, or we may find that a tried and true recipe does not work in a given
situation. We could conceivably meet an actual contemporary (for example, the person
who sorts our mail) and revise our typifications of such a person on the basis of the encounter. Or we could be forced to revise our typifications if the actual person *did not
behave as we expected*. We may, for example, expect a post-office employee to sort
our mail accurately, but we may be forced to revise that typification if we constantly
receive the wrong mail. Remember, however, that while we may revise our own typifications, the cultural typifications remain untouched.

SCIENTIFIC PROCEDURES

While Schutz was well aware of the ability of actors to revise typifications in the real
world, he constructed a scientific world in which actors lack this kind of freedom. In
developing such a science Schutz utilized concepts that tried to capture the meaning of

the social world from the actor's perspective. In Schutz's (1962:59) words: "The thought objects constructed by the social scientist, in order to grasp . . . reality, have to be founded upon the thought objects constructed by the commonsense thinking of men, living their daily life within their social world." However, in order to meet the demands of "science" the meaning of the world from the actor's perspective must be captured in abstraction from its unique and unpredictable expression within immediate reality.

How does the social scientist proceed? The investigator must first establish a scientific attitude. There are three crucial differences between the commonsense and scientific attitudes toward the social world. First, the commonsense actor is pragmatically oriented to the social world. The scientist, in contrast, is disinterested; the theorizing of the scientist serves no pragmatic purpose in the actor's everyday world. Second, the stock of knowledge of the commonsense actor is derived from the everyday world, whereas that of the scientist is scientifically derived. Third, the scientist must become detached from his or her personal biographical situation during the investigative process. Typifications within the commonsense world, in contrast, receive a unique *biographical* expression. Once the social scientist has established detachment, the first step, attaining a scientific attitude, has been reached.

In the second step the investigator mentally replaces actual human beings with puppets (homunculi) created by the social scientist (Schutz, 1962:40). The content of the puppets' consciousness is restricted to what is necessary to perform the typical course of action relevant to the scientific problem. The puppets are not embedded in biographical situations. They do not selectively perceive objects in their environment that are relevant for the solution of problems at hand. The puppets do not choose, nor do they have knowledge outside of the typical knowledge imputed to them by the social scientist. In short, the homunculi are completely determined by typifications; they are animated and constrained entirely by social forces.

Finally, with the construction of homunculi, the social scientist is ready to perform a series of thought experiments. A puppet is placed in a number of hypothetical situations. The objective is to delineate the ideal-typical courses of action that the puppet should take in such situations. Since the puppet lacks consciousness, its courses of action are completely determined by social forces. This scientific orientation conveys the importance of cultural and social constraints in Schutz's thinking about social life. This theme of external constraint is also prominent in his thoughts on the topic of the next section, the life world.

THE LIFE WORLD

To Schutz the concept *life world* encompasses the cultural, taken-for-granted framework of social life and its impact on the thoughts and actions of actors. While he was interested in the impact of cultural forces on actors, Schutz accorded at least as great significance to the cultural level itself. He was most interested in culturally prescribed and socially transmitted patterns of belief and conduct. The cultural components of the life world both precede and will succeed us in time. This framework, imposed on us from outside, is not a continuing individual construction of reality. It serves to constrain actors, to set limits on their everyday conduct. Actors are provided with ready-made courses of action, solutions to problems, interpretations of the social world, and so forth. As a result, in nonproblematic situations actors tend to be reduced to habitual response patterns. In the *mitwelt* actors are likely to experience few problematic situations and therefore have little need to question the taken-for-granted cultural framework. However, in the *umwelt* more problematic situations are likely to arise in face-to-face relations, with the result that typifications are more likely to be called into question. For example, meeting a semiliterate college professor would lead us to question our typifications of professors.

The life world includes the totality of typifications upon which all experience, knowledge, and conduct are based. It is a world taken for granted by the typical actor; it is simply there. While particular typifications may be questioned, the larger structure of typifications ordinarily is not. That the social world is, to a large extent, predefined by cultural impositions leads, paradoxically, to more freedom for actors. Because actors do *not* have to negotiate every aspect of every situation, and can rely on definition by type and conduct by recipe, they are then free to modify knowledge and conduct in particular problematic parts of their lives.

COMPONENTS OF THE LIFE WORLD: CULTURE AND THE INDIVIDUAL

Schutz was interested in specific components of the life world, for example, the three routine elements of knowledge that are part of the taken-for-granted reality of everyday life—knowledge of skills, useful knowledge, and knowledge of recipes. Each is part of the social stock of knowledge and leads to more or less habitual action.

Knowledge of skills is the most basic form of knowledge in that it rarely becomes problematic and is thus accorded a high degree of certainty. An example is the skill of walking. (A rare exception would be in the case of a temporary paralysis.)

Useful knowledge is a definite solution to a problem that was once problematic. Although this type of knowledge is not absolutely trustworthy, it has achieved a high level of certainty. Examples include courses of action, such as driving a car or playing a piano, as well as intellectual perspectives, such as philosophy.

Knowledge of recipes, the third form of habitual knowledge, is the most variable but is still standardized. In certain situations, recipes are called forth as standard ways to cope. Whenever possible an actor will employ a recipe. For example, in dealing with most customers a salesperson can use time-tested techniques, but should the situation become problematic and the customer behave in unusual ways, the salesperson can employ an alternative recipe or even come up with an innovative response.

Schutz was also aware that all the elements of the cultural realm can and often do vary from individual to individual because personal experience differs. In Schutz's terms, the stock of knowledge is "biographically articulated." It has a private component. However, even this unique and private component of the stock of knowledge is not solely of the actor's own making: "It must be stressed . . . that sequence, experiential depth and nearness, and even the duration of experiences and the acquisition of knowledge, are socially objectivated and determined. In other words, there are social categories of biographical articulation" (Schutz and Luckmann, 1973:113).

Because of their source in individual biography, private stocks of knowledge are not part of the life world. Since they are biographical in nature, Schutz did not feel that the unique and private components of knowledge are amenable to scientific study. They are, in Schutz's view, nonetheless important components of the everyday life of actual actors.

RELATIONSHIPS IN THE LIFE WORLD   Within the life world are both we and they relations. Schutz felt that only the latter could be studied scientifically. To understand why, we need to look at both sorts of relations.

We relations are defined by a relatively high degree of intimacy, which is determined by the extent to which the actors are acquainted with one another's personal biographies. The pure we relation is a face-to-face relationship "in which the partners are aware of each other and sympathetically participate in each other's lives for however short a time" (Schutz, 1932/1967:164). The we relation encompasses the consciousness of the participants as well as the patterns of action and interaction that characterize face-to-face interaction. To put it another way, the we relation is characteristic of the *umwelt*. Relations at this level are far too problematic, far too subject to idiosyncratic negotiation by actors, to be treated by scientific sociology. Finally, the we relation is distinguished from the they relation by the particular orientation to the other person in the interaction. Specifically, the we relation is characterized by a "thou orientation," which "is the universal form in which the other is experienced 'in person'" (Schutz and Luckmann, 1973:62). In other words, we relations are highly personal and immediate.

The immediacy of interaction has two implications for social relations. First, in a we relation, unlike in a they relation, there are abundant indicators of the other's subjective experience. Immediacy allows each actor to enter into the consciousness of the other. Second, when entering any social relation, we or they, an individual has only typical knowledge of the other. However, in the continuing process of a face-to-face interaction, typifications of the other are tested, revised, re-enacted, and modified. That is, interaction with others necessarily modifies typologies.

Schutz not only offered a number of insights into we relations per se, but also linked these relationships to cultural phenomena in the real world. For example, in we relations actors learn the typifications that allow them to survive socially. Without recipes, actors would have to invent a proper response in every new situation. Clearly people need typifications in order to live socially. They are learned within the everyday life world through socialization by parents, teachers, and peers, generally in we relations. This socialization takes place throughout the life cycle as people acquire the recipes they need in order to survive in different settings.

People not only learn recipes in we relations but use them there as well—trying them out, altering them when they prove ineffective or inappropriate. In general, people use recipes as long as they work; they "try to determine new situations as familiar" (Schutz and Luckmann, 1973:141). However, because the everyday world often proves unreceptive to typical courses of action, a recipe that has worked many times in the past may prove ineffective. In these circumstances actors, using their creative minds, abandon a typical strategy and invent a new one appropriate to this particular circumstance or person. Although Schutz recognized that this happens in the everyday world, he did not regard it as an appropriate subject matter for a scientific sociology, since it is so unpredictable. Schutz could and did philosophize about such matters, but he did not believe they could be studied scientifically. However, as we will see later in this chapter, some of his modern disciples, especially in ethnomethodology, disagreed and sought to study we relations scientifically.

Schutz was aware that there is considerable give-and-take among actors in we relations. People try out different courses of action on other people. They may quickly abandon those that elicit hostile reactions while they continue to use those that are accepted. People may also find themselves in situations where recipes do not work at all, and they must create appropriate and workable sets of actions. In other words, in we relations people are constantly adjusting their actions to those with whom they interact.

People also adjust their conceptions of others. They enter a given relationship with certain assumptions about what the other actors are thinking. In general, people assume that the thinking of others is of the same order as their own. Sometimes this is confirmed by what they find, but in other circumstances the facial expressions, the movements, the words, and the actions of others may be inconsistent with people's sense of what others are thinking. People must then revise their view of others' thought processes and then adjust their responses on the basis of this new image of what others are thinking. This is an indirect process, since people cannot actually know what others are thinking. Thus they may tentatively change their actions in the hope that this will elicit responses consistent with what they now think is going on in others' minds. People may be forced to revise their conception of others' thought processes and their actions a number of times before they are able to understand why others are acting in a particular way. It is even conceivable that in some instances people cannot make an adequate number of adjustments, with the result that they are likely to flee the particular interaction completely confused. In such a case, they may seek out more comfortable situations where familiar recipes can be applied.

Even within we relations in everyday life most action is guided by recipes. People do not *usually* reflect on what they do or on what others do. However, when they encounter problems, inappropriate thoughts and actions, they must abandon their recipes and reflect on what is going on in order to create an appropriate response. This is psychologically costly to people, who prefer to act and interact in accord with recipes.

In contrast to we relations, they relations can be studied scientifically. What interested Schutz as a scientist are routine aspects of social reality, those that are dominated by cultural forces. They relations—which are found within the realm of Schutz's interest, the *mitwelt*—fall into this category. *They relations* are characterized by interaction with impersonal contemporaries (for example, the unseen postal employee who sorts our mail) rather than associates (for example, a personal friend). In they relations the thoughts and actions of people are dominated by anonymous typifications.

In the "pure" they relation the typical schemes of knowledge used to define other actors are not available for modification. Since we do not interact with actual people but with impersonal contemporaries, information that varies from our typifications is not provided to us. In other words, new experiences are not constituted in they relations. Cultural typifications determine action, and they cannot be altered by the thoughts and actions of actors in a they relationship. Thus, whereas we relations are subject to negotiation, they relations are not. A science of typifications is possible in they relations. Although Schutz held this view, he was aware that these typifications have their historical roots in a group of people's thoughts and actions: "The first and originally objective solution of a problem was still largely dependent on the subjective relevance awareness of the individual" (Schutz and Luckmann, 1973:225). However, these solutions ultimately become more typified and anonymous—in short, more and more a part of the cultural realm.

CONSCIOUSNESS

If the action and interaction patterns of we relations are not amenable to scientific study, then it is far less likely that one can study scientifically what goes on in individual consciousness. Schutz believed that in the everyday life world, as long as things are proceeding smoothly in accord with recipes, actors pay little attention to what is going on in the minds of others. Similarly, he believed (in contrast to Husserl) that in a science of sociology one can also ignore individual consciousness (Schutz, 1932/ 1967:190). In fact, because Schutz found the mind impervious to scientific study, and because he wanted to focus instead on cultural typifications, he admitted that in his own work he was going to "abandon the strictly phenomenological method," which has historically focused on mental processes (Schutz, 1932/1967:97). We thus have the paradoxical situation of a sociologist who is the field's best-known phenomenologist saying that he is abandoning the subject matter he is best known for.

Despite Schutz's avowed position on science, he offered many philosophical insights into consciousness. In fact, Schutz (1932/1967:11) argued that the base of all of his sociological concerns lay in the "processes of meaning establishment and understanding occurring within individuals, processes of interpretation of the behavior of other people and processes of self-interpretation."

The philosophical basis of Schutz's image of the social world, albeit a basis that is, for him, not amenable to scientific study, is deep consciousness (*durée*), in which is found the processes of meaning establishment, understanding, interpretation, and self-interpretation. A phenomenological sociology must be based on "the way meaning is constituted in the individual experience of the solitary Ego. In so doing we shall track meaning to its very point of origin in the inner time consciousness in the duration of the ego as it lives through its experience" (Schutz, 1932/1967:13). This is the domain that was of central concern to Schutz's philosophical predecessors, Henri Bergson and Edmund Husserl. They were interested in philosophizing about what went on in the mind, but Schutz wanted to turn this interest into a scientific sociological concern.

Schutz was drawn to the work of Max Weber, particularly that part of Weber's work concerned with social action, because it reflected, he thought, both an interest in consciousness and a concern for a scientific sociology. But Weber was a less-than-satisfying model for Schutz. To Schutz, the problem with Weber's work was that there were inadequacies in his conception of consciousness. Weber failed to distinguish among types of meanings and he failed to distinguish meanings from motives. In clarifying what Weber failed to do, Schutz told us much about his own conception of consciousness.

In distinguishing meanings from motives, Schutz differentiated between two subtypes of both meanings and motives. Although he did not always succeed in keeping them neatly separated, for Schutz *meanings* concern how actors determine what aspects of the social world are important to them, while *motives* involve the reasons actors do what they do. One type of meaning is the *subjective* meaning context. That is, through our own independent mental construction of reality, we define certain components of reality as meaningful. However, while this process is important in the everyday life world, Schutz did not see it as amenable to scientific study because it is too idiosyncratic.

What is of concern to scientific sociology is the second type of meaning, the *objective* meaning context, the sets of meanings that exist in the culture as a whole and that are the shared possession of the collectivity of actors. Since these sets of meanings are shared rather than idiosyncratic, they are as accessible to sociologists as to anyone else. Since they have an objective existence, they can be studied scientifically by the sociologist, and they were one of Schutz's main concerns. Schutz was critical of Weber for failing to differentiate between subjective and objective meaning and for failing to make it clear that only objective meaning contexts can be scrutinized in scientific sociology.

Schutz also differentiated between two types of motives—"in order to" and "because." Both involve the meaningful reasons for an individual's actions, but only because motives are accessible to the sociologist. *In-order-to motives* are the reasons an actor undertakes certain actions in an effort to bring about some future occurrence. They are only apparent when the action is taking place. They are part of deep consciousness, the continuing stream of consciousness, and as such are inaccessible to the scientific sociologist. Sociology cannot concern itself with in-order-to motives because they cannot be studied scientifically. But sociology can study *because motives*, or retrospective glances at the factors that have caused individuals to behave as they did. Since the actions have already occurred, the motives for them are accessible to both the social scientist and the actor. In fact, however, Schutz was as little inclined to scientifically study because motives as in-order-to motives. Both are much too subjective, much too individualistic, for his scientific work, although that did not stop him from philosophizing about them.

SOCIAL ACTION AND PROBLEMATIC SITUATIONS

Action is conduct that is based on a preconceived plan. The plan makes action meaningful from the point of view of the social actor. Without it, behavior becomes mere unconscious doing. If the plan or project takes into account another actor, then it becomes social action. Further, all action necessarily involves choice among projects. If there were no alternatives to choose among, conduct would require no project and, once again, behavior would be reduced to mere unconscious doing. Action, involving the process of ascertaining and choosing between alternative projects, becomes necessary only when the application of recipes to typically defined situations is no longer adequate to accomplish practical purposes, that is, when situations become problematic.

When situations become problematic, typical knowledge and routine patterns of conduct are no longer sufficient for the mastery of situations. At this point the actor must consciously choose a behavioral response to the problematic situation. Action necessarily involves choosing among plans, projects, or alternative lines of conduct. In the enactment of the chosen project of action new experiences are constituted; an addition has been made to the existing stock of knowledge.

When problematic situations are social, then the solution, the choosing and enactment of a plan, is "social" action, action that is oriented toward another actor. The dynamics of consciousness that underlie social action (the coming to be of a "problem," the positing of alternative courses of conduct, and the ultimate choice and enactment of a project) are the foundations upon which we relations are based. A we relation is a relation in which the subjective consciousness of one actor is oriented toward the consciousness of another actor. We relations presume social action. The implication is that in every immediate, intense, and vivid interaction in which there is a reciprocal thou orientation (each actor is oriented to the consciousness of the other), perceptions of the social world are available for modification; new types are formed; and the social stock of knowledge is enlarged.

Action, according to Schutz's formulation of the concept, represents the manifestation of voluntarism at the individual level. The actor is a "free agent" in choosing among projects of action, although choosing is limited by one's stock of knowledge on hand. The stock of knowledge, the set of types that underlies the actor's conception of and behavior within the social world, is the base. The conscious choice of conduct in response to a problematic situation is what modifies or enlarges the stock of knowledge.

INTERPRETING SCHUTZIAN THEORY

As we noted at the beginning of this section, some commentators praise Schutz for his micro focus on how actors create the social world. Others criticize him for this. Still others see Schutz as having a large-scale cultural focus. All three positions are defensible, at least to some degree. The first two rely on Schutz's philosophical ideas, while the third focuses on his thoughts about scientific sociology. Followers of the first position applaud Schutz for creating a philosophical sociology of consciousness. Those who take the second position criticize Schutz for this orientation and for his failure to deal adequately with social structures. Supporters of the third position see Schutz as creating a scientific sociology of the cultural constraints on actors. That such diverse interpretations are all defensible tells us much about the richness of, and the confusions in, Schutzian theory.

Current Phenomenological Sociology: Types and Common Characteristics

Because of the influence of Husserl and (mainly) Schutz, a number of phenomenologically inspired sociologies have been developed.

There is one type of sociology that is phenomenological only in a very loose sense of the term. That is, all that those who practice this type of sociology share with phenomenology is a concern with consciousness and the importance of subjective meaning in the interpretation of social action. In this category we could include the sociological theories of Cooley and Mead as well as those of their followers. These sociologists had little or no familiarity with the phenomenology of Husserl and Schutz, however.

A second type of phenomenological sociology does make explicit use of phenomenological philosophy as its intellectual starting point. A few of these sociologists operate from a Husserlian base, but the vast majority take their inspiration from the more sociologically relevant ideas of Schutz. Those working in this tradition try to relate Schutz's ideas to work by traditional sociologists. The work of Peter Berger and Thomas Luckmann (1967), which we will discuss later in this chapter, is a good example of this kind of phenomenological sociology.

A third type of phenomenological sociology, well illustrated by Heap and Roth's own work, is a more truly phenomenological approach. One of the defining characteristics of such an orientation, and of the Heap and Roth essay, is its *reflexivity*. As they put it, in this approach sociology would have to be treated as both "*in* and *about* the very life world that it studies" (Heap and Roth, 1973:342). Phenomenological sociology would not only have to examine the hidden, implicit, taken-for-granted aspects of the social world, but also its *own* hidden assumptions. In their essay Heap and Roth were more interested in the phenomenology of sociology than in the phenomenology of the social world.

Finally, Heap and Roth argued that ethnomethodology is a fourth type of phenomenological sociology. In their view, it combines phenomenology and sociology into a unique and independent type of study.

In spite of this variability, some general statements can be made about the nature of phenomenological sociology, although these characterizations will not be completely true of any one of the current types. In a sense, what we need at this point is an ideal-typical characterization of phenomenological sociology.

At the broadest level, phenomenological sociology is that sociology which operates on the basis of philosophical phenomenology. It tries, without doing too much damage to its original sources, to apply the principles of philosophical phenomenology to sociological questions. In this, the work of philosophers such as Husserl, as well as Henri Bergson, Franz Brentano, and Maurice Merleau-Ponty, provides its ultimate source, and the work of Schutz, its closest source.

Can we find a clear statement that gives us a good idea about what phenomenology in general, and phenomenological sociology in particular, do? Alexander Blumenstiel's (1973:189) rather disarming definition of phenomenology goes a long way toward this end: "Phenomenology is, essentially, the trick of making things whose meanings seem clear meaningless and then discovering what they mean. By doing this we reveal meanings that are not actually apparent to the uncritical mind but which nevertheless are present at some other level of consciousness." This unveiling of the basic structure of consciousness—defined in terms of intentionality—is the basic philosophical presupposition of a phenomenologically oriented sociology. As a result of its phenomenological orientation, this sociology takes as its objective the *description* of the universal structure of *subjective* orientations (Psathas, 1973a). While Husserl's subjective concerns were at the level of consciousness, Schutz combined this interest with a larger-scale subjective interest in cultural recipes, typifications, and the like. Phenomenological sociology thus seeks the features of society that rest on a universal subjective base (Psathas, 1973a). Like phenomenological philosophy, phenomenological sociology is a science because of its rigorous, systematic, and critical attempt to uncover the basic realities of social life.

Examples of Current Phenomenological Sociology

Up to this point we have presented abstract generalities about phenomenology and phenomenological sociology. In part, this reflects the fact that a good portion of the field is content with such a level of discourse and that those who work within it regularly produce theoretical tracts. However, it is possible to be more concrete about phenomenological sociology, to illustrate its application to sociological concerns.

We will now deal with three examples of phenomenological sociology. The first, by George Psathas and Frances C. Waksler (1973), on face-to-face interaction, illustrates the micro-level focus of much of phenomenology.[4] The second example is the work of Peter Berger and Thomas Luckmann (1967), and their effort to integrate small-scale phenomenological insights with more traditional large-scale sociological work. The third example is Alan Blum and Peter McHugh's (1971) micro-level analysis of motives. This work illustrates that modern phenomenological sociology attempts to bring together many different currents, including traditional sociology, ethnomethodology, linguistics, and even structuralism.

FACE-TO-FACE INTERACTION

Psathas and Waksler (1973) started with the assumption that face-to-face interaction is the basis of the more complex, larger-scale social phenomena; however, they opted to concentrate on the individual levels of analysis, especially consciousness.

By outlining their argument we can follow the structure the authors used. They divide the elements of face-to-face interaction into three basic components: features of the actors, features of the relations between actors, and features of action.

1. Features of the Actors (Psathas and Waksler, 1973:168–170)
    a. Both Ego and Other are conscious and they are aware of that consciousness. It is significant for phenomenological sociology that Psathas and Waksler began their analysis of face-to-face interaction with consciousness. True to their intellectual roots, they did not focus on action but turned directly to consciousness. Also, they conceived of consciousness as intentional; consciousness may be of something that "is real or ideal, existent or imaginary" (Psathas and Waksler, 1973:168).
        In this phase of the analysis of face-to-face interaction the observer must ascertain whether Ego and Other are both conscious and see themselves as conscious. Face-to-face interaction cannot be said to occur unless the parties are conscious and aware that they are conscious.
    b. Both Ego and Other have constituted a self. In order for interaction to occur, both parties must have a sense of themselves; that is, they must "see themselves as unitary beings, acted upon and acting on the world." Having a self also involves the actors' seeing themselves "as having a past, present and future" and being "capable of reacting to the other and eliciting reactions in him." Finally, for sociologists to be assured that the parties have selves, they

---

[4] Although micro-level studies are the norm in current phenomenological sociology, Psathas (1973a) believed that the discipline would also study larger-scale phenomena, such as organizations, groups, cultures, and societies.

"must judge that each is at least potentially effective in his world" (Psathas and Waksler, 1973:169).

c. Both Ego and Other have acquired and are able to use a stock of knowledge and a system of relevance. For interaction to occur and to be comprehensible to both actors, during their socialization they must have acquired bodies of knowledge as well as schemes for interpreting knowledge and information. However, if the two parties have entirely different, nonoverlapping bodies of knowledge and systems of relevance, then they cannot interact. They must share at least some knowledge and systems of relevance for them to be able to interact.

d. Both Ego and Other are able to communicate and to use a symbolic system of meaning. In order to interact, the parties must be able to communicate with each other using both *signs* and *symbols* in the sense that Mead meant. That is, signs are such things as physical gestures that stand for themselves, whereas symbols involve both physical and verbal phenomena that can stand for something else. Actors do not have to use symbols every time they communicate, but the symbols must be at least potentially available to them. Symbolic systems of meaning serve two very important functions. First, they make the ensuing steps in the interaction process possible. Second, they make "possible that internal conversation by means of which the person interprets the meaning of his experiences" (Psathas and Waksler, 1973:170).

e. Both Ego and Other are motivated to act. This means simply that both parties are ready to act and interested in acting.

f. Both Ego and Other view their bodies as fields of experience. This means that, in lay terms, "body language" is important to interaction. In order to deal with each other, actors must be able to "read" the meaning of such things as facial expressions, body tension, and body movements. And in fact, we all do pay a great deal of attention to such phenomena during the interaction process.

2. Features of the Relations Between Actors (Psathas and Waksler, 1973:170–172)

a. Both Ego and Other are present. Physical presence of the actors is a necessary but not sufficient condition for interaction to occur. Each party may be within reach of the other without interaction occurring. However, being close enough to use one's senses in order to interact is a precondition of face-to-face interaction.

b. Ego and Other are each aware of the other's bodily presence. In order for interaction to occur mere physical presence must be supplemented by a mutual awareness that the potential actors are in each other's presence.

c. Ego and Other constitute each other as actors with the features of actors. Another prerequisite for interaction is that Ego and Other attribute to each other all the characteristics discussed above; in other words, each must think of the other as an actor. In Schutz's terms, a we relationship can be said to exist when each party is conscious of the other. That awareness is involved in the next two aspects of the process delineated by Psathas and Waksler.

d. Both Ego and Other are aware that each is conscious of the other person's presence.

e. Both Ego and Other are aware that each constitutes the other as an actor. Each party must be aware not only of the other's bodily presence, but also of the other's consciousness of him as being present and being accepted as an actor. As a result of this mutual awareness, both parties are in a position to receive and interpret information about the other's subjective experiences as they are occurring.

3. Features of Action (Psathas and Waksler, 1973:172–173)
    a. Both Ego and Other project action of affecting-the-other type. Even at this
        stage in the process, action has not yet occurred. We are still at the stage of
        the psychological formulation of a plan of action. To use Schutz's terms
        again, Ego's "in order to" motive is to cause some kind of conscious ex-
        perience for the Other.
    b. Both Ego and Other develop an act on the basis of their plan of action. On the
        basis of the plan developed mentally, each party develops a plan of action.
    c-1. Ego acts. At this point we move from the psychological presuppositions of
        action to the arena of action. One party has now acted, but interaction can-
        not be said to have occurred yet. The following stages are needed.
    d-1. Other is aware of Ego's act as arising from his plan of action. We return
        here to consciousness, since in order for interaction to occur Other must in-
        terpret Ego's act as meaningful and as arising out of Ego's plan for action.
    c-2. Other acts.
    d-2. Ego is aware of Other's act as arising from his project of action. Thus, for
        interaction to occur, we must have not only mutual action but also mutual
        awareness of each party's consciousness.

With this return to consciousness, Psathas and Waksler completed the analysis at
the same level that they began. Of course, in the real world one set of actions and reactions rarely closes an interactional episode; rather, the process is likely to continue.

A few generalizations can be derived from Psathas and Waksler's analysis and applied to phenomenological sociology. First, the analysis illustrates the preoccupation
of many contemporary phenomenologists with the individual level of analysis. Second,
at this level, consciousness is more interesting to phenomenologically oriented sociologists than is action or interaction; they are more concerned with the psychological
prerequisites for action than with action itself. Although Psathas and Waksler set out to
deal with interaction, they devoted most of their analysis to consciousness. Third,
Psathas and Waksler used no data, in the conventional sense of the term; that is, their
analysis was not empirical. This reflects the fact that phenomenological sociology remains highly descriptive, theoretical, and philosophical. Phenomenological sociologists seem more interested in thought experiments than in studies in the real world.
Still, an analysis such as that of Psathas and Waksler is relevant to an understanding of
the real world.

THE SOCIAL CONSTRUCTION OF REALITY

The preoccupation with individual thought and action was undoubtedly one of the
reasons for Berger and Luckmann's book *The Social Construction of Reality* (1967),
which tried to extend the concerns of phenomenological sociology to social structures
and institutions. Furthermore, the authors sought to integrate the individual and
societal levels. We will be concerned not only with what they have done but with how
successful they have been in achieving their ambitious objectives.

Berger and Luckmann's (1967) work is one of the most widely read and influential
books in contemporary sociology. One of its main attractions is that it translated Alfred
Schutz's sometimes arcane phenomenology into the terms of mainstream sociological
theory. Berger and Luckmann also attempted to go beyond Schutz's work, to buttress it

with Mead's social psychology and to complement both Schutz's and Mead's work with the work of Marx and Durkheim on society and culture. They attempted to integrate Weber's work on social action with Durkheim's thoughts on social facts as external realities. In relating these thinkers to one another, Berger and Luckmann (1967:18) made it quite clear that they wanted to deal in an integrated fashion with "the dual character of society in terms of objective facticity *and* subjective meaning." Even more explicit is this statement, which seems to give the essence of an approach to social reality that integrates a concern with large- and small-scale phenomena: "*Society is a human product. Society is an objective reality. Man is a social product*" (Berger and Luckmann, 1967:61). In other words, people are the products of the very society they create.

The book's subtitle, *A Treatise in the Sociology of Knowledge,* provides the key to their analysis. Their view of the sociology of knowledge is unusual. To them, it is concerned with the social construction of reality. In articulating this view, their goal was to move the sociology of knowledge away from the study of intellectual history and to the everyday construction of reality, the process of everyday knowledge production in which we all engage. However, despite their intent to deal with both large- and small-scale phenomena, and their commitment to deal with the work of people such as Marx and Durkheim, they said little about objectivity, especially large-scale social structures, even though the longest chapter in their book is titled "Society as Objective Reality."

EVERYDAY LIFE Berger and Luckmann began their analysis at the individual level with the reality of everyday life, the commonsense world. Here Berger and Luckmann relied almost exclusively on the work of Schutz.

Berger and Luckmann were particularly interested in people's phenomenological tendency to view subjective processes as objective realities. In their view, people tend to apprehend everyday life as an ordered reality; that is, social reality seems to the actor to be independent of the actor's apprehension of it. It appears already objectified, and it seems to impose itself on the actor. Crucial to this tendency toward objectification is language, which "continuously provides [people] with the necessary objectifications and posits the order within which these make sense and within which everyday life has meaning for [people]" (Berger and Luckmann, 1967:23). We take the reality of everyday life for granted; although we could question it, we suspend that ability in order to live comfortably within it. The thrust of Berger and Luckmann's discussion was a view of the social world as the cultural product of conscious processes.

Berger and Luckmann's discussion of face-to-face interaction is welcome, although it adds little to Schutz's work and lacks the detail of Psathas and Waksler's (1973) work. What is significant about their micro-level analysis is that Berger and Luckmann, unlike Schutz, were willing to include the individual level in their sociology. In their description of face-to-face interactions, which, following Schutz, they called "we relationships," Berger and Luckmann emphasized that such relationships involve an immediate interchange of meanings. In we relationships there is much less typification than in they relationships (which involve anonymous others). In other words, instead of relating to people on the basis of culturally defined recipes, in we relationships people relate to each other in more personalized ways. Since we relationships are less dominated by typifications, there is more latitude for negotiations among the actors. As we move away from immediate, face-to-face relationships to relationships with people with whom we are less intimate, or even strangers, there is more likelihood of typification and less of interpersonal negotiation. In other words, our relationships with others in the they relationship grow progressively more impersonal and stereotypic. The importance of typifications to Berger and Luckmann is illustrated by their definition of social structures, a definition clearly not in line with an objective view of such structures. They define *social structures* as "the sum total of these typifications and of the recurrent patterns of interaction established by means of them" (Berger and Luckmann, 1967:33).

As with many phenomenologists, language is very important to Berger and Luckmann, especially as it relates to the typification process. Berger and Luckmann viewed language as a specific form of the process of "signification," a subtype of objectification distinguished by the explicit purpose that it serves as standing for a wide range of subjective meanings. Language is a system of vocal symbols, the most important symbol system in society. The reason for its importance is that language can be detached from the here and now, from face-to-face interaction, and can communicate meanings that are not immediate expressions of subjectivity. Language also allows us to deal with things that we never have experienced, and perhaps never will experience, ourselves. It can also help us accumulate meanings and knowledge that can then be passed on to future generations. In these and other ways language is, in Berger and Luckmann's system, the most important social structure: "I encounter language as a facticity external to myself and it is coercive on me" (Berger and Luckmann, 1967:38). Here they self-consciously took the position that language is an external and coercive social fact. However, this is an exception to their general tendency to pay little attention to social structures, or the objective components of society.

OBJECTIVE COMPONENTS OF SOCIETY   Despite their perspective on language, Berger and Luckmann are weakest on the objective components of society. For example, they defined social structure as nothing more than recurrent patterns of action. In their chapter "Society as an Objective Reality," they were interested primarily in the process by which that world, such as it is, is produced and how a *sense* of its objectivity is created. They carefully reminded readers that this sense, as well as whatever objective reality there "really" is out there, is produced by people.

INSTITUTIONALIZATION   Beneath this process by which a sense of social reality is constructed lies the fact that people must externalize; that is, they must do such things as produce what they need to survive and interact with others. In the process of externalizing, people are prone to develop habitualized patterns of acting and interacting in recurrent situations. Life would be impossible without habits. It would be very difficult to decide the proper action in every new situation.

Habitualized actions set the stage for the development of institutionalization. This occurs when people develop typifications of what others are likely to do in a given situation. Berger and Luckmann (1967) defined an institution as a kind of reciprocal process of typification. This is a very microscopic conception of an institution and one that is quite different from most sociological conceptions of institutions. Although to

Berger and Luckmann institutions are not large-scale phenomena, they are nonetheless external and coercive. They argued that institutions "*control* human conduct by setting up predefined patterns of conduct" (Berger and Luckmann, 1967:55).

The stream of history allows these institutions to acquire objectivity. However, when Berger and Luckmann considered these institutions, they were inclined to think of them subjectively also:

> This means that the institutions that now have been crystallized . . . are *experienced* as existing over and beyond the individuals who "happen to" embody them at the moment. In other words, the institutions are now *experienced* as possessing a reality of their own, a reality that confronts the individual as an external and coercive fact.
> (Berger and Luckmann, 1967:58; italics added)

By emphasizing the *experience* of institutions, rather than their external reality, Berger and Luckmann made their subjective biases quite clear, even when they were supposedly dealing with external realities.

Children perceive the institutional world as an objective reality; that is, it was there before they were born and it will be there after they die. As individuals mature they apprehend their biographies as episodes within the objective history of society.

The various institutions within society tend to "hang together," but in Berger and Luckmann's view this is due not to their objective qualities but to the tendency of people to perceive them in that way. In other words, what is crucial is the knowledge people have of society. Thus sociology should focus on how people reconstruct their knowledge of social reality, not only in the historical production of the world but also in the continuing creation of that world on a day-to-day basis.

ROLES   Berger and Luckmann's definition of roles is typical of their sense of objective social reality. To them, roles are typifications of what can be expected of actors in given social situations. Roles are not to be confused with objective positions, as they tend to be in the work of many others. The role was particularly important to Berger and Luckmann because it constitutes a mediation or link between the large- and small-scale worlds. In Berger and Luckmann's hands, it served to mediate *only* between culture and consciousness: "The analysis of role is of particular importance to the sociology of knowledge because it reveals the mediations between the macroscopic *universe of meaning* objectivated in a society and the ways in which these universes are *subjectively* real to individuals" (Berger and Luckmann, 1967:79; italics added).

REIFICATION   Berger and Luckmann defined *reification* solely as a subjective phenomenon: "the apprehension of human phenomena as if they were things, that is, in nonhuman or possibly supra-human terms" (Berger and Luckmann, 1967:89). Reification is the tendency to *perceive* human products as if they were something else, "such as facts of nature, results of cosmic laws, or manifestations of divine will" (Berger and Luckmann, 1967:89). In other words, people simply lose sight of the dialectical relationship between them and their products. People can objectify social phenomena without reifying them; that is, they can produce objects and view the world in objective terms without forgetting that people produce them. However, Berger and

Luckmann gave absolutely no sense of the other aspect of reification—that is, the degree to which society, as a result of the subjective processes they describe, objectively comes to acquire a life of its own. Marxian sociologists are more interested in the latter aspect of reification as well as its relationship to the subjective processes involved in reification.

LEGITIMATIONS   Also telling, in terms of their tendency to ignore objective structures, was Berger and Luckmann's extensive treatment of *legitimations*, or the explanations and justifications of the institutional system. Again, instead of dealing with the structures themselves, Berger and Luckmann focused on the knowledge that is used to support their existence: "Legitimation 'explains' the institutional order by ascribing cognitive validity to its objectivated meaning. Legitimation justifies the institutional order by giving a normative dignity to its practical imperatives" (Berger and Luckmann, 1967:83). The focus is not on the structures being legitimated but on the means by which they are legitimated.

CRITICISMS   Berger and Luckmann's chapter on society as objective reality really deals with subjective phenomena. In their next chapter, on society as a subjective reality, Berger and Luckmann discussed the socialization process, the process by which cultural phenomena are communicated to, and internalized in, consciousness. This chapter added little beyond elementary knowledge about socialization.

Berger and Luckmann provided an almost purely subjective characterization of the social world. However, this might not be a fair criticism, since their stated intention was to present a sociology of knowledge. Furthermore, near the end of their work they admitted the need for a structural sociology to complement their subjective orientation (Berger and Luckmann, 1967:186). Still, they are vulnerable to criticism because they promised more than simply a subjective sociology, including integrating Freud, Mead, and Weber on social action with Marx and Durkheim on social structures—and they did not deliver. More important was what they promised in their pivotal statement: "*Society is a human product. Society is an objective reality. Man is a social product*" (Berger and Luckmann, 1967:61). They failed to produce any sense of society as an objective reality; as a result, their entire dialectic loses much of its significance. In Marx's hands a similar discussion is much more powerful, because of his strong sense of the obdurate structures of the social world and the difficulties involved in overcoming these structures. Berger and Luckmann were right to state that they needed Marx's sociology, but unfortunately, they did not follow through on this.

In spite of the harsh criticisms leveled at Berger and Luckmann in this section, they are to be praised for the effort to extend phenomenology from its traditional (Husserlian) focus on consciousness to a more Schutzian concern for culture. Their failure to deal satisfactorily with objective social structures, despite their avowed desire to do so, does not mean that phenomenological sociology *cannot* integrate a concern with social structure into its approach, but it does mean that it will be difficult. Phenomenological sociology *may* be able to deal with larger-scale social structures, but that remains to be demonstrated. Its strengths continue to lie in the understanding of consciousness and its relationship to action and interaction, and in the study of culture and its constraining effects on actors.

MOTIVES

We close this section on phenomenological sociology with a discussion of an essay by Alan Blum and Peter McHugh (1971) on motives. Their essay illustrates that many works in phenomenological sociology integrate it with one or more other theories. Blum and McHugh's essay has strong elements of phenomenology, along with components of linguistics, structuralism, and ethnomethodology.

Phenomenology is manifest in Blum and McHugh's work in various ways. For example, they accepted the basic idea that consciousness involves intentionality, that is, the relationship between actors and objects. As a result, they rejected the ideas that consciousness involves private internal states or is an antecedent variable causing people to do certain things. Also, Blum and McHugh adopted the basic phenomenological idea of reflexivity. They took it as their obligation to understand not only how actors use motives, but also how sociologists employ the idea of motives to understand what actors do.

This led Blum and McHugh to an interest in the grammar of motives, an interest obviously stimulated by linguistics as well as conversational analysis in ethnomethodology. As a grammatical form, motives involve a set of terms used "by actors to accomplish their routine affairs" (Blum and McHugh, 1971:100). Also grammatically, motives are used by sociologists to help them do what they do, that is, explain the routine actions of laypeople. Thus, a layperson may act in a certain way because he or she feels motivated to do so, and a sociologist may explain that action with reference to the actor's motives. Thus motives are grammatical tools that allow both laypeople and sociologists to accomplish their routine tasks.

This idea is linked to the view held by many ethnomethodologists that there is little difference between laypeople and sociologists—both are observers of the social scene. All observers must know the basic grammar of motives in order to understand what is going on around them.

Blum and McHugh were influenced not only by phenomenology, ethnomethodology, and linguistics but also by structuralism. This led them to look for the deep structures of the mind that generate the various motives an actor may cite at any given time.[5] This would seem to imply that actors are governed totally by invariant rules, by deep mental structures. However, Blum and McHugh, true to their roots in phenomenology and ethnomethodology, were careful to point out that although people are guided by these deep structures, they are not governed by them. People are seen as possessing creativity, the ability to make independent decisions, although these decisions are guided by deep structures that are unknown to them at a conscious level.

Although it shows a number of phenomenological influences, this is a very different kind of phenomenology from those discussed previously. The reason is that it reflects a variety of theoretical orientations, including the ethnomethodological approach, to which we now turn.

---

[5]We will have more to say about "deep structures" in the final chapter, but they are basically the unconscious logical structures of the mind that to the structuralist determine what people think and do as well as the larger structures and institutions they create.

ETHNOMETHODOLOGY

Ethnomethodology was "invented" by Harold Garfinkel in the 1940s. Since that time it has expanded enormously and moved in a number of different directions. This led Don Zimmerman to conclude that there is no longer one ethnomethodology, but several. As Zimmerman (1978:6) put it, ethnomethodology now "encompasses a number of more or less distinct and sometimes incompatible lines of inquiry." We will start with this diversity and describe a number of different studies done from an ethno-methodological perspective. The heart of ethnomethodology lies in these specific studies and not in general theoretical or programmatic statements. Nevertheless, ethnomethodology does have a core of shared ideas that we will discuss after the analysis of the specific studies.

Examples of Ethnomethodology

DOING WALKING

Few of us ever give more than a passing thought to the act of walking, let alone subject it to serious sociological analysis, but that is precisely what A. Lincoln Ryave and James N. Schenkein (1974) did. Their concern was not simply with walking but with "doing" walking. Although we all possess routine, methodical practices for walking, we must actually use those routines to "do" walking. Furthermore, we must do it in concert with the other people who walk with, by, or toward us; in other words, walking is the concerted accomplishment of members of the community. Ryave and Schenkein (1974:165) examined walking not just to understand this specific act but to understand a wide range of such phenomena: "In treating this commonplace phenomenon as the problematic achievement of members, we hope to build towards a greater understanding of social phenomena as on-going situated accomplishments."

Their basic resource in this study was a series of video tapes of people walking. Their central concern was the ways in which people navigate and avoid collisions. In order for successful walking to occur, the parties must not only *recognize* what they are doing but also *produce* the appropriate walking strategy. This is a striking example of how, using ethnomethodology, sociologists can take a mundane situation and demonstrate its problematic character.

Let us take the issue of how walking together is accomplished. In order to walk together, people have to produce a collective pattern to their walking. For example, they must maintain a certain proximity to each other. If one participant gets too far ahead or behind, that person will engage in "repair work" in order to restore walking together. The individual might hurry up, slow down, or explain (at the time or later on) why he or she was out of step. If the participant refuses to engage in repair work and continues out of step, it becomes a serious threat to the reality of walking together.

The act of walking together also makes possible a set of walking together activities: "For example, such activities as conversing, being available for conversation, touching, laughing, offering of offerables such as cigarettes or sweets, parting, and so on, are made relevant, and expectable, by the sheer fact of walking together" (Ryave and Schenkein, 1974:272).

Ryave and Schenkein also viewed the phenomenon of walking alone as a social accomplishment. For example, how does the lone walker avoid the appearance of walking together when he or she passes another walker on the street? Ryave and Schenkein's video tapes indicate that the individual manipulates direction, pace, and body attitude so that the moment of co-presence is only fleeting. Similarly, it takes work to avoid engaging in violations while walking. For example, an individual could easily seem to be "following" someone in the street. Or the manner of one's approach could appear to be a threat to others. To avoid such violations, or appearances of violations, walkers not only must be conscious that these acts are possible but also must be ready and able to take actions that would prevent their occurrence.

TELEPHONE CONVERSATIONS: IDENTIFICATION AND RECOGNITION

Emanuel A. Schegloff (1979:24) viewed his examination of the way in which telephone conversations are opened as part of a larger effort to understand the orderly character of social interaction:

> The work in which my colleagues and I have been engaged is concerned with the *organization of social interaction*. We bring to the materials with which we work—audio and videotapes of *naturally occurring* interaction, and transcripts of those tapes—an interest in *detecting* and *describing* the *orderly* phenomena of which conversation and interaction are composed, and an interest in depicting the *systematic organizations* by reference to which those phenomena are produced.
>
> (Schegloff, 1979:24; italics added)

The interest of Schegloff and his colleagues extended to various orderly phenomena within interaction, such as the organization of turn taking in conversations and the ways in which people seek to repair breaches in normal conversational procedure. Beyond this, they were interested in the overall structure of a conversation including openings, closings, and regularly recurring internal sequences.

In this context Schegloff (1979:25) looked at the opening of a phone conversation, which he defined as "a place where the type of conversation being opened can be proffered, displayed, accepted, rejected, modified—in short, incipiently constituted by the parties to it." Although the talk one hears on the phone is no different from that in face-to-face conversations, the participants lack visual contact. Schegloff focused on one element of phone conversations not found in face-to-face conversations, the sequence by which the parties who have no visual contact identify and recognize each other.

In his research Schegloff drew on data from 450 telephone openings. On the one hand, he found that telephone openings are often quite straightforward and standardized:

A.   Hello?
B.   Shar'n?
A.   Hi!

Or:

A. Hello.
B. Hello, Charlie?
A. Oh, hi.

(Schegloff, 1979:52)

On the other hand, some openings "look and sound idiosyncratic—almost virtuoso performances" (Schegloff, 1979:68).

A. Hello.
B. Hello Margie?
A. Yes.
B. hhh We do painting, antiquing,
A. is that right.
B. eh, hh—hhh
A. hnh, hnh, hnh
B. nhh, hnh, hnh! hh
A. hh
B. keep people's pa'r tools
A. y(hhh)! hnh, hnh
B. I'm sorry about that—that—I din' see that.

(Adapted from Schegloff, 1979:68)

Although these may be different from the usual openings, they are not without their organization. They are "engendered by a systematic sequential organization adapted and fitted by the parties to some particular circumstances" (Schegloff, 1979:68). For example, the preceding conversation is almost incomprehensible until we understand that B is calling to apologize for keeping some borrowed power tools too long. B makes a joke out of it by building it into a list (painting, antiquing), and it is only at the end when both are laughing that the apology comes.

Schegloff's conclusion was that even where cases are very idiosyncratic, they are to be examined for their organizational pattern:

> Particular cases can, therefore, be examined for their local, interactional, biographical, ethno-graphic, or other idiosyncratic interest. The same materials can be inspected so as to extract from their local particularities the formal organization into which their particularities are infused. For students of interaction, the organizations through which the work of social life gets accomplished occupy the center of attention.

(Schegloff, 1979:71)

INVITING LAUGHTER

Gail Jefferson (1979) looked at the question of how one knows when to laugh in the course of a conversation. The lay view is that laughter is a totally free event in the course of a conversation or interaction. However, Jefferson found that there are several basic structural characteristics of an utterance that are designed to induce the other party to laugh. The first is the placement, by the speaker, of a laugh at the end of his utterance:

Dan.   I thought that was pretty out of sight. Did you hear me say you're a junkie . . .
          heh, heh
Dolly. heh, heh, heh.

(Adapted from Jefferson, 1979:80)

The second device reported by Jefferson is within-speech laughter—for example, in mid-sentence:

A.   You know I didn't . . . you know
B.   Hell, *you* know I'm on ret (haha);
A.   ehh, yeh, ha ha.

(Adapted from Jefferson, 1979:83)

Jefferson concluded from these examples that the occurrence of laughter is more organized than we realize:

> It appears, then, that the order of alternative responses to a candidate laughable is not organized as freely as one might suppose; i.e., the issue is not that *something* should occur, laughter *or* whatever else, but that *laughter* should occur, on a volunteer basis *or* by invitation.
> (Jefferson, 1979:83)

But Jefferson was interested not only in the decision to laugh but also in the declining of an invitation to laugh. She found that silence after an invitation is not enough, that a clear signal is required indicating refusal of the invitation. If, for example, someone refuses to laugh, a strategy would be to commence, just after the onset of the speaker's laugh, a serious pursuit of the topic.

THE INTERACTIVE EMERGENCE OF SENTENCES

Charles Goodwin (1979) challenged the traditional linguistic assumption that sentences can be examined in isolation from the process of interaction in which they occur. His view was that "sentences emerge with conversation" (Goodwin, 1979:97). The fact is that the "speaker can reconstruct the meaning of his sentence *as he is producing it* in order to maintain its appropriateness to its recipient of the moment" (Goodwin, 1979:98; italics added).

Goodwin's essential point was that speakers pay acute attention to listeners as they are speaking. As the listeners react verbally, facially, or with body language, the speaker adjusts the sentence as it is emerging on the basis of these reactions. The reactions allow the speaker to decide whether his or her point is being made, and if not, to alter the structure of the sentence. In a rather complicated conversation that he analyzed, Goodwin described some of the alterations that took place in a particular sentence sequence:

> In the course of its production the unfolding meaning of John's sentence is reconstructed twice, a new segment is added to it, and another is deleted prior to its production but replaced

with a different segment. The sentence eventually produced emerges as the product of a dynamic process of interaction between speaker and hearer as they mutually construct the turn of talk.

(Goodwin, 1979:112)

In other words sentences are the products of collaborative processes.

FORMULATIONS

J. C. Heritage and D. R. Watson (1979) were interested in the general issue of orderliness within conversations. They placed this issue within the general context of ethnomethodological concerns:

> A central focus of ethnomethodological work is the analysis of the practical sociological reasoning through which social activity is rendered accountable and orderly. Assumed by this concern is the notion that all scenic features of social interaction [for example, biographies, events, personalities, locations] are occasioned and established as a concerted practical accomplishment, in and through which the parties display for one another their competence in the practical management of social order. As analysts, our interest is to explicate, in respect of naturally occurring occasions of use, the methods by which such orderliness can be displayed, managed, and recognized by members.

(Heritage and Watson, 1979:123–124)

Their specific concern was the issue of when conversational order itself becomes a topic of conversation for the participants. Specifically, they looked at *formulations*, which they defined as a part of a conversation used to describe that conversation. In particular, their concern was a specific type of formulation, one in which an actor seeks to "characterize states of affairs already described or negotiated (in whole or in part) in the preceding talk" (Heritage and Watson, 1979:126).

The conversations that Heritage and Watson used are too lengthy to include here, but the following should give a sense of what they meant by formulations:

A.   I was so depressed that . . .
B.   Yes
A.   . . . that I climbed on the railing of the bridge
B.   *You were prepared to commit suicide because* . . .
A.   Yes, I am so overweight.

In this example, in saying that A was prepared to commit suicide, B is formulating what A was trying to say in his previous two statements.

Such formulations illustrate the practical management of conversations. A formulation is a part of a conversation in which the objective "is manifestly and specifically to exhibit participants' understanding" (Heritage and Watson, 1979:129). A formulation is one example of how members demonstrate their understanding of what is occurring.

"THE RADIO RAIDERS" STORY

Jim Schenkein was struck by the following headline in a British newspaper: "Police Inquiry Into Why They Missed The Radio Raiders" (Schenkein, 1979:188). To the casual observer this is a highly perplexing statement. Among other things, it raises the following questions: What kind of inquiry did the police undertake? Did they miss a radio show? If so, why did they miss the show? What kind of show is "The Radio Raiders"? Or, did somebody raid a radio station? If so, why would anyone raid a radio station? And, why did the police fail to capture the raiders? The fact is that all of these questions are far off the mark; the story was, as we will see, about something completely different. However, we could not have known that—but the author of the story did, as did the usual readers of the paper. Although we don't usually think of it in that way, reading a newspaper is a practical accomplishment of people on a day-to-day basis. Newspaper headlines, and even stories, do not speak for themselves; they are what Schenkein called "referential puzzles"—a creation of the author and the readers, who fill in the details behind a few very vague words. Readers have a variety of acquired skills that allow them to do this. In addition, to make sense of a story such as this, readers must have read the stories that have led up to it. The person who wrote the headline in question assumed that the audience was familiar with the previous stories and thus would be able to make sense out of this one's ambiguous words.

What, then, was this story about? The following is an excerpt from it:

> An informal inquiry is to be held in London with a view of tightening policy procedures after the Baker Street bank raid discovered yesterday. . . . Scotland Yard officials recognise "disturbing aspects" of the case.
> Valuables estimated as worth several hundred thousand pounds were stolen from private safe deposit boxes at Lloyds bank branch—in spite of an early warning from an amateur radio enthusiast, who . . . picked up the thieves' walkie-talkie conversation.
>
> (cited in Schenkein, 1979:188)

With this information, the headline now makes sense to us. However, regular readers of the paper already had this background from previous stories, and thus the headline "made sense" to them. Making sense of the news, and most other aspects of social life, is an accomplishment requiring considerable learned skills and knowledge.

MAKING AND MANAGING MEANING IN TRAFFIC COURT

Melvin Pollner (1979) raised the issue of how people deal with a situation in which they lack the prior experience that enables them to anticipate what behavior is expected of them. Traffic court is the example Pollner used of a situation that is largely unknown to the actor. How, he asked, do people in this setting develop some sense of what is expected from them? He found, after studying several traffic courts, that they are their own socializing agents. That is, the participants are usually allowed to observe several cases before their turn comes, which enables them to see how the judge has handled various people. As a result, they learn some of the subtleties of behavior in this traffic court. Behavior in this setting emerges both from the earlier observation and in the actual interaction. Even the judge, who has prior knowledge of such settings, cannot structure the process ahead of time. The participants, the nature of the cases, and the nature of the participants' relationship to the judge are different in each case. Thus the judge, as well as the defendants, must make and manage meaning in traffic court.

DIRECTIONAL MAPS

As we have seen, many ethnomethodologists have focused on oral communication; however, that need not always be the case, as Psathas has shown:

> Just as spoken materials can be examined to discover the methods of practical reasoning which their users depend upon to make what they say understandable, so written materials can be studied with the same purpose . . . letters, diaries, notes, reports, essays, and the like can, on close examination, be found to contain methods of practical reasoning.
>
> (Psathas, 1979a:203)

To illustrate his point, Psathas focused on the maps we all have occasion to draw in order to give people directions on how to get places. Despite his choice of materials, Psathas shared the traditional ethnomethodological concern with the ordered properties of practical reasoning.[6] He contended that the goal of his analysis is "to discover the methods of practical reasoning which members must and do use to make and read the map. These methods have their ordered properties discernible in and through the careful examination of the maps" (Psathas, 1979a:224).

Three basic conclusions emerge from Psathas's analysis of map making and map reading. First, there are "methodical and orderly" aspects of a map that make it "recognizable, readable, and interpretable" as a map to the potential reader. The lines, the names of streets, the words, and other elements make it clear that the object is a map drawn for a certain specific use, namely, getting to an ultimate destination. Second, the map maker only does part of the work involved; map readers accomplish the work of the map through their reading of it. Finally, the map provides readers with methods (arrows, words) that allow them to find the ultimate destination.

As Psathas (1979a:224) concluded: "It is remarkable that a number of lines on paper can be interpreted by members as being about a world." Map makers, through a few lines and words, and readers, through their interpretive procedures, are able to "make" a map that allows one to get to a destination. Map making and map reading are practical accomplishments.

ACCOMPLISHING GENDER

It seems incontrovertible that one's gender—male or female—is biologically based. People are seen as simply manifesting the behaviors that are an outgrowth of their biological makeup. People are not usually thought of as accomplishing their gender. In contrast, sexiness is clearly an accomplishment; people need to speak and act in certain ways in order to be seen as sexy. However, it is generally assumed that one does not have to do or say *anything* to be seen as a man or a woman. Ethnomethodology has investigated the issue of sexuality, with some very unusual results.

The ethnomethodological view is traceable to one of Garfinkel's (1967) now classic demonstrations of the utility of this orientation. In the 1950s Garfinkel met a person

---

[6]By *practical reasoning*, ethnomethodologists mean the logic used by people in everyday life rather than formal logic.

named Agnes, who seemed unquestionably a woman. Not only did she have the figure of a woman, but it was virtually a ''perfect'' figure with an ideal set of measurements. She also had a pretty face, a good complexion, no facial hair, and plucked eyebrows— and she wore lipstick. This was clearly a woman, or was it? Garfinkel discovered that Agnes had not always appeared to be a woman. In fact, at the time he met her, Agnes was trying to convince officials that she needed an operation to remove her male genitalia and create a vagina.

Agnes was defined as a male at birth. In fact, she was by all accounts a boy until she was sixteen years of age. At that age, sensing something was awry, Agnes ran away from home and started to dress like a girl. She soon discovered that dressing like a woman was not enough; she had to *learn to act* like a woman if she was to be accepted as one. She did learn the accepted practices and as a result came to be defined, and to define herself, as a woman. The more general point here is that we are not simply born men or women; we all also learn and routinely utilize the practices that define us as men or women. It is only in doing this that we come to be, in a sociological sense, a man or a woman.

BREACHING EXPERIMENTS

In its early years ethnomethodology gained much notoriety for its use of the *breaching experiment*. Despite the name, even Garfinkel (1967) recognized that these are not really experiments in the formal sense of the term and might better be called ''breaching demonstrations.'' In these demonstrations, social reality is ''breached'' in order to demonstrate the basic principles of ceaseless reality construction. The assumption behind this research is not only that the social construction of reality occurs all the time, but also that the participants are generally unaware that it is occurring. The objective of the breaching experiment is to disrupt normal procedures so that the process by which reality is constructed, or reconstructed, can be observed. In his work, Garfinkel discussed a number of examples of breaching experiments, most of which were undertaken by his students in order to illustrate the basic principles of ethnomethodology. Let us give one example to illustrate the procedure.

Garfinkel (1967:47–49) asked his students to spend between fifteen minutes and an hour in their homes imagining that they were boarders and then acting on the basis of that assumption. ''They were instructed to conduct themselves in a circumspect and polite fashion. They were to avoid getting personal, to use formal address, to speak only when spoken to'' (Garfinkel, 1967:47). In the vast majority of cases, family members were dumbfounded by such behavior: ''Reports were filled with accounts of astonishment, bewilderment, shock, anxiety, embarrassment, and anger, and with charges by various family members that the student was mean, inconsiderate, selfish, nasty, or impolite'' (Garfinkel, 1967:47). These reactions indicate how important it is that people act in accord with the unspoken assumptions about how they are supposed to behave.

What was most interesting to Garfinkel were the ways in which the family members sought to cope with such a breach. On the one hand, they demanded explanations from the students for their behavior. In their questions, they often implied an explanation of the aberrant behavior:

"Did you get fired?"
"Are you sick?"
"Are you out of your mind or are you just stupid?"

(Garfinkel, 1967:47)

Family members also sought to explain the behaviors to themselves in terms of previously understood motives. For example, a student was thought to be behaving oddly because she was working too hard or had had a fight with her fiancé. Such explanations are important to participants—the other family members, in this case—because the explanations help them feel that under normal circumstances interaction would occur as it always had.

If the student did not acknowledge the validity of such explanations, family members were likely to withdraw and to seek to isolate, denounce, or retaliate against the culprit. Deep emotions were aroused because the effort to restore order through explanation was rejected by the student. The other family members felt that more intense statements and actions were necessary to restore the equilibrium:

"Don't bother with him, he's in one of his moods again."
"Why must you always create friction in our family harmony?"
"I don't want any more of *that* out of *you* and if you can't treat your mother decently you'd better move out!"

(Garfinkel, 1967:48)

In the end, the students explained the experiment to their families, and in most situations harmony was restored. However, in some instances hard feelings lingered.

Breaching experiments are undertaken to illustrate the way people make sense out of their everyday lives. These experiments also reveal the fragility of social reality and the ways in which people seek to understand, and to heal, breaches. It is assumed that the way people handle these breaches tells us much about how they handle their everyday lives (Handel, 1982:59). Although these experiments seem innocent enough, they often lead to highly emotional reactions. These extreme reactions reflect how important it is to people to engage in routine, everyday activities. The reactions to breaches are sometimes so extreme that Hugh Mehan and Houston Wood (1975:113) have cautioned about their use: "*Interested persons are strongly advised not to undertake any new breaching studies.*"

Criticisms of Traditional Sociology

A good way to begin a discussion of the theoretical orientation of ethnomethodology is to look at how ethnomethodologists set themselves apart from mainstream sociologists; specifically, how they criticize the way sociology is most often practiced.

As we have seen, the idea of reflexivity is basic to ethnomethodology. This means, on the one hand, that actors are seen as self-conscious about their activities. On the other, and more germane at this point, it means that ethnomethodologists believe that sociologists should be self-conscious and self-critical about their own activities. Sociology must be studied using the same basic strategies used to study any social phenomenon. In fact, one of the ethnomethodologists' basic criticisms of sociology is that it has not been sufficiently self-critical.

Ethnomethodologists criticize traditional sociologists for imposing *their* sense of social reality on the social world (Mehan and Wood, 1975:37). They believe sociology has not been attentive enough, and true enough, to the everyday life world that should be its ultimate source of knowledge. Enamored of their own view of the social world, sociologists have tended not to share the same social reality as those they study. As Mehan and Wood (1975:63) put it, "in attempting to do a social *science*, sociology has become alienated from the social."

Within this general orientation Mehan and Wood leveled a number of specific criticisms at sociology. The concepts used by sociologists are said to distort the social world, to destroy its ebb and flow. Further distortion is caused by sociology's reliance on scientific techniques and statistical analyses of data. Statistics simply do not usually do justice to the elegance and sophistication of the real world. The coding techniques used by sociologists, when they translate human behavior into their preconceived categories, distort the social world. Furthermore, the seeming simplicity of the codes conceals the complicated and distorting work involved in turning aspects of the social world into the sociologists' preconceived categories. Sociologists are also seen as tending to accept unquestioningly a respondent's description of a phenomenon rather than looking at the phenomenon itself. Thus, a description of a social setting is taken to *be* that setting, rather than one conception of that setting. Finally, Mehan and Wood argued that sociologists are prone to offer abstractions of the social world that are increasingly removed from the reality of everyday life.

Taking a slightly different approach, Don Zimmerman and Melvin Pollner (1970) argued that conventional sociology has suffered from a confusion of *topic* and *resource*. That is, the everyday social world is a resource for the favorite topics of sociology, but it is rarely a topic in its own right. This can be illustrated in a variety of ways. For example, Roy Turner (1970) argued that sociologists usually look at everyday speech, not as a topic in itself, but as a resource with which to study hidden realities such as norms, values, attitudes, and so on. However, instead of being a resource, everyday speech can be seen as one of the ways in which the business of social life is carried on—a topic in itself. Matthew Speier (1970) argued that when sociologists look at childhood socialization, they look not at the processes themselves but at a series of abstract "stages" generalized from those processes. Speier (1970:189) argued that *"socialization is the acquisition of interactional competencies."* Thus, the ethnomethodologist must look at the way these competencies are acquired and utilized in the everyday reality of the real world.

Another analysis of childhood socialization, by Robert W. Mackay (1974), is even more useful as a critique of traditional sociology, and the confusion of topic and resource. Mackay contrasted the "normative" approach of traditional sociology with the interpretive approach of ethnomethodology. The normative approach is seen as arguing that socialization is merely a series of stages in which "complete" adults teach "incomplete" children the ways of society. Mackay viewed this as a "gloss" that ignores the reality that socialization involves an interaction between children and adults. Children are not passive, incomplete receptacles; rather, they are active participants in the socialization process, since they have the ability to reason, invent, and acquire knowledge. Socialization is a two-sided process. Mackay (1974:183) believed that the ethnomethodological orientation "restores the interaction between adults and children based on interpretive competencies as the phenomenon of study."

Don Zimmerman and Melvin Pollner (1970) cited other examples of the confusion of topic and resource. For example, they argued that sociologists normally explain action in bureaucracies by the rules, norms, and values of the organization. However, had they looked at organizations as topics, they would have seen that actors often simply make it *appear*, through their actions, that those actions can be explained by the rules. It is not the rules, but the actors' *use* of the rules, that should be the topic of sociological research. Zimmerman and Pollner then cited the example of a code of behavior among prison convicts. Whereas traditional sociology would look at the ways in which actors are constrained by a convict code, ethnomethodologists would examine how the convicts use the code as an explanatory and persuasive device. Don Zimmerman and Lawrence Wieder offered the following generalization on the confusion of topic and resource:

> The ethnomethodologist is *not* concerned with providing causal explanations of observably regular, patterned, repetitive actions by some kind of analysis of the actor's point of view. He *is* concerned with how members of society go about the task of *seeing, describing,* and *explaining* order in the world in which they live.
>
> (Zimmerman and Wieder, 1970:289)

Social order is not a reality in itself to the ethnomethodologist but an accomplishment of social actors.

Another way of putting this argument is in terms of Garfinkel's (1967) view that sociology treats its actors as "judgmental dopes." Sociology sees actors as constrained by external forces, unable to make independent judgments or take independent action. Ethnomethodology, however, accepts the idea that actors make crucially important judgments and, in fact, makes this fact a centerpiece of the orientation.

These criticisms of traditional sociology give us an overview of ethnomethodology, but in negative terms. We turn now to a more positive characterization of this theory, starting with Mehan and Wood's (1975) program statement.

Ethnomethodology: A Basic Program

Mehan and Wood (1975) have offered ethnomethodology's most basic program statement. Their approach is similar to that of Berger and Luckmann: "The person begins with certain materials that set limits, and then acts and in acting alters those limits. These new limits form the material of another creative act, ad infinitum" (Mehan and Wood, 1975:203). This is a very strong statement of the relationship between people and the structures they create. However, Mehan and Wood tended to discuss this only in contemporary terms and paid insufficient attention to the historically created social structures that constrain activity.

In developing their approach, Mehan and Wood attempted to set themselves apart from those ethnomethodologists who go too far and regard the "objective reality of social facts" as nonexistent except for the practices by which they are constituted by actors. They accepted the importance of meaning constructions but refused to fall into the trap of arguing that there are no objective realities: "People create meanings, but the world comes to them independently of their interpretive activities" (Mehan and Wood, 1975:194). They concluded that "the facticity of an objective world is now an explicit feature of the theory" (Mehan and Wood, 1975:197).

Mehan and Wood also rejected the idea that ethnomethodology should focus on mental activities. Rather, they focused on the action and interaction that flows from mental activities. In this, they viewed themselves as following in the tradition of Garfinkel, who stated:

> I shall exercise a theorist's preference and say that meaningful events are entirely and exclusively events in a person's behavioral environment. . . . Hence there is no reason to look under the skulls since nothing of interest is to be found there but brains. The skin of the person will be left intact.
>
> (Garfinkel, 1963:190)

Once again, we are confronted with the reluctance of sociologists to focus on mental activities, even among ethnomethodologists, who, one would presume, would be concerned with them.

The heart of Mehan and Wood's program statement lies in the view that ethnomethodology sees social reality as:

> dependent upon ceaseless (1) reflexive use of (2) bodies of social knowledge in (3) interaction. As this reflexive interactional work assembles the reality, without it, the reality could not be sustained. Hence, each reality (4) is fragile. Insofar as people may experience more than one reality, realities are said to be (5) permeable.
>
> (Mehan and Wood, 1975:6)

This position involves five basic views of the nature of social reality:

1. *Reality as reflexive activity.* To ethnomethodologists, we are all engaged in the process of creating social reality through our thoughts and actions. However, we are rarely aware of this process, usually because we conceal it from ourselves. (This is why ethnomethodologists use breaching experiments.) When we say hello to someone and the person responds similarly, we are not conscious of the reflexive work both parties are doing. On the other hand, when the other person scowls and walks away in response to our "hello," we become aware that we were trying to create a certain social reality and that we failed. We may then often try to reaffirm the world of greetings as we know it by trying to explain away the individual's inappropriate response ("He didn't hear me" or "He wasn't feeling well").

2. *Reality as a coherent body of knowledge.* People in their everyday lives, as well as sociologists studying them, organize the world into coherent realities. Problems arise when the social scientist imposes an order that is not the same as the one used by the participants. Ethnomethodologists, with their basic commitment to the study of reflexivity, would generally be more aware of this problem and strive to limit the distortions.

3. *Reality as interactional activity*. Social reality is not simply "out there." Rather, its existence depends on the ceaseless reciprocal interaction and social construction of reality of the participants.
4. *The fragility of realities*. Social realities are not hardened structures but highly fragile creations that can be disrupted in various ways. This view is another of the bases of the ethnomethodologist's interest in breaching experiments. Because of their fragility, social realities can be breached by both the ethnomethodologist and the layperson. The ethnomethodologist can do this consciously in order to study the process of reality construction.
5. *The permeability of realities*. People live within a variety of social worlds and can move from one reality to another. For instance, on a day-to-day basis we move easily from classroom to athletic field, two very different areas of social life. A more extreme case occurs when people pass from being "straight" to dope addiction, or from atheism to religious fundamentalism. Behaviors (for instance, cannibalism) that we find objectionable in one context might be acceptable in another (for instance, survival techniques for those involved in a plane crash on a desolate mountain).

SOME BASIC CONCEPTS

As Mehan and Wood made clear, ethnomethodologists have developed some interesting and unusual concepts. We now examine several of these concepts to gain an idea of both the problems and the essential nature of ethnomethodology.

ACCOUNTS   *Accounting* is the process by which people make sense out of the world (Handel, 1982:24). *Accounts* are the ways in which actors do such things as describe, analyze, criticize, and idealize specific situations (Bittner, 1973:115). Ethnomethodologists devote a lot of attention to analyzing people's accounts, as well as to the ways in which accounts are offered and accepted (or rejected) by others. This is one of the reasons ethnomethodologists are preoccupied with conversational analysis. To take an example, when a student explains to her professor why she failed to take an examination, she is offering an account. The student is trying to make sense out of an event for her professor. Ethnomethodologists are interested in the nature of that account, as well as the accounting process by which the student offers the account and whether it is either accepted or rejected by the professor. At a very different level, the work of ethnomethodologists—indeed, of all sociologists—should be seen as a series of accounts that are analyzable in the same way as all other accounts.

INDEXICALITY   The term "indexicality" is drawn from linguistics, where it deals with sentences that may have different meanings in different contexts. " 'It's raining' has different meanings: on the day of a long awaited picnic, at the end of a drought, when the rivers are already overflowing their banks, or when one is driving and the temperature is near freezing" (Handel, 1982:41). Ethnomethodologists adopt the view that all accounts—in fact, all expressions and all practical actions—must be interpreted within their particular context. This means that the ethnomethodologists must not impose their view of reality on the actors. Instead, they must try to put themselves in the actors' place in order to understand what is transpiring.

ETCETERA PRINCIPLE   All situations involve incomplete aspects that must be filled in by the participants. A good example is the "Radio Raiders" story discussed above. Despite being confronted with ambiguities, we carry on our social life. In a given situation, we allow unclear information to pass on the assumption that it will be clarified later on. As the action proceeds, we seek information within the context that allows us to clarify and grasp what happened. If we stopped to question every ambiguity, little social life would take place. We must all practice the etcetera principle if social life is to be possible.

DOCUMENTARY METHOD   Both laypeople and sociologists utilize the documentary method, which involves an effort to identify "an *underlying pattern* behind a series of appearances such that each appearance is seen as referring to, an expression of, or a document of, the underlying pattern" (T. Wilson, 1970:68; italics added). Neither the layperson nor the sociologist is content with the analysis of isolated events; both need to uncover the underlying pattern.

NATURAL LANGUAGE   This system of practices allows people to speak, hear, and witness the objective production and display of social life. Natural language is not the same as linguistic categories; rather, it is a concern with the basic structure of speaker-hearer interaction. Examples of this include the way in which people take turns in conversations or seek to cope with disruptions in a conversation (Zimmerman, 1978).

The Strain Toward Structural Constraint

Ethnomethodology has always encompassed an impossible dichotomy. On the one hand, its adherents have talked of the actor as a constructor of social reality, and they have excoriated mainstream sociology for seeing the actor as overly constrained by large-scale structures. On the other hand, many ethnomethodologists have adopted the view that the field should focus on the more micro-level constraints on actors, the constraints that exist within "natural language," for example. Zimmerman (1978:10) came to be a strong supporter of this latter position, as witnessed by his view that natural language is both "(1) prior to and independent of any particular speaker, that is, external, and (2) less preferential than obligatory, that is, constraining." This sounds remarkably like Durkheim's treatment of social facts, which the ethnomethodologists have been so critical of, but at the individual rather than the social-cultural level. Zimmerman has often sounded like a structuralist as he examined the "invariant" properties of natural language. However, he also spoke of natural language as a resource used by actors in the accomplishment of social life. It is unclear whether actors are "judgmental dopes" or active creators of their social lives. There is an unresolved strain in Zimmerman's work, as well as in ethnomethodology in general.

This strain toward structuralism is even clearer in the work of another important ethnomethodologist, Aaron Cicourel (1974). Cicourel criticized traditional sociology for seeing the actor as overly constrained by large-scale structures. He viewed the actor as a creator of social reality. Simultaneously, however, he adopted a structuralist view of cognitive processes and viewed the interpretive procedures actors use as similar to deep-structure grammatical rules. These deep structures allow actors to cope with their social setting, yet they are not enslaving. They enable "the actor to generate appropriate (*usually innovative*) responses to changing situated settings" (Cicourel, 1974:27). He viewed interpretive procedures that have *invariant* properties as allowing the actor to behave *innovatively*. One of the ways that Cicourel sought to handle this paradox was to argue that interpretive procedures emerge developmentally through the life cycle. Thus the actor is constantly developing new procedures to handle new situations.

Cicourel developed a complicated theory that sought to integrate ethnomethodology with linguistics (deep structures) and traditional sociology (normative or surface rules). Social life emerges from the interaction of creative actors, deep structures, and normative constraint. The crucial issue here, indeed for all ethnomethodologists who study the deep structures of linguistics, is how such structures allow for creativity. On the surface, it would appear that they constrain, if not determine, what actors think and do. Ethnomethodologists with this orientation need to demonstrate better how such determinism is consistent with their view of actors as creators.

The Move Toward Social Structure

Given the historical concern of ethnomethodology with small-scale phenomena, a number of observers (for instance, Zimmerman, 1978) have started to think about how ethnomethodology can be integrated with a concern for social structures. Zimmerman (1978:12) viewed cross-fertilization with macro sociology as "an open question, and an intriguing possibility." Indeed, Zimmerman and others (for instance, Chua, 1977) have discussed the relationship between ethnomethodology and Marxian theory. Little work has been done in this area up to the present, but is is an area of ethnomethodology that will probably continue to develop in the future.

SUMMARY

In this chapter we discuss two separate but related theories—phenomenological sociology and ethnomethodology. We begin with a treatment of the general similarities of the two theories. For instance, they have a common intellectual base in the work of Edmund Husserl and Alfred Schutz, and they both focus on individual thought and action. It is sometimes difficult to classify their work as belonging to one or the other school; in fact, some individuals have created material that at one time can be associated with one school and at another time with the other school.

Next we discuss the important differences between the two theories. Most generally, ethnomethodology seems to have taken phenomenology and fused it with traditional sociology to produce a unique perspective. Among the specific differences, ethnomethodologists tend to emphasize empirical research, whereas phenomenologists concentrate on "think pieces"; ethnomethodologists tend to focus more on action and interaction, whereas phenomenologists are more concerned with consciousness and culture; and ethnomethodologists tend to emphasize the freedom of actors, whereas phenomenologists see them as rather constrained. Thus, in spite of the similarities, there are enough differences between them to make it necessary to deal with the two approaches separately.

The discussion of phenomenology begins with a few of the most relevant ideas of Edmund Husserl, including his notions of the natural attitude, bracketing, a science of consciousness, and intentionality. Although contemporary phenomenologists often trace their roots to Husserl's philosophy, they often distort his orientation.

A large portion of this chapter is devoted to the work of Alfred Schutz, the most important figure in the development of both phenomenological sociology and ethno-methodology. Schutz offered a complex, often confusing theory that is difficult to summarize and has been subject to conflicting analyses.

Schutz's work becomes clearer when we discuss his differentiation between philosophy and science. In his philosophical work, the everyday world—the thoughts and actions of individuals—is very important. However, these micro phenomena, especially consciousness, are not amenable to scientific sociological analysis. Amenable to scientific study are the cultural aspects of the social world. We see this illustrated in various ways in Schutz's work.

At one level, Schutz differentiated among four basic realms of the social world. The realms of successors, the future (*folgewelt*), and predecessors, the past (*vorwelt*), are of marginal importance from a scientific point of view. The *umwelt*, the world of directly experienced social reality, is important, but it cannot be analyzed scientifically. What can be studied scientifically is the *mitwelt*, or the world of indirectly experienced social reality. In this realm people deal with abstract types rather than with actual people in face-to-face interaction. Since people do not deal with actual others in this realm, their thoughts and actions are determined by various cultural phenomena such as "typifications." People learn "recipes" and then simply employ them at the appropriate moment. They do not deal with actors but simply with types.

In this effort to demarcate a realm of scientific sociology, Schutz sometimes went even further and substituted homunculi, or puppets, for real actors. Such homunculi are incapable of thought and action; they are totally determined by cultural phenomena like typifications.

We also discuss Schutz's analysis of cultural forces in the life world, which involves the general, taken-for-granted framework of social life and its impact on actors' thoughts and actions. The life world is a framework imposed on actors from without; it is the totality of typifications upon which all experience, knowledge, and conduct is based. The actor takes an unquestioning attitude to the life world and adopts what Schutz called the "natural attitude." We discuss as well several of Schutz's specific components of the life world such as skills, useful knowledge, and knowledge of recipes. Schutz recognized that in the everyday world these elements receive specific biographical articulations, or personal expressions; they become private stocks of knowledge.

The distinction between we and they relationships in the life world is taken up next. Although the personal, face-to-face interaction of we relationships is important, and Schutz offers many philosophical insights about it, it is not amenable to scientific analysis in his view. However, they relationships, which involve indirect interaction with impersonal contemporaries rather than personal associates, can be the subject of scientific study. In they relationships, thoughts and actions of people are dominated by anonymous typifications.

Although his definition of scientific sociology excludes consciousness, Schutz offered many insights into the concept. In this area, we analyze his work on meanings and motives. Schutz also offered useful ideas on how people act in the face of problematic situations.

Given the background of the ideas of Husserl and especially Schutz, we then seek to develop some sense of the nature and diversity of contemporary phenomenological sociology. To this end, we discuss several examples of this theory. First we look at how George Psathas and Frances Waksler examined face-to-face interaction from the point of view of micro-level phenomenology. Although such small-scale analyses predominate within phenomenology, there are also broader efforts, such as Peter Berger and Thomas Luckmann's important, but aborted, attempt to integrate the small-scale concerns of phenomenology with larger-scale issues. Finally, we return to the individual level for a discussion of Alan Blum and Peter McHugh's analysis of motives. This work illustrates the tendency of some phenomenologists to fuse phenomenological sociology with ethnomethodology as well as other theories.

Since ethnomethodology is dominated by empirical studies, the bulk of the second part of this chapter is devoted to a series of examples of the kind of research undertaken by ethnomethodologists. We look at studies devoted to how people ''do'' walking, open telephone calls, invite laughter, produce sentences in the course of interaction, formulate summaries during a conversation, understand newspaper stories, understand what to do in settings that they have not previously encountered, read directional maps, accomplish their gender, and repair breaches in interactional encounters.

We also discuss a number of the ethnomethodologists' criticisms of traditional sociology, especially its tendency to impose *its* sense of reality on the social world rather than letting the sense emerge from the setting itself. To the ethnomethodologists, the sociologist's concepts, techniques, and statistics distort the true nature of social reality. Furthermore, ethnomethodologists have argued that although the real social world has been a resource for the analyses of traditional sociologists, it has rarely been a topic in its own right for them. Finally, they attack traditional sociologists for treating actors as ''judgmental dopes'' rather than as active creators of their social worlds.

The work of Hugh Mehan and Houston Wood is offered as a basic program statement of ethnomethodology. It involves five basic propositions:

1. Reality involves reflexive activity.
2. Reality is organized into coherent bodies of knowledge.
3. Reality is the product of ceaseless interaction.
4. Reality is fragile.
5. Reality is permeable.

We also discuss several of the basic concepts of ethnomethodology, including accounts, indexicality, the etcetera principle, documentary method, and natural language. We note that some ethnomethodologists have tended to move away from an image of the actor as creator and toward a more structural interpretation. We close with a discussion of the possibility of integrating the micro orientation of ethnomethodology with larger-scale theories.

In sum, despite some similarities, there are important differences between phenomenological sociology and ethnomethodology. Still, in the future there may well be an increased effort to integrate the two.

CHAPTER SEVEN
Exchange Theory and Behavioral Sociology

THE next discussion concerns two rather curious sociological theories—exchange theory and behavioral sociology. They are unique for several reasons. First, they take their inspiration primarily from psychology, specifically from the behaviorism of B. F. Skinner (Tarter, 1973). Second, another influence, especially in exchange theory, is economics, also outside the domain of sociology. Third, in their most extreme forms they constitute an outright rejection of all the other sociological theories discussed in this book.

Given the preeminent place of B. F. Skinner and his behaviorism in exchange theory, we will begin this chapter with his general orientation. Next, we will discuss behavioral sociology, since it represents the most pristine translation of Skinner's ideas into sociological principles. Finally, we will turn to exchange theory per se, particularly as it is presented in the work of its two foremost sociological practitioners—George Homans and Peter Blau.[1]

There are a number of sociologists who focus on behavior and exchange without accepting much, if any, of Skinner's behavioral sociology and Homans's and Blau's versions of exchange theory. Alvin Gouldner's (1960) classic essay on reciprocity and William Goode's (1960) work on role strain illustrate this long-standing tradition of nonbehavioristic exchange theory. This version of exchange theory emphasizes the reciprocal nature of social relationships and how power and prestige grow out of imbalances in reciprocity

---

[1]Homans and Blau are not the only exchange theorists of note. Also of importance is the work of John Thibaut and Harold H. Kelley (1959), Richard Emerson (1972a; 1972b; 1976; 1981), B. F. Meeker (1971), and Robert L. Hamblin and John K. Kunkel (1977).

(Goode, 1978). While these thinkers are likely to think of themselves as exchange theorists, they are not likely to think of themselves as either sociological or psychological behaviorists. In this chapter we will focus on the sociological work on behavior and exchange that is heavily influenced by psychological behaviorism. We will not be concerned with work of this genre done from nonbehavioristic perspectives.

Although all of the chapters in this book are shaped, at least in part, by the author's sense of sociology's multiple paradigms (see Appendix) as well as the place of various theorists and theories within them, this perspective plays a far greater role in this chapter. Since it plays such a central role in the following pages, we will discuss that schema briefly, and in the process we can consider the theories discussed thus far as components of sociology's multiple paradigms.

In the author's (Ritzer, 1975a; 1975b) view, sociology is composed of three major paradigms—the social facts, social definition, and social behavior paradigms. Each paradigm has four major components, but of importance to us at the moment are only the paradigms' images of the subject matter of sociology and the theories each encompasses. The social facts paradigm takes as the subject matter of sociology large-scale social structures and institutions and their coercive effect on actors and their thoughts and actions. Structural functionalism, conflict theory, and several varieties of neo-Marxian theory are associated with the social facts paradigm. The social definition paradigm accepts as the primary concern of sociology actors, the ways in which they construct social reality, and the action that results from such construction. Thus actors, to the social definitionist, are relatively free and creative, while to the social factist they are largely determined by large-scale structures and institutions. Symbolic interactionists, phenomenologists, ethnomethodologists, and at least some neo-Marxists operate within this paradigm. Finally, there is the social behavior paradigm, in which the subject matter of sociology is individual behavior and the reinforcers and punishers that affect it. The theories we are about to discuss, behavioral sociology and exchange theory, are encompassed by this paradigm.

The multiple paradigm schema just outlined plays an especially key role in this chapter. First, it attunes us to the main concerns of the two theories—behavior, reinforcement, and punishment. Second, it alerts us to the fact that the theorists associated with this paradigm are not primarily concerned with, and some even reject an interest in, large-scale structures and institutions as well as the social construction of reality and social action. Third, although many associated with this paradigm have adopted a dogmatic position on what it should and should not concern itself with, there are some others who have sought to integrate the traditional concerns of social behaviorism with those of social factism and social definitionism. Throughout this chapter we will try to sort out the complex interrelationships that exist between social behaviorism and the other sociological paradigms.

SKINNER AND BEHAVIORISM

Behaviorism has a long history in the social sciences, and in particular in psychology. However, modern behaviorism in all the social sciences, and in particular in sociology, can be traced to the work of B. F. Skinner. Skinner's work, while steadfastly devoted to the principles of behaviorism, has covered a broad spectrum, including scientific tracts (Skinner, 1938), a utopian novel (Skinner, 1948), polemical and political essays (Skinner, 1971), and practical applications of behaviorism. His scientific, utopian, political, and practical works have all played a role in the development of a sociological version of behaviorism.

First, let us examine Skinner's attitudes toward other sociological theories. He regarded them as rather mystical enterprises. This goes for the macro theories associated with the social facts paradigm, such as structural functionalism and conflict theory, as well as the micro theories associated with the social definition paradigm, such as symbolic interactionism, ethomethodology, and phenomenology. He saw these theories as constructing mystical entities that serve to distract the sociologist from the only concrete entities of study—behavior and the consequences that make that behavior more or less likely to occur (Molm, 1981:160). Take, for example, Skinner's criticism of the concept of culture, often defined by a typical social factist as "traditional (i.e., historically derived and selected) ideas and especially their attached values" (Skinner, 1971:121). He argued that this definition has created unnecessary mystical elements such as "ideas" and "values." Scientists do not see ideas and values when they look at society. Instead, they see "how people live, how they raise their children, how they gather or cultivate food, what kinds of dwellings they live in, what they wear, what games they play, how they treat each other, how they govern themselves, and so on" (Skinner, 1971:121). The culture of a community is composed of behaviors. In order to understand behaviors we do not need concepts such as ideas and values; rather, we need to understand such things as rewards and costs.

Skinner leveled his strongest criticisms at the theories of social definitionism. One of Skinner's major goals in *Beyond Freedom and Dignity* (1971) was to eliminate the idea that he labels "autonomous man" from the social sciences—indeed, from the world. The idea of an autonomous man is an integral part of the social definition paradigm (for example, Mead's "I" is close to Skinner's hated autonomous man), and an attack on it thus means an attack on the social definitionists. Skinner, speaking for social behaviorism, did not want to reconcile his differences with the social definitionists. In fact, he was interested in eliminating the theories associated with the social definition paradigm.

What is this notion of an autonomous man that Skinner sought to eliminate? We imply that people are autonomous when we attribute to them such things as feeling, thinking, freedom, and dignity. People, in this view, have an inner core from which their actions emanate. This inner core enables them to initiate, originate, and create. This active, creative, voluntaristic view of people is clearly in line with the social definitionist position, and Skinner's effort to destroy this idea is, indirectly, an effort to destroy the theories of social definitionism.

To Skinner (1971:12), the idea that people have an inner, autonomous core is a mystical, metaphysical position of the kind that must be eliminated from the social sciences: "Autonomous man serves to explain only the things we are not yet able to explain in other ways. His existence depends on our ignorance, and he naturally loses status as we come to know more about behavior." Behavior, as well as the conditions that produce behavior, primarily other behaviors, are the primary subject matter to Skinner. He believed we should not focus on such concepts as "feelings"; we should mainly focus on the examination (and control) of behavior and the contingencies that affect it.[2] Linda Molm (1981:161) amplified this point by arguing that Skinner was concerned with what he called "private events," or "events that take place inside an individual and that are not directly observable by others." In this category he included thoughts, feelings, and perceptions. However, Skinner was only willing to accept a concern with such internal states under two conditions. First, they cannot be independent, or mediating, variables but can only occupy the role of dependent variables in a behaviorist's schema. In other words, they cannot be explanatory variables, only variables to be explained by other factors. Second, they must be observable in some way. The self-reports of actors (as well as their behaviors) count as observable phenomena. Such a limited, scientific view of mental states is not likely to be acceptable to those who adopt the social definition paradigm.

Skinner and social behaviorists in general are interested in the relationship between individuals and their environment (Molm, 1981:160), which is composed of a variety of social and nonsocial objects. The social behaviorist argues that the principles that govern the relationship between an individual and a social object are the same as those that govern the relationship between an individual and a nonsocial object.[3] Don Bushell and Robert Burgess (1969:27) defined the nature of the subject matter of behaviorists as "the behavior of individuals that operates on the environment in such a way as to produce some consequence or change in it which, in turn, modifies subsequent performances of that behavior." Thus they focus on the "functional relationship" between behavior and changes in the environment of the actor. This means that a child tossing a stone into a river is an object of study to the behaviorist in exactly the same way as a mother scolding a child, a teacher instructing a class, or a business executive meeting a board of directors.

Social behaviorists claim they are interested in an interaction process, but the process is conceptualized very differently from the way it is in the theories of the social definitionists. Actors, to the social definitionist, are dynamic, creative forces in the interaction process (Perinbanayagam, 1981:167). They do not simply respond to stimuli but interpret them and act on the basis of their definitions of them. The social behaviorist, on the other hand, allows the individual far less freedom. The individual's response is determined by the nature of the external stimuli. The image is of a much more mechanical person than that conceived by the social definitionists.[4]

The image of actors in social factist theories (for example, structural functionalism) is almost as mechanistic as in the social behaviorist paradigm. The social factist sees the individual as determined by external norms, values, structures, and the like. The difference between social factism and social behaviorism lies in the source of control

---

[2]A number of behaviorists are willing to include such things as cognition, emotion, the "mind" in their domain. For example, Arthur Staats (1976) made the case for including the mind in behaviorism. John Baldwin and Janice Baldwin (1978) argued that behaviorists, indeed all sociologists, should use both traditional scientific techniques and the *verstehen* methodology to understand a variety of social phenomena, including subjectivity and meaning.

[3]This is another place in which Molm disagreed with more traditional social behaviorists, such as Homans. She took pains to differentiate between the orientations of behavioral psychologists and behavioral sociologists.

[4]As we will see, this is still another point on which Molm disagreed.

over the individual. To the social factist, large-scale structures and institutions control the individual. Social behaviorists are concerned with the relationship between individuals and the consequences that make a behavior more or less likely to occur.

We turn now to a discussion of behavioral sociology. It is increasingly important in itself, and it is a useful link between our discussions of Skinner's behaviorism and the exchange theories of Homans and Blau.

BEHAVIORAL SOCIOLOGY

Behavioral sociology represents an effort to apply the principles of psychological behaviorism to sociological questions. The behavioral sociologist is concerned with the relationship between the effects of an actor's behavior on the environment and their impact on the actor's later behavior. To put this more concretely, an actor emits some behavior. One might almost think of this, at least initially, as a random behavior. The environment in which the behavior exists, be it social or physical, is affected by the behavior and in turn ''acts'' back in various ways. That reaction, positive, negative, or neutral, will have an effect on the actor's later behavior. If the reaction has been rewarding to the actor, the same behavior is likely to be emitted in the future in similar situations. If the reaction has been painful or punishing, the behavior is less likely to occur in the future. What the behavioral sociologist is interested in is the relationship between the *history* of environmental reactions or consequences and the nature of present behavior. The behavioral sociologist is saying that the past consequences of a given behavior govern its present state. By knowing what elicited a certain behavior in the past, we can predict whether an actor will produce the same behavior in the present situation.

Basic Concepts

A key concept in behavioral sociology is *reinforcement*, which may be defined as a reward. Nothing inherent in an object makes it serve as a reward. Reinforcers cannot be defined on a priori grounds apart from their effects on behavior. Thus a ''reward'' that does not affect the actor is not a reinforcer. Food might generally be considered a reward in our society, but if a given individual is not hungry, it will not serve as a reinforcer. One crucial determinant of whether a given reward will, in fact, serve as a reinforcer is the actors' level of deprivation. If actors have been deprived of food, for example, they will be hungry and food will act as a reinforcer. If, on the other hand, they have just eaten, their level of deprivation will be minimal and food will not be an effective reinforcer. This is an example of physiological deprivation. If we deny people food, sex, water, or air, they will serve as potent reinforcers. If, however, these physiological needs are well met, they will not be useful reinforcers. However, reinforcers are not just physiological; they can also be learned. That is, we learn to need certain things. Once we learn to need these things, they serve as reinforcers when we are deprived of them.

Reinforcers may be either positive or negative. Positive reinforcement occurs when environmental changes take the form of rewards, ''which thereby increase the probability of behavior occurring in the future'' (Bushell and Burgess, 1969:28–29). In this situation the actor is rewarded; for example, the salesperson knocks on a door and makes a sale. Behavioral theory would view the sale as a positive reinforcement, *if* the salesperson then knocks on more doors in the hopes of repeating the success. Negative reinforcement also increases the likelihood of a behavior occurring in the future, but it takes the form of removing something from the environment. Turning off a noisy radio, for example, may improve a person's ability to write or read. In the future, a person's ability to write or read may be improved when the radio is turned off.

In considering reinforcers, *punishment* must also be taken into account: "A consequence which decreases the frequency of the response that precedes it is a *punisher*" (Bushell and Burgess, 1969:29). For example, a whip, or even the mere threat of a whip, may serve to prevent someone from repeating a given act. However, what is a punishment to one person may be a reward to another. A masochist, for instance, may find the whip rewarding and would be more likely to repeat a given act. Thus in order to determine whether something will be a reward or a punishment, we must know the personal history as well as the physiological properties of the individual.

Punishments, like reinforcers, can be either positive or negative, but remember, punishers are aimed at reducing the frequency of a response. Striking a child every time he cries is an example of a positive form of punishment. Punishment takes a negative form when we remove or threaten to remove a reward. This is labeled *response cost*, or loss of reinforcers. If we remove or threaten to remove privileges enjoyed by a child because he is crying, we are employing a negative form of punishment. Bushell and Burgess (1969:30) argued that response cost "is the mainstay of control procedures in social organizations." Rather than reward or positively punish, most social organizations prefer to remove, or threaten to remove, rewards already being enjoyed.

As pointed out earlier, the behavioral sociologist is concerned primarily with the relationship between actors and their environment. The reinforcement-punishment relationship between actors and their environment occurs in patterns, some of which are naturally determined (for example, by food deprivation) and some of which are socially determined. In the simplest pattern, reinforcement follows each and every act. This pattern of continuously reinforced behavior is most likely to be found in childhood where, for example, a child's cry is immediately followed by attention from parents. This pattern is less likely to occur in adulthood. In fact, adult reinforcement is much more likely to be intermittent, with reinforcement occurring at an uneven pace. Traveling salespeople do not expect every knock on a door to produce a sale; obviously, though, knocks on doors do lead to some sales, which keep salespeople on the job. If they were never rewarded with a sale, their sales behavior would be *extinguished*, and they would cease functioning as salespeople. Interestingly, continuously reinforced behavior is more easily extinguished than intermittently rewarded behavior. Salespeople become accustomed to intermittent reward, and a good deal of time passes after the last sale before they realize that they may not be rewarded again. Thus extinguishing their sales behavior takes a long time. If they had been rewarded continuously, and the rewards suddenly stopped, they might continue working for only a short time. They would cease their activities far more quickly than they would had they been rewarded intermittently.

Reinforcement is far more complex than simply doing something and receiving the desired (or undesired) reaction. Many conditions in the environment determine the probability for reinforcement of a given act. Some conditions make the response likely, whereas others make it less likely. These conditions are things that have in the past been associated with a reinforcement or a punishment. If, for example, the person doing the reinforcing has always worn some sort of uniform, that uniform may elicit a given response even when it is worn by someone else. Similarly, if a classroom has always been associated with punishment, a response to punishment will be elicited even if the student is transferred to a rewarding classroom situation. This is the process by which originally neutral stimuli—for example, the uniform—become *secondary,* or *conditioned, reinforcers.* Once transformed, a neutral stimulus can become a positive reinforcer. Since reinforcement rarely occurs in a vacuum, a number of secondary reinforcers inevitably become associated with the original one. By this process the number of reinforcers mushrooms.

Although many reinforcers are specific to a given situation, there are some that are *generalized reinforcers.* These are defined by Bushell and Burgess as reinforcers that:

> have great power and importance in social analyses because they retain their effectiveness in the absence of any specific deprivation. The term "generalized" refers to the fact that these stimuli stand for, represent, or provide access to a wide range of other reinforcers, both unconditioned and conditioned, which may differ from time to time and from person to person.
>
> (Bushell and Burgess, 1969:38)

Money and status are two good examples of generalized reinforcers. They can be used to acquire many other desirable things. Since generalized reinforcers represent a number of other different things, they become more and more reinforcing in themselves. The behavioral sociologist sees the individual as difficult to satiate in terms of such generalized reinforcers. Large amounts of money or status are not likely to dull the desire for more.

Behavior Modification

When a given response is reinforced, a whole series of other responses similar to the one being rewarded are almost inevitably reinforced at the same time. This fact allows the behavioral sociologist to speak of *shaping behavior,* or *behavior modification.* Figure 7.1 illustrates this process.

FIGURE 7.1   Behavior Modification: Existing and Desired Behaviors

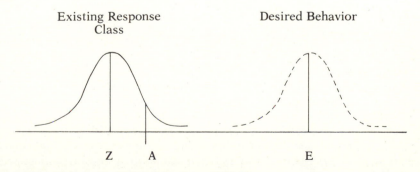

Source: Adapted from Bushell and Burgess, 1969:40.

Because we possess a given reward, we are able to elicit behavior Z from an individual. In eliciting this behavior, we also elicit a number of similar behaviors, including A. Suppose the behavior we really want to elicit is E. How do we get our subject to respond with behavior E? We begin by rewarding A, which is already in our range of elicited responses. By repeatedly eliciting A, we move the center of the curve over A and bring behaviors closer to E, the desired behavior, within our range. Ultimately, we will elicit behavior E. The process is illustrated in Figure 7.2.

FIGURE 7.2   Behavior Modification: Eliciting the Desired Behavior

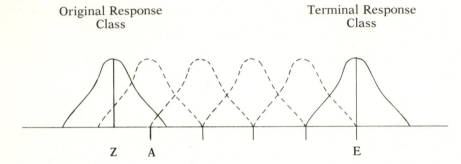

Original Response Class   Terminal Response Class

Z   A   E

Source: Adapted from Bushell and Burgess, 1969:41.

The process of *behavior modification* has been adapted to therapeutic situations. Behavior modification is seen as a six-step process:

1. Therapists must identify the specific final behaviors that they want to elicit.
2. They must determine the nature of the existing response class of the subject, that is, what range of behaviors is currently being elicited and how close this is to the desired behavior.
3. Therapists must construct a favorable training site. "This means eliminating distracting stimuli, the possibility of conflicting or incompatible behavior, and providing stimuli which are discriminative for the desired response" (Bushell and Burgess, 1969:43).
4. Therapists must establish motivation in the subject by acquiring an effective reinforcer. Although specific reinforcers can be used, general reinforcers such as money, social attention, and social status are most often used.
5. Therapists must begin the shaping process by "differential reinforcement of responses that are successively closer to the terminal state" (Bushell and Burgess, 1969:43–44).
6. Finally, when the modification has "taken," therapists should apply the reinforcers more intermittently. The reinforcement should eventually come less from an artificial device and more from the natural world.

The applications of behavioral sociology—for example, to behavior modification—set it apart from other sociological theories, including exchange theory. Although there are such instances as the human relations school of industrial sociology, which seeks to manipulate group processes in order to increase the productivity of workers, behavioral sociology has far more of an applied character than any other sociological theory. Behavior modification has been used with retarded children (Birnbauer et al., 1965), autistic children (Brawley et al., 1969), preschool children (Bushell, Wrobel, and Michaelis, 1969), and even college students (Miller, 1970).

EXCHANGE THEORY

Exchange theory constitutes an effort to take the principles of behaviorism, fuse them with other ideas, and apply them to the concerns of sociologists. Although exchange theory can be traced back many years (Knox, 1963), it underwent a boom in the 1950s and 1960s in the work of George Homans (Beniger and Savory, 1981). Much of Homans's exchange theory can be viewed as a reaction to the social facts paradigm and its sociological theories, especially structural functionalism.

Homans and Durkheim

Homans (1969) confronted the structural functionalists by directly attacking the work of Emile Durkheim on three points: the issue of emergence, his view of psychology, and his method of explanation. Homans recognized Durkheim's view that during interaction new phenomena emerge. He felt that such a view is acceptable to social behaviorists. However, how do we explain what emerges from interaction? Homans took the position that no new propositions, beyond those already applying to simple individual behavior, are needed. He said: "All the usual examples of emergent social phenomena can readily be shown to follow from psychological propositions" (Homans, 1969:14). Thus, Durkheim thought that emergent forms could only be explained by sociology, while Homans felt they could be explained by psychological principles.

Homans pointed out correctly that since Durkheim wrote in the late nineteenth century, the psychology he knew was extremely primitive. Psychology in his day focused primarily on instinctive forms of behavior and assumed that human nature was the same in all individuals. Thus Durkheim was right to disentangle sociology from the psychology of his day. "Sociology is surely not a corollary of the kind of psychology Durkheim had in mind" (Homans, 1969:18). However, contemporary psychology is far more sophisticated and complex than the psychology of Durkheim's time; that Durkheim was able to separate psychology from sociology does not mean that the same feat can be accomplished today.

Finally, Homans attacked Durkheim for his method of explanation. Homans argued that Durkheim considered something explained if we were able to find its cause or causes. More specifically, a social fact is explained when we can find the social facts that cause it. Homans admitted that social facts are often the cause of other social facts, but such a finding does not in his view constitute an explanation. To Homans, what needs to be explained is the *relationship* between cause and effect, why one social fact causes another social fact. Homans thought that explanation was inevitably psychological. (It should be noted that when Homans used the term "psychological" he meant *behavioral*, "the behavior of men as men," as he put it.) Homans's explanation of a particular historical cause and effect is instructive:

The price rise of the sixteenth century, which I take to be a social fact, was certainly a determining cause of the enclosure movement among English landlords. But were we to construct
an explanation why this particular cause has this particular effect, we should have to say that
the price rise presented English landlords both with great opportunities for monetary gain and
great risks of monetary loss, that enclosure tended to increase the gain and avoid the loss, that
the landlords found monetary gain rewarding (which is a state of individual consciousness, if
you like), and finally, that men are likely to take actions whose results they find rewarding—
which, as I cannot repeat too often, is a general psychological proposition.

(Homans, 1969:19)

Thus individual responses (behavior) always intervene between social facts. Homans
argued that social facts lead to individual responses, which in turn lead to new social
facts. However, the essential factor is the behavior, not the social fact.

GEORGE CASPAR HOMANS: An Autobiographical Sketch

How I became a sociologist, which was largely a matter
of accident, I have described in other publications. My
sustained work in sociology began with my association,
beginning in 1933, with Professors Lawrence Henderson
and Elton Mayo at the Harvard Business School. Henderson, a biochemist, was studying the physiological characteristics of industrial work, Mayo, a psychologist, the
human factors. Mayo was then and later the director of
the famous researches at the Hawthorne Plant of the
Western Electric Company in Chicago.

I took part in a course of readings and discussions
under Mayo's direction. Among other books Mayo asked
his students to read several books by prominent social
anthropologists, particularly Malinowski, Radcliffe-Brown, and Firth. Mayo wanted us to
read these books so that we should understand how in aboriginal, in contrast to
modern, societies social rituals supported productive work.

I became interested in them for a wholly different reason. In those days the cultural
anthropologists were intellectually dominant, and friends of mine in this group, such as
Clyde Kluckhohn, insisted that every culture was unique. Instead I began to perceive
from my reading that certain institutions of aboriginal societies repeated themselves in
places so far separated in time and space that the societies could not have borrowed
them from one another. Cultures were not unique and, what was more, their similarities
could only be explained on the assumption that human nature was the same the world
over. Members of the human species working in similar circumstances had independently created the similar institutions. This was not a popular view at the time. I am
not sure it is now.

By this time I had also been exposed to a number of concrete or "field" studies of
small human groups both modern and aboriginal. When I was called to active duty in
the Navy in World War II, I reflected on this material during long watches at sea. Quite
suddenly, I conceived that a number of these studies might be described in concepts
common to them all. In a few days I had sketched out such a conceptual scheme.

Back at Harvard with a tenured position after the war, I began working on a book,
later entitled *The Human Group*, which was intended to apply my conceptual scheme

Homans and Lévi-Strauss

Homans reacted not only against Durkheim but also against those who followed in the Durkheimian tradition. Peter P. Ekeh (1974) has argued that Homans's orientation was shaped directly as a reaction against the work of neo-Durkheimian anthropologist Claude Lévi-Strauss (Homans and Schneider, 1955). In fact, what Homans reacted against was Lévi-Strauss's neo-Durkheimian version of exchange theory. (We will encounter a very different aspect of Lévi-Strauss's theory in Chapter Eight.) We learn a good deal about Homans's exchange theory by examining his reaction to Lévi-Strauss's orientation to the same theoretical perspective.

Ekeh's basic position was that exchange theory emerged out of two "nonmarriageable" traditions. On the one hand, Lévi-Strauss (1949) developed his view of ex-

---

to the studies in question. In the course of this work it occurred to me that a conceptual scheme was useful only as the starting-point of a science. What was next required were propositions relating the concepts to one another. In *The Human Group* I stated a number of such propositions, which seemed to hold good for the groups I had chosen.

I had long known Professor Talcott Parsons and was now closely associated with him in the Department of Social Relations. The sociological profession looked upon him as its leading theorist. I decided that what he called theories were only conceptual schemes, and that a theory was not a theory unless it contained at least a few propositions. I became confident that this view was correct by reading several books on the philosophy of science.

Nor was it enough that a theory should contain propositions. A theory of a phenomenon was an explanation of it. Explanation consisted in showing that one or more propositions of a low order of generality followed in logic from more general propositions applied to what were variously called given or boundary conditions or parameters. I stated my position on this issue in my little book *The Nature of Social Science* (1967).

I then asked myself what general propositions I could use in this way to explain the empirical propositions I had stated in *The Human Group* and other propositions brought to my attention by later reading of field and experimental studies in social psychology. The general propositions would have to meet only one condition: in accordance with my original insight, they should apply to individual human beings as members of a species.

Such propositions were already at hand—luckily, for I could not have invented them for myself. They were the propositions of behavioral psychology as stated by my old friend B. F. Skinner and others. They held good of persons both when acting alone in the physical environment and when in interaction with other persons. In the two editions of my book *Social Behavior* (1961 and revised in 1974), I used these propositions to try to explain how, under appropriate given conditions, relatively enduring social structures could arise from, and be maintained by, the actions of individuals, who need not have intended to create the structures. This I conceive to be the central intellectual problem of sociology.

Once the structures have been created, they have further effects on the behavior of persons who take part in them or come into contact with them. But these further effects are explained by the same propositions as those used to explain the creation and maintenance of the structures in the first place. The structures only provide new given conditions to which the propositions are to be applied. My sociology remains fundamentally individualistic and not collectivistic.

change theory, at least in part, in the French collectivist tradition, of which Durkheim was the major exponent. On the other, Homans was the inheritor of the British individualistic tradition, of which Herbert Spencer was a major spokesman. With such different orientations, it is not surprising that Lévi-Strauss and Homans came to have such different images of exchange theory. In Ekeh's view, Lévi-Strauss developed his orientation first, and Homans shaped his own ideas in reaction to the collectivist thrust of Lévi-Strauss's work.

In his dispute with Lévi-Strauss, Homans believed that he was doing battle with a newer version of Durkheimian theory, with its focus on collectivities and its tendency to view the individual as nonessential. Homans (1962:8) saw Durkheim's work (and therefore Lévi-Strauss's) as an assault on ''one of the unstated assumptions of the western intellectual tradition, the notion that the nature of individuals determined finally the nature of society.'' Homans (1962:23) said of Durkheimian functionalism, with its focus on the functions of social facts for society as a whole: ''I was suspicious of it from the beginning without learning why. It had been a splinter under my skin that has taken me a long time to get out.'' And Homans did get the ''splinter'' of functionalism out, in large part in his critique of Lévi-Strauss's neo-Durkheimian exchange theory: ''His reading of Lévi-Strauss . . . was the last straw that broke his patience with functionalism of the Durkheimian type'' (Ekeh, 1974:88).

Durkheim saw the actor as constrained by social facts, especially the collective conscience, but Lévi-Strauss went further, because he believed in a collective *unconscious*, which is buried deep in humanity and is unknown to the actors themselves. This was, from Homans's point of view, even more constraining, pernicious, and mystifying than Durkheim's ideas of collective conscience and social facts. As Ekeh (1974:42) put it: ''In Lévi-Strauss' work the individual is accorded less of a place in social processes than in Durkheim's sociology.'' With this general background, we now turn to a brief outline of Lévi-Strauss's exchange theory and, more important, Homans's critical reaction to it.

According to Ekeh, Lévi-Strauss erected his exchange theory on two basic assumptions. First, he believed that social exchange is a distinctively human process of which lower animals are incapable. By implication, one cannot learn about human exchange from the behavior of nonhuman animals. Humans are capable of culturally directed action, whereas lower animals can only respond naturally. Similarly, Lévi-Strauss saw actors as capable of creative, dynamic action, whereas animals behave in a static way. Homans's reaction to this was that there is no distinctive difference between humans and lower animals. Thus he rejected all of Lévi-Strauss's ideas about the distinctiveness of human behavior.

Second, Lévi-Strauss rejected the idea that human exchange can be explained in terms of individual self-interest. He did not deny that such self-interest may be involved, but he argued that it is not sufficient to sustain social relationships based on exchange. Lévi-Strauss argued that social exchange is sustained by supraindividual forces, by collective forces, by cultural forces. Thus human exchange is seen by Lévi-Strauss as symbolic rather than self-interested.

Society plays a variety of roles in the exchange process. Where there is scarcity society must intervene to provide rules of appropriate conduct in order to forestall destructive human conduct. In some situations a social exchange is justified in terms of social expectations rather than the benefits the exchange brings those involved. This is done in order to inhibit the development of disruptive negative feelings. For example, people hold a wedding reception because it is the custom rather than because they want to benefit from the gifts received. Finally, customs may develop in which one feels obliged to reciprocate another's action not by repaying him or her but by rewarding a third party. For example, instead of repaying parents for all they have done, children may instead pass similar benefits on to their own children. In general, what Levi-Strauss saw here is a *moral system of exchange* rather than the operation of individual self-interest.

Homans, of course, rejected all of this. He focused on two-party exchanges rather than on the more extended societal forms of exchange implied in the last example of parent and child. Homans also rejected the emphasis on a moral system, arguing instead that the basis of human exchange lies in self-interest based on a combination of economic and psychological needs.

Homans and Structural Functionalism

In addition to these specific attacks on Durkheim and Levi-Strauss, Homans also attacked the structural-functionalist explanation of *institutions*, which he defined as "relatively persistent patterns of social behavior to whose maintenance the actions of many men contribute" (Homans, 1969:6). He argued that four types of explanation have been used in analyzing institutions; the two he rejected are associated with structural functionalism.

The first type of explanation is *structural*; it argues that a "particular institution exists because of its relation to other institutions in a social system" (Homans, 1969:6). For Homans, the assertion that certain institutions are correlated with others does not explain them. The second type of explanation, which is *functional*, contends that "the institution exists because the society could not survive or remain in equilibrium without it" (Homans, 1969:6). This is a vulgarized form of functional explanation that ignores the modern work on the subject, such as that of Robert Merton (1949/1968). Having set up the functional explanation as a straw man, Homans then attacked it:

> The trouble with functional explanations in sociology is not a matter of principle but of practice. From the characteristic general proposition of functionalism we can draw the conclusion in logic that a society failing to survive did *not* possess institutions of type x—whatever x may be. Now there are societies—a very few—that have not survived in any sense of the word. For some of these societies we have accounts of the social organization before their disappearance, and it turns out that they did not possess institutions of type x. If these societies failed to survive, it was not for lack of social institutions, unless resistance to measles and alcohol be a social institution. That is, there is inadequate evidence so far for the truth of the general propositions of functionalism—and after all truth does make a difference. It is conceivable that the difficulties will be overcome, that better statements of the conditions for the survival or equilibrium of any society may be devised, from which nothing but true conclusions will be drawn. But in spite of endless efforts nothing of the sort is in sight. Whatever its status in principle, functional explanation in sociology is in practice a failure.
>
> (Homans, 1969:9)

Had Homans taken on Merton's functional paradigm, rather than a vulgarized form of functionalism that no contemporary functionalist would support, we could take Homans more seriously. Having taken on only easy targets, Homans could cavalierly conclude that structural explanation is no explanation at all and functional explanation is unsatisfactory, since it leads to both true and false conclusions.

Homans (1969:6) used the label *historical* for the third type of explanation of institutions. Here the institution is seen as the end-product of a historical process. Interestingly, he saw historical explanation as basically a *psychological* explanation, his fourth type of explanation. He saw institutional change as ubiquitous and its study as central to sociology. When we perform a historical analysis correctly we must conclude that the explanation of this change lies at the psychological level:

> All human institutions are products of processes of historical change. In fact, most institutions are continually changing. When we have enough factual information, which we often do not, even to begin explaining historical change, and when we try to supply the major premises of our unstated deductive systems, we find that there are certain premises we absolutely cannot avoid using, and that these premises are not propositions about the interrelations of institutions, as in structural explanation, or propositions about the conditions for the survival of societies, as in functional explanation, but . . . propositions about the behavior of men as men. . . . That is, they are psychological propositions: in their major premises history and psychology are one.
>
> (Homans, 1969:11)

In sum, Homans argued that institutional change must be explained by sociologists, and that any explanation of change will be psychological at its base. Homans illustrated this with the example of the introduction of power-driven machinery into the English textile industry in the eighteenth century. He argued that this event was of great sociological importance, since it was one of the first steps in the Industrial Revolution that led to many of our present-day institutions. His starting point was the growth in English cotton exports in the eighteenth century:

> [This] led to an increased demand on the part of the industrial entrepreneurs for supplies of cotton thread, a demand that was not fully met by the existing labor force, spinning thread by hand on spinning wheels, so that the wages of spinners began to rise, threatening to raise the price of cloth and thus check the expansion of trade.
>
> (Homans, 1969:10)

To prevent this rise in wages, costs, and prices, and reduction in trade, entrepreneurs in the textile industry, who already knew of power-driven machines in other industries, developed machines driven by water power or steam that could spin several threads at a time. Driven by the thought of higher profits, many tried to develop such machines, and some succeeded.

Homans argued that this process can be reduced to a deductive system that would explain why entrepreneurs took the actions they did. This deductive system, based upon psychological principles, takes the following form:

1. Men are likely to take actions that they perceive are, in the circumstances, likely to achieve rewarding results.

2. The entrepreneurs were men.
3. As entrepreneurs, they were likely to find results in the form of increasing profits rewarding (Homans, 1969:11).

Starting with his basic assumption about the psychological nature of human beings, Homans argued that he had explained the coming of power-driven machines to the eighteenth-century English textile industry. Using this example, Homans concluded that historical change can be explained only by psychological principles. Homans drummed structural functionalism out of sociology and argued that the only true sociology is based on psychological principles. However, Homans was more than simply polemical; he tried to develop a theory based on psychological principles.

Homans's Basic Propositions

Although some of Homans's basic propositions deal with at least two interacting individuals, he was careful to point out that his propositions are based on psychological principles. According to Homans, they are psychological for two reasons. First, "they are usually stated and empirically tested by persons who call themselves psychologists" (Homans, 1967:39–40). Second, and more important, they are psychological because of the level at which they deal with the individual in society: "They are propositions about the behavior of individual human beings, rather than propositions about groups or societies as such; and *the behavior of men, as men,* is generally considered the province of psychology" (Homans, 1967:40; italics added). As a result of this position, Homans (1974:12) admitted to being "what has been called—and it is a horrid phrase—a psychological reductionist."

Although Homans made the case for psychological principles, he did not think of individuals as isolated. He recognized that people are social and spend a considerable portion of their time interacting with other people. He attempted to explain social behavior with psychological principles: "What the position [Homans's] does assume is that the general propositions of psychology, which are propositions about the effects on human behavior of the results thereof, do not change when the results come from other men rather than from the physical environment" (Homans, 1967:59). Homans did not deny the Durkheimian position that something new emerges from interaction. Instead, he argued that those emergent properties can be explained by psychological principles; there is no need for new sociological propositions to explain social facts. He used the basic sociological concept of a norm to illustrate this:

> The great example of a social fact is a social norm, and the norms of the groups to which they belong certainly constrain towards conformity the behavior of many individuals. The question is not that of the existence of constraint, but of its explanation. . . . The norm does not constrain automatically: individuals conform, when they do so, because they perceive it is to their net advantage to conform, and it is psychology that deals with the effect on behavior of perceived advantage.
>
> (Homans, 1967:60)

In numerous publications Homans detailed a program to, in his words, "bring men back in[to]" sociology, but he also tried to develop a theory that focuses on psychology, people, and the "elementary forms of social life." That theory has come to be called *exchange theory*. According to Homans, it "envisages social *behavior* as an exchange of activity, tangible or intangible, and more or less rewarding or costly, between at least two persons" (Homans, 1961:13; italics added).

In the example discussed above, Homans sought to explain the development of power-driven machinery in the textile industry, and thereby the Industrial Revolution, through the psychological principle that people are likely to act in such a way as to increase their rewards. More generally, in his version of exchange theory, he sought to explain elementary social behavior in terms of rewards and costs. He was motivated in part by the work of the social factists, in particular the structural-functional theories of his acknowledged "colleague and friend," Talcott Parsons. He argued that such theories "possess every virtue except that of explaining anything" (Homans, 1961:10). To Homans, the structural functionalists did little more than create conceptual categories and schemes. Homans admitted that a scientific sociology needs such categories, but sociology "also needs a set of general propositions about the relations among the categories, for without such propositions explanation is impossible. No explanation without propositions!" (Homans, 1974:10). Homans, therefore, set for himself the task of developing those propositions that focus on the psychological level; these form the groundwork of exchange theory.

In *Social Behavior: Its Elementary Forms* (1961, 1974),[5] Homans acknowledged that his exchange theory is derived from both behavioral psychology and elementary economics. Homans began his development of exchange theory, his brand of social behaviorism, with a discussion of the exemplar of the behaviorist paradigm, B. F. Skinner, in particular of Skinner's study of pigeons.

> Suppose, then, that a fresh or naive pigeon is in its cage in the laboratory. One of the items in its inborn repertory of behavior which it uses to explore its environment is the peck. As the pigeon wanders around the cage pecking away, it happens to hit a round red target, at which point the waiting psychologists or, it may be, an automatic machine feeds it grain. The evidence is that the probability of the pigeon's emitting the behavior again—the probability, that is, of its not just pecking but pecking on the target—has increased. In Skinner's language the pigeon's behavior in pecking the target is an *operant*; the operant has been *reinforced*; grain is the *reinforcer;* and the pigeon has undergone *operant conditioning*. Should we prefer our language to be ordinary English, we may say that the pigeon has learned to peck the target by being rewarded for doing so.
>
> (Homans, 1961:18)

Skinner was interested in this instance in pigeons; Homans's concern was humans. According to Homans, Skinner's pigeons are not engaged in a true exchange relationship with the psychologist. The pigeon is engaged in a one-sided exchange relationship, while human exchanges are always two-sided. The pigeon is being reinforced by the grain, but the psychologist is not truly being reinforced by the pecks of the pigeon.

---

[5]In the following discussion we move back and forth between the two editions of Homans's book. We do not restrict ourselves to the revised edition since many aspects of the first edition more clearly reflect Homans's position. In the preface to the revised edition he said that although it is a thorough revision, he had not "altered the substance of the underlying argument" (Homans, 1974:v). Thus we feel safe in dealing simultaneously with both volumes.

The pigeon is carrying on the same sort of relationship with the psychologist as it would with the physical environment. Since there is no reciprocity, Homans defined this as individual behavior. Homans seemed to relegate the study of this sort of behavior to the psychologist, whereas he urged the sociologist to study social behavior "where the activity of each of at least two animals reinforces (or punishes) the activity of the other, and where accordingly each influences the other" (Homans, 1961:30). However, it is significant that, according to Homans, *no new propositions* are needed to explain social behavior as opposed to individual behavior. The laws of individual behavior as developed by Skinner in his study of pigeons explain social behavior as long as we take into account the complications of mutual reinforcement. Homans admitted that he might ultimately have to go beyond the principles derived by Skinner, but only reluctantly.

Next we look at the kind of behavior Homans focused on. In his theoretical work he restricted himself to everyday social interaction. It is clear, however, that he believed that a sociology built on his principles would ultimately be able to explain all social behavior. Here is the case Homans used to exemplify the kind of exchange relationship he was interested in:

> Suppose that two men are doing paperwork jobs in an office. According to the office rules, each should do his job by himself, or, if he needs help, he should consult the supervisor. One of the men, whom we shall call Person, is not skillful at the work and would get it done better and faster if he got help from time to time. In spite of the rules he is reluctant to go to the supervisor, for to confess his incompetence might hurt his chances for promotion. Instead he seeks out the other man, whom we shall call Other for short, and asks him for help. Other is more experienced at the work than is Person; he can do his work well and quickly and be left with time to spare, and he has reason to suppose that the supervisor will not go out of his way to look for a breach of rules. Other gives Person help and in return Person gives Other thanks and expressions of approval. The two men have exchanged help and approval.
>
> (Homans, 1961:31–32)

Although Homans would ultimately deal with more complex social behavior, initially he aimed his exchange theory at this level. Focusing on this sort of situation, and basing his ideas on Skinner's findings on pigeons, Homans developed several propositions. These are the basis of his exchange theory of social behavior.

THE SUCCESS PROPOSITION

> For all actions taken by persons, the more often a particular action of a person is rewarded, the more likely the person is to perform that action.
>
> (Homans, 1974:16)

In terms of Homans's Person-Other example involving an office situation, this proposition means that a person is more likely to ask others for advice if he or she has been rewarded in the past with useful advice. Furthermore, the more often a person received useful advice in the past, the more often he or she will request more advice. Similarly, the other person will be more willing to give advice, and give it more frequently, if he or she has often been rewarded with approval in the past. More generally, behavior in accord with the success proposition involves three stages: first, a person's action; next, a rewarded result; and finally, a repetition of the original action, or at minimum, one similar in at least some respects.

Homans specified a number of things regarding the success proposition. First, although it is generally true that increasingly frequent rewards lead to increasingly frequent actions, this cannot go on indefinitely. At some point individuals simply cannot act that way as frequently. Second, the shorter the interval between behavior and reward, the more likely a person is to repeat the behavior. Conversely, long time spans between behavior and reward lead to a lower likelihood of repeat behavior. Finally, it was Homans's view that intermittent rewards are more likely to elicit repeat behavior than regular rewards. Regular rewards lead to boredom and satiation, whereas rewards at irregular intervals (as in gambling) are very likely to elicit repeat behaviors.

THE STIMULUS PROPOSITION

> If in the past the occurrence of a particular stimulus, or set of stimuli, has been the occasion on which a person's action has been rewarded, then the more similar the present stimuli are to the past ones, the more likely the person is to perform the action, or some similar action.
>
> (Homans, 1974:23)

Again looking at Homans's office example: if, in the past, Person and Other found the giving and getting of advice rewarding, then they are likely to engage in similar actions in similar situations in the future. Homans (1974:23) offered an even more down-to-earth example: "A fisherman who has cast his line into a dark pool and has caught a fish becomes more apt to fish in dark pools again."

Homans was interested in the process of *generalization;* that is, the tendency to extend behavior to similar circumstances. In the fishing example, one aspect of generalization would be to move from fishing in dark pools to fishing in any pool with any degree of shadiness. Similarly, success in catching fish is likely to lead from one kind of fishing to another (for instance, fresh water to salt water) or even from fishing to hunting. However, the process of *discrimination* is also operant. That is, the actor may fish only under the specific circumstances that proved successful in the past. For one thing, if the conditions under which success occurred were too complicated, then similar conditions may not stimulate behavior. Or if the crucial stimulus occurs too long before behavior is required, then it may not actually stimulate that behavior. An actor can become oversensitized to stimuli, especially if they are very valuable to the actor. In fact, the actor could respond to irrelevant stimuli, at least until the situation is corrected by repeated failures. All of this is affected by the individual's alertness or attentiveness to stimuli.

THE VALUE PROPOSITION

> The more valuable to a person is the result of his action, the more likely he is to perform the action.
>
> (Homans, 1974:25)

In the office example, if the rewards each offers to the other are considered valuable, then the actors are more likely to perform the desired behaviors than if the rewards were less valuable. At this point Homans introduced the concepts of rewards and punishments. Rewards are actions with positive values; an increase in rewards is more likely to elicit the desired behavior. Punishments are actions with negative values; an increase in punishment means that the actor is less likely to manifest undesired behaviors. Homans found punishments to be an ineffective means of getting people to change their behavior. It is preferable to simply not reward undesirable behavior, since it will eventually become extinguished. Punishments are even less likely to work as a means of getting someone to do something. Rewards are clearly to be preferred, but they may be in short supply. Homans did make it clear that his is not simply a hedonistic theory; rewards can be either materialistic (for example, money) or altruistic (helping others).

THE DEPRIVATION-SATIATION PROPOSITION

> The more often in the recent past a person has received a particular reward, the less valuable any further unit of that reward becomes for him.
>
> (Homans, 1974:29)

In the office, Person and Other may reward each other so often for giving and getting advice that the rewards can cease to be valuable to both parties. The recent past is crucial here; people are less likely to become satiated if particular rewards are stretched over a long period of time.

At this point Homans defined two other critical concepts: cost and profit. The *cost* of any behavior is defined as the rewards an actor has lost in forgoing alternative lines of action. *Profit* in social exchange is seen as the greater number of rewards gained over costs incurred. These concepts led Homans (1974:31) to recast the deprivation-satiation proposition as ''the greater the profit a person receives as a result of his action, the more likely he is to perform the action.''

THE AGGRESSION-APPROVAL PROPOSITION

> *Proposition A:* When a person's action does not receive the reward he expected, or receives punishment he did not expect, he will be angry; he becomes more likely to perform aggressive behavior, and the results of such behavior become more valuable to him.
>
> (Homans, 1974:37)

In the office case, if Person did not get the advice he or she expected and Other did not receive the praise he or she anticipated, then both are likely to be angry.[6] We are surprised to find the concepts of frustration and anger in Homans's work since they would seem to refer to mental states. In fact, Homans (1974:37) admitted as much: ''When a person does not get what he expected, he is said to be frustrated. A purist in behaviorism would not refer to the expectation at all, because the word seems to refer . . . to a state

---

[6]Although Homans still called this the ''law of distributive justice'' in the revised later edition, he developed the concept more extensively in the first edition. *Distributive justice* refers to whether the rewards and costs are distributed fairly among the individuals involved. In fact, Homans (1961:75) originally stated it as a proposition: ''The more to a man's disadvantage the rule of distributive justice fails of realization, the more likely he is to display the emotional behavior we call anger.''

of mind.'' Homans went on to argue that frustration of such expectations need *not* refer ''only'' to an internal state. It can also refer to ''wholly external events,'' observable not just by Person but also by outsiders.

Proposition A on aggression-approval refers only to negative emotions, whereas Proposition B deals with more positive emotions:

> *Proposition B:* When a person's action receives the reward he expected, especially a greater reward than he expected, or does not receive punishment he expected, he will be pleased; he becomes more likely to perform approving behavior, and the results of such behavior become more valuable to him.
>
> (Homans, 1974:39)

For example, in the office, when Person gets the advice he or she expects and Other gets the praise he or she expects, both will be pleased and more likely to get or give advice. Advice and praise will become more valuable to each.

In the end, Homans's theory can be condensed to a view of the actor as a rational profit seeker. However, Homans was unable to completely eradicate mental states or large-scale structures from his system. For example, Homans was forced to admit that institutional history makes a difference in individual behavior. On consciousness Homans (1974:45) admitted the need of a ''more fully developed psychology.''

Despite such admissions Homans remained a behaviorist who worked resolutely at the behavioral level and who argued that large-scale structures can be understood if we adequately understand elementary social behavior. He contended that these exchange processes are ''identical'' at the individual and societal levels, although he admitted that at the societal level ''the way the fundamental processes are combined is more complex'' (Homans, 1974:358).

Criticisms of Homans's Theory of Society and Culture

Homans's exchange theory called forth strong criticism in sociology, a debate that continues to this day (see, for example, Abrahamsson, 1970; Ekeh, 1974; Mitchell, 1978; Molm, 1981). We will focus on the two crucial weaknesses in Homans's theory as well as criticisms of them by other sociologists. The key problems are Homans's failure to deal adequately with the cultural and societal levels and his failure to deal with internal mental processes.

Ekeh (1974), for example, criticized Homans for focusing solely on two-person, or dyadic, exchange and for ignoring more large-scale patterns of exchange. Ekeh was also critical of Homans for ignoring the norms and values that symbolically shape exchange relations. However, the criticisms of Talcott Parsons, from a social factist point of view, best illustrate the problems in Homans's work at the societal level.

PARSONS VERSUS HOMANS

Parsons pinpointed two basic differences between himself and Homans. First, he contended that Homans tended to ''slur'' the difference between the behavior of people and that of lower animals. Parsons, however, saw a very clear dividing line. To Parsons, the principles used to explain human behavior are qualitatively different from those used to explain animal behavior. Parsons objected to Homans's derivation of human exchange principles from Skinner's study of pigeons.

Parsons's second objection is even more crucial: "The most general formulations applicable to men as men (which *I* would call principles of *action*, rather than psychological) do *not* suffice to explain . . . the complex subsystems of action" (Parsons, 1964:216). In other words, psychological principles do not, indeed cannot, explain social facts. Homans had been unable to show how psychological principles apply at the societal level. As Parsons (1964:216) said: "Homans is under obligation to show how his principles can account for the principal structural features of large scale social systems." He concluded that even if Homans were to try to do this, he would inevitably fail, because social facts are variables capable of explaining, and being explained, without reference to Homans's psychological principles:

> The alternative to this [Homans's] emphasis is to see acting units as part of organized systems, which have properties other than those attributable to . . . the . . . interaction between "men as men." They have languages, cultural values, legal systems, various kinds of institutional norms and generalized media. Concrete behavior is not a function simply of elementary properties, but of the kinds of systems, their various structures and the processes taking place within them. From this point of view it is quite legitimate to be concerned with the organization of complex systems . . . long before their properties can be derived from elementary principles.
>
> (Parsons, 1964:219)

In reply to Parsons, Homans maintained that the key issue concerns explanations of the structures and institutions of complex societies: "Here is the nub of the matter. Parsons thinks psychological propositions do not suffice to explain them; I think they do" (Homans, 1971:375). Homans recognized that social facts emerge out of interaction, but he thought they could be explained by psychological principles. Conversely, Parsons thought that only social facts could explain social facts.

Homans replied to the attack by Parsons and others with a counterattack aimed at social factists:

> Let them therefore specify what properties of social behavior they consider to be emergent and show, by constructing the appropriate deductive systems, how they propose to explain them without making use of psychological propositions. I guarantee to show either that the explanations fail to explain or that they in fact use psychological propositions, in however disguised a form.
>
> (Homans, 1971:376)

What has occurred between Homans and Parsons is a series of charges and counter-charges, with each party claiming that the other's theory has little explanatory power. Replying to Parsons's statements that he is under an obligation to show how his principles can explain the structural features of large-scale societies, Homans (1971:376) said: "I am under no more obligation than Parsons is under himself, who has not shown how his principles can explain the existence of these principal structural features. Indeed, it is not at all clear what his principles *are*." What we are left with is an unresolved argument in which Parsons says Homans has not explained structure and Homans says Parsons has not explained structure. However, the dialogue does clarify once again the battle lines between the social facts and social behaviorist paradigms in general and between structural functionalism and exchange theory in particular.

Blau's Large-Scale Exchange Theory

Whereas Homans and Parsons can manage nothing better than a simple declaration of the boundaries that separate them, Peter Blau (1964) went a good deal further in his effort to develop an exchange theory that combines social behaviorism and social factism. (We will encounter a very different form of Blau's theorizing in Chapter Eight.) Blau's (1964:2) goal was "an understanding of social structure on the basis of an analysis of the social processes that govern the relations between individuals and groups. The basic question . . . is how social life becomes organized into increasingly complex structures of associations among men." Blau's intention, as stated here, was to go beyond Homans's concern with elementary forms of social life and into an analysis of complex structures. Homans was content to work at the behavioral level, but Blau (1964:13) viewed such work only as a means to a larger end: "The main sociological purpose of studying processes of face-to-face interaction is to lay the foundation for an understanding of the social structures that evolve and the emergent social forces that characterize their development."

Blau focused on the process of exchange, which, in his view, directs much of human behavior and underlies relationships among individuals as well as among groups. In effect, Blau envisioned a four-stage sequence leading from interpersonal exchange to social structure to social change:

Step one: Personal exchange transactions between people give rise to . . .
Step two: Differentiation of status and power, which leads to . . .
Step three: Legitimation and organization, which sow the seeds of . . .
Step four: Opposition and change.

Let us examine each of these steps to see how Blau sought to bridge the gap between Homans's exchange theory and Parsons's structural functionalism.

On the individual level Blau and Homans were interested in similar processes. However, Blau's concept of social exchange is limited to actions that are contingent, that depend on rewarding reactions from others—actions that cease when expected reactions are not forthcoming. People are attracted to each other for a variety of reasons that induce them to establish social associations. Once initial ties are forged, the rewards they provide to each other serve to maintain and enhance the bonds. The opposite situation is also possible: with insufficient rewards an association will weaken or break. Rewards that are exchanged can be either intrinsic (for instance, love, affection, respect) or extrinsic (for instance, money, physical labor). The parties cannot always reward each other equally; when there is inequality in the exchange a difference of power will emerge within an association.

When one party needs something from another but has nothing comparable to offer in return, four alternatives are available. First, people can force other people to help them. Second, they can find another source to obtain what they need. Third, they can attempt to get along without what they need from the others. Finally, and most important, they can subordinate themselves to the others, thereby giving the others "generalized credit" in their relationship; the others can then draw on this credit when they want them to do something. (This latter alternative is, of course, the essential characteristic of power.)

Up to this point Blau's position is similar to Homans's position, but Blau extended his theory to the level of social facts. He noted, for example, that we cannot analyze processes of social interaction apart from the social structure that surrounds them. Social structure emerges from social interaction, but once this occurs social structures have a separate existence that affects the process of interaction.

Social interaction exists first within social groups. People are attracted to a group when they feel that the relationships will offer more rewards than those in other groups. Because they are attracted to the group, they want to be accepted. In order to be accepted they must offer group members rewards. This involves impressing the group members by showing the members that associating with the new people will be rewarding. The relationship with the group members will be solidified when they have impressed the group—when members have received the rewards they expected. Newcomers' efforts to impress group members generally lead to group cohesion, but competition and ultimately social differentiation can occur when too many people actively seek to impress each other with their abilities to reward.

The paradox here is that while group members with the ability to impress can be attractive associates, their impressive characteristics can also arouse fears of dependence in other group members and cause them to acknowledge their attraction only reluctantly. In the early stages of group formation, competition for social recognition among group members actually acts as a screening test for potential leaders of the group. Those best able to reward are most likely to end up in leadership positions. Those group members with less ability to reward will want to continue to receive the rewards offered by the potential leaders, and this will usually more than compensate for their fears of becoming dependent on them. Ultimately, those individuals with the greater ability to reward emerge as leaders and the group is differentiated.

The inevitable differentiation of the group into leaders and followers creates a renewed need for integration. Once they have acknowledged the leader's status, followers have an even greater need for integration. Earlier, followers flaunted their most impressive qualities. Now, in order to achieve integration among fellow followers, they display their weaknesses. This is, in effect, a public declaration that they no longer want to be leaders. This self-deprecation leads to sympathy and social acceptance from the other also-rans. The leader (or leaders) also engages in some self-deprecation at this point, in order to improve overall group integration. By admitting that subordinates are superior in some areas, the leader reduces the pain associated with subordination and demonstrates that he or she does not seek control over every area of group life. These types of forces serve to reintegrate the group despite its new, differentiated status.

All of this is reminiscent of Homans's discussion of exchange theory. Blau, however, moved to the societal level and differentiated between two types of social organization. Exchange theorists and behavioral sociologists also recognize this emergence, but there is, as we will see, a basic difference between Blau and "purer" social behaviorists on this issue. The first type, in which Blau recognized the emergent properties of social groups, emerges from the processes of exchange and competition discussed above. The second type of social organization is not emergent but is explicitly established to achieve specified objectives—for example, manufacturing goods that can be sold for a profit, participating in bowling tournaments, engaging in collective bargaining, and winning political victories (Blau, 1964:199). In discussing these two types of organization Blau clearly moved beyond the "elementary forms of social behavior" that are typically of interest to social behaviorists.

In addition to a concern with these organizations, Blau was interested in the subgroups within them. For example, he argued that leadership and opposition groups are found in both types of organization. In the first type, these two groups emerge out of the process of interaction. In the second, leadership and opposition groups are built into the structure of the organization. In either case, differentiation between the groups is inevitable and this lays the groundwork for opposition and conflict within the organization between leaders and followers.

Having moved beyond Homans's elementary forms of behavior and into complex social structures, Blau knew that he must adapt exchange theory to the societal level. Blau (1964:253) recognized the essential difference between small groups and large collectivities, whereas Homans minimized this difference in his effort to explain all social behavior in terms of basic psychological principles.

> The complex social structures that characterize large collectives differ fundamentally from the simpler structures of small groups. A structure of social relations develops in a small group in the course of social interaction among its members. Since there is no direct social interaction among most members of a large community or entire society, some other mechanism must mediate the structure of social relations among them.
>
> (Blau, 1964:253)

This statement requires careful scrutiny. On the one hand, Blau clearly ruled out social behaviorism as an adequate paradigm for dealing with complex social structures. On the other, he ruled out the social definitionist paradigm, since he argued that social interaction and the social definitions that accompany it do not occur directly in a large-scale organization. Thus, starting from the social behavior paradigm, Blau aligned himself with the social facts paradigm in dealing with more complex social structures. Let us explore how Blau sought to transform exchange theory into social factism.

For Blau, the mechanisms that mediate between the complex social structures are the norms and values (the value consensus) that exist within society:

> Commonly agreed upon values and norms serve as media of social life and as mediating links for social transactions. They make indirect social exchange possible, and they govern the processes of social integration and differentiation in complex social structures as well as the development of social organization and reorganization in them.
>
> (Blau, 1964:255)

Other mechanisms mediate between social structures, but Blau focused upon value consensus. Looking first at social norms, Blau argued that they serve to substitute indirect exchange for direct exchange. One member conforms to the group norm and receives approval for that conformity and implicit approval for the fact that conformity contributes to the group's maintenance and stability. In other words, the group or collectivity is now engaged in an exchange relationship with the individual. This is in contrast to Homans's simpler notion, which focused on interpersonal exchange. Blau offered a number of examples of collectivity-individual exchanges replacing individual-individual exchanges:

> Staff officials do not assist line officials in their work in exchange for rewards received from them, but furnishing this assistance is the official obligation of staff members, and in return for discharging these obligations they receive financial rewards from the company.
> Organized philanthropy provides another example of indirect social exchange. In contrast to the old-fashioned lady bountiful who brought her baskets to the poor and received their gratitude and appreciation, there is no direct contact and no exchange between individual donors and recipients in contemporary organized charity. Wealthy businessmen and members of the upper class make philanthropic contributions to conform with the normative expectations that prevail in their social class and to earn the social approval of their peers, not in order to earn the gratitude of the individuals who benefit from their charity.
> (Blau, 1964:260)

The concept of norm in Blau's formulation moves Blau to the level of exchange between individual and collectivity, but it is the concept of values that moves him to the largest-scale societal level and to the analysis of the relationship *between collectivities*. Blau said:

> Common values of various types can be conceived of as media of social transactions that expand the compass of social interaction and the structure of social relations through social space and time. Consensus on social values serves as the basis for extending the range of social transactions beyond the limits of direct social contacts and for perpetuating social structures beyond the life span of human beings. Value standards can be considered media of social life in two senses of the term; the value context is the medium that molds the form of social relationships; and common values are the mediating links for social associations and transactions on a broad scale.
> (Blau, 1964:263–264)

In Blau's view there are four basic types of values, each of which performs different functions. First are *particularistic* values, which are the media of integration and solidarity. These values serve to unite the members of a group around such things as patriotism or the good of the school or the company. These are seen as similar at the collective level to sentiments of personal attraction that unite individuals on a face-to-face basis. However, they extend integrative bonds beyond mere personal attraction. Particularistic values also differentiate the ingroup from the outgroup, thereby enhancing their unifying function.

The second type of values is *universalistic* values. These are standards by which the relative worth of the various things that can be exchanged is assessed. The existence of these standards allows for the possibility of indirect exchange. An individual may make a contribution to a segment of a community, and universalistic values allow the community to assess the value of the contribution and to reward the individual in an appropriate manner (for example, by higher social status).

The values that *legitimate authority* are the third type. The value system that accords some people (for example, bosses, presidents) more power than others extends the scope of organized social control. This is related to the fourth type of value—values of *opposition*. Opposition (or revolutionary) values allow for the spread of a feeling for a need for change far beyond that possible merely by personal contact among those who oppose the established order. These values (for example, socialism and anarchism in a capitalist society) legitimate opposition to those whose power is legitimated by authority values.

Blau's four types of values have carried us far from Homans's version of exchange theory. The individual and individual behavior, paramount for Homans, have almost disappeared in Blau's conception. Taking the place of the individual are a wide variety of *social facts*. For example, Blau discussed groups, organizations, collectivities, societies, norms, and values. Blau's analysis is concerned with what holds large-scale social units together and tears them apart, clearly traditional concerns of the social factist.

Although Blau argued that he was simply extending exchange theory to the societal level, in so doing he twisted exchange theory beyond recognition. He was even forced to admit that processes at the societal level are fundamentally different from those at the individual level. In his effort to extend exchange theory, Blau managed only to transform it into another theory congruent with the social facts paradigm. Blau seemed to recognize that exchange theory is primarily concerned with face-to-face relations. As a result, it needs to be complemented by other theoretical orientations that focus mainly on complex structures with institutionalized values.

Criticisms of Homans's Theory of Consciousness

The other major criticism of Homans's theory was of its failure to do an adequate analysis of consciousness. Bengt Abrahamsson (1970:283), for example, argued that Homans tends to focus on overt behaviors and ignore the inner experiences of the actors: "Knowing the *experience* of individuals and their perceptions of rewards of certain acts is often of great importance for understanding and predicting their behavior." Jack N. Mitchell (1978:81) was also critical of Homans's reductionism and his failure to deal with the dynamics of consciousness: "Any theory that purports to explain or 'get to' the nature of man's social behavior cannot assume explicitly or tacitly that interaction is merely the working out of the rationality of needs, biological or psychological—or of economic processes. What is lacking . . . is a sense of . . . uncertainty, problematics and negotiation." To overcome the limitations of exchange theory in the analysis of consciousness, Mitchell argued for the incorporation into exchange theory of insights from the work of social definitionists such as Goffman and Garfinkel.

INTEGRATING EXCHANGE THEORY AND SYMBOLIC INTERACTIONISM

Singelmann (1972) has made an explicit effort to integrate the main concepts of symbolic interaction and exchange theory. Singelmann began with Mead's categories of mind, self, and society in his effort to establish convergences between these two theories.

MIND   Singelmann (1972:416) stated that to the symbolic interactionist the concept of mind "reflects the human capacity to *conceive* what the organism *perceives*, define situations, evaluate phenomena, convert gestures into symbols, and exhibit pragmatic and goal-directed behavior." According to Singelmann, the actor is an active agent to both the symbolic interactionist and the exchange theorist. He argued that the symbolic interactionist concept of the mind has been "explicitly recognized" by exchange theorists. As evidence that such a concept of mind exists among exchange theorists, he cited discussions by exchange theorists of such things as individuals' awareness of alternatives, aspirations, and expectations. He also detected evidence of mental processes in Homans's concept of distributive justice. One must subjectively evaluate different rewards in order to determine whether the law of distributive justice has been violated.

On the basis of this kind of analysis Singelmann (1972:417) concluded: "Current exchange theory has thus gone beyond the purely 'behavioristic' approach of many reinforcement theories by recognizing, more or less explicitly, that the human mind mediates the relationships between stimuli and behavioral responses." Thus, a reward is not a reward in itself but must be *defined* as a reward in order to operate as a reinforcer. In Singelmann's view, this process of definition brings exchange theory in line with the symbolic interactionist position.

Most behaviorists would agree with Singelmann that there is nothing inherent in an object that makes it a reward. A reward may be defined as a reinforcer if it in fact affects behavior. However, Singelmann aside, behaviorists, though aware of the process of social definition, are not concerned with it. They are concerned only with the behavioral manifestations of the definition process, not the process itself.

Singelmann's efforts at reconciliation, as well as Blau's similar effort to extend exchange theory to the level of social facts, show that all of these levels *can be integrated*. However, many exchange theorists are likely to reject this aspect of both Singelmann's and Blau's work. Singelmann, in fact, transformed exchange theory into a social definitionist perspective. It is no longer exchange theory, nor does it fall within the behaviorist paradigm. Similarly, Blau's extension of exchange theory to the societal level is no longer within the behaviorist paradigm.

SELF   Singelmann (1972:417) pointed out that symbolic interactionists are concerned with the idea of self both in the sense used by Mead, as "as process in which actors reflect on themselves as objects," and in the sense of the self-concept held by actors. Singelmann suggested that at some level exchange theorists understand that an individual has a self and a self-concept, and that these ideas are perfectly appropriate to exchange theory. For exchange relationships to develop and persist, each party must be able to take the role of the other, as well as the generalized other, in order to determine what rewards they should offer and what rewards they are likely to receive. Although this is a useful insight, many exchange theorists are not likely to find it relevant to their concerns. They are not concerned with the process by which individuals decide what rewards they will offer, but only in the exchange relationship itself. Pure exchange theorists would want to know about behavior and not about such concepts as self, generalized other, and taking the role of the other. These are for a philosopher to dabble in, not something of concern to the "scientist" who identifies with the behaviorist paradigm. Thus, for example, Skinner (1971:189) defined the self as simply "a repertoire of behavior," a definition very different from that of symbolic interactionists.

SOCIETY   Singelmann argued that both symbolic interactionists and exchange theorists focus on the micro-social level in analyzing social structure. In addition, he saw
two other points of convergence. First, he argued that symbolic interactionists focus on
how people fit their interaction patterns together, while Homans is concerned with the
stabilization of relationships on the basis of the most profitable exchanges. Both imply
a constant construction and reconstruction of interaction patterns. Second, Singelmann
(1972:419) argued that ''exchange may be conceptualized as symbolic interaction,''
meaning that exchange entails a communication of symbols. This is a clue to Singelmann's implicit argument that exchange theory can be subsumed under symbolic interactionism. Exchange theory is transformed into something very different by Singelmann, but symbolic interactionism remains unscathed.

Interestingly, Singelmann is weakest on the societal level of integration, which
reflects his orientation toward symbolic interactionism. To him society seems to be little
more than patterned interaction and symbols. The real strength of Singelmann's analysis is in his discussion of mind and self and how the insights of symbolic interactionism
and exchange theory are mutually reinforcing on those issues. In his conclusion,
Singelmann attempted a theoretical synthesis involving four basic points:

1. In exchange, actors construct normative and existential definitions of themselves,
    others, actions, goals, and assessments of ''fairness.''
2. These definitions are not only subjectively constructed but to a large extent socially
    shared and thus constitute a constraint external to the individual actors.
3. In exchange, the hedonistic strivings of actors are limited and qualified by the nature of
    the subjective and socially shared definitions of the objective world which includes the
    self and others.
4. In exchange, actors will change their behaviors or definitions when:
    a. changes in the objective world render existing behaviors and definitions problematic,
    b. changes in some of their subjective definitions render other definitions or existing
        objective conditions and behaviors problematic. (Singelmann, 1972:422)

The word ''definition'' appears over and over in Singelmann's four propositions. He
has transformed exchange theory beyond recognition and placed it within social definitionism.[7] In so doing, he actually did the same thing that Blau did in trying to move exchange theory into the social facts camp. Nevertheless, both Blau and Singelmann did try
to reconcile the disparate theories. It is problematic, however, whether transforming one
theory into another really contributes to the reconciliation of theoretical differences.

THE CURRENT STATUS OF
BEHAVIORAL THEORIES

It is appropriate at this point to offer some thoughts on the current status and future
prospects of behavioral sociology and exchange theory, as well as the social behavior
paradigm in general.

---

[7]Social behaviorists published a bitter reply to Singelmann in the *American Sociological Review*. In effect, they accused Singelmann of distorting behaviorism by integrating it with social definitionism. They
were resisting Singelmann's effort to destroy ''pure'' behaviorism with this political attack on him (see
Abbott, Brown, and Crosbie, 1973).

First, it is clear that this is one of the genuine growth areas in contemporary sociology in general, and in theory in particular (Beniger and Savory, 1981). Much of importance has been published in recent years (for example, Chadwick-Jones, 1976; Hamblin and Kunkel, 1977; Michaels and Green, 1978; Molm and Wiggins, 1979), and one can safely predict considerable work on the theories, and in the empirical work derived from them, in the coming years.

Second, although some remain tied to a very dogmatic view of psychological behaviorism as the basis of sociological work in this area, others seem willing and anxious to move it beyond its traditional bounds to encompass consciousness as well as large-scale structures and institutions (for example, Bredemeier, 1978; Emerson, 1981).

Third, one can anticipate an acceleration of the criticisms of sociological behaviorism as the paradigm gains momentum. Sentiments expressed by Kurt Back are likely to be repeated even more stridently in the future:

> Many scientists exhibit a tremendous talent, even a joy, in finding some human behavior which can be explained in a nonhuman way by reference either to an animal model or to a completely mechanical model. . . . When the history of current social science is written, it will be largely a story of treating social science as if it were something else, or trying to get away from the human properties of human beings, and of the strange faith of scientists who can measure exactly stimulus and response to reinforcement.
>
> (Back, 1970:1100)

In this context it is instructive to look in detail at a recent work by Linda Molm (1981), in which the major criticisms of social behaviorism were reviewed and responses to those criticisms offered.

Molm's basic position is that social behaviorism is a legitimate form of sociology, one that is not as different from other sociological approaches as many believe. Molm (1981:153) blamed both behaviorists and their opponents for a distorted view of this perspective: "In attempting to establish the behavioral perspective as a distinctive approach, behavioral sociologists tended to emphasize their differences from other sociologists and these differences were sometimes distorted, in the course of debate, into wide gulfs." She concluded that the differences from other sociological theories "are based more on misunderstanding than on fact" (Molm, 1981:154). It is in the context of this view of the misunderstandings surrounding sociological behaviorism that Molm looked at the three basic criticisms of it.

The first criticism is that social behaviorism is reductionistic, since it focuses on individual behavior. This, in her view, is certainly not true of macro behaviorists (such as Blau), but further she felt that it is not even true of micro-behavioral sociologists. While she agreed that behavioral psychologists are reductionistic, she argued that behavioral sociologists are not. Behavioral psychologists "study how a single subject's behavior is affected by *individual* or independent contingencies: relationships in which the individual's reinforcers are contingent solely on his own behavior" (Molm, 1981:154). Behavioral sociologists, on the other hand, "study how two or more subjects' behaviors are jointly affected by mutual *social* contingencies: relationships in which each person's reinforcers are at least partially contingent on the behaviors of one or more other persons" (Molm, 1981:154).

While Homans and other purists focus on how one individual's behavior is affected by another person's behavior, many behavioral sociologists "are asking how the *relationship* between persons' *behaviors* is affected by the *relationship* between their *behaviors and rewards*" (Molm, 1981:155). Social behaviorists are not reductionistic because they look at the "*structural relationships* between persons, and thus they are clearly within the domain of sociology. They are not characteristics of individuals or aggregations of individual characteristics; they are truly *relational* variables" (Molm, 1981:155).

In fact, Molm went further and argued that social behaviorism is actually less reductionistic than other sociological theories:

> The behavioral sociologists' study of dyadic or group behavior stands in sharp contrast to most of contemporary social psychology and much of structural sociology, in which the individual is the unit of analysis, and aggregated, nonrelational variables are studied. At the same time, it should be evident that behavioral sociologists who study social contingencies *are* studying structural variables, albeit micro structures.
>
> (Molm, 1981:156)

Molm is certainly correct in saying that much of the rest of sociology is reductionistic when it conducts empirical research (McPhail, 1981; Akers, 1981), but this does not constitute a solid defense against behaviorism's reductionism. Robert Perinbanayagam (1981:168) made this point when he argued that Molm's position "hardly meets the criticism: the charge of reductionism is applied when the key explanatory variables do not take into account the emergent properties of interactions, exchanges, groups, and even situations."

The second criticism of behavioral sociology is that it leaves many things unexplained, especially norms and values. On the one hand, Molm argued that behaviorists have done no worse on this score than other sociologists. On the other hand, she argued that they do have a theory of the formation of norms and values, albeit in the author's view a very questionable theory, extending individual behavioristic principles to large-scale units: "To understand the formation of norms, we must examine the learning history of the group, institution, or culture under consideration, just as we would examine the learning history of an individual to understand individual behavior" (Molm, 1981:158).

The third criticism of social behaviorism is that it operates with a mechanical and unfeeling conception of the actor. Molm (1981:160) countered this claim by arguing that operant behaviors "are not automatically elicited by any prior stimulus; they simply occur—they are emitted by the organism, not *elicited* by a stimulus." But this is hardly an active, creative image of the actor, as Perinbanayagam (1981:166) pointed out: "Such claims, far from meeting the criticism of mechanism, merely confirm it. They neatly capture the behaviorist image of a human as a passive, machinelike entity, incapable to volition and originality, that 'emits' behaviors." In other words, Molm's image of the actor has nothing to say about "*constructing a social act*" (Perinbanayagam, 1981:166).

SUMMARY

In this chapter we discuss behavioral sociology and exchange theory as well as their roots in psychological behaviorism. We trace exchange theory back to its basic source in the work of behavioral psychologist B. F. Skinner. Skinner is a virtually pure behaviorist, and as such he rejected the basic tenets of theories associated with social definitionism (for instance, symbolic interactionism, phenomenology, ethnomethodology) *and* social factism (for instance, structural functionalism and conflict theory).

The focus of behavioral sociologists is almost single-mindedly microscopic. Their concern is with the relationship between the history of environmental consequences and the nature of present behavior. In short, individuals are seen as likely to repeat behaviors that in the past have been rewarding, whereas those that proved costly are likely to be extinguished. In this context, we discuss a number of the concepts of central importance to the behavioral sociologist—positive and negative reinforcers, positive and negative punishments, response cost, generalized reinforcers, and behavior modification.

Next we examine exchange theory, the major representative of behaviorism in sociology. The most important spokesperson for exchange theory is George Homans, who was heavily and directly influenced by the work of B. F. Skinner. Homans criticized the macro-level explanations of social behavior of such people as Durkheim, Parsons, and Lévi-Strauss. Instead, he sought to explain social behavior in terms of psychological principles—that is, behaviorism. He believed that psychological principles can be used to explain not only individual behavior but also social structures *and* social change. The heart of Homans's theory lies in the following basic propositions:

1. *The success proposition:* "For all actions taken by persons, the more often a particular action of a person is rewarded, the more likely the person is to perform that action."
2. *The stimulus proposition*: "If in the past the occurrence of a particular stimulus, or set of stimuli, has been the occasion on which a person's action has been rewarded, then the more similar the present stimuli are to the past ones, the more likely the person is to perform the action, or some similar action, now."
3. *The value proposition*: "The more valuable to a person is the result of his action, the more likely he is to perform the action."
4. *The deprivation-satiation proposition*: "The more often in the recent past a person has received a particular reward, the less valuable any further unit of that reward becomes for him."
5. *The aggression-approval proposition*: A. "When a person's action does not receive the reward he expected, or receives punishment he did not expect, he will be angry; he becomes more likely to perform aggressive behavior, and the results of such behavior become more valuable to him." B. "When a person's action receives the reward he expected, especially a greater reward than he expected, or does not receive punishment he expected, he will be pleased; he becomes more likely to perform approving behavior, and the results of such behavior become more valuable to him."

Given its orientation to individual behavior, Homans's theory has been criticized by social factists for ignoring large-scale structures and by social definitionists for ignoring mental processes. The debate between Parsons and Homans can be seen in terms of the differences between the social factist and the social behaviorist orientations. Although such a dialogue is important, even more significant was the effort by Peter Blau to extend exchange theory from the individual to the societal levels. Blau outlined a four-stage sequence leading from interpersonal exchange to social structure to social change:

1.   Personal exchange transactions between people give rise to . . .
2.   Differentiation of status and power, which leads to . . .
3.   Legitimation and organization, which sow the seeds of . . .
4.   Opposition and change.

Blau's work, although commendable, transforms exchange theory at the societal level so that it is no longer identifiable as a behavioristic orientation.

   In addition to being criticized for its weaknesses at the societal level, exchange theory has also been criticized for its inattention to mental processes. In this context, we look at Singelmann's work as an effort to integrate symbolic interactionism and exchange theory. Although also commendable, Singelmann's work seems to be vulnerable to the same criticism as Blau's; that is, it transforms exchange theory so that its behaviorism is no longer recognizable. The chapter closes with an assessment of the current status and future prospects of sociological behaviorism, in light of Molm's effort to respond to the major criticisms of this orientation.

PART THREE
CONCLUSIONS

CHAPTER EIGHT
Sociological Theory Today

ALTHOUGH we do summarize, and reflect here on, the general status of sociological theory, the most significant part of this chapter is the discussion of a number of theories not yet examined in the text—action theory, systems theory, sociobiology, structuralism, macrostructural theory, and existential sociology. Most (although not all) of these are of great contemporary significance, some representing the latest developments in sociological theory. Some are the rising stars of sociological theory, others are fading, and at least one has all but disappeared, although it remains significant in understanding more contemporary theories.

The theories discussed in the first part of this chapter represent a diverse set of circumstances. Action theory, which is traceable to Max Weber's work on action, found its most important expression in Talcott Parsons's early work. Action theory, while still of historical interest, is of declining importance in sociological theory. Systems theory imported ideas from the hard sciences. It enjoyed a meteoric rise in popularity in the 1960s and an equally meteoric fall in the 1970s. Sociobiology is a theoretical approach whose popularity has varied over the years. At the moment it is popular, but it remains to be seen whether this is a long-term development or just another peak in the cycle of love and hate between sociology and biology. There is also the question of whether sociobiology is really a theory, or is better thought of as a new discipline or a new sociological paradigm. Similar questions can be asked about structuralism, another "hot" new approach in sociology; it is unclear whether structuralism is best seen as a theory, a paradigm, or a discipline. Macrostructural theory is something of a throwback to early sociological theory, particularly Durkheimian theory that focuses on material social facts. Existential theory is another of the "creative" sociologies (along with phenomenology and ethnomethodology), but with some distinctive characteristics.

In thinking about these theories the reader is advised to keep in mind at least two of the ground rules detailed in Chapter One for according a set of ideas the status of a sociological theory:

1. Does the set of ideas grapple with, or is it applicable to, important social issues?
2. Does the set of ideas deal with, or is it relevant to, a wide range of social phenomena?

All the theories discussed throughout the previous chapters, and in this chapter, qualify in terms of these two criteria. However, some are more popular than others at the moment—some are ascending, others descending. This leads us to conclude that there are sometimes other bases (for example, the internal politics of the discipline) that affect the status of sociological theories.

ACTION THEORY: ON THE VERGE OF DISAPPEARANCE

Not too many years ago, a book on sociological theory would have devoted a great deal of attention to action theory. Today, however, interest in action theory has faded. First, many of its basic ideas have been subsumed under more attractive and popular theories. Second, some of its crucial problems and ambiguities were never adequately resolved. Nevertheless, action theory enjoyed a great deal of attention in the 1930s and early 1940s (Znaniecki, 1934, 1936; MacIver, 1931, 1942; Parsons, 1937).

Action theory had its origin in Max Weber's work on social action. Weber developed a perspective that sought to determine how individuals in some social contexts experience, perceive, understand, and interpret that context and then act on those bases. But action theory has always had an unresolved ambiguity. That is, Weber talked about action as it related to individuals, yet in his historical studies he shifted his focus to the social and cultural levels. This contradiction lay at the base of action theory and it was one of the reasons for its later decline. Actually, what action theorists extracted from Weber's work was often not true to the way Weber used action theory. Although Weber embedded his work in assumptions on actors and action, his real interest was in the cultural and structural constraints on them. Instead of focusing on this aspect of Weber's work, action theory operated at the level of individual thought and action. This is clear from Roscoe Hinkle's summary of the fundamental tenets of action theory:

1. Men's social activities arise from their consciousnesses of themselves (as subjects) and of others and the external situations (as objects).
2. As subjects, men act to achieve their (subjective) intentions, purposes, aims, ends, objectives, or goals.

3. They use appropriate means, techniques, procedures, methods, and instruments.
4. Their courses of action are limited by unmodifiable conditions or circumstances.
5. Exercising will or judgment, they choose, assess, and evaluate what they will do, are do-
    ing, and have done.
6. Standards, rules, or moral principles are invoked in arriving at decisions.
7. Any study of social relationships requires the researcher to use subjective investigative
    techniques such as "*verstehen*," imaginative or sympathetic reconstruction, or vicarious
    experience. (Hinkle, 1963:706–707)

Of course, these premises were not novel to action theory. According to Hinkle
(1963:707), they were present in many classical and contemporary works in literature,
philosophy, psychology, and sociology.

There is some evidence that such a small-scale action approach was anticipated by
pre–World War I sociologists such as Lester Ward, E. A. Ross, Franklin Giddings,
Albion Small, and Charles H. Cooley, although their link to modern action theory is
tenuous. Most of these early sociologists were preoccupied with the large-scale question of societal evolution. They discussed an active, creative view of the individual,
but tended to give society coercive power over the individual.

The exception to this tendency was Cooley. Although he accepted some of the
tenets of his contemporaries, and their interest in evolution, "what became ultimately
significant in social life [were] subjective consciousness and personal feelings, sentiments, ideas, or ideals in terms of which men initiate and terminate their actions
toward one another" (Hinkle, 1963:709). Cooley's methodological approach allowed
the sociologist to understand the personal experience of each actor. Cooley objected to
the application of the methods of the natural sciences to sociology because they implied
a mechanistic conception of human beings. He also opposed statistical analyses
because they concentrated on behavior rather than consciousness. Instead, Cooley urged
the use of *verstehen*, or the methodology of putting oneself in the place of the actor being studied in order to comprehend the reasons for his or her thoughts and actions.

Sociologists who worked between the end of World War I and the Depression ex-
hibited far more connection with later action theory. Among the more important of
these sociologists were Robert Park, Ellsworth Faris, W. I. Thomas, George Herbert
Mead, and Talcott Parsons. Parsons was the major inheritor of the Weberian orientation,
and his use of action theory in his early work gave that approach its widest audience.

Parsons, like all other social action theorists, was anxious to differentiate action
theory from behaviorism. In fact, he chose the term "action" because it had a different
connotation from that of "behavior." Behavior implied mechanical response to stimuli, whereas action implied an active, creative, "mental" process. Parsons (1937:
77–78) was careful to differentiate action theory from behaviorism: "A theory which,
like behaviorism, insists on treating human beings in terms which exclude his subjective aspect, is not a theory of action."

From the beginning Parsons (1937) made it clear that action theory could not adequately explain social structures and institutions, although it could deal with the most
elementary forms of social life.[1] This foreshadowed Parsons's later work, in which,

---

[1] As we saw in Chapter Seven, Parsons's conception of the most elementary forms of social analysis
does not coincide with that of such social behaviorists as George Homans.

many people feel, he almost totally abandoned action theory for a theoretical orientation more appropriate to the study of social structures and culture.

The basic unit in Parsons's action schema is the *unit act*, in which an actor is seen seeking a goal in a situation in which there are norms that orient his choice of means. Yet these norms do not determine the choice of means to the ends. This ability to choose is Parsons's well-known notion of *voluntarism*. The actor, in behaving voluntaristically, "is essentially an active, creative, evaluating creature" (Parsons, 1934–1935:282). Despite this voluntarism, Parsons never viewed the actor as totally free, as having free will. Ends, conditions, and norms, as well as other situational exigencies, all restrict the freedom of the actor.

This orientation led Parsons to a methodological position similar to Weber's interpretative understanding: "The schema is inherently subjective. . . . This is most clearly indicated by the fact that the normative elements can be conceived of 'existing' only in the mind of the actor" (Parsons, 1937:733). However, this methodology played a small role in Parsons's later work, as it did in Weber's. Most of Parsons's later work was at the level of social facts, which he examined *as if* they were separable from the minds of people. Although Parsons paid lip service to action theory in his later works, it is relatively insignificant.[2]

This is the crucial ambiguity and problem in action theory. The approach was long perceived as oriented toward individual thought and action, but its two major exponents, Weber and Parsons, devoted most of their attention to the constraints imposed by cultural phenomena. This ambiguity is clarified when we realize that while Weber and Parsons assumed that actors were dynamic and creative, the bulk of their sociology was devoted to analyses of cultural constraints. Action theory was most influential in the development of such theories as symbolic interactionism and phenomenology, but because its major focus is on the societal level, it really should have had at least as large a role in the development of larger-scale theories. To give one example, the methodology of *verstehen* is usually interpreted as a tool for understanding the relationship between consciousness and action, when it was in fact more useful, and was in the past more likely to be used, as a tool for understanding the normative constraints on actors. The idea was for sociologists to place themselves in the place of the actors they were studying in order to understand the constraints on them.

Thus one of the main reasons for the demise of action theory was that certain confusions were built into it from the beginning. Also, most of its basic assumptions about consciousness, action, and interaction have been taken over and dealt with much more consistently by other micro-oriented theories—for example, symbolic interactionism, phenomenology, and ethnomethodology. These assumptions are quite compatible with other aspects of these theories, indeed they are probably more compatible with them than they ever were with the other components of action theory. Still it is unfortunate that the large-scale orientation of action theory seems to have largely been lost on these

---

[2]Many people have criticized Parsons for abandoning action theory (for example, Scott, 1963; Tiryakian, 1965:684; Buckley, 1967:19). However, Jonathan Turner and Leonard Beeghley (1974) attacked these critics, arguing that Parsonsian theory has been continuous, especially in terms of its voluntaristic thesis. Among other things, they pointed out that in many of Parsons's later works, voluntaristic action theory tends to reappear. Also arguing for continuity in Parsons's work is Richard Münch (1981, 1982).

other theories. Even though action theory never really adequately integrated its large-scale and small-scale concerns, that does not mean that it could not be done .

In sum, since action theory was riddled by contradictions from the beginning, and since many of its basic tenets have since been subsumed by other theories, it is difficult to see how it can stage a comeback. Action theory seems on its way to becoming merely a footnote in the history of sociological theory. Its continuing importance seems to lie almost exclusively in helping us understand more contemporary theories.

SYSTEMS THEORY:
METEORIC RISE AND FALL

While action theory has experienced a gradual decline since peaking in the 1930s and early 1940s, systems theory has in less than two decades experienced a meteoric rise and a precipitous fall. Systems theory, which rose and fell in the 1960s and 1970s, has not yet fulfilled, and may never fulfill, the promise its early supporters thought it had. As a result, in recent years it has lost some ground in sociology, and today merits little more than a brief discussion.

Systems theory is the product of a variety of scientific ideas imported into sociology from other fields, including cybernetics, information theory, operations research, and economic systems theory (Lilienfeld, 1978). These ideas were then remolded to apply to social life. In *Sociology and Modern Systems Theory* (1967) Walter Buckley answered the question of what sociology has to gain from systems theory.

First, since systems theory is derived from the hard sciences and since it is, at least in the eyes of its proponents, applicable to *all* behavioral and social sciences, it promises a common vocabulary to unify them. Second, systems theory is multileveled and can be applied equally well to the largest-scale and the smallest-scale, to the most objective and the most subjective, aspects of the social world. Third, systems theory is interested in the varied relationships of the many aspects of the social world and thus operates against piecemeal analyses of the social world. The argument of systems theory is that the intricate relationship of parts cannot be treated out of the context of the whole. Systems theorists reject the idea that society, or other large-scale components of society, should be treated as unified social facts. Rather the focus is on relationships or processes at various levels within the social system. Buckley described the focus:

> The kind of system we are interested in may be described generally as a complex of elements or components directly or indirectly related in a causal network, such that each component is related to at least some others in a more or less stable way within any particular period of time.
> (Buckley, 1967:41)

Richard A. Ball offered a clear conception of the relational orientation of systems theory, or what he calls General Systems Theory (GST):

> GST begins with a processual conception of reality as consisting fundamentally of relationships among relationships, as illustrated in the concept of "gravity" as used in modern physics. The term "gravity" does not describe an entity at all. There is no such "thing" as gravity. It

is *a set of relationships*. To think of these relationships as entities is to fall into reification. . . . The GST approach demands that sociologists develop the logic of relationships and conceptualize social reality in relational terms.

(Ball, 1978:66)

Fourth, the systems approach tends to see all aspects of the sociocultural system in process terms, especially as networks of information and communication. Fifth, and perhaps most important, systems theory is inherently integrative. Buckley, in his definition of the perspective, saw it involving the integration of large-scale objective structures, symbol systems, action and interaction, and "consciousness and self-awareness." Ball (1978:68) also accepted the idea of integration of levels: "The individual and society are treated equally, not as separate entities but as mutually constitutive fields, related through various 'feedback' processes." In fact, systems theory is so attuned to integration that Buckley criticized the tendency of other sociologists to make analytical distinctions among levels:

We note the tendency in much of sociology to insist on what is called an "analytical distinction" between "personality" (presumably intracranial), symbol systems (culture), and matrices of social relations (social systems), though the actual work of the proponents of the distinctions shows it to be misleading or often untenable in practice.

(Buckley, 1967:101)

(Buckley was somewhat unfair here, since he did much the same thing throughout his own work. Making analytical distinctions is apparently acceptable to systems theorists as long as one is making such distinctions in order to make better sense out of the interrelationships among the various aspects of social life.) Finally, systems theory tends to see the social world in dynamic terms, with an overriding concern for "sociocultural emergence and dynamics in general" (Buckley, 1967:39).

Buckley discussed the relationship between sociocultural systems, mechanical systems, and organic systems. Buckley focused on delineating the essential differences among these systems. On a number of dimensions a continuum runs from mechanical systems to organic systems to sociocultural systems—going from least to most complexity of the parts, from least to most instability of the parts, and from lowest to highest degree to which the parts are attributable to the system as a whole.

On other dimensions the systems differ qualitatively rather than simply quantitatively. In mechanical systems the interrelationships of the parts are based on transfers of energy. In organic systems the interrelationships of the parts are based more on exchange of information than on energy. In sociocultural systems the interrelationships are based even more on information exchange.

The three types of systems also differ in the degree to which they are open or closed —that is, in the degree of interchange with aspects of the larger environment. A more open system is better able to respond selectively to a greater range and detail of the endless variety of the environment. In these terms, mechanical systems tend to be closed; organic systems more open; and sociocultural systems the most open of the three. The degree of openness of a system is related to two crucial concepts in systems theory: *entropy*, or the tendency of systems to run down; and *negentropy*, or the tendency of systems to elaborate structures. Closed systems tend to be entropic, whereas open systems tend to be negentropic. Sociocultural systems also tend to have more tension built into them than the other two. Finally, sociocultural systems can be purposive and goal-seeking because they receive feedback from the environment that allows them to keep moving toward their goals.

Feedback is an essential aspect of the cybernetic approach that systems theorists take to the social system. This is in contrast to the equilibrium approach, which is characteristic of many sociologists who purportedly operate from a systems approach. Using feedback enables cybernetic systems theorists to deal with friction, growth, evolution, and sudden changes. The openness of a social system to its environment and the impact of environmental factors on the system are important concerns to these systems theorists.

A variety of internal processes also affect social systems. Two other concepts are critical here. *Morphostasis* refers to those processes that help the system maintain itself, whereas *morphogenesis* refers to those processes that help the system change, grow more elaborate. Social systems develop more and more complex "mediating systems" that intervene between external forces and the action of the system. Some of these mediating systems help the system to maintain itself, while others help it to change. These mediating systems grow more and more independent, autonomous, and determinative of the actions of the system. In other words, these mediating systems permit the social system to grow less dependent on the environment.

These complex mediating systems perform a variety of functions in the social system. For example, they allow the system to adjust itself temporarily to external conditions. They can direct the system from harsh to more congenial environments. They can also allow the system to reorganize its parts in order to deal with the environment more effectively.

Buckley (1967) moved from a discussion of general principles to the specifics of the social world in order to show the applicability of systems theory. He began at the individual level, where he was very impressed by Mead's work, in which consciousness and action are interrelated. In fact, Buckley recast the Meadian problematic in systems theory terms. Action begins with a *signal* from the environment, which is transmitted to the actor. However, the transmission may be complicated by *noise* in the environment. When it gets through, the signal provides the actor with *information*. On the basis of this information, the actor is allowed to *select* a response. The key here is the actor's possession of a mediating mechanism—self-consciousness. Buckley discussed self-consciousness in the terminology of systems theory:

> In the language of cybernetics, such self-consciousness is a mechanism of internal feedback of the system's own states which may be mapped or compared with other information from the situation and from memory, permitting a selection from a repertoire of actions in a goal-directed manner that takes one's own self and behavior explicitly into account.
>
> (Buckley, 1967:100)

To Mead, and the symbolic interactionists and systems theorists, consciousness is not separated from action and interaction, but rather is an integral part of both.

Despite his views that consciousness and interaction are interrelated, and that levels should not be separated from one another, Buckley did move from consciousness to the interactional domain. Patterns of interaction—namely, imitation and response—clearly fit into a systemic view of the world. More important, Buckley tied the interpersonal realm directly to the personality system; indeed he saw the two as mutually determinative. Finally, Buckley turned to the large-scale organization of society, especially roles and institutions, which he saw in systemic terms and as related to, if not indistinguishable from, the other levels of social reality.

Buckley concluded by discussing some of the general principles of systems theory as they apply to the sociocultural domain. First, the systems theorist accepts the idea that tension is a normal, ever-present, and necessary reality of the social system. Second, there is a focus on the nature and sources of variety in the social system. The emphasis on both tension and variety makes the systems perspective a dynamic one. Third, there is a concern for the selection process at both the individual and the interpersonal levels, whereby the various alternatives open to the system are sorted and shifted. This lends further dynamism. Fourth, the interpersonal level is seen as the basis of the development of larger structures. The transactional processes of exchange, negotiation, and bargaining are the processes out of which emerge relatively stable social and cultural structures. Finally, despite the inherent dynamism of the systems approach, there is a recognition of the processes of perpetuation and transmission. As Buckley (1967:160) put it, "Out of the continuous transactions emerge some relatively stable accommodations and adjustments."

An interesting note: there are a number of rather striking similarities between systems theory and the dialectical approach, even though they are derived from extremely different sources (one scientific, the other philosophical) and have very different vocabularies (Ball, 1978). Similarities between them include a focus on relations, process, creativity, and tension.

Criticisms of Systems Theory

Despite the initial excitement about systems theory, it has failed to become the major sociological theory that most of its adherents had hoped. Robert Lilienfeld (1978) criticized systems theory on several grounds. He argued that when it has been employed in sociology, as well as in other fields, systems theory has been a failure. To exemplify this Lilienfeld (citing Hoos) noted the case of the San Francisco Bay Area Rapid Transit system, which is based on a systems approach:

> The Bay Area Rapid Transit system . . . built lines through and to many places [which were] so laid waste by the protracted and inept construction stages that it may be years before former use patterns will be restored, if ever. Terminals are out in the fields and way stations stand as sole occupants of once prosperous and now desolate business sections.
> (Lilienfeld, 1978:123)

Lilienfeld found analogous, if not so enormous, failures in the products of sociological systems theorists.

Lilienfeld criticized the scientific pretensions of sociological systems theorists. He maintained that they tended to pick up details from the sciences that supported their view and to disregard those that did not. Lilienfeld also assailed the systems theorists' love of analogies (or "isomorphisms") between one field and another. While these may be esthetically appealing, they are not necessarily accurate. Then Lilienfeld (1978:192) criticized the generality of systems theory, arguing that it "achieves its all-encompassing 'universality' only by its very abstractness," by ignoring "the specific, the concrete, the substantive."

Lilienfeld (1978:227) found systems theory to be highly speculative, a general problem that is exacerbated as systems theory "migrates" from the "hard" sciences to other fields, where it "becomes ever more loosely defined and impressionistic in usage." He viewed it as a mixture of speculation and empirical data that is satisfying as neither. When systems theorists venture into the social world their work suffers because of their ignorance of the way it works. Lilienfeld argued that no new findings based on systems theory can be found in any science. Finally, he contended that systems theory cannot be tested and thus cannot be proven right or wrong.

Lilienfeld concluded that systems theory should be seen more as an ideological system than as a scientific approach. He saw it as a form of consciousness and a way of interpreting and understanding the world that justifies and maintains specific relations of power. To Lilienfeld, systems theory not only supports the status quo but also tends to have authoritarian implications.

The future of systems theory is uncertain. Its openness to a multileveled, integrative approach to the social world is attractive, but it needs to overcome a number of its weaknesses before it will gain the broad sociological audience it once promised to attract.

SOCIOBIOLOGY

Early sociological theory was heavily influenced by ideas derived from the biological sciences. For example, all of the early evolutionary theories of society owe a deep debt to biological theories of evolution. Also, many early theorists, especially structural functionalists, drew analogies between organic structures and functions and societal structures and functions. Later the tendency to use such analogies came under heavy attack. Sociological theory could even be said to have developed in opposition to biological theory. More recently, sociobiology has gained renewed attention as a result of the publication of Edward O. Wilson's *Sociobiology: The New Synthesis* (1975); it has generated an enormous controversy as well as much thought and research (Caplan, 1978; Ruse, 1979).

As we will see, there is a great deal to sociobiology, but at its base it argues that human behavior is genetically shaped, and some would even argue genetically determined. Sociobiologists build on the idea that the process of evolution for humans is just like that for any other species: behavioral adaptations that are most conducive to survival are passed on genetically. Thus, patterns of human behavior are probably the result of genetically inherited tendencies. An illustration of a sociobiological explanation will help to clarify this orientation.

Many people believe that men and women have different sexual appetites. Men are thought to have greater sexual desires and therefore to want a variety of sexual partners. Women are thought to be more limited in their sexual desires and to be satisfied with one partner. In the past men's allegedly greater sexual interest was attributed to

EDWARD O. WILSON: A Biographical Sketch

Edward O. Wilson was born in Birmingham, Alabama, on June 10, 1929. He received his bachelor's and master's degrees from the University of Alabama and his doctorate from Harvard, where he is now Frank B. Baird Jr. Professor of Science. Wilson is not a sociologist but a biologist. In fact, he is recognized as one of the world's leading experts on ants. The obvious question is: Why should there be a biographical sketch of a biologist in a book on sociological theory? The answer is that many sociologists have found Wilson's work relevant to their theorizing, and other theorists have found cause to be highly critical of his orientation.

Up until 1975 Wilson was, as viewed from the field of sociology, a rather innocent analyst of insects. He had achieved wide recognition in his field but was almost completely unknown in sociology. All that changed in 1975 when he published his best-known book, *Sociobiology: The New Synthesis*. Although it was almost totally devoted to an analysis of animals, *Sociobiology* also argued that the principles underlying the study of animal societies are applicable to the study of human beings. This argument attracted much attention as well as a firestorm of criticism. While the book was well-received by journal reviewers, it was roundly attacked in a variety of forums. Those who prefer to see human action as emanating from some variant of free will were repulsed by the association of human and animal societies. Many others saw an implicit kind of racism in Wilson's work. They felt that it could be used as academic support for the view that there is a biological basis for differences in human races. Public protests were organized and Wilson was harangued and jeered at professional meetings, including at least one professional sociological meeting.

However, the most important criticism, at least academically, was that Wilson's thesis, at least on the surface, constituted a direct threat to the social sciences, or at least it was so interpreted by some social scientists. They argued that social, cultural, and environmental, not biological, forces shaped human behavior. However, Wilson himself downplayed the significance of biological forces, arguing that while only about 10 percent of human behavior is biological, the rest is explained environmentally.

In addition to downplaying the significance of biological forces, Wilson was miffed by those critics who argued that he should not have presented his ideas, since they might be of use to certain political forces (racists). He defended his right to present his scientific views, arguing that scientific ideas can always be misused by those who wish to do so.

Wilson has been very active since 1975 and has published more and more on the links between biology and human behavior. His 1978 book, *On Human Nature*, won the Pulitzer prize. In this work he extended his analysis of the role of biology in human behavior to such things as aggression, sex, altruism, religion, and homosexuality. Although he continued to believe that biology does not play a dominant role in human behavior, he does argue that genes exercise constraint on culture. In 1982 a new book coauthored with Charles T. Lumsden, *An Outline of the Theory of Gene-Culture Coevolution*, is scheduled to come out. As of this writing, the book has yet to appear, but the authors contend in a prepublication advertisement that it "extends the field of sociobiology in a first attempt to explain the origin of mind and cultural diversity." This kind of extension seems to confirm the fears of those social scientists who felt that sociobiology was out to swallow them up. It remains to be seen how far Wilson intends to extend his ideas and how many of them sociologists will accept.

a stronger "sex drive." Today, some sociobiologists offer a different explanation.

Sociobiologists begin with the assumption that a primary human objective is to have one's genes passed on through offspring. Women usually have only one egg each month that can be fertilized and through which, therefore, they can pass on their genes. By contrast, men's genes are passed on through the sperm, of which there are billions during a lifetime. A child (and therefore the genes of the woman) is more likely to survive if the woman can get the man who impregnates her to assist and support her and the child. The man's genes are most likely to survive if he can impregnate as many women as possible; he has to give them only as much support as is necessary to assure the survival of the offspring.

Thus, the sociobiologists argue that as a result of a long evolutionary process men are predisposed by their genetic makeup to want as many sexual relationships as possible. Women, on the other hand, are predisposed by their genes to attempt to "tie down" one man, and to do so they must employ a variety of pressures and enticements (Trivers, 1972). Most sociologists do not accept such a genetic explanation of sexual relationships, but it is illustrative of the kind of work done by at least some sociobiologists.

But what is sociobiology? A theory? A set of theories? A sociological paradigm?[3] A new discipline? An established discipline? As the following discussion will make clear, there are those who subscribe to each of these views.

Sociobiology: An Academic Discipline?

A number of observers believe that sociobiology is a separate discipline, although they disagree whether it is already established, newly erected, or en route to being established. E. O. Wilson (1978:xi) saw it as an established field: "sociobiology is a discipline, not a particular theory." Arthur L. Caplan (1978:31), on the other hand, viewed it as a perspective struggling to gain disciplinary status: "Sociobiology stands as an instance of a rarely observed intellectual phenomena: the attempt to produce and legitimize a new scientific discipline." And Penelope J. Greene, Charles J. Morgan, and David P. Barash (1979:414) adopted the middle-ground position that "sociobiology is a *new discipline* that applies biology to the analysis of social behavior" (italics added).

The consensus seems to be that sociobiology is indeed a discipline. It has, or is in the process of acquiring, its own membership. Academicians from both the biological and the social sciences seem to be identifying with it. However, others have remained within their own fields and adapted sociobiology to those fields. This is true of some biologists as well as those in the social sciences, including sociology.

Sociobiology: A New Sociological Paradigm?

George Ritzer (1975a) argued that sociobiology has the potential to gain the status of a new sociological paradigm and, as a result, it was seen as likely to cause considerable political conflict in sociology:

---

[3]The concept of a sociological paradigm has been discussed briefly in the preceding chapter. It is discussed in greater depth in the Appendix. Here it is important to keep in mind that a paradigm—a broader unit than a theory—encompasses two or more theories, methods, or other component parts. For still more detail, see the author's *Sociology: A Multiple Paradigm Science* (1975a).

> An intriguing possibility for paradigmatic status in sociology is the burgeoning interest in biological factors and their role in social phenomena. . . . Were it to be demonstrated that biology plays a greater role in social phenomena than has heretofore been recognized, many of the ideas associated with all of the current sociological paradigms would be called into question. The political conflict [previously discussed] . . . would be minor in terms of the battle that would occur were a biological paradigm to begin to gain a significant foothold in sociology.
>
> (Ritzer, 1975a:226)

In a reanalysis in 1980, sociobiology was viewed as an even stronger contender for paradigmatic status in sociology:

> In my earlier work [1975a] I contended that sociobiology and critical sociology were showing signs of achieving paradigmatic status within the discipline. If anything, these perspectives show even more vitality today than they did a few years ago. The strength of sociobiology is reflected in the enormous amount of publicity devoted to Edward Wilson's *Sociobiology* . . . which has been the subject of great attention in the major sociological journals. Although this may simply be another cycle in sociology's longstanding love-hate relationship with the issue of how much social behavior can be explained biologically, it could also be that sociologists will finally overcome their historical insecurity about biology and begin an era in which a number of them make this the focus of their work.
>
> (Ritzer, 1980:234)

Sociobiology has thus made some strides toward achieving paradigmatic status in sociology.

To be considered a paradigm, sociobiology must acquire the formal characteristics of a sociological paradigm and attract enough supporters to achieve paradigmatic status. First, sociobiologists would need to articulate the subject matter of sociology from a distinctively sociobiological point of view. The various efforts to accomplish this have differed on several grounds, especially the degree to which biology was used to explain behavior. The most extreme view, which few hold publicly, is that most, if not all, social behavior is to be explained biologically. If this view came ultimately to be supported by the evidence, sociobiology would not only become a sociological paradigm, it would become *the* sociological paradigm: sociobiology would be sociology. Lee Ellis (1977) articulated the worst fears of many sociologists. He envisioned a process whereby sociobiology begins to absorb sociology so that by the end of the twentieth century a situation exists in which "essentially nothing remains of sociology within the academic community" (Ellis, 1977:56).

Most sociobiologists make more modest claims for sociobiology, seeing it as potentially but one of several paradigms in sociology. Wilson (1978:xi), for example, in a statement made after he wrote *Sociobiology* (1975), concluded only that: "*some* variability in human social behavior has a genetic base, and, as a consequence, at least *some* behavior is genetically constrained" (italics added). Penelope Greene, Charles Morgan, and David Barash (1979:424) took a similar limited view: "Precisely how much of the subject matter of traditional sociology is reducible in this [sociobiological] fashion is not yet clear, but theoretical treatments and empirical studies now strongly suggest that at least some parts of our social structure are suitable for this type of analysis." To the degree that such limited views of sociobiology prevail, it does have the potential to become a new paradigm coexisting with the others within sociology.

Interestingly, whether sociobiologists have espoused the extreme or the more modest view, they have met with significant opposition within sociology. Some of this is simply a result of normal politics in sociology, but there are some additional factors involved. For one thing, sociologists, at least since the early years, have been very resistant to biological reductionism. As Scott McNall (1979a:397) put it: "There has been an inordinate amount of resistance to biological explanations of human behavior in the social sciences, partly because the social sciences evolved in opposition to biological reductionism." Then, too, sociologists have been inclined to see a sharp discontinuity between people and other animals (van den Berghe, 1974). Thus they resisted the idea that insights derived from work on lower animals are relevant to humans; that is, that cross-species comparisons can teach us about humans. Pierre van den Berghe, an ardent supporter of sociobiology, found this position indefensible:

> Human behavior is not radically discontinuous from that of other species. Man is *not* unique in transmitting socially learned behavior, and there is no reason to assume that our biological make-up does not affect our behavior when it so clearly affects that of other species. Indeed, it makes no sense to divorce behavior from biology, since the behavior of any species is so directly linked with its biological evolution.
>
> (van den Berghe, 1974:777–778)

Still, many sociologists are likely to resist the development of a sociobiological paradigm. This has led Michael Ruse (1979:192) to conclude that in sociology "the contributions of sociobiology are going to remain slight, at least for some time to come."

Sociobiology is unlikely to acquire paradigmatic status in sociology until its image of the subject matter of sociology is more unified. It is far better off on the second component of a paradigm—an *exemplar*, or a body of work that stands as a model for those who work within the paradigm (see the Appendix for more discussion of exemplars). It seems clear that the work of E. O. Wilson has already acquired exemplary status. Its methods should not be problematic, since there is a set of well-established methods in biology that could be applied to sociobiological issues.

Sociobiology: A Sociological Theory?

The view taken in this book is that sociobiology is better seen as either a separate discipline or a potential paradigm than as a theory. In fact, since sociobiology is not a theory, in our view, it should not even be discussed in this book. However, as either a discipline or a paradigm, sociobiology does encompass at least two theoretical orientations, and probably more. The work of Greene, Morgan, and Barash (1979) is quite useful here because it differentiates between proximate and ultimate causes of behavior. Sociobiological theories split along these lines. On the one hand, there is the view that proximate biological factors lead people to behave as they do; for example, chemical changes in the body, hormonal changes, weight gain or loss, and the various components of maturation and aging may all influence human behavior. At least some human behaviors can be traced to such proximate biological causes.

On the other hand, there is the more important sociobiological theory that deals with ultimate causes of human behavior and focuses on evolutionary factors (Quadagno,

1979). Most of the attention and controversy in sociology has been over the utility of evolutionary theory in explaining human behavior. Greene, Morgan, and Barash delineated the basic components of evolutionary theory.

1. Living organisms possess an inherent capacity to overreproduce.
2. Natural populations tend to remain numerically stable over time. . . .
3. This balance derives from the competition of individuals, which insures that some are more successful reproductively than others.
4. Individuals differ from each other in their competitive prowess, and to some extent, these differences are inheritable by their offspring.
5. Ultimately, the genetic composition of a population changes, reflecting the characteristics of the more successful individuals who have left more offspring.
      Over time, the genes carried by the more successful individuals become more common in the gene pool of the population. It is this change in gene frequency that *is* evolution.

(Greene, Morgan, and Barash, 1979:415)

Although the evolutionary theory may be clear, its applicability to human behavior is not. Jill S. Quadagno (1979:108) closed her controversial analysis of evolutionary theory by concluding "that in terms of method and logic, sociobiology is not applicable to the study of human social behavior."

Of the three views of sociobiology—as discipline, paradigm, or theory—the first two seem more defensible. In the future sociobiology is likely to emerge as a separate discipline or as a distinctive paradigm within sociology and other fields. The one thing that sociobiology is not is a theory, since it encompasses at least two, and probably more, theories of the role of biological factors in social behavior. The precise nature of these theories and their relevance to sociological issues will undoubtedly be further developed in the years to come as sociobiology acquires disciplinary or paradigmatic status.

STRUCTURALISM

Although we have already looked at it several times in this book, it is now time to discuss systematically another of the most debated perspectives in contemporary sociology —structuralism. In discussing structuralism we are confronted with the same issues that we encountered in the discussion of sociobiology: What, exactly, is structuralism? Is it best seen as a sociological theory? A new sociological paradigm? A new discipline?

Structuralism: A New Academic Discipline?

A very strong case can be made that structuralism is a new academic discipline that is emerging from diverse developments in various fields. The basic source of modern structuralism, and its strongest bastion to this day, is linguistics. The work of Ferdinand de Saussure (1857–1913) stands out in the development of structural linguistics, and ultimately structuralism in various other fields (Culler, 1976). Of particular interest to us is Saussure's differentiation between *langue* and *parole*, which was to have enormous significance. *Langue* is the formal, grammatical system of language. It is a system of phonic elements whose relationships are governed, Saussure and his followers believed, by determinate laws. Much of linguistics since Saussure's time has been oriented to the discovery of those laws. The existence of *langue* makes *parole* possible. *Parole* is actual speech, the way speakers use language to express themselves. Although Saussure recognized the significance of people's use of language in subjective and often idiosyncratic ways, he believed that that cannot be the concern of the scientifically oriented linguist. Such a linguist must look at *langue*, the formal system of language, not the subjective ways in which it is used by actors.

The concern for structure has been extended beyond language to the study of all sign systems. This focus on the structure of sign systems has been labeled semiotics and has attracted many followers (Hawkes, 1977). *Semiotics* is broader than structural linguistics, since it encompasses not only language but also other sign systems, such as facial expressions, body language, literary texts, indeed all forms of communications.

Many of the fields to which structuralism has been extended are concerned in one way or another with communication. These include Marxism, psychiatry, the plastic arts, musical theater, literature, and—most important for the development of a structural sociology—anthropology, especially in the work of Claude Lévi-Strauss (Ehrmann, 1970). Although there are a number of similarities in the use of structuralism in these various fields, there are also a number of important differences. Structuralism is far from a unified perspective at the present time. We will now look at several examples of structuralism in psychiatry and anthropology, as well as some additional characteristics of structural Marxism.

First, a few words about the work of Jacques Lacan in psychiatry (Miel, 1970). Lacan was interested in the development of psychiatry as a science and was highly critical of Freudians, who adopted a subjective view of the unconscious. Subjective approaches can never, in his view, produce a science of psychiatry. Instead, in a science of psychiatry the verbal reports of patients must be the basic source of all psychiatric information. In this way the structural mode of analysis developed by linguists could be used to make a systematic and objective study of the unconscious. Lacan and his followers sought to extend the ideas of structural linguistics to the study of the structure of the unconscious.

CLAUDE LÉVI-STRAUSS

The most important work in structuralism, as far as sociology is concerned, has been done in anthropology by Claude Lévi-Strauss. Over the years he has produced an enormous body of complex work that has dramatically altered the field of anthropology—and other fields as well. Structuralists in sociology have been strongly influenced by Lévi-Strauss's work.

One of the reasons for the complexity of Lévi-Strauss's work is that various types of structures are to be found in it. The first type, the large-scale structures and institutions of the social world, is the kind that he took pains to deny are structures. While these are structural realities to most anthropologists and sociologists, to Lévi-Strauss they serve to conceal the real underlying structures of society. This leads to the second, and more important, type of structure in Lévi-Strauss's work, the model that the social scientist constructs to get at the underlying structure of society. But there is a third, and most important, type of structure to Lévi-Strauss, and that is the structure of the human brain

(Leach, 1974). The models of the social world that social scientists construct take similar forms in diverse societies because human products around the world have the same basic source, the human brain. *It is the structure of the mind that is the ultimate structure in Lévi-Strauss's work.*

At one level, Lévi-Strauss can be seen as simply extending Saussure's work on language to anthropological issues—for example, to myths in primitive societies. However, Lévi-Strauss went further and applied structuralism more broadly to all forms of communication. His major innovation was to reconceptualize a wide array of social phenomena (for instance, kinship systems) as systems of communication and thereby make them amenable to structural analysis (Burris, 1979). The exchange of spouses, for example, can be analyzed in the same way as the exchange of words. Both are social exchanges that can be studied through the use of structural anthropology.

We can illustrate Lévi-Strauss's (1967:34) thinking with the example of the similarities between linguistic systems and kinship systems. First, terms used to describe kinship, like phonemes in language, are basic units of analysis to the structuralist. Second, neither the kinship terms nor phonemes have meaning in themselves. Rather, both acquire meaning only when they are integral parts of a larger system. The overall structure of the system gives each of the component parts meaning. Third, Lévi-Strauss admitted that there is empirical variation from setting to setting in both phonemic and kinship systems, but even these variations can be traced to the operation of general, although implicit, laws. Finally, and ultimately in terms of Lévi-Strauss's sense of structure, both phonemic systems and kinship systems are the products of the structures of the mind. However, they are not the products of a conscious process. Instead, they are the products of the unconscious, logical structure of the mind. These systems, as well as the logical structure of the mind from which they are derived, operate on the basis of general laws.

Lévi-Strauss subjected anthropological data to structural analysis in much the same way that Saussure analyzed linguistic data. In contrast, most anthropologists, and sociologists for that matter, are likely to accept the subjective reports of respondents. To Lévi-Strauss, such reports are simply the basic resources out of which to construct the underlying structures. In his analyses of primitive societies Lévi-Strauss was interested in uncovering the underlying structure of myths and kinship systems, indeed of the entire society.

Although Lévi-Strauss devoted his attention to primitive societies, he believed that all societies, including modern ones, have a similar underlying structure. He focused on primitive societies because there is less distortion and it is easier to discover the structure. In modern societies a series of conscious models, or normative systems, have been developed to conceal the structural reality. Lévi-Strauss did not totally denigrate the importance of such models. These normative systems, including their biases and distortions, are important products of people in a society. However, these systems are not of primary importance, since "cultural norms are not of themselves structures" (Lévi-Strauss, 1967:274).

Most anthropologists study what people say and do, but Lévi-Strauss was more concerned with their human products (Rossi, 1974b). He was concerned with the objective structure of these products, not their subjective meanings or their origins in subjective processes. In looking at various human products—myths, kinship systems, and others—

Lévi-Strauss was interested in their interrelationships. The charting of such interrelationships is *the* structure, or at least a structure. Since a structure is created by the observer, different observers can construct different structures. Two important points need to be underscored here. First, structures are the creations of observers. Second, the structures that are created do not exist in the real world. As Lévi-Strauss (1967:271) put it: "The term 'social structure' has nothing to do with empirical reality but with models which are built up after it."

Lévi-Strauss was not interested in simply charting the structure of a simple primitive society. Rather, his concern was in comparing a wide array of available data on a number of such societies. He hoped that such comparative analyses would yield an underlying structure common to all societies. Although he searched for such structure, Lévi-Strauss did not adopt the dogmatic point of view that structures are the same for all places and for all times. Contrary to the view of most observers, there is flexibility in his system.

Lévi-Strauss rejected the traditional orientations of anthropologists. For example, he rejected the idea that myths can be explained either by their narrative content or by their functions for society. Instead, the meaning of myths must be sought at the unconscious structural level. Lévi-Strauss's methodology for analysis of myths can be broken down into a series of steps. First, he would examine a number of variants of a particular myth. Second, he would isolate in these variants the basic thematic elements. Third, he would chart the complex patterns in which thematic elements within each variant are interwoven. Fourth, he would construct "a table of possible permutations between these terms" (Lévi-Strauss, 1963:16). Fifth, the table itself would become the structure, "the general object of analysis which, at this level only, can yield necessary connections, the empirical phenomenon considered at the beginning being only one possible combination among others" (Lévi-Strauss, 1963:16). Finally, such a table, or structure, would allow the analyst not only to understand the myth in general but also to hypothesize about the meaning of a particular myth within a particular society.

On the surface, it would appear that Lévi-Strauss's structures are the same as Durkheim's social facts; both seem to have a life of their own that is external to, and coercive of, the actor. However, Lévi-Strauss did not operate at the societal level, at the level of social facts. Lévi-Strauss was influenced by Durkheim's later work on primitive classification rather than his earlier work on social facts. Lévi-Strauss's actors are constrained, but not by social facts. People, in his view, are constrained by the structures of the mind.

Perhaps, then, it was Sigmund Freud, not Durkheim, who was closest to Lévi-Strauss in orientation and a major influence on his work. It would appear that Lévi-Strauss accepted the view of Freudian psychiatry that actors are determined by unconscious forces. Although Lévi-Strauss was interested in the unconscious, there is a crucial difference between Lévi-Strauss and Freud on this issue (Rossi, 1974a). Freud conceived of the unconscious largely in terms of its hidden emotional content; actors are seen as impelled by emotions that are unknown to them at a conscious level. However, Lévi-Strauss was clearly not interested in the emotional aspects of the unconscious; his focus in the unconscious was "the permanent and logical structures of the mind" (Rossi, 1974a:19). Lévi-Strauss's actors are constrained not by unconscious emotions, but by the unconscious, logical structures of their minds. Here is one way in which Lévi-Strauss expressed his interest in the unconscious:

> If, as we believe to be the case, the unconscious activity of the mind consists in imposing forms upon content, and, if these forms are fundamentally the same for all minds—ancient or modern, primitive or civilized . . . then it is necessary and sufficient to grasp the unconscious structure underlying each institution and each custom in order to obtain a principle of interpretation valid for other institutions and other customs, provided, of course, that the analysis is carried far enough.
>
> (Lévi-Strauss, 1967:21–22)

Lévi-Strauss's view, of course, led to a problem common in the social sciences: that the mind is not accessible to immediate observation (Scheffler, 1970). This caused Lévi-Strauss to focus on the human products discussed above and their interrelationships. Here his interest was not in those products in themselves, but in what they can tell us about the logical structure of the mind. Thus his studies of the structure of the primitive world in general, and kinship and mythical systems in particular, are not ends in themselves but rather means to help him understand basic mental structures.

In his search for the basic structures of the mind, it would seem that Lévi-Strauss undertook a project resembling those of at least some phenomenologists. However, Lévi-Strauss, like most structuralists, had a deep distaste for phenomenology (Petit, 1975). In his view, phenomenologists seek to place human, subjective consciousness at the center of the social sciences. To structuralists, consciousness is not amenable to scientific analysis. Whereas phenomenologists (and others associated with this approach, such as ethnomethodologists and existentialists) are seen as engaged in an effort to humanize the social sciences, structuralists almost self-consciously seek to *dehumanize* those fields. They want to remove people from the center of the social sciences and substitute various structures, such as the logical structure of the mind, language, various components of society, or society in general. Charles Lemert (1979), for example, was pleased to see that the social sciences are witnessing the approach of the demise of people as the heart of their fields. In the view of most structuralists, a focus on people, especially on their subjective processes, retards, if not prevents, the development of social *science*. To engage in a science, the focus must shift from people to some sort of objective structure.

Lévi-Strauss's orientation and interest in mental structures would suggest that he was engaged in an enterprise similar to that undertaken by the philosopher Immanuel Kant. Although there are some similarities, there is also a crucial difference between them. As a philosopher, Kant sought to uncover the basic mental categories through introspection or philosophizing, or both. As a social *scientist*, Lévi-Strauss rejected such methods and sought instead to examine empirically the structures of the social world, in order to shed light on mental structures.

Thus, although it seems that Lévi-Strauss was doing work resembling that of a number of other thinkers, a closer examination indicates important differences between Lévi-Strauss and all of them. Indeed, this is a measure of Lévi-Strauss's distinctive and important contribution to the social sciences.

STRUCTURAL MARXISM

In addition to the anthropological structuralism of Lévi-Strauss, another important variant of structuralism is the French structural Marxism of Louis Althusser, Nicos Poulantzas and Maurice Godelier, whom we have considered earlier.

In this section we will focus on what is distinctive about French structural Marxism, differentiating it from other varieties of structuralism, particularly that of Lévi-Strauss. First, however, we will look at the similarities between structuralism in general and structural Marxism (Glucksmann, 1974)—in other words, the reasons that the work of Althusser, Poulantzas, and others *is* structuralism.

Although we have presented the case that modern structuralism began with Saussure's work in linguistics, there are those who argue that it started with the work of Karl Marx: "When Marx assumes that structure is not to be confused with visible relations and explains their hidden logic, he inaugurates the modern structuralist tradition" (Godelier, 1972b:336). Although structural Marxism and structuralism in general are both interested in "structures," each field conceptualizes structure differently.

At least some structural Marxists share with structuralists an interest in the study of structure as a prerequisite to the study of history. As Maurice Godelier (1972b:343) said: "The study of the internal functioning of a structure must precede and illuminate the study of its genesis and evolution." In another work Godelier (1972a:xxi) said: "The inner *logic* of these systems must be analyzed *before* their *origin* is analyzed." Another view shared by structuralists and structural Marxists is that structuralism should be concerned with the structures, or systems, that are formed out of the interplay of social relations. Both schools see structures as real (albeit invisible), although they differ markedly on the nature of the structure that they consider real. For Lévi-Strauss, the real structure is the model, while for structural Marxists it is the underlying structure of society.

Perhaps most important, both structuralism and structural Marxism reject empiricism and accept a concern for underlying invisible structures. Godelier (1972a:xviii) argued: "What both structuralists and Marxists reject are the empiricist definitions of what constitutes a social structure." Godelier also made this statement:

> For Marx as for Lévi-Strauss a structure is *not* a reality that is *directly* visible, and so directly observable, but a *level of reality* that exists *beyond* the visible relations between men, and the functioning of which constitutes the underlying logic of the system, the subjacent order by which the apparent order is to be explained.
>
> (Godelier, 1972a:xix)

Godelier (1972a:xxiv) went even further and argued that such a pursuit defines all science: "What is visible is a *reality* concealing *another*, deeper reality, which is hidden and the discovery of which is the very purpose of scientific cognition."

Despite the similarities between structural Marxism and structuralism, in general there are major differences between structuralism (Marxian and non-Marxian) and at least the main thrust of Marxian theory. First, the two schools use different modes of logic. Marxists generally adopt dialectical reasoning, whereas structuralists are more inclined to employ analytic reason. Structuralists expound on the need to do synchronic studies; Marxists are more likely to see the need for diachronic analyses. Humanistic Marxists are likely to focus on the human subject, but structuralists (Marxian and non-Marxian) see such a concern as nonscientific (Burris, 1979). Marxists believe that theory can help in social change. The argument of the structuralists is that, given the universality of certain structures and that people, especially in modern society, are inclined to mystify the social world, the chance of meaningful political change is small (Glucksmann, 1974).

Perhaps the ultimate difference between structuralism in general and Marxism in general lies in their levels of analysis. In Val Burris's (1979) terms, the difference is between materialism and psychological reductionism. Marxists tend to focus on the structures of society (economic, political, ideological), whereas structuralists are concerned with the ''deep structures'' of the mind. Thus Marx and most Marxists are concerned with the underlying logic of the large-scale structures of capitalist society. Although structuralists may deal with large-scale structures, it is usually not as an end in itself, but only a means to understand the ultimate subject, the structure of the mind. Some structuralists are interested in the societal level and some Marxists in structures of the mind, but there is a basic difference in focus.

In this light, it is interesting to underscore a point made by Godelier. As a French structural Marxist trained in Lévi-Strauss's structuralism, Godelier was in a good position to analyze the relationship between French structural Marxism and structuralism. Although he recognized some overlap and some differences, Godelier argued for an integration of the two, so that their strengths would be fused and their weaknesses overcome. For example, in discussing the weaknesses in Lévi-Strauss's work, Godelier stated that:

> What is lacking is analysis of the precise functions of these forms of thought, of the circulation of these forms of ideology with other levels of social reality, and of the conditions of their transformation. . . . To go further than a structural morphology means, therefore, trying to account for the forms, functions, modes of articulation and conditions of transformation of the social structures within the concrete societies studied by the historian and the anthropologist. It is precisely in order to accomplish this complex task, which presupposes a combination of several theoretical methods, that Marx's hypothesis of the determination, in the last analysis, of the forms and the evolution of societies by the conditions of production and reproduction of their material life is needed as the central hypothesis.
>
> (Godelier, 1972a:xli)

Godelier's main sympathies seem to lie with Marxism. However, true integration would require serious attention to the strengths and weaknesses of both orientations.

To return to the central theme of this section, strong evidence exists that the term ''discipline'' does, or will soon, apply to structuralism. There have been developments in a number of specific fields that show enough broad similarities for structuralism to be considered at least the beginnings of a new intellectual discipline. However, we also need to examine the other possible interpretations of structuralism—as a sociological paradigm and as a sociological theory.

Structuralism: A New Sociological Paradigm?

Although structuralism in sociology is a fairly recent arrival, it could possibly now become a sociological paradigm. This is essentially the position taken by Bruce Mayhew

(1980, 1981), who saw structuralism as the alternative to the individualism rampant in American sociology. Ritzer's paradigmatic analysis of sociology concluded:

> It seems clear now that structuralism also has the *potential* of emerging as a new sociological paradigm. At the moment it remains largely on sociology's periphery, with the most notable inputs stemming from linguistics and anthropology, particularly in the work of Lévi-Strauss. . . . Sociology now has its own practitioners . . . and defenders . . . of structuralism, and we can anticipate greater interest in the future.
>
> (Ritzer, 1980:234–235)

Although the potential is there, structuralism has not yet become a paradigm. Let us examine, following David Goddard (1976), at least some of the factors that make it attractive to sociologists, as well as some of the barriers to its acceptance.

Structuralism holds a number of attractions for sociologists, especially those oriented to the development of a science of sociology. For example, it has a highly abstract system of thought that allows a good deal of analytical rigor. It promises the possibility of formal modeling as well as the use of sophisticated statistical and mathematical techniques. It also seems to offer a transhistorical perspective on social life. Above all, it offers a perspective with great scope capable of dealing with everything from the structure of the mind to the structure of society to the structure of the natural world.

For these reasons and others, at least some sociologists have gravitated toward a structuralist orientation in recent years. For example, some ethnomethodologists, most notably Aaron Cicourel, have sought to employ a structuralist orientation. Cicourel (1974:27) argued that ethnomethodologists should be interested in actors' basic interpretive procedures, which he sees as being "like deep structure grammatical rules." Interestingly, Cicourel, with his roots in ethnomethodology, a "creative sociology," saw these deep structures in a nondeterministic way, that is, as generating *innovative* responses to social situations.

The work of Erving Goffman, especially his later works, including *Frame Analysis* (1974), also illustrates the drift toward structuralism. George Gonos (1977:854) argued that Goffman's work constitutes "an American variant of contemporary structuralism." Goffman's recent task has been to look beyond and behind everyday situations in a search for the structures that invisibly govern them. Goffman labeled these invisible structures "frames." While situations may vary in their particularities, the frames retain stable rules of operation. Gonos provided other structural characteristics of frames:

> From Goffman's analyses of particular framed activities, we can derive certain principal characteristics of frames. A frame is not conceived as a loose, somewhat accidental amalgamation of elements put together over a short time-span. Rather, it is constituted of a set number of essential components, having a definite arrangement and stable relations. These components are not gathered from here and there, as are the elements of a situation, but are always found together as a system. The standard components cohere and are complete. . . . Other less essential elements are present in any empirical instance and lend some of their character to the whole. . . . In all this, frames are very close in conception to "structures."
>
> (Gonos, 1977:860)

Goffman seems to be offering a conception of structures of interaction that promises the possibility of integration with Lévi-Strauss's mental structures and the French structural Marxists' large-scale structures.

Despite these trends, structuralism has far to go to achieve paradigmatic status in sociology. There are some almost insurmountable barriers it must overcome. As Goddard (1976) so well understood, structuralism not only has little to offer to traditional sociological concerns, but also constitutes a deep threat to those interests. For example, structuralists are generally little interested in such traditional small-scale sociological topics as creative consciousness, actors, action, behavior, and interaction. The actor and various individual-level processes are difficult to find in structuralism. Moreover, structuralism, except for French structural Marxism, seems almost totally inapplicable to the traditional large-scale concerns of sociologists:

> To put it bluntly, if there were laws of structural organization in large-scale, heterogeneous societies—laws relating to significant phenomena such as class, bureaucracy, power, change, development, solidarity, and the varied interrelations between these phenomena—structural analysis could not provide the requisite assumptions, methods or theories which would lead to the discovery of such laws.
>
> (Goddard, 1976:126)

To Goddard and many others, structuralism represents a frontal assault on many of the basic premises of sociology. In fact, Goddard (1976:132) saw dire consequences should sociologists adopt a structural paradigm: since such an approach would "compromise absolutely what is perhaps its own fundamental premise . . . that ideas and symbols are formed in their material context of given social milieux . . . the idea of a sociological materialism which inaugurated sociology as a special discipline would have to be completely abandoned." Given such harsh attacks, it will be difficult for structuralism to achieve paradigmatic status. However, were there not a strong possibility that structuralism might achieve this status, it would not be singled out for such attacks.

Structuralism: A Sociological Theory?

The last question is whether structuralism is a sociological theory. As with sociobiology, this is the least defensible of the three positions. It is more likely that structuralism will emerge as a new sociological paradigm; if so, then it will probably encompass several theories, all of which can be lumped under such a paradigm. Let us look at some of the possible theories, examining the considerable overlap among them, the possibility that some combined forms will emerge, and the differences among them.

First, we could conceive of a sociological theory oriented primarily toward the study of mental structures. One could interpret Lévi-Strauss as developing a theory of this type, although it is too limiting to conceive of his approach as concerned solely with mental structures. Other thinkers fit more comfortably into this type of theory. One is Sigmund Freud, whose work can be seen as an effort to uncover the basic structures, primarily emotional, of the mind. Another is Edmund Husserl, who searched for the transcendental ego. However, most structuralists would reject his work and any phenomenological theory that flowed from it as too subjective.

A second possible theory is one that focuses on "real" interactional or larger-scale phenomena that constrain or determine what actors think or do. At the interactional level, at least some aspects of the work of structural linguists, as well as that of sociologists such as Cicourel and Goffman, would be instructive. At the societal level, the French structural Marxists have led the way. The ambiguity in much of this work is how much structure is seen as existing in the real world and how much of it is simply a model constructed by the social scientist.

This leads to a third possible theory, which is that to structuralists "reality" does not exist in the real world but only in the models they construct. Their subject matter *is* those models. At times this is implied in the work of many structuralists. In this view, the actor is conceived of in a very different way than in the preceding theoretical possibilities. Actors are not determined by large or small-scale structures. Structural models are nothing more than charts of the nature of social life.

The fourth possible theory is the most complicated: structuralism deals with *all* the above possibilities in a dialectical fashion. Lévi-Strauss's work probably fits best here. That is, he is concerned with the dialectical interplay of large- and small-scale structures and their relationship to the models constructed by the social scientist. These models are simply other manifestations of the basic structure that pervades all sectors of the social, and even the natural, world. In the end, this theory would see everything as involved in essentially the same structural dynamics.

The above are four possibilities for theoretical status should structuralism gain the status of a paradigm in sociology. However, structuralism could prove to be another intellectual fad that is of little lasting importance at any level—as discipline, theory, or paradigm.

MACROSTRUCTURAL THEORY

One of the more interesting developments in recent years has been the rebirth of interest in macrostructural theory—that is, a return to the roots of sociology in Emile Durkheim's concept of social facts. This rebirth has been led by many of the leaders of sociology's "old guard," including such people as Robert Merton, Lewis Coser, William Goode, Seymour Martin Lipset, and most important, Peter Blau. Having witnessed their traditional orientations under attack from various sides, they felt the need to reiterate their focus on large-scale structures.

The politics of this revival are rather interesting and tell us a good deal about macrostructural theory. Lewis Coser (1975a) was particularly upset that many of his colleagues in sociology seemed to have succumbed to "a veritable orgy of subjectivism" in adopting such small-scale theories as phenomenology and ethnomethodology. He argued that the study of large-scale structures is the "cornerstone" of sociology. Sociologists are urged not to give in to the subjectivists, but rather to return to the work of Durkheim, as well as to that of Simmel and Marx, which teaches "us that individual striving is not sufficient to free us from the grip of societal constraints" (Coser, 1975b:210). The ultimate focus of sociology should be on the "stubborn facticity of structural arrangements" (Coser, 1975b:210).

It is not that Coser wanted to focus exclusively on large-scale structures, but rather that he wanted to treat them as the ultimate determinants of the other aspects of social reality. His basic model is that social structures impinge on social processes (for instance, social conflict), which in turn affect individual behavior. Coser exemplified his theoretical approach in terms of the issue of race relations:

> The last ten or fifteen years have seen large-scale changes in the social consciousness, the construction of reality, of both whites and blacks, but these depended not only on underlying structural shifts in the relations between the races, but also on specific conflict strategies and specific mobilization of black militants that helped transform mere potentialities into concrete results.
>
> (Coser, 1975b:212)

The *ultimate source* of all this lies at the level of large-scale phenomena.

The other major "enemy" of the macrostructuralists is the group of sociologists who have focused on the cultural level, on the normative systems of society (Goode, 1975).[4] One of those whom William J. Goode had in mind here must have been Parsons, with his brand of cultural determinism. Goode suggested that, instead of focusing on such normative or cultural forces, we focus instead on such structural phenomena as communication systems, authority systems, paths of travel, and the physical layout of housing. Peter Blau (1975a) extended this list by including the following large-scale structures: class structure, structural change, division of labor, associations that structure social relations, status sets and role sets, structural roots of deviance and rebellion, and the interrelationship among the environment, population, and social structure. In addition to this enumeration, Blau (1975a:3) offered a definition: "Social structure refers to the patterns discernible in social life, the regularities observed, the configurations detected." Blau (citing Homans, 1975a:3) also defined the antithesis of social structure: "chaos, formlessness, idiosyncratic human behavior that exhibits no regularities and hence is unstructured."

Robert K. Merton (1975) clearly supported a large-scale structural approach. He recognized that it is not the answer to all sociological problems, but it is the best we have. Characteristically, Merton wanted macrostructural work to focus on the link between societal and individual levels, although he stated that it is social structure that structures individual alternatives. In discussing deviance, for instance, Merton argued that social structure generates different rates of deviant behavior. However, Merton was generally inclined to take a more balanced approach to the relationship between societal and individual levels. He argued that each new cohort enters a social structure that it never created and by which it is constrained, but it also proceeds to modify that structure. Structures are changeable and, more important, cannot exhaustively explain all of social life.

Not surprisingly, some Marxists, such as Tom Bottomore (1975), were attracted to macrostructural sociology. In fact, Bottomore (citing Macdonald) offered a good description of the structural realities that attract the interest of Marxists:

> I remember once walking in the street and suddenly really *seeing* the big heavy buildings in their obstinate actuality and realizing I simply couldn't imagine all this recalcitrant matter transformed by socialism. How would the street *look* when the workers took it over, how would, how could revolution transfigure the miles and miles of stubborn stone?
>
> (Bottomore, 1975:159)

Bottomore did not see all social structures as rocklike; however, he was unwilling to go to the other extreme and see them as a ceaseless and formless flux of events.

---

[4]Interestingly, Lipset (1975), supposedly operating from a macrostructural perspective, focused on the normative system. He was clearly out of line with the rest of this group.

As a Marxist, Bottomore was interested in developing a conception of large-scale structures, but one that allows for conflict and change. In his view, we must describe these structures but in such a way that we do not neglect "the flow of historical action by individuals and social groups which sustains, re-creates, revises, or destructs this order" (Bottomore, 1975:160). What preoccupied Bottomore were the sources of variation in social structures. The first source of variation is the circulation of membership. The new people who enter are never totally socialized into the group so that they construct new subgroups, alter their roles, and so on. Second, the growth in knowledge and the resulting expansion of science and technology lead to continual structural change. Third, the progressive processes of social differentiation lead to changes in social structure. New positions and roles lead to new ideas, mental orientations, social definitions, and social interests. Finally, there is the possibility of change within structures themselves and in their impact on culture and consciousness.

Peter Blau's Macrostructuralism

The work of Peter Blau (1975b; 1977a; 1977b) is the most important representation of this "reborn" macrostructuralism. (For a more recent set of essays on this and other varieties of structuralism, see Blau and Merton, 1981.) Blau offered a rather extreme version of this structural orientation. For one thing, he clearly defined the task of sociology in structural terms: "The most distinctive task of sociology is the structural analysis of various forms of differentiation, their interrelations, the conditions producing them and changes in them and their implications for social relations" (Blau, 1977a: 6–7). In this definition, Blau pointedly eliminated cultural- and individual-level variables from sociology. On the cultural issue, Blau (1977a:x) stated: "I am a structural determinist, who believes that the structures of objective social positions among which people are distributed exert more fundamental influences on social life than do cultural values and norms." Blau wanted to look at social structures, but without the cultural and functional connotations of structural functionalism. Furthermore, he was going to ignore the individual levels. From his point of view, the parts of society are groups or classes of people, not actors and their thoughts and actions. "The focus is on structures of differentiated positions and their influences on the relations of human beings, not on the intensive analysis of the sociopsychological processes involved in human relations" (Blau, 1977a:4). Blau recognized the importance of such factors but stated that he would not deal with them. This means that there is an inherent limitation in his approach: "To be sure, these theorems are deterministic only for groups, not for individuals, for whom they are only probabilistic" (Blau, 1977a:7).

Blau also found it necessary to differentiate himself from Lévi-Strauss's brand of structuralism. He examined Lévi-Strauss's claim that in his system the concept of social structure has nothing to do with empirical reality, but rather with theoretical models built about this reality. Blau took the opposite position, arguing that the social structures with which he was concerned were *real social phenomena*. Furthermore, while Lévi-Strauss saw structures as invisible, Blau (1977a:2) argued that they are "observable aspects of social life, not theories about it."

Blau (1975b:221) also defined social structure: "population distributions among social positions along various lines—positions that affect people's role relations and social interaction." There are two key elements of this definition: positions and popu-

PETER M. BLAU: A Biographical Sketch

Peter Blau was born in Vienna, Austria, on February 7, 1918. He emigrated to the United States in 1939 and became a United States citizen in 1943. In 1942 he received his bachelor's degree from the relatively unknown Elmhurst College in Elmhurst, Illinois. His schooling was interrupted by World War II, and he served in the United States Army and was awarded the Bronze Star. After the war he returned to school and completed his education, receiving his Ph.D. from Columbia University in 1952.

Blau first received wide recognition in sociology for his contributions to the study of formal organizations. His empirical studies of organizations, as well as his textbooks on formal organizations, are still widely cited in that subfield, and he continues to be a regular contributor to it. He is also noted for a book he coauthored with Otis Dudley Duncan, *The American Occupational Structure*, which won the prestigious Sorokin Award from the American Sociological Association in 1968. That work constitutes a very important contribution to the sociological study of social stratification.

While he is well known for a range of work, what interests us here is Blau's contribution to sociological theory. What is distinctive about it, as reflected in the way in which it has been treated in this book, is that Blau has made important contributions to two distinct theoretical orientations. As we saw in Chapter Seven, his 1964 book *Exchange and Power in Social Life* is a major component of contemporary exchange theory. Blau's chief contribution there was to take the primarily small-scale exchange theory and try to apply it to larger-scale issues. Although it has some notable weaknesses, it constitutes an important effort to theoretically integrate large- and small-scale sociological issues. More recently, as is discussed in this chapter, Blau has been in the forefront of what is termed here macrostructural theory. During his term as president of the American Sociological Association (1973–1974), he made this the theme of the annual meeting of the association. Since then he has published a number of books and articles designed to clarify and to extend macrostructural theory.

Since 1970 Blau has been professor of sociology at Columbia University, and since 1979 he has simultaneously held the position of distinguished professor at the State University of New York at Albany.

lation. Social positions define social structures. They are, in turn, defined by the various parameters that are the criteria implicit in the social distinctions that people make in their social interaction. Examples of these parameters include age, sex, race, and socioeconomic status. Blau (1975b:222) contended that his basic thesis "is that the study of the various forms of differentiation among people, their interrelations, the conditions producing them, and their implications is *the* distinctive task of sociology."

As implied above, Blau was interested in both the differentiation and interrelationship of social positions. In terms of interrelationships, Blau saw two factors linking social positions: first, the various social associations among people; second, the process of social mobility, which he defined very broadly as *all* movements of persons between social positions.

In discussing differentiation, Blau outlined two major types of structural parameters. The first type is *nominal* parameters, which serve to differentiate a population
without ranking the different subsets. Each subset has a distinct boundary. Among the
nominal parameters that Blau discussed are sex and race. The second type is *graduated*
structural parameters, which serve to differentiate people on status dimensions. The
differences are stated in terms of gradations, and there are no clear dividing lines between subsets (for example, income and wealth).

Based on his differentiation between parameters, Blau presented two types of social
positions, each of which is distinguished by a given structural parameter. A *group* is
determined on the basis of nominal parameters, whereas a *status* is determined on the
basis of graduated parameters.

Building on parameters and social positions, Blau developed two generic forms of
differentiation. The first is *heterogeneity,* which involves the distribution of a population among various groups in terms of nominal parameters. The second is *inequality*,
which is determined by status distributions in terms of graduated parameters. We see
reflected here Blau's values: there is too much inequality in society, and there can
never be too much heterogeneity.

Blau explained in great detail what he meant by parameters of social structure. He
did this by explaining what his macrostructural theory does, or does not, concern itself
with. For example, he would not be interested in the ethnic backgrounds of individual
actors, but he would be concerned with the ethnic heterogeneity of a population. Or, he
would not be concerned with occupational performance but would be interested in the
division of labor. In short, Blau was interested in large-scale structural factors and not
in small-scale behavioral and attitudinal factors.

To illustrate his approach, Blau identified several problem areas that would be the
focus of macrostructural analyses. One is the issue of social *differentiation and integration.* Unlike Lipset and Parsons, Blau did not believe that such factors as culture,
values, and norms produce social integration. Rather, the degree of structural differentiation produces integration among groups and individuals. Blau's parameters,
especially nominal parameters, determine the degree of integration. In general, integration occurs when a segment of the population has a high degree of similarity in parameters such as age, sex, race, occupation, and neighborhood. A great deal of heterogeneity, on the other hand, tends to produce barriers to social integration. At some
point, however, when heterogeneity is too great, the barriers tend to break down. With
enough differentiation people will prefer outgroup associates to no associates at all. In
fact, in modern society numerous nominal parameters produce multiform heterogeneity, which means that virtually everyone belongs to a multitude of groups and has
multiple roles. Such a structure "*compels* people to have associates outside their own
groups" (Blau, 1975b:233; italics added). This is the most characteristic form of
macrostructural sociology—social structures determining individual action.

More recently, Blau (1980) published a "fable" in which he tried to illustrate his
theory. He described a fictional spaceship, carrying, among others, two sociologists,
that lands on a planet called Stellar 8R. There they encounter "Aytars," or living
creatures that Blau (1980:777) described as being "more like people than like pro-
tozoa." The Aytars, who live in small villages on an island, are all alike expect for two
things. First, they come in two colors, blue and green (a *nominal* parameter). Second,

they vary in height from ten to thirty inches (a *graduated* parameter). There were no differentiations in sex, nor in age, for although time elapsed, it did not change them.

Although the people varied only in these two characteristics, the "research sociologists" found that the villages that the Aytars lived in varied along five dimensions. First, the villages varied in population size from many to comparatively few Aytars. Second, the ratio of blue to green Aytars varied among the villages; some villages were disproportionately blue, others disproportionately green. Third, the villages differed in terms of the average height of the Aytars. Some villages had comparatively tall populations; others had populations that were smaller on the average. Fourth, the differences in height led to inequality in some villages where the population was not homogeneous. "Since size was the only quantitative difference among Aytars, large ones could dominate small ones; they could simply roll over them" (Blau, 1980:777). Fifth, the villages varied in the extent to which size and color were related. Some villages were dominated numerically by tall green Aytars, others by short blue ones. In sum, although the population differed on only two characteristics, these differences led to major differences in the structure of the villages in which they lived.

Blau's sociologists then discovered that there were other islands on Stellar 8R and that there were more villages on each of these islands. The individuals were the same—that is, varying only in height and color—but these villages could be differentiated on eight dimensions. The first five dimensions were the same as those that differentiated the Aytars on the first island. Sixth, although the ratio of blue to green Aytars on two or more islands might be the same, it could be the result of very different ratios within the villages on each island. Thus, a one-to-one ratio could be the result of a one-to-one ratio within most villages, or it could be the result of great variations between villages that tended to cancel each other out. Seventh, Blau made the same point about height. That is, the average height on an island could come about because all or most of villages on the island were similar in height or from the canceling out of some villages dominated by tall Aytars by others dominated by small Aytars. Eighth, the same issue was raised about the relationship between color and size. Again, there could be a similar correlation in most villages, or some villages might be peopled mostly by taller greens and others by smaller blues. Thus, although the demographic characteristics of two islands might be the same, the ecological structures of the villages on the two islands could be very different. Blau's biggest interest was the effect of such ecological (that is, structural) differences on social relationships. As Blau (1980:780) said: "The composition and ecological structure of villages and islands influence the social relations of Aytars independent of their psychological preferences."

Blau began with the assumption that in general people prefer to associate with others like themselves. However, Blau's hypothetical scientists discovered that Aytars of different size and color were sometimes found in each other's company. In their "survey" they uncovered some representative comments: "At least we have the same color, and there is nobody my size around here." "Sure, my friend is green, but to me size is more important than color" (Blau, 1980:780). Blau argued that the chance of one Aytar having outgroup friends is the product of several structural realities. For example, if one's own kind is a small minority in a village, one is more likely to have outgroup friends. Or if one exists within small groups, then the chances of outgroup friendships are increased because one will have fewer people with similar characteristics to choose from. Finally, the intersection of parameters tends to inhibit outgroup choices. That is, if size and color are substantially related (if, for example, green Aytars are also likely to be short), the intersection of these two factors tends to cause the factors to reinforce each other and make ingroup choices even more likely.

Macrostructural theory includes some very old sociological ideas (as, for example, from Simmel and Durkheim) cast in a new form. It remains to be seen how far macrostructural theory can go in sociology, with its exclusive focus on the large-scale structural level of social reality. Although that strict focus might appear to limit its explanatory power, compared to some of the more integrative sociological theories, macrostructuralism appeals to some very basic propensities of sociologists. It will probably prove attractive especially to those sociologists who reject subjective or small-scale factors as primary concerns of sociology.

EXISTENTIAL SOCIOLOGY

We have already encountered a number of micro-oriented theories in this book that can be grouped together as social definitionism (Ritzer, 1975a, 1975b), creative sociologies (M. Morris, 1977), or sociologies of everyday life (Douglas, 1970; Douglas et al., 1980). Included under all of these similar headings are such theories as symbolic interactionism, phenomenological sociology, and ethnomethodology. Existential sociology can be added to this list. We have left it for the final chapter because it has not achieved the status of the other social definitionist theories; however, it has been the subject of increasing interest in recent years. It will probably become clear in the next decade whether existential sociology is to occupy a more central position in sociological theory or recede into the background.

First we will offer a preliminary definition of existential sociology: "the study of human experience in the world . . . in all its forms" (Douglas and Johnson, 1977:vii). It is oriented to the study of the way people live, feel, think, and act. It accords special importance to the "problematic and situated nature of meaningful experience" (Douglas and Johnson, 1977:xiii). In accepting such a view, existential sociology rejects any monocausal view of human life. To the existential sociologist, "Man is varied, changeable, uncertain, conflictful, and partially free to choose what he will do and what he will become, because he must be so to exist in a world that is varied, changeable, uncertain, and conflictful" (Douglas, 1977:14). This underscores a dominant theme in existential sociology; people are both free *and* constrained.

This idea, as well as many other aspects of existential sociology, derives from the work of Jean-Paul Sartre, the French novelist and philosopher. Of particular interest to sociologists was Sartre's effort to relate individual freedom and societal constraints. Sartre sought to fuse his early phenomenological interests and his later Marxian concerns into a dialectical whole. In Ian Craib's (1976; see also Hayim, 1980) view, Sartre's thought underwent evolution. In his early work Sartre focused on the individual level, especially on individual freedom. At that point he adhered to the view that people are not subject to or determined by any social laws. In other words, man "cannot justify his actions by reference to anything outside himself" (Craib, 1976:4). However, later in his career, Sartre became more intrigued by Marxian theory and as a result shifted his focus to the "*free* individual situated in a *massive and oppressive social structure* which limits and alienates his activities" (Craib, 1976:9; italics added). Sartre did not simply shift to a societal level of concern, but sought to combine it with his earlier interest in the actor. Craib (1976:12) concluded that later in his career Sartre succeeded in unifying large- and small-scale theory.

A good illustration of existential sociology was offered by Andrea Fontana, who drew it from George Orwell's short story "Shooting an Elephant":

> As soon as I saw the elephant I knew with perfect certainty that I ought not to shoot him. . . . I decided that I would watch him for a little while to make sure that he did not turn savage again, and then go home. . . .
>
>   But at that moment I glanced round at the crowd that had followed me. It was an immense crowd. . . . They were watching me. . . . They did not like me, but with the magical rifle in my hands I was momentarily worth watching. And suddenly I realized that I should have to shoot the elephant after all. The people expected it of me and I had got to do it; I could feel their two thousand wills pressing me forward, irresistibly.
>
> (Fontana, 1980:172)

This vignette illustrates several basic components of existential thought. First, the focus is on the actor, in this case the hunter, and his thoughts and actions. Second, there is the situated and problematic character of social life. Left to his own devices, the hunter would not have shot the elephant. However, he found himself in a situation in which he was led to change his course of action. Third, there is the social setting, the crowd, which "forced" the hunter to shoot the elephant. Finally, there is Sartre's theme of "bad faith." The hunter did not have to shoot the elephant, as he claimed. He could have said no to the pressure. This illustrates the political theme of existentialism. Despite the existence of external pressures, one can always say no. The Nazi concentration camp officer is practicing bad faith when he tells us that he was just carrying out orders; he could have said no.

Although it leads to distinct political conclusions about actions, the basic orientation of existential sociology is not easily differentiated from that of the other social definitionist theories that allow the actor some autonomy even within certain external constraints. However, the unique characteristics of existential sociology do become clearer when we distinguish it from its closest theoretical neighbor, phenomenological sociology.[5]

Existentialism and Phenomenology

Existential sociology and phenomenological sociology have similar philosophical sources. Both have deep roots in philosophical phenomenology, especially the work of Edmund Husserl. While phenomenological sociologists have acknowledged this source, existential sociologists have tried to dissociate themselves from both philosophical and sociological phenomenology. For example, Craib (1976) noted that while

---

[5]Some of the earlier work in existential sociology (Tiryakian, 1962, 1965; Manning, 1973) made little effort to do this. In fact, it often seemed that existential sociologists were trying to show how everything was at least to some degree existential.

Sartre was influenced by Husserl, he was not inclined to accept the idea of essences, or invariant structures of consciousness. By excising them from his theory, Sartre left consciousness "empty" of eternal structures; consciousness was to be conceived of as a relationship within the actor and with the outside world.

Herbert Spiegelberg (1967) took great care to differentiate Sartre's existentialism from Husserl's phenomenology. First, phenomenology aspires to be a rigorous science, but existentialism has no similar aspirations. Second, phenomenology brackets, or sets aside, the everyday world in order to get at the essence of consciousness, whereas existentialism focuses on the everyday world. Although existentialists do not focus on consciousness per se, they admit that individual consciousness is a crucial ingredient in the everyday world they study. Third, phenomenologists rely on intuition and description as their methodologies, whereas existentialism eschews a commitment to a single method. Fourth, while phenomenologists seek to get at the essence of consciousness, existentialists try to comprehend the larger situation in which thought and action take place. Finally, phenomenologists study all types of beliefs and do not express a preference for any one type, whereas existentialists enunciate a preference for a special mode of existence, one they call "authentic existence." To illustrate this last idea in terms of the example discussed above, the elephant hunter was not involved in authentic existence. The objective of the existentialist would be to awaken in the hunter the sense that he was not forced to shoot the elephant.

Andrea Fontana (1980) extended Spiegelberg's differentiation between existentialism and phenomenology. First, Fontana argued that, while phenomenology aims at making universal statements, existentialism emphasizes a particularistic orientation. Second, whereas phenomenology tends to be abstract and uninvolved, existentialism is concrete and engaged in the real world.

Fontana also made the useful point that the two philosophies are not coterminous with the two sociologies derived from them. For one thing, existential sociology is different from existential philosophy in that the former seeks to discover the systematic structure of everyday life. However, at the same time, it does not deny the situational and problematic character of everyday life. Nor does it lose sight of the fact that its own knowledge of everyday life is itself problematic. In addition, although existential sociology is not limited to any particular method, its adherents have tended to rely on personal observation and participant observation.

Among the differences between existential sociology and phenomenological sociology, Fontana pointed out that, because of its basic nature, existential sociology is not as detached from the everyday world as phenomenological sociology. In addition, while phenomenological sociologists tend to focus on the routine elements of social life, existential sociologists are not similarly restricted and concern themselves with all facets of everyday life.

Inevitably, comparisons between the theories imply preferences for one or the other. Fontana, for example, seems to prefer the more tangible and more political existential sociology. Spiegelberg (1967) seems to take the opposite position, at least as far as the two philosophies are concerned. He admitted that the two philosophies are comparable, but he criticized Sartrean existentialism for its selective emphasis, its hasty interpretations, and its inadequate descriptions. Spiegelberg (1967:266) concluded: "Existentialism may be on the trail of more vital, more fruitful insights than pure phenomenology. But it has still to learn a few lessons from the older phenomenology, particularly from Husserl.''

Existential Sociology: Primary Concerns

Existential sociology has a deep commitment to the naturalistic study of actors and their thoughts, feelings, and actions. Within this general arena, it emphasizes several phenomena. For one thing, existential sociologists (for instance, Manning, 1973; Kotarba, 1979) have a strong interest in feelings, sentiments, and the like, in stark contrast to the propensity of most sociologists, who emphasize the rational aspects of human existence (a notable exception being Kemper, 1978a; 1978b; 1981). Joseph A. Kotarba (1979:350) made clear precisely how important the study of feelings is to the existential sociologist: "Underlying all the work, however, is an emphasis on and a deep commitment to understanding how feelings form the foundations of our lives, as well as the intricate social realities we construct." In other words, our understanding, not only of people but of their social products as well, is made possible by the study of human feelings.

Another crucial concern of the existential sociologist is the *self,* or the "individual's total experience of being." The self, to the existentialist, cannot be separated from the physical body in which it is found. The relationship between the mental and physical dimensions of life is deemed important and worthy of study (Kotarba, 1977). Furthermore, the self is viewed not as a static structure but as a process, something constantly in a state of becoming. That is, the self is creative and spontaneous, highly affected by its immediate situation. In this definition, the self is always seen as at least partially problematic and situational.

Future Prospects

What are the future prospects of existential sociology? In order to achieve a more central position, it will need to overcome several problems. First, its practitioners will have to convince a larger number of sociologists that it offers something different from and superior to that which is offered by the other, more established sociologies of everyday life. Second, in spite of Sartre's later work, existential sociology does not yet have much to offer to our understanding of large-scale structures and their relationship to small-scale processes. Third, existentialism will need a better sense of history; it seems to many to be largely ahistorical. Kotarba (1979) sought to deal with this issue directly by arguing that existential sociology is historical, since it leads the researchers to be critical of historical documents as "deceitful" products of a particular historical context. In addition, he urged existentialists to utilize empathic immersion in history as a research strategy.

One final issue bears on the future of existential sociology: it sometimes seems that it was chosen as the favorite of the young, bourgeois intelligentsia only because it spoke to their voguish concerns. In his analysis, Kotarba (1979:358) reinforced this view: "Feelings are more crucial to sociology than ever before. Our society is increasingly marked by the dominance of feelings. This is fairly obvious in the areas of sex, drug use, and violent behavior." The observer is led to wonder whether existential sociology will outlive the voguish concerns of this generation's intelligentsia. Although existential sociology has some strong theoretical roots, its long-term appeal remains to be seen.

CONCLUSIONS

Most of this chapter has been devoted to a variety of theories that are at various stages in the cycle of acceptance and rejection in sociology. Action theory seems to be near its demise as a result of its internal contradictions as well as the fact that its basic premises and most useful derivatives have been taken over by more popular theories. Systems theory enjoyed a brief boom, but in the last few years it has declined as a result of attacks on it for, among other things, showing modest results, being pseudo-scientific, and being ideologically conservative. Sociobiology, probably better seen as a discipline or a paradigm than as a theory, is attracting a good deal of attention these days in sociological theory. Its future depends on several factors, perhaps the most important of which is how far sociobiologists are interested in pressing their claims. If they claim that sociobiology explains a large portion of social and cultural life, their ideas are likely to be rejected once again. If, however, they argue that biology is only one of many factors explaining the social world, their ideas are more likely to be accepted.

We examined three very different sociological theories that are currently increasing in popularity—structuralism, macrostructural theory, and existential sociology. Structuralism constitutes an effort to import into sociology a perspective developed in such fields as linguistics and anthropology. Although structuralism seems to have considerable promise, structuralists have yet to demonstrate the applicability of the theory to a wide range of social issues. Macrostructural theory rejects outright structuralism's interest in invisible structures. Its concern is with visible social structures. Whereas structuralism imported ideas from other fields, macrostructural theory returns to sociology's Durkheimian roots. Existential sociology, the third theory, is part of the boom in theories associated with the social definitionist paradigm, which also includes phenomenology and ethnomethodology. It is not interested in either visible or invisible structures; it has instead a focus on actors, their thoughts and actions. The future of existential sociology is tied to that of social definitionism in general—continuing as part of the boom, being subsumed by either phenomenological sociology or ethnomethodology, or finding itself of declining significance.

SOME FINAL OBSERVATIONS

Students of sociological theory would be wise to watch carefully the theories discussed in the latter parts of this chapter, but they should not lose sight of the theories discussed throughout this book, because they continue to be the most important in sociology. They all deal with, or are relevant to, important areas of social life; they are rather wide in scope; and they have demonstrated at least some long-term staying power. On this last criterion they contrast with several theories discussed in this chapter, which have yet to demonstrate their long-term appeal to sociologists. Because the theories to which we have devoted the bulk of this book have been shown to have lasting significance, we close this book with a few words about them.

Not too many years ago, a text on sociological theory would have been dominated by structural functionalism, conflict theory, and the debate between them. Until recent years, sociological theory was considered to be coterminous with structural functionalism and conflict theory, with a dash of symbolic interactionism thrown in. That view has, of course, changed dramatically and is likely to continue to change in the future. As you will recall, only one of the eight chapters in this book has been devoted to structural functionalism and conflict theory, and developments in sociological theory would seem to imply that they will occupy an even smaller role in the future. Structural functionalism, under attack from many sides for a number of years, has been badly damaged in the process. At one time, it seemed that conflict theory, the major alternative to structural functionalism, would replace it at the center of sociological theory. However, no sooner had conflict theory begun to attract significant attention than it too was attacked. Some of the attacks were defensive measures by structural functionalists, but the more devastating attacks came from Marxian theorists who saw conflict theory as little more than structural functionalism in reverse. Nonetheless, conflict theory still has some life, especially in the new directions taken by people such as Randall Collins.

Symbolic interactionism, the other sociological theory that had dominated American sociological theory, also faces a bleak future. Although it was highly relevant to a number of important social issues, it was always limited in scope. Most of its major exponents are either dead, retired, or geographically dispersed; its basic texts, except for Mead's *Mind, Self and Society*, are largely unread; and it has long since lost its geographical center at Chicago. Cognizant of the threat to their theory, surviving symbolic interactionists have sought to counterattack by establishing professional societies (such as the Society for Symbolic Interaction) and journals (*Studies in Symbolic Interaction*). However, these appear to be largely futile gestures. The potential constituency for a revived symbolic interactionism seems much more likely to be attracted to the newer and more sophisticated varieties of social definitionism—phenomenology, ethnomethodology, and existentialism. Furthermore, there seems to be no up-and-coming theorist with the capacity to inject new life into symbolic interactionism. At one time, Erving Goffman seemed likely to take that role; however, his most recent work moves away from symbolic interactionism and toward a more structural mode of analysis.

Exchange theory and behavioral sociology have somewhat different pasts, and are likely to have different futures, than the other theories discussed here. Always narrow in scope and significance, exchange theory and behavioral sociology have traditionally had a small but vociferous following in sociology. However, the tendency toward psychologism among at least some of their supporters has dimmed their attraction for many sociologists. Exchange theory and behavioral sociology are likely to remain attractive to a small group of sociologists but not likely to achieve theoretical hegemony in sociology.

In contrast, both phenomenology and ethnomethodology are likely to grow even stronger in the coming years, and to be refined and expanded. They have strong philosophical and theoretical roots, and both have already spawned significant bodies of thought and research. These two theories are likely to be attractive to the large number of sociologists who used to gravitate toward symbolic interactionism. However, some of their limitations in scope and relevance will need to be addressed. For instance, their relationship to the other major variant of social definitionism—existentialism—will need resolution. Supporters of each of the theoretical variants of the social definition paradigm will probably try to gain preeminence in the area. It is to be hoped that in so doing they will not ignore the need to refine their theoretical orientations and deal with the links between them.

Some of the most exciting work in sociology is being done in the various types of neo-Marxian theories. The neo-Marxian perspectives, taken collectively, have great scope and significance and great promise. However, they face some serious tests in the future. Sociological theory has generally been conservative and anti-Marxist, and such sentiments remain strong. It is thus likely that neo-Marxian theory will be tested by many strong attacks. However, Marxian theory has long faced such attacks and flourished nonetheless. What is almost as troublesome are the internal problems one can anticipate within neo-Marxian theory. For one thing, the contemporary importance of the different neo-Marxian theories varies greatly. Economic determinism and Hegelian Marxism are of little more than historical importance, while the others are more relevant today. Then, too, the bitter disputes that already exist among the various branches of neo-Marxian theory show every sign of accelerating in the future and of tearing neo-Marxian theory apart, leaving a series of isolated and warring camps. Instead of pointless political warfare, more work is needed on cementing the common bonds that exist, or can be uncovered, among the various branches of neo-Marxian theory, especially in the face of the hostility neo-Marxists are likely to encounter from without.

Greater integrative efforts by *all* sociological theorists would heal many wounds and aid in theoretical development. It is not that theoretical differences should be ignored where they are relevant and important; rather, the tendency to exaggerate differences and minimize similarities for political reasons is a threat to all of sociological theory. A healthy regard for both potential points of integration and basic differences should be basic to sociological theory.

APPENDIX
A Schema for Analyzing Sociological Theory

THE IDEAS OF THOMAS KUHN

SOCIOLOGY: A MULTIPLE PARADIGM SCIENCE
  MAJOR SOCIOLOGICAL PARADIGMS

TOWARD A MORE INTEGRATED SOCIOLOGICAL PARADIGM
  LEVELS OF SOCIAL REALITY: A REVIEW OF THE LITERATURE
  LEVELS OF SOCIAL REALITY: A MODEL

ALTHOUGH it has been played down, this book has an underlying organizational schema. Since the primary objective of the text has been to present sociological theory, it was decided to make the organizing principles as unobtrusive as possible. Thus, all chapters, as well as the book as a whole, can be read without knowledge of the organizing schema that undergirds them. However, some students may be interested in that schema, either early in their reading of the book or after they have finished it. This appendix provides an overview of the book's organization. It constitutes a brief summary of two of my earlier books, *Sociology: A Multiple Paradigm Science* and *Toward an Integrated Sociological Paradigm: The Search for an Exemplar and an Image of the Subject Matter*. Those who are interested in the issues raised in this appendix are referred to those two books for more detailed discussion.

The concerns of this appendix lead us into a field known as the sociology of sociology (Friedrichs, 1970). Few fields other than sociology can study themselves. A physics of physics or a biology of biology does not make any sense. But sociologists (and the other social scientists) *can* analyze themselves. A sociology of sociology is just as legitimate as a sociology of the family, of religion, or of work.

As a subfield of sociology, the sociology of sociology has been growing in importance in recent years and encompasses a number of specific concerns. The sociologist of sociology might study such issues as the personal backgrounds of sociologists (Glenn and Weiner, 1969) and the kinds of students in introductory sociology courses (Oksanen and Spencer, 1975). But we are not interested in all of the sociology of sociology in this appendix. Rather our concern is with the sociological study of sociological *theory*. Of all of the areas within the sociology of sociology, this one has gained the greatest attention. In fact, so much work has been done in it that it has acquired a name of its own—*metasociology* (Furfey, 1953; Snizek et al., 1979; Lemert, 1979).

As there are many sociological theories and many facets of a sociology of sociology, it should come as no surprise that there are also different metasociologies—many theories of sociological theory (for example, Gouldner, 1970; Mullins, 1973; Ritzer,

1975a, 1975b; Eisenstadt and Curelaru, 1976; Strasser, 1976; Goudsblom, 1977; Snizek et al., 1979; Lemert, 1979). However, there is one metasociology, inspired by the work of the philosopher Thomas Kuhn (1962, 1970), that dominates all of the others.

THE IDEAS OF THOMAS KUHN

In 1962 the philosopher of science Thomas Kuhn published a rather slim volume entitled *The Structure of Scientific Revolutions*. Since this work grew out of philosophy, it appeared fated to a marginal status within sociology. This seemed especially likely since it focused on the hard sciences (physics, for example) and had little directly to say about the social sciences. However, the theses of the book proved extremely interesting to people in a wide range of fields (for example, Searle, 1972, in linguistics; Stanfield, 1974, in economics; Hollinger, 1980, in history), and to none was it more important than to sociologists. In 1970 Robert Friedrichs published the first important work from a Kuhnian perspective, *A Sociology of Sociology*. Since then there has been a steady stream of work from this perspective (Lodahl and Gordon, 1972; Effrat, 1972; Fredrichs, 1972a, 1972b; D. Phillips, 1973, 1975; Ritzer, 1975a, 1975b; Eisenstadt and Curelaru, 1976; Snizek, 1976; Snizek et al., 1979; Quadagno, 1979, Eckberg and Hill, 1979; Ritzer, 1981b). There is little doubt that Kuhnian theory dominates metasociology, but what exactly is Kuhn's approach?

One of Kuhn's goals in *The Structure of Scientific Revolutions* was to challenge commonly held assumptions about the way in which science changes. In the view of most laypeople, and many scientists, science advances in a cumulative manner, with each advance building inexorably on all that preceded it. Science has achieved its present state through slow and steady increments of knowledge. It will advance to even greater heights in the future. This conception of science was enunciated by the famous physicist Isaac Newton, who said, "If I have seen further, it is because I stood on the shoulders of giants." But Kuhn regarded this conception of cumulative scientific development as a myth and sought to debunk it.

Kuhn acknowledged that accumulation plays some role in the advance of science, but the truly major changes come about as a result of revolutions. Kuhn offered us a theory of how major changes in science occur. He saw a science at any given time as dominated by a specific *paradigm* (defined for the moment as a fundamental image of the science's subject matter). *Normal science* is a period of accumulation of knowledge in which scientists work to expand the reigning paradigm. Such scientific work inevitably spawns *anomalies*, or findings that cannot be explained by the reigning paradigm. A *crisis* stage occurs if these anomalies mount, and this crisis may ultimately end in a scientific revolution. The reigning paradigm is overthrown as a new one takes it place at the center of the science. A new dominant paradigm is born, and the stage is set for the cycle to repeat itself. Kuhn's theory can be depicted diagrammatically:

Paradigm I → Normal Science → Anomalies →
Crisis → Revolution → Paradigm II

It is during periods of revolution that the truly great changes in science take place. This view clearly places Kuhn at odds with most conceptions of scientific development.

The key concept in Kuhn's approach, as well as in this appendix, is the *paradigm*. Unfortunately, Kuhn is vague on what he means by a paradigm. According to Margaret Masterman (1970), he used it in at least twenty-one different ways. But we will employ a definition of paradigm that we feel is true to the sense and spirit of his early work.

A paradigm serves to differentiate one scientific community from another. It can be used to differentiate physics from chemistry or sociology from psychology. These fields have different paradigms. It can also be used to differentiate between different historical stages in the development of a science. The paradigm that dominated physics in the nineteenth century is different from the one that dominated it in the early twentieth century. There is a third usage of the paradigm concept, and it is the one that is most useful to us here. Paradigms can be used to differentiate among subcommunities *within* the same science. Contemporary psychoanalysis, for example, is differentiated into Freudian, Jungian, and Horneyian paradigms (among others)—that is, there are *multiple paradigms* in psychoanalysis—and the same is true of sociology and of most other fields.

We can now offer a definition of paradigm that we feel is true to the sense of Kuhn's original work:

> A paradigm is a fundamental image of the subject matter within a science. It serves to define what should be studied, what questions should be asked, how they should be asked, and what rules should be followed in interpreting the answers obtained. The paradigm is the broadest unit of consensus within a science and serves to differentiate one scientific community (*or subcommunity*) from another. It subsumes, defines, and interrelates the exemplars, *theories* [italics added], and methods and instruments that exist within it.
>
> (Ritzer, 1975a:7)

With this definition we can begin to see the relationship between paradigms and theories. *Theories are only part of larger paradigms*. To put it another way, a paradigm may encompass two or more *theories*, as well as different *images* of the subject matter, *methods* (and instruments), and *exemplars* (specific pieces of scientific work that stand as a model for all of those who follow). An objective of this appendix will be to identify the basic paradigms in sociology.

SOCIOLOGY: A MULTIPLE-PARADIGM SCIENCE

The idea that sociology is a multiple-paradigm science has received some empirical support (Lodahl and Gordon, 1972), but most of the analyses of the paradigmatic status of sociology have been nonempirical.

In the earliest systematic application of Kuhnian ideas to sociology, Robert Friedrichs (1970) presented two different images of the paradigmatic status of sociology, but both affirmed the idea that sociology was a multiple-paradigm science. At one level, Friedrichs argued that despite greater consensus in the past, sociology is split largely between a *system* paradigm (emphasizing societal integration and consensus) and a *conflict* paradigm (emphasizing societal disintegration and coercion) with a wide array of other perspectives as potential paradigms. These paradigms are based on the fundamental images of the subject matter of sociology, but Friedrichs thinks of them as being of secondary importance to two other paradigms that focus on sociologists' images of themselves as scientific agents. These are the *prophetic* and the *priestly* paradigms. While prophetic sociologists perceive themselves as agents of social change, priestly sociologists conceive of themselves as "value-free" scientists. The crucial point for our purposes is that, whether Friedrichs looks at images of the subject matter or images of the sociologists themselves, he concludes that sociology is a multiple-paradigm science.

Andrew Effrat (1972) clearly aligned himself with those who see sociology as a multiple-paradigm science, although he mistook more specific theories for paradigms. Effrat ended up with a cumbersome list of paradigms, including Marxian, Freudian, Durkheimian, Weberian, phenomenological, ethnomethodological, symbolic interactionist, and exchange theory. As we will see, all of these are best viewed as theoretical components of sociology's multiple paradigms, but Effrat was on the right track in his multiparadigmatic image of sociology.

S. N. Eisenstadt and M. Curelaru (1976) differentiated among discrete, closed-system, and open-system paradigms. They framed their paradigms in terms of the historical development of the field. The earliest is the *discrete paradigm*, in which the focus was on separate concrete entities such as ecological properties, size of groups, or racial and psychological characteristics. Given this image of the world as a set of isolated units, those who operated within this paradigm had difficulty dealing with such relational issues as emergence, innovation, and creativity. This early and primitive paradigm left only a small mark on the development of sociology and persists today in only isolated domains. It was replaced, historically, by the *closed-system model*, whose supporters saw society as composed of separate but interrelated elements. Those who operated within this paradigm tended to see one element as dominant over the others. In Eisenstadt and Curelaru's view (but not this author's), Marx was operating within this paradigm with his emphasis on the economic sector. This paradigm was replaced, in turn, by the *open-system model*, which focuses on the "internal systemic dynamics, interconnections, and continuous feedback processes among the components of the social order" (Eisenstadt and Curelaru, 1976:92). Although the evolution of these paradigms follows "no simple, natural, chronological trend," and there is "considerable temporal and operative overlapping of the several approaches," there is in Eisenstadt and Curelaru's view a long-term trend toward the open-system paradigm.

Charles Lemert (1979) argued that rather than being composed of multiple paradigms, sociology is unified in its *homocentrism*, "the peculiarly nineteenth-century idea which holds that *man* is the measure of all things" (Lemert, 1979:13). While it is true that sociology is person-centered, it is questionable whether this is really evidence that sociology is unified. One equally plausible conclusion is that there are multiple paradigms in sociology and that the sources of their differences are their varied interpretations *of* humankind. In the author's view, the ideas of homocentrism and multiple paradigms are not mutually exclusive.

Lemert concluded that in spite of their homocentrism there are important paradigmatic differences among the various modes of sociological discourse. He differentiated among them on a linguistic basis. The first is *lexical sociology*, which is primarily technical in orientation. Second is *semantical sociology*, which focuses on the interpretation of meaning that only people (not animals) are capable of producing. Finally, there is *syntactical sociology*, which is much more political in its orientation to sociology. Thus, for Lemert, there *are* multiple paradigms, at least in contemporary sociology.

Major Sociological Paradigms

Although all the preceding perspectives have some degree of utility, it is my own earlier work on the paradigmatic status of sociology (Ritzer, 1975a, 1975b, 1980) that provides the basis for the metasociological perspective that has guided the analysis of sociological theory throughout this book. Like most of those discussed above, I conceive of sociology as a multiple paradigm science. In my view there are *three* paradigms that dominate contemporary sociology, with several others having the potential to achieve paradigmatic status. I label the three paradigms the *social facts, social definition,* and *social behavior* paradigms. Each paradigm is analyzed in terms of the four components of a paradigm outlined in the definition discussed earlier.

THE SOCIAL FACTS PARADIGM

1. *Exemplar.* The model for social factists is the work of Emile Durkheim, particularly *The Rules of Sociological Method* and *Suicide.*
2. *Image of the subject matter.* Social factists focus on what Durkheim termed *social facts,* or large-scale social structures and institutions. Those who subscribe to the social facts paradigm focus not only on these phenomena but on their effect on individual thought and action.
3. *Methods.* Social factists are more likely than those who subscribe to the other paradigms to use the interview-questionnaire[1] and historical-comparative methods.
4. *Theories.* The social facts paradigm encompasses a number of theoretical perspectives. *Structural-functional* theorists tend to see social facts as neatly interrelated and order as maintained by general consensus. *Conflict* theorists tend to emphasize disorder among social facts as well as the notion that order is maintained by coercive forces in society. Although structural functionalism and conflict theory are the dominant theories in this paradigm, there are others that are discussed in this book, including *systems* theory.

THE SOCIAL DEFINITION PARADIGM

1. *Exemplar.* To social definitionists, the unifying model is Max Weber's work on social action.
2. *Image of the subject matter.* Weber's work helped lead to an interest among social definitionists in the way actors define their social situations and the effect of these definitions on ensuing action and interaction.
3. *Methods.* Social definitionists, although they are most likely to use the interview-questionnaire method, are more likely to use the observation method than those in any other paradigm. In other words, observation is the distinctive methodology of social definitionists.

---

[1]William Snizek (1976) has shown that the interview-questionnaire is dominant in *all* paradigms.

4. *Theories*. There are a wide number of theories that can be included within social definitionism: *action theory, symbolic interactionism, phenomenology, ethnomethodology,* and *existentialism.*

THE SOCIAL BEHAVIOR PARADIGM

1. *Exemplar.* The model for sociologists who accept the social behavior paradigm is the work of the psychologist B. F. Skinner.
2. *Image of the subject matter.* The subject matter of sociology to social behaviorists is the unthinking *behavior* of individuals. Of particular interest are the rewards that elicit desirable behaviors and the punishments that inhibit undesirable behaviors.
3. *Methods.* The distinctive method of social behaviorism is the experiment.
4. *Theories.* There are two theoretical approaches in sociology that can be included under the heading of social behaviorism. The first is *behavioral sociology,* which is very close to pure psychological behaviorism, and the second, and much more important, is *exchange theory.*[2]

TOWARD A MORE INTEGRATED SOCIOLOGICAL PARADIGM

In addition to detailing the nature of sociology's multiple paradigms, I also sought in my earlier work to make the case for more paradigmatic integration in sociology. Although there is reason for extant paradigms to continue to exist, there is also a need for a more integrated paradigm. Extant paradigms tend to be one-sided, focusing on specific levels of social reality while paying little or no attention to the others. This is reflected in the social factists' concern with macrostructures; the social definitionists' interest in action, interaction, and the social construction of reality; and the social behaviorists' focus on behavior. It is this kind of one-sidedness that has led to what I perceive to be a growing interest in a more integrated approach among a wide range of sociologists. (This is but part of what I see as a growing interest in integration within, and even among, many social sciences; see, especially, Mitroff and Kilmann, 1978). For example, Robert Merton (1975:30), representing social factism, saw it and social definitionism as mutually enriching, as "opposed to one another in about the same sense as ham is opposed to eggs: they are perceptively different but mutually enriching." Among social definitionists Hugh Mehan and Houston Wood (1975:180) argue that one theoretical component of social definitionism (ethnomethodology) accepts at least one basic tenet of social factism, "the reality of an external and constraining world." Among social behaviorists Arthur Staats (1976) seeks to integrate creative mental processes (a key element of social definitionism) with traditional behaviorism. Calls for a more integrated paradigm are clearly important, but what is necessary is an effort to delineate what such a paradigm might look like.

---

[2]Analyses of Ritzer's paradigm schema include Snizek (1976), Staats (1976), Eckberg and Hill (1979), Friedheim (1979), and Harper, Sylvester, and Walczak (1980).

The key to an integrated paradigm is the notion of *levels* of social reality (Ritzer, 1979; 1981a). As the reader is well aware, *the social world is not "really" divided into levels*. In fact, social reality is best viewed as an enormous variety of social phenomena that are involved in continuing interaction and change. Individuals, groups, families, bureaucracies, the polity, and numerous other highly diverse social phenomena represent the bewildering array of phenomena that make up the social world. It is extremely difficult to get a handle on such a large number of wide-ranging and mutually interpenetrating social phenomena. Some sort of conceptual schema is clearly needed, and sociologists have developed a number of such schema in an effort to deal with the social world. The idea of levels of social reality employed here should be seen as but one of a large number of such schema that can be, and have been, used for purposes of dealing with the complexities of the social world.

Levels of Social Reality: A Review of the Literature

Although the idea of levels is implicit in much of sociology, it has received relatively little explicit attention. In concentrating on levels here, we are doing little more than making explicit what has been implicit in sociology.

The close of this appendix will offer a conceptualization of the major levels of social reality. To understand adequately that conceptualization some preliminary differentiations must be made. As will be seen two continua of social reality are useful in developing the major levels of the social world. The first is the *macroscopic-microscopic* continuum. Thinking of the social world as being made up of a series of entities ranging from those large in scale to those small in scale is relatively easy, because it is so familiar. Most people in their day-to-day lives conceive of the social world in these terms. In the academic world, a number of thinkers have worked with a macro-micro continuum (including Edel, 1959; Wagner, 1964; Gurvitch, 1964; Korenbaum, 1964; Bosserman, 1968; Blalock and Wilken, 1979; Collins, 1981; and Johnson, 1981:54–59). For laypeople and academics alike the continuum is based on the simple idea that social phenomena vary greatly in size. At the macro end of the continuum are such large-scale social phenomena as groups of societies (for example, the capitalist and socialist world systems), societies, and cultures. At the micro end are individual actors and their thoughts and actions. In between are a wide range of groups, collectivities, social classes, and organizations. We have little difficulty recognizing these distinctions and thinking of the world in macro-micro terms. There are no clear dividing lines between the macro social units and the micro units. Instead, there is a continuum ranging from the micro to the macro ends.

The second continuum is the *objective-subjective* dimension of social reality. At each end of the macro-micro continuum we can differentiate between objective and subjective components. At the micro, or individual, level, there are the subjective mental processes of an actor and the objective patterns of action and interaction in which he or she engages. Subjective here refers to something that occurs solely in the realm of ideas, while objective relates to real, material events. This same differentiation is also found at the macro end of the continuum. A society is made up of both objective structures, such as governments, bureaucracies, and laws, and subjective phenomena, such as norms and values. The objective-subjective continuum is more complicated than the macro-micro range, and it is even, as we will see, more complicated than is implied in this introduction. To try to clarify matters and to work toward greater complexity, let us look at a concrete example as well as at the work of a number of sociologists on the objective-subjective continuum.

Consider the purchase of a new automobile. At the micro-subjective level we would focus on the attitudes and orientations of the individual buyer that will influence the kind of car to be purchased. But—and this is the key distinction between the micro-subjective and micro-objective levels of analysis—the buyer may desire (subjective state) a sports car and actually buy (objective act) an economy compact. Some sociologists are interested in subjective mental states, others in objective acts. In many cases it is useful and important to understand the interplay between these two micro levels.

The macro level also has subjective and objective dimensions. For many years most Americans shared a set of preferences for larger and ever more powerful cars. This was a subjective set of attitudes shared by a large number of people. Then a series of objective changes at the societal level had an impact on these shared attitudes. OPEC was formed, oil deliveries to the United States were curtailed, and the government played a more active role in oil-related matters. These and other macro-structural changes led to changes in the shared preferences of large numbers of people. Almost overnight many people came to prize small, fuel-efficient automobiles. This change, in turn, led to a massive alteration in the structure of the American automobile companies. Also affected were the thoughts and actions of many individual Americans. Thus, the purchase of a car as well as most other mundane and extraordinary activities involve the complex interaction of the macro-micro and objective-subjective components of social life.

Now let us turn to the work of several sociologists on the objective-subjective continuum. As we saw in Chapter One, an important influence on Karl Marx was German idealism, particularly the work of G. W. F. Hegel. The Hegelian dialectic was a subjective process taking place within the realm of ideas. Although affected by this view, Marx, and before him the Young Hegelians, were dissatisfied with the dialectic because it was not rooted in the objective, material world. Marx, building on the work of Ludwig Feuerbach and others, sought to extend the dialectic to the material world. On the one hand, this meant that he was concerned with real, sensuous actors rather than idea systems. On the other hand, he came to focus on the objective structures of capitalist society, primarily the economic structure. Marx became increasingly interested in the real material structures of capitalism and the contradictions that exist among and within them. This is not to say that Marx lost sight of subjective ideas; in fact, notions of false and class consciousness play a key role in his work. It is the materialism-idealism split, as manifest in the work of Marx and others, that is one of the major philosophical roots of the objective-subjective continuum in modern sociology.

We can also find this continuum, although in a different form, in the work of Emile Durkheim (1895/1964). In his classic work on methodology, Durkheim differentiated between material (objective) and nonmaterial (subjective) social facts. In *Suicide*, Durkheim (1897/1951:313) said: "The social fact is sometimes materialized as to become an element of the external world.'' He discussed architecture and law as two examples of material (objective) social facts. However, most of Durkheim's work emphasizes nonmaterial (subjective) social facts:

> Of course it is true that not all social consciousness achieves such externalization and materialization. Not all aesthetic spirit of a nation is embodied in the works it inspires; not all morality is formulated in clear precepts. The greater part is diffused. There is a large collective life which is at liberty; all sorts of currents come, go, circulate everywhere, cross and mingle in a thousand different ways, and just because they are constantly mobile are never crystallized in an objective form. Today a breath of sadness and discouragement descends on society: tomorrow, one of joyous confidence will uplift all hearts.
>
> (Durkheim, 1897/1951:315)

These social currents do not have material existence; they can only exist within the consciousness of individuals and between them. In *Suicide*, Durkheim concentrated on examples of this kind of social fact. He related differences in suicide rates to differences in social currents. For example, where there are strong currents of anomie (normlessness), we will find high rates of anomic suicide. Social currents such as anomie, egoism, and altruism clearly do not have a material existence, although they may have a material effect by causing differences in suicide rates. Rather, they are intersubjective phenomena that can only exist in the consciousness of people.

More recently, Peter Blau (1960) has been in the forefront of those employing an objective-subjective continuum. His differentiation between institutions (subjective entities) and social structures (objective entities) is of this genre. He defined subjective institutions as ''the common values and norms embodied in a culture or subculture'' (Blau, 1960:178). Conversely, there are social structures that are ''the networks of social relations in which processes of social interaction became organized and through which social positions of individuals and subgroups become differentiated'' (Blau, 1960:178).

It can be argued that the objective-subjective continuum plays a crucial role in the thought of people like Marx, Durkheim, Blau, and many others. But there is a rather interesting problem involved in their use of the continuum: they employ it almost exclusively at the macroscopic level. However, it also can be applied at the microscopic level. Before giving an example of this, we need to underscore the point that we must deal not only with the macroscopic-microscopic and objective-subjective continua *but also with the interaction between them.*

One example of the use of the objective-subjective continuum at the microscopic level is an empirical study by Mary and Robert Jackman (1973) of what they called ''objective and subjective social status.'' Their micro-subjective concern was ''the individual's perception of his own position in the status hierarchy.'' Micro subjectivity in this study involved the feelings, the perceptions, and the mental aspects of the actors' positions in the stratification system. These are related to various components of the micro-objective realm that include the actor's socioeconomic status, social contacts, amount of capital owned, ethnic group membership, or status as a breadwinner or a union member. Instead of dealing with actors' feeling, these dimensions involve the more objective characteristics of the individuals—the patterns of action and interaction in which they actually engage.

At a more general level, the microscopic aspect of the objective-subjective continuum is manifest in both the social definition and social behavior paradigms, as well as in the differences between them. While both tend to focus on the micro-objective patterns of action and interaction, they split on the micro-subjective dimension. All of the theoretical components of the social definition paradigm (for example, symbolic interactionism, ethnomethodology, and phenomenology) share an interest in micro subjectivity—the feelings and thoughts of actors. However, the social behaviorists reject the idea that it is necessary to study the micro-subjective components of social life. This is exemplified by B. F. Skinner's (1971) attack on what he called the idea of "autonomous man." To Skinner, we imply that people are autonomous when we attribute to them such ideas as feeling, minding, freedom, and dignity. People are held to possess some sort of inner core from which their actions emanate. They are able to initiate, originate, and create because of this inner core of micro subjectivity. To Skinner, the idea that people have an inner, autonomous core is a mystical, metaphysical position of the kind that must be eliminated from the social sciences: "Autonomous man serves to explain only the things we are not yet able to explain in other ways. His existence depends on our ignorance, and he naturally loses status as we come to know more about behavior" (Skinner, 1971:12). Although we need to reject this kind of political diatribe, the key point is this: the microscopic level has *both* a subjective and an objective dimension.

Levels of Social Reality: A Model

The most important thinker on the issue of levels of social reality was the French sociologist Georges Gurvitch. Although he did not use the same terms, Gurvitch had a sense of *both* the macro-micro and objective-subjective continua. Even more important, he had a profound sense of how these two continua were related. To his credit, he also steadfastly refused to treat the two continua and their interrelationships as static tools but used them to underscore the dynamic quality of social life. But Gurvitch has one major difficulty: his analytical schema is extremely complex and cumbersome. The social world is very complicated and in order to get a handle on it we need relatively simple models.

The simple model we are seeking is formed out of the intersection of the two continua of levels of social reality discussed in the last several pages. The first, the macroscopic-microscopic continuum, can be depicted as in Figure A.1:

FIGURE A.1 The Macroscopic-Microscopic Continuum, with Indentification of Some Key Points on the Continuum

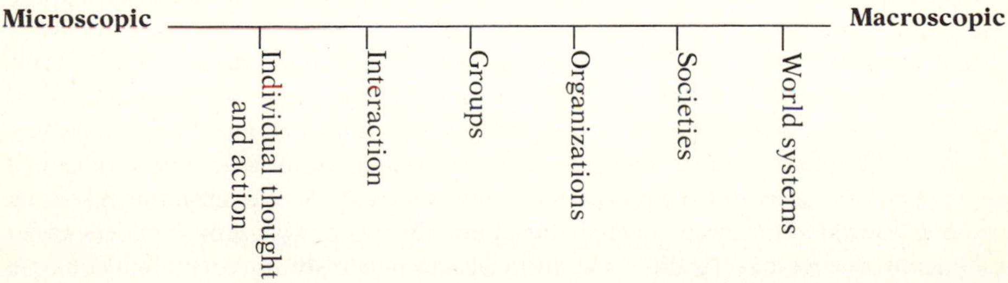

Microscopic ————————————————————————— Macroscopic

Individual thought and action
Interaction
Groups
Organizations
Societies
World systems

The objective-subjective continuum presents greater problems, yet it is no less important than the macro-micro continuum. In general, an objective social phenomenon is one that has a real, material existence. We can think of the following, among others, as objective social phenomena: actors, action, interaction, bureaucratic structures, law, and the state apparatus. It is possible to see, touch, or chart all of these objective phenomena. However, there are social phenomena that exist *solely* in the realm of ideas; they have no material existence. These are sociological phenomena such as mental processes, the social construction of reality (Berger and Luckmann, 1967), norms, values, and many elements of culture. The problem with the objective-subjective continuum is that there are many phenomena in the middle that have *both* objective and subjective elements. The family, for example, has a real material existence as well as a series of subjective mutual understandings, norms, and values. Similarly, the polity is composed of objective laws and bureaucratic structures as well as subjective political norms and values. In fact, it is probably true that the vast majority are mixed types of social phenomena representing some combination of objective and subjective elements. Thus it is best to think of the objective-subjective continuum as two polar types with a series of variously mixed types in the middle. Some of these types may have more objective than subjective characteristics, while others may have the reverse combination. Figure A.2 is the objective-subjective continuum.

FIGURE A.2   The Objective-Subjective Continuum, with Identification of Some Mixed Types

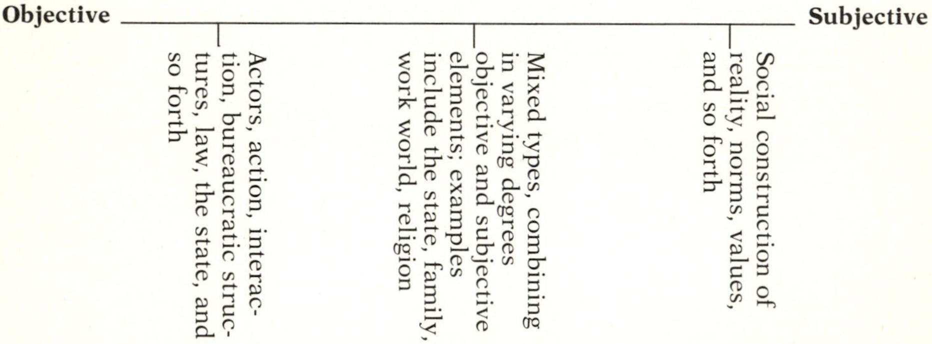

Objective _____ Subjective

Actors, action, interaction, bureaucratic structures, law, the state, and so forth

Mixed types, combining in varying degrees objective and subjective elements; examples include the state, family, work world, religion

Social construction of reality, norms, values, and so forth

While these continua are interesting in themselves, it is the interrelationship of the two continua that concerns us here. Figure A.3 is a schematic representation of the intersection of these two continua and the four major levels of social reality that are derived from it.

It is the contention here that an integrated sociological paradigm must deal with the four basic levels of social reality identified in the figure and their interrelationships. It must deal with macroscopic objective entities like bureaucracy, macro-subjective structures like values, micro-objective phenomena like patterns of interaction, and micro-subjective facts like the process of reality construction. We must remember that in the real world all of these gradually blend into the others as part of the larger social continuum, but we have made some artificial and rather arbitrary differentiations in order to be able to deal with social reality. These four levels of social reality are posited for heuristic purposes and are not meant to be accurate depictions of the social world.

FIGURE A.3   Major Levels of Social Reality

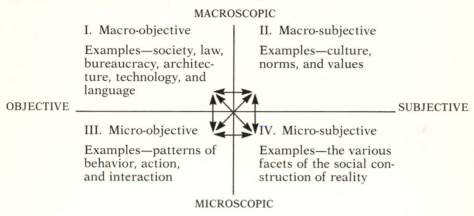

MACROSCOPIC

I. Macro-objective

Examples—society, law, bureaucracy, architecture, technology, and language

II. Macro-subjective

Examples—culture, norms, and values

OBJECTIVE _____ SUBJECTIVE

III. Micro-objective

Examples—patterns of behavior, action, and interaction

IV. Micro-subjective

Examples—the various facets of the social construction of reality

MICROSCOPIC

An obvious question is how these four levels relate to the three paradigms outlined in my earlier work as well as to the integrated paradigm. Figure A.4 relates the four levels to the three paradigms.

FIGURE A.4   Levels of Social Reality and the Major Sociological Paradigms

LEVELS OF SOCIAL REALITY	SOCIOLOGICAL PARADIGMS	
Macro-subjective	Social Facts	Integrated Sociological Paradigm
Macro-objective		
Micro-subjective	Social Definition	
Micro-objective		
	Social Behavior	

The social facts paradigm focuses primarily on the macro-objective and macro-subjective levels. The social definition paradigm is largely concerned with the micro-subjective world and that part of the micro-objective world that depends on mental processes (action). The social behavior paradigm deals with that part of the micro-objective world that does not involve the minding process (behavior). Whereas the three extant paradigms cut across the levels of social reality horizontally, an integrated paradigm cuts across vertically. This depiction makes it clear why the integrated paradigm does not supersede the others. Although each of the three existing paradigms deals with a given level or levels in great detail, the integrated paradigm deals with all levels but does not examine any given level in anything like the degree of intensity of the other paradigms. Thus the choice of a paradigm depends on the kind of question being asked. Not all sociological issues require an integrated approach, but it is certain that at least some do.

What has been outlined in the preceding pages is a model for the image of the subject matter of an integrated sociological paradigm. This is obviously a sketch that will need to be detailed in future years with a sharper image of the subject matter, a new exemplar, and the delineation of appropriate methods and theories. But that is another task (see Ritzer, 1981a). The goal of this discussion is not the development of a new sociological paradigm, but the delineation of a metasociological schema that allows us to analyze sociological theory in a coherent fashion. The model developed in Figure A.3 forms the basis for this analysis.

Each of the sociological theories in the text is analyzed using the four levels of social reality depicted in Figure A.3. This figure provides us with a metatheoretical tool that can be used in the comparative analysis of sociological theories. It enables us to analyze both the strengths and weaknesses of a theoretical perspective and its assets and liabilities relative to every other sociological theory. We begin with the assumption that any good sociological theory will deal with the relationship between *at least* two major levels of social reality and that the strongest will deal in the most balanced fashion with *all* major levels of the social world. We are concerned not only with whether a theory touches on two or more levels but also with the quality of its insights into each specific level. A ''good'' sociological theory, one with wide scope, not only deals with multiple levels but also deals with each level in great depth and with great insight.

One thing to be avoided at all costs is the simple identification of a theory or a theorist with specific levels of social reality. Although it is true, given the preceding description of the current paradigmatic status of sociology, that sociological theorists who adhere to a given paradigm tend to focus on a given level or levels of social reality, it often does them an injustice simply to equate the breadth of their work with one or more levels. For example, Karl Marx is often thought of as focusing on macro-objective structures—in particular, the economic structures of capitalism. But the use of the multiple levels of social reality schema allows us to see that Marx had rich insights regarding all levels of social reality and their mutual interrelationships. Similarly, symbolic interactionism is generally considered as a perspective that deals with micro-subjectivity and micro-objectivity, but it is not devoid of insights into the macroscopic levels of social reality (Maines, 1977).

It is also important for the reader to remember that the use of levels of social reality to analyze any theory tends to break up the wholeness, the integrity, and the internal consistency of the work. While the levels are useful in understanding a theory and comparing it to others, one must take pains to deal with the interrelationship among levels and with the theoretical totality of the work.

In sum, the metasociological schema outlined in Figure A.3, whose development was traced in this appendix, provides the basis for the analysis of the various sociological theories discussed in this book.

BIBLIOGRAPHY

Abbott, Carroll, Brown, Charles R., and Crosbie, Paul V.
1973   "Exchange as Symbolic Interaction: For What?" *American Sociological Review* 38:504–506.

Aberle, D. F. et al.
1950/1967   "The Functional Prerequisites of a Society." In Nicholas Demerath and Richard Peterson (eds.), *System, Change and Conflict*. New York: Free Press: 317–331.

Abrahamson, Mark
1978   *Functionalism*. Englewood Cliffs, N.J.: Prentice-Hall.

Abrahamsson, Bengt
1970   "Homans on Exchange." *American Journal of Sociology* 76:273–285.

Abrams, Philip
1968   *The Origins of British Sociology: 1834–1914*. Chicago: University of Chicago Press.

Abrams, Philip, Deem, Rosemary, Finch, Janet, and Rock, Paul
1981   *Practice and Progress: British Sociology 1950–1980*. London: Allen and Unwin.

Agger, Ben (ed.)
1978   *Western Marxism: An Introduction*. Santa Monica, Calif.: Goodyear.

Akers, Ronald
1981   "Reflections of a Social Behaviorist on Behavioral Sociology." *The American Sociologist* 16:177–180.

Althusser, Louis
1969   *For Marx*. Harmondsworth, Eng.: Penguin.
1977   *Politics and History*. London: NLB.

Althusser, Louis, and Balibar, Etienne (eds.)
1970   *Reading Capital*. New York: Pantheon.

Amin, Samir
1977   *Unequal Development: An Essay on the Social Formations of Peripheral Capitalism*. New York: Monthly Review Press.

Anderson, Perry
1976   *Considerations on Western Marxism*. London: NLB.

Andreski, Stanislav (ed.)
1974   *The Essential Comte*. New York: Barnes & Noble.

Antonio, Robert J.
1979   "Domination and Production in Bureaucracy." *American Sociological Review* 44:895–912.
1981   "Immanent Critique as the Core of Critical Theory: Its Origins and Development in Hegel, Marx and Contemporary Thought." *British Journal of Sociology* 32:330–345.

Appelbaum, Richard
1979   "Born-Again Functionalism? A Reconsideration of Althusser's Structuralism." *The Insurgent Sociologist* 9:18–33.

Back, Kurt
1970   Review of Robert Burgess and Don Bushell, *Behavioral Sociology*. *American Sociological Review* 35:1098–1100.

Baldwin, Alfred
1961   "The Parsonian Theory of Personality." In Max Black (ed.), *The Social Theories of Talcott Parsons.* Englewood Cliffs, N.J.: Prentice-Hall: 153–190.

Baldwin, John D., and Baldwin, Janice I.
1978   "Behaviorism on Verstehen and Erklären." *American Sociological Review* 43:335–347.

Ball, Richard A.
1978   "Sociology and General Systems Theory." *The American Sociologist* 13:65–72.

Baran, Paul, and Sweezy, Paul M.
1966   *Monopoly Capital: An Essay on the American Economic and Social Order.* New York: Monthly Review Press.

Bauman, Zygmunt
1976   *Towards a Critical Sociology: An Essay on Commonsense and Emancipation.* London: Routledge and Kegan Paul.

Bellah, Robert
1980   "The World Is the World Through Its Theorists—In Memory of Talcott Parsons." *American Sociologist* 15:60–62.

Beniger, James R., and Savory, Laina
1981   "Social Exchange: Diffusion of a Paradigm." *The American Sociologist* 16:240–250.

Berger, Peter, and Luckmann, Thomas
1967   *The Social Construction of Reality.* Garden City, N.Y.: Anchor.

Bierstedt, Robert
1963   "The Common Sense World of Alfred Schutz." *Social Research* 30:116–121.

Birnbauer, J. S. et al.
1965   "Classroom Behavior of Retarded Pupils with Token Reinforcement." *Journal of Experimental Child Psychology* 2:219–235.

Bittner, Egon
1973   "Objectivity and Realism in Sociology." In George Psathas (ed.), *Phenomenological Sociology: Issues and Applications.* New York: John Wiley: 109–125.

Blalock, Hubert, and Wilken, Paul
1979   *Intergroup Processes: A Micro-Macro Perspective.* New York: Free Press.

Blau, Peter
1960   "Structural Effects." *American Sociological Review* 25:178–193.
1964   *Exchange and Power in Social Life.* New York: John Wiley.
1975a   Introduction, "Parallels and Contrasts in Structural Inquiries." In Peter Blau (ed.), *Approaches to the Study of Social Structure.* New York: Free Press: 1–20.
1975b   "Parameters of Social Structure." In Peter Blau (ed.), *Approaches to the Study of Social Structure.* New York: Free Press: 220–253.
1977a   *Inequality and Heterogeneity: A Primitive Theory of Social Structure.* New York: Free Press.
1977b   "A Macrosociological Theory of Social Structure." *American Sociological Review* 83:26–54.
1980   "A Fable About Social Structure." *Social Forces* 58:777–788.

Blau, Peter, and Merton, Robert K. (eds.)
1981   *Continuities in Structural Inquiry.* Beverly Hills, Calif.: Sage Publications.

Bleich, Harold
1977   *The Philosophy of Herbert Marcuse.* Washington, D.C.: University Press of America.

Blum, Alan, and McHugh, Peter
1971   "The Social Ascription of Motives." *American Sociological Review*
              36:98–109.
Blumenstiel, Alexander D.
1973   "The Sociology of Good Times." In George Psathas (ed.), *Phenomenological
              Sociology: Issues and Applications*. New York: John Wiley: 187–215.
Blumer, Herbert
1954/1969   "What Is Wrong with Social Theory?" in Herbert Blumer, *Symbolic Inter-
              action:* 140–152.
1955/1969   "Attitudes and the Social Act." In Herbert Blumer, *Symbolic Interaction:*
              90–100.
1956/1969   "Sociological Analysis and the 'Variable.'" In Herbert Blumer, *Symbolic
              Interaction:* 127–139.
1962/1969   "Society as Symbolic Interaction." in Herbert Blumer, *Symbolic Interaction:*
              78–89.
1969a   *Symbolic Interaction: Perspective and Method*. Englewood Cliffs, N.J.:
              Prentice-Hall.
1969b   "The Methodological Position of Symbolic Interactionism." In Herbert
              Blumer, *Symbolic Interaction:* 1–60.
1974   "Comments on 'Parsons as a Symbolic Interactionist.'" *Sociological Inquiry*
              45:59–62.
1980   Comment: "Mead and Blumer: The Convergent Methodological Perspectives
              of Social Behaviorism and Symbolic Interactionism." *American Sociological
              Review* 45:409–419.
Bosserman, Phillip
1968   *Dialectical Sociology: An Analysis of the Sociology of Georges Gurvitch*.
              Boston: Porter Sargent.
Bottomore, Tom
1975   "Structure and History." In Peter Blau (ed.), *Approaches to the Study of
              Social Structure*. New York: Free Press: 159–171.
Bourricaud, François
1981   *The Sociology of Talcott Parsons*. Chicago: University of Chicago Press.
Braverman, Harry
1974   *Labor and Monopoly Capital: The Degradation of Work in the Twentieth Cen-
              tury*. New York: Monthly Review Press.
Brawley, Eleanor et al.
1969   "Behavior Modification of an Autistic Child." *Behavioral Science* 14:87–96.
Bredemeier, Harry C.
1978   "Exchange Theory." In Tom Bottomore and Robert Nisbet (eds.), *A History
              of Sociological Analysis*. New York: Basic Books: 418–456.
Buckley, Walter
1967   *Sociology and Modern Systems Theory*. Englewood Cliffs, N.J.: Prentice-Hall.
Burger, Thomas
1976   *Max Weber's Theory of Concept Formation: History, Laws and Ideal Types*.
              Durham, N.C.: Duke University Press.
1977   "Talcott Parsons, the Problem of Order in Society, and the Program of an
              Analytical Sociology." *American Journal of Sociology* 83:320–334.
Burgess, Robert, and Bushell, Don
1969a   "A Behavioral View of Some Sociological Concepts." In Robert Burgess and
              Don Bushell (eds.), *Behavioral Sociology*. New York: Columbia University
              Press: 273–290.

Burgess, Robert, and Bushell, Don (eds.)
1969b   *Behavioral Sociology.* New York: Columbia University Press.
Burris, Val
1979   Introduction, "The Structuralist Influence in Marxist Theory and Research."
               The Insurgent Sociologist 9:4–17.
Bushell, Don, and Burgess, Robert
1969   "Some Basic Principles of Behavior." In Robert Burgess and Don Bushell
               (eds.), *Behavioral Sociology.* New York: Columbia University Press: 27–48.
Bushell, Don, Wrobel, Ann, and Michaelis, Mary Louise
1969   "Applying 'Group' Contingencies to the Classroom Study of Behavior of Pre-
               school Children." In Robert Burgess and Don Bushell (eds.), *Behavioral
               Sociology.* New York: Columbia University Press: 219–230.
Campbell, Colin
1982   "A Dubious Distinction? An Inquiry into the Value and Use of Merton's Con-
               cepts of Manifest and Latent Function." *American Sociological Review*
               47:29–44.
Caplan, Arthur L. (ed.)
1978   *The Sociobiology Debate.* New York: Harper & Row.
Chadwick-Jones, J. K.
1976   *Social Exchange Theory: Its Structure and Influence in Social Psychology.*
               London: Academic Press.
Charon, Joel
1979   *Symbolic Interaction: An Introduction, an Interpretation, an Integration.*
               Englewood Cliffs, N.J.: Prentice-Hall.
Chua, Beng-Huat
1977   "Delineating a Marxist Interest in Ethnomethodology." *American Sociologist*
               12:24–32.
Cicourel, Aaron
1974   *Cognitive Sociology: Language and Meaning in Social Interaction.* New York:
               Free Press.
Cohen, Jere, Hazelrigg, Lawrence, and Pope, Whitney
1975   "DeParsonizing Weber: A Critique of Parsons' Interpretation of Weber's
               Sociology." *American Sociological Review* 40:229–241.
Cohen, Percy
1968   *Modern Social Theory.* New York: Basic Books.
Coleman, James
1968   Review of Harold Garfinkel, *Studies in Ethnomethodology. American
               Sociological Review* 33:126–130.
1971   "Community Disorganization and Conflict." In Robert Merton and Robert
               Nisbet (eds.), *Contemporary Social Problems,* 3rd ed. New York: Harcourt
               Brace Jovanovich: 657–708.
Colfax, J. David, and Roach, Jack L.
1971   *Radical Sociology.* New York: Basic Books.
Collins, Randall
1975   *Conflict Sociology: Toward an Explanatory Science.* New York: Academic
               Press.
1981   "On the Microfoundations of Macrosociology." *American Journal of Sociol-
               ogy* 86:984–1014.
Connerton, Paul (ed.)
1976   *Critical Sociology.* Harmondsworth, Eng.: Penguin.

Cooley, Charles H.
1902/1964   *Human Nature and the Social Order.* New York: Scribner's.
Coser, Lewis
1956   *The Functions of Social Conflict.* New York: Free Press.
1975a   Presidential Address: "Two Methods in Search of a Substance." *American Sociological Review* 40:691–700.
1975b   "Structure and Conflict." In Peter Blau (ed.), *Approaches to the Study of Social Structure.* New York: Free Press: 210–219.
Craib, Ian
1976   *Existentialism and Sociology: A Study of Jean-Paul Sartre.* Cambridge: Cambridge University Press.
Culler, Jonathan
1976   *Ferdinand de Saussure.* Harmondsworth, Eng.: Penguin.
Dahrendorf, Ralf
1958   "Out of Utopia: Toward a Reorientation of Sociological Analysis." *American Journal of Sociology* 64:115–127.
1959   *Class and Class Conflict in Industrial Society.* Stanford, Calif.: Stanford University Press.
1968   *Essays in the Theory of Society.* Stanford, Calif.: Stanford University Press.
Davis, Kingsley
1959   "The Myth of Functional Analysis as a Special Method in Sociology and Anthropology." *American Sociological Review* 24:757–772.
Davis, Kingsley, and Moore, Wilbert
1945   "Some Principles of Stratification." *American Sociological Review* 10:242–249.
Demerath, Nicholas, and Peterson, Richard (eds.)
1967   *System, Change and Conflict.* New York: Free Press.
Devereaux, Edward C.
1961   "Parsons's Sociological Theory." In Max Black (ed.), *The Social Theories of Talcott Parsons.* Englewood Cliffs, N.J.: Prentice-Hall: 1–63.
DiTomaso, Nancy
1982   "'Sociological Reductionism' From Parsons to Althusser: Linking Action and Structure in Social Theory." *American Sociological Review* 47:14–28.
Dobb, Maurice
1964   *Studies in the Development of Capitalism.* Rev. ed. New York: International Publishers.
Douglas, Jack
1977   "Existential Sociology." In Jack D. Douglas et al. (eds.), *Existential Sociology.* Cambridge: Cambridge University Press: 3–73.
1980   "Introduction to the Sociologies of Everyday Life." In Jack Douglas et al. (eds.), *Introduction to the Sociologies of Everyday Life.* Boston: Allyn and Bacon: 1–19.
Douglas, Jack (ed.)
1970   *Understanding Everyday Life.* Chicago: Aldine.
Douglas, Jack, and Johnson, John
1977   "Introduction." In Jack Douglas et al. (eds.), *Existential Sociology.* Cambridge: Cambridge University Press: vii–xv.
Douglas, Jack et al. (eds.)
1980   *Introduction to the Sociologies of Everyday Life.* Boston: Allyn and Bacon.
Durkheim, Emile
1893/1964   *The Division of Labor in Society.* New York: Free Press

1895/1964   *The Rules of Sociological Method.* New York: Free Press.
1897/1951   *Suicide.* New York: Free Press.
1912/1965   *The Elementary Forms of Religious Life.* New York: Free Press.
Eckberg, Douglas Lee, and Hill, Lester
1979   "The Paradigm Concept and Sociology: A Critical Review." *American Socio-logical Review* 44:925–937.
Edel, Abraham
1959   "The Concept of Levels in Social Theory." In Llewellyn Gross (ed.), *Symposium on Sociological Theory.* Evanston, Ill.: Row Peterson: 167–175.
Effrat, Andrew
1972   "Power to the Paradigms: An Editorial Introduction." *Sociological Inquiry* 42:3–33.
Ehrmann, Jacques
1970   "Introduction." In Jacques Ehrmann (ed.), *Structuralism.* Garden City, N.Y.: Anchor: vii–xi.
Eisen, Arnold
1978   "The Meanings and Confusions of Weberian 'Rationality.'" *British Journal of Sociology* 29:57–70.
Eisenstadt, S. N., with M. Curelaru
1976   *The Form of Sociology: Paradigms and Crises.* New York: John Wiley.
Ekeh, Peter P.
1974   *Social Exchange Theory: The Two Traditions.* Cambridge, Mass.: Harvard University Press.
Ellis, Lee
1977   "The Decline and Fall of Sociology, 1975–2000." *American Sociologist* 12:56–66.
Emerson, Richard M.
1972a   "Exchange Theory, Part I: A Psychological Basis for Social Exchange." In Joseph Berger, Morris Zelditch, Jr., and Bo Anderson (eds.), *Sociological Theories in Progress,* vol. 2. Boston: Houghton-Mifflin: 38–57.
1972b   "Exchange Theory, Part II: Exchange Relations and Networks." In Joseph Berger et al. (eds.), *Sociological Theories in Progress,* vol. 2. Boston: Houghton-Mifflin: 58–87.
1976   "Social Exchange Theory." In Alex Inkeles, James Coleman, and Neil Smelser (eds.), *Annual Review of Sociology,* vol. 2. Palo Alto, Calif.: Annual Reviews, Inc.: 335–362.
1981   "Social Exchange Theory." In Morris Rosenberg and Ralph H. Turner (eds.), *Social Psychology: Sociological Perspectives.* New York: Basic Books: 30–65.
Engels, Friedrich
1890/1972   "Letter to Joseph Bloch." In Robert C. Tucker (ed.), *The Marx-Engels Reader.* New York: Norton: 640–642.
Farganis, James
1975   "A Preface to Critical Theory." *Theory and Society* 2:483–508.
Faris, R. E. L.
1970   *Chicago Sociology: 1920–1932.* Chicago: University of Chicago Press.
Faught, Jim
1980   "Presuppositions of the Chicago School in the Work of Everett Hughes." *The American Sociologist* 15:72–82.
Fontana, Andrea
1980   "Toward a Complex Universe: Existential Sociology." In Jack D. Douglas, et

al. (eds.), *Introduction to the Sociologies of Everyday Life.* Boston: Allyn and
Bacon: 155–181.

Frank, André Gunder
1966/1974   "Functionalism and Dialectics." In R. Serge Denisoff, Orel Callahan, and
Mark H. Levine (eds.), *Theories and Paradigms in Contemporary Sociology.*
Itasca, Ill.: Peacock: 342–352.

Frankfurt Institute for Social Research
1973   *Aspects of Sociology.* London: Heinemann.

Freeman, C. Robert
1980   "Phenomenological Sociology and Ethnomethodology." In Jack D. Douglas et
al. (eds.), *Introduction to the Sociologies of Everyday Life.* Boston: Allyn and
Bacon: 113–154.

Friedheim, Elizabeth
1979   "An Empirical Comparison of Ritzer's Paradigms and Similar Metatheories: A
Research Note." *Social Forces* 58:59–66.

Friedrichs, Robert
1970   *A Sociology of Sociology.* New York: Free Press.
1972a   "Dialectical Sociology: Toward a Resolution of Current 'Crises' in Western
Sociology." *British Journal of Sociology* 13:263–274.
1972b   "Dialectical Sociology: An Exemplar for the 1970's." *Social Forces*
50:447–455.

Furfey, Paul
1953   *The Scope and Method of Sociology: A Metasociological Treatise.* New York:
Harper.

Gans, Herbert
1972   "The Positive Functions of Poverty." *American Journal of Sociology*
78:275–289.

Garfinkel, Harold
1963   "A Conception of and Experiment with 'Trust' as a Condition of Concerted
Stable Actions." In O. J. Harvey (ed.), *Motivations and Social Interaction.*
New York: Ronald Press.
1967   *Studies in Ethnomethodology.* Englewood Cliffs, N.J.: Prentice-Hall.
1974   "The Origins of the Term 'Ethnomethodology.'" In Roy Turner (ed.), *Ethnomethodology.* Harmondsworth, Eng.: Penguin: 15–18.

Gerth, Hans, and Mills, C. Wright
1953   *Character and Social Structure.* New York: Harcourt, Brace and World.

Glenn, Norval, and Weiner, David
1969   "Some Trends in the Social Origins of American Sociologists." *American
Sociologist* 4:291–302.

Glucksmann, Miriam
1974   *Structural Analysis in Contemporary Social Thought: A Comparison of the
Theories of Claude Lévi-Strauss and Louis Althusser.* London: Routledge and
Kegan Paul.

Goddard, David
1976   "On Structuralism and Sociology." *American Sociologist* 11:123–133.

Godelier, Maurice
1972a   *Rationality and Irrationality in Economics.* London: NLB.
1972b   "Structure and Contradiction in *Capital*." In Robin Blackburn (ed.), *Readings
in Critical Social Theory.* London: Fontana: 334–368.

Goffman, Erving

1959   *Presentation of Self in Everyday Life.* Garden City, N.Y.: Anchor.

1961   *Encounters: Two Studies in the Sociology of Interaction.* Indianapolis: Bobbs-Merrill.

1963a   *Behavior in Public Places: Notes on the Social Organization of Gatherings.* Glencoe, Ill.: Free Press.

1963b   *Stigma: Notes on the Management of Spoiled Identity.* Englewood Cliffs., N.J.: Prentice-Hall.

1967   *Interaction Ritual: Essays on Face-to-Face Behavior.* Garden City, N.Y.: Anchor.

1971   *Relations in Public: Microstudies of the Public Order.* New York: Basic Books.

1972   *Strategic Interaction.* New York: Ballantine.

1974   *Frame Analysis: An Essay on the Organization of Experience.* New York: Harper Colophon.

1976   *Gender Advertisements.* New York: Harper Colophon.

Gonos, George

1977   "'Situation' Versus 'Frame': The 'Interactionist' and the 'Structuralist' Analyses of Everyday Life." *American Sociological Review* 42:854–867.

Goode, William J.

1960   "A Theory of Role Strain." *American Sociological Review* 25:483–496.

1975   "Homans' and Merton's Structural Approach." In Peter Blau (ed.), *Approaches to the Study of Social Structure.* New York: Free Press: 66–75.

1978   *The Celebration of Heroes: Prestige as a Social Control System.* Berkeley: University of California Press.

Goodwin, Charles

1979   "The Interactive Construction of a Sentence in Natural Conversation." In George Psathas (ed.), *Everyday Language: Studies in Ethnomethodology.* New York: Irvington: 97–121.

Gorman, Robert A.

1975a   "Alfred Schutz: An Exposition and Critique." *British Journal of Sociology* 26:1–19.

1975b   "The Phenomenological 'Humanization' of Social Science: A Critique." *British Journal of Sociology* 26:389–405.

1977   *The Dual Vision: Alfred Schutz and the Myth of Phenomenological Social Science.* London: Routledge and Kegan Paul.

Goudsblom, Johan

1977   *Sociology in the Balance: A Critical Essay.* New York: Columbia University Press.

Gouldner, Alvin

1959/1967   "Reciprocity and Autonomy in Functional Theory." In Nicholas Demerath and Richard Peterson (eds.), *System, Change and Conflict.* New York: Free Press: 141–169.

1960   "The Norm of Reciprocity." *American Sociological Review* 25:161–178.

1970   *The Coming Crisis of Western Sociology.* New York: Basic Books.

Gramsci, Antonio

1971   *Selections from the Prison Notebooks.* New York: International Publishers.

Grathoff, Richard (ed.)

1978   *The Theory of Social Action: The Correspondence of Alfred Schutz and Talcott Parsons.* Bloomington: Indiana University Press.

Greene, Penelope J., Morgan, Charles J., and Barash, David P.
1979   "Sociobiology." In Scott McNall (ed.), *Theoretical Perspectives in Sociology*.
              New York: St. Martin's Press: 414–430.
Greisman, Harvey C., and Ritzer, George
1981   "Max Weber, Critical Theory and the Administered World." *Qualitative
              Sociology* 4:34–55.
Gurney, Patrick J.
1981   "Historical Origins of Ideological Denial: The Case of Marx in American
              Sociology." *The American Sociologist* 16:196–201.
Gurvitch, Georges
1964   *The Spectrum of Social Time*. Dordrecht, Neth.: D. Reidel.
Habermas, Jurgen
1968   *Knowledge and Human Interests*. Boston: Beacon Press.
1970   *Toward a Rational Society*. Boston: Beacon Press.
1975   *Legitimation Crisis*. Boston: Beacon Press.
Hamblin, Robert L., and Kunkel, John H.
1977   *Behavioral Theory in Sociology*. New Brunswick, N.J.: Transaction.
Handel, Warren
1982   *Ethnomethodology: How People Make Sense*. Englewood Cliffs, N.J.:
              Prentice-Hall.
Harper, Diane Blake, Sylvester, Joan, and Walczak, David
1980   "An Empirical Comparison of Ritzer's Paradigms and Similar Metatheories:
              Comment on Friedheim." *Social Forces* 59:513–517.
Hawkes, Terence
1977   *Structuralism and Semiotics*. London: Metheun.
Hawthorn, Geoffrey
1976   *Enlightenment and Despair*. Cambridge: Cambridge University Press.
Hayim, Gila
1980   *The Existential Sociology of Jean-Paul Sartre*. Amherst: University of
              Massachusetts Press.
Hazelrigg, Lawrence
1972   "Class, Property and Authority: Dahrendorf's Critique of Marx's Theory of
              Class." *Social Forces* 50:473–487.
Heap, James L., and Roth, Phillip A.
1973   "On Phenomenological Sociology." *American Sociological Review*
              38:354–367.
Held, David
1980   *Introduction to Critical Theory: Horkheimer to Habermas*. Berkeley: Univer-
              sity of California Press.
Heritage, J. C., and Watson, D. R.
1979   "Formulations as Conversational Objects." In George Psathas (ed.), *Everyday
              Language: Studies in Ethnomethodology*. New York: Irvington: 187–201.
Heyl, John D., and Heyl, Barbara S.
1976   "The Sumner-Porter Controversy at Yale: Pre-Paradigmatic Sociology and In-
              stitutional Crisis." *Sociological Inquiry* 46:41–49.
Himes, Joseph
1966   "The Functions of Racial Conflict." *Social Forces* 45:1–10.
Hinkle, Roscoe
1963   "Antecedents of the Action Orientation in American Sociology Before 1935."

American Sociological Review 28:705–715.

1980   *Founding Theory of American Sociology: 1881–1915.* London: Routledge and Kegan Paul.

Hinkle, Roscoe, and Hinkle, Gisela

1954   *The Development of American Sociology.* New York: Random House.

Hobsbawm, Eric J.

1965   *Primitive Rebels.* New York: Norton.

Hofstadter, Richard

1959   *Social Darwinism in American Thought.* New York: Braziller.

Hollinger, David

1980   "T. S. Kuhn's Theory of Science and Its Implications for History." In Gary Gutting (ed.), *Paradigms and Revolutions.* Notre Dame, Ind.: Notre Dame University Press: 195–222.

Homans, George C.

1958   "Social Behavior as Exchange." *American Journal of Sociology* 63:597–606.

1961   *Social Behavior: Its Elementary Forms.* New York: Harcourt, Brace and World.

1962   *Sentiments and Activities.* New York: Free Press.

1967   *The Nature of Social Science.* New York: Harcourt, Brace and World.

1969   "The Sociological Relevance of Behaviorism." In Robert Burgess and Don Bushell (eds.), *Behavioral Sociology.* New York: Columbia University Press: 1–24.

1971   "Commentary." In Herman Turk and Richard Simpson (eds.), *Institutions and Social Exchange.* Indianapolis: Bobbs-Merrill: 363–374.

1974   *Social Behavior: Its Elementary Forms.* Rev. ed. New York: Harcourt Brace Jovanovich.

Homans, George C., and Schneider, David M.

1955   *Marriage, Authority and Final Causes: A Study of Unilateral Cross-Cousin Marriage.* New York: Free Press.

Hook, Sidney

1965   "Pareto's Sociological System." In James H. Meisel (ed.), *Pareto and Mosca.* Englewood Cliffs, N.J.: Prentice-Hall: 57–61.

Horowitz, Irving L.

1962/1967   "Consensus, Conflict, and Cooperation." In Nicholas Demerath and Richard Peterson (eds.), *System, Change and Conflict.* New York: Free Press: 265–279.

Huaco, George

1966   "The Functionalist Theory of Stratification: Two Decades of Controversy." *Inquiry* 9:215–240.

Husserl, Edmund

1931   *Ideas.* London: George Allen and Unwin.

Jackman, Mary R., and Jackman, Robert W.

1973   "An Interpretation of the Relation Between Objective and Subjective Social Status." *American Sociological Review* 38:569–582.

Jay, Martin

1973   *The Dialectical Imagination.* Boston: Little, Brown.

Jefferson, Gail

1979   "A Technique for Inviting Laughter and Its Subsequent Acceptance Declination." In George Psathas (ed.), *Everyday Language: Studies in Ethnomethodology.* New York: Irvington: 79–96.

Johnson, Doyle Paul
1981   *Sociological Theory: Classical Founders and Contemporary Perspectives.* New
               York: John Wiley.
Kalberg, Stephen
1980   "Max Weber's Types of Rationality: Cornerstones for the Analysis of Ration-
               alization Processes in History." *American Journal of Sociology* 85:1145–1179.
Kando, Thomas
1976   "L'année Sociologique: From Durkheim to Today." *Pacific Sociological
               Review* 19:147–174.
Kemper, Theodore
1978a   "Toward a Sociological Theory of Emotions: Some Problems and Some Solu-
               tions." *The American Sociologist* 13:30–41.
1978b   *A Social Interactional Theory of Emotions.* New York: Wiley.
1981   "Social Constructionist and Positivist Approaches to the Sociology of Emo-
               tions." *American Journal of Sociology* 87:336–362.
Knox, John
1963   "The Concept of Exchange in Sociological Theory: 1884 and 1961." *Social
               Forces* 41:341–346.
Kockelmans, Joseph J.
1967a   *Phenomenology: The Philosophy of Edmund Husserl and Its Interpretations.*
               Garden City, N.Y.: Anchor.
1967b   "Some Fundamental Themes of Husserl's Phenomenology." In Joseph J.
               Kockelmans (ed.), *Phenomenology: The Philosophy of Edmund Husserl and Its
               Interpretations.* Garden City, N.Y.: Anchor: 24–36.
Kohn, Melvin L.
1976   "Occupational Structure and Alienation." *American Journal of Sociology*
               82:111–127.
Kolb, William L.
1944   "A Critical Evaluation of Mead's 'I' and 'Me' Concepts." *Social Forces*
               22:291–296.
Korenbaum, Myrtle
1964   Translator's preface to Georges Gurvitch, *The Spectrum of Social Time.*
               Dordrecht, Neth.: D. Reidel: ix–xxvi.
Kotarba, Joseph A.
1977   "The Chronic Pain Patient." In Jack Douglas et al. (eds.), *Existential Sociol-
               ogy.* Cambridge: Cambridge University Press: 257–272.
1979   "Existential Sociology." In Scott McNall (ed.), *Theoretical Perspectives in
               Sociology.* New York: St. Martin's Press: 348–368.
Kuhn, Manford
1964   "Major Trends in Symbolic Interaction Theory in the Past Twenty-five
               Years." *The Sociological Quarterly* 5:61–84.
Kuhn, Thomas
1962   *The Structure of Scientific Revolutions.* Chicago: University of Chicago Press.
1970   *The Structure of Scientific Revolutions.* 2nd ed. Chicago: University of
               Chicago Press.
Lachman, L. M.
1971   *The Legacy of Max Weber.* Berkeley, Calif.: Glendessary Press.
Leach, Edmund
1974   *Claude Lévi-Strauss.* New York: Penguin Books.

Lefebvre, Henri
1968   *The Sociology of Marx.* New York: Vintage.
Lemert, Charles
1979   *Sociology and the Twilight of Man: Homocentrism and Discourse in
              Sociological Theory.* Carbondale: Southern Illinois University Press.
Lengermann, Patricia Madoo
1979   "The Founding of the *American Sociological Review." American Sociological
              Review* 44:185–198.
Lenzer, Gertrud (ed.)
1975   *Auguste Comte and Positivism: The Essential Writings.* Magnolia, Mass.: Peter
              Smith.
Levine, Donald, Carter, Ellwood B., and Gorman, Eleanor Miller
1976a   "Simmel's Influence on American Sociology—I." *American Journal of
              Sociology* 81:813–845.
1976b   "Simmel's Influence on American Sociology—II." *American Journal of
              Sociology* 81:1112–1132.
Lévi-Strauss, Claude
1949   *Les Structures Elementaires de la Parente.* Paris: Presses Universitaires de
              France.
1963   *Totemism.* Boston: Beacon Press.
1967   *Structural Anthropology.* Garden City, N.Y.: Doubleday Anchor.
Lilienfeld, Robert
1978   *The Rise of Systems Theory: An Ideological Analysis.* New York: Wiley-
              Interscience.
Lipset, Seymour M.
1975   "Social Structure and Social Change." In Peter Blau (ed.), *Approaches to the
              Study of Social Structure.* New York: Free Press: 172–209.
Lockwood, David
1956   "Some Remarks on *The Social System." British Journal of Sociology*
              7:134–146.
1958   *The Blackcoated Worker: A Study in Class Consciousness.* London: George
              Allen and Unwin.
Lodahl, Janice B., and Gordon, Gerald
1972   "The Structure of Scientific Fields and the Functioning of University Graduate
              Departments." *American Sociological Review* 37:57–72.
Lukács, George
1922/1968   *History and Class Consciousness.* Cambridge, Mass.: MIT Press.
Lyman, Stanford, and Scott, Marvin
1970   *A Sociology of the Absurd.* New York: Appleton-Century-Crofts.
MacCrae, Donald G.
1974   *Max Weber.* Harmondsworth, Eng.: Penguin.
MacIver, Robert
1931   *Society: Its Structure and Changes.* New York: Ray Long and Richard R.
              Smith.
1942   *Social Causation.* Boston: Ginn.
Mackay, Robert W.
1974   "Words, Utterances and Activities." In Roy Turner (ed.), *Ethnomethodology:
              Selected Readings.* Harmondsworth, Eng.: Penguin: 197–215.
Maines, David R.
1977   "Social Organization and Social Structure in Symbolic Interactionist Thought."

In Alex Inkeles, James Coleman, and Neil Smelser (eds.), *Annual Review of Sociology* 3:259–285.

Manis, Jerome, and Meltzer, Bernard (eds.)
1978   *Symbolic Interaction: A Reader in Social Psychology.* 3rd ed. Boston: Allyn and Bacon.

Manning, Peter
1973   "Existential Sociology." *The Sociological Quarterly* 14:200–225.

Marcuse, Herbert
1964   *One-Dimensional Man.* Boston: Beacon Press.
1969   *An Essay on Liberation.* Boston: Beacon Press.

Marks, Stephen R.
1974   "Durkheim's Theory of Anomie." *American Journal of Sociology* 82:329–363.

Marx, Karl
1847/1963   *The Poverty of Philosophy.* New York: International Publishers.
1857–1858/   *Pre-Capitalist Economic Formations*, Eric J. Hobsbawm (ed.). New York:
1964   International Publishers.
1857–1858/   *The Grundrisse: Foundations of the Critique of Political Economy.* New York:
1974   Random House.
1859/1970   *A Contribution to the Critique of Political Economy.* New York: International Publishers.
1867/1967   *Capital: A Critique of Political Economy*, vol. 1. New York: International Publishers.
1932/1964   *The Economic and Philosophic Manuscripts of 1844*, Dirk J. Struik (ed.). New York: International Publishers.

Marx, Karl, and Engels, Friedrich
1845/1956   *The Holy Family.* Moscow: Foreign Language Publishing House.

Masterman, Margaret
1970   "The Nature of a Paradigm." In Imre Lakatos and Alan Musgrove (eds.), *Criticism and the Growth of Knowledge.* Cambridge: Cambridge University Press: 59–89.

Matthews, Fred H.
1977   *Quest for an American Sociology: Robert E. Park and the Chicago School.* Montreal: McGill University Press.

Mayhew, Bruce
1980   "Structuralism Versus Individualism: Part 1, Shadowboxing in the Dark." *Social Forces* 59:335–375.
1981   "Structuralism Versus Individualism: Part II, Ideological and Other Obfuscations." *Social Forces* 59:627–648.

McLellan, David (ed.)
1971   *The Thought of Karl Marx.* New York: Harper Torchbooks.

McNall, Scott
1979a   Introduction to Part VII, "Biology and Human Behavior." In Scott McNall (ed.), *Theoretical Perspectives in Sociology.* New York: St. Martin's Press: 397–398.

McPhail, Clark
1981   "The Problems and Prospects of Behavioral Perspectives." *The American Sociologist* 16:172–174.

McPhail, Clark, and Rexroat, Cynthia
1979   "Mead vs. Blumer." *American Sociological Review* 44:449–467.

1980   Rejoinder: "*Ex Cathedra* Blumer or *Ex Libris* Mead?" *American Sociological Review* 45:420–430.

Mead, George Herbert
1934/1962   *Mind, Self and Society: From the Standpoint of a Social Behaviorist.* Chicago: University of Chicago Press.

Meeker, B. F.
1971   "Decisions and Exchange." *American Sociological Review* 36:485–495.

Mehan, Hugh, and Wood, Houston
1975   *The Reality of Ethnomethodology.* New York: Wiley.

Meltzer, Bernard
1964/1978   "Mead's Social Psychology." In Jerome Manis and Bernard Meltzer (eds.), *Symbolic Interaction: A Reader in Social Psychology.* 3rd ed. Boston: Allyn and Bacon: 15–27.

Meltzer, Bernard, Petras, James, and Reynolds, Larry
1975   *Symbolic Interactionism: Genesis, Varieties and Criticisms.* London: Routledge and Kegan Paul.

Merton, Robert K.
1949/1968   "Manifest and Latent Functions." In *Social Theory and Social Structure*: 73–138.
1968   *Social Theory and Social Structure.* New York: Free Press.
1975   "Structural Analysis in Sociology." In Peter Blau (ed.), *Approaches to the Study of Social Structure.* New York: Free Press: 21–52.
1980   "Remembering the Young Talcott Parsons." *American Sociologist* 15:68–71.

Mészáros, István
1970   *Marx's Theory of Alienation.* New York: Harper Torchbooks.

Michaels, James W., and Green, Dan S.
1978   "Behavioral Sociology: Emergent Forms and Issues." *The American Sociologist* 13:23–29.

Miel, Jan
1970   "Jacques Lacan and the Structure of the Unconscious." In Jacques Ehrmann (ed.), *Structuralism.* Garden City, N.Y.: Anchor: 94–101.

Miliband, Ralph
1972   "Reply to Nicos Poulantzas." In Robin Blackburn (ed.), *Ideology in Social Science: Readings in Critical Social Theory.* London: Fontana: 253–262.
1974   *The State in Capitalist Society.* London: Quartet.

Miller, L. Keith
1970   "A Token Economy for the University Classroom." Paper read at meetings of the American Psychological Association, Miami, Fla.

Mills, C. Wright
1951   *White Collar.* New York: Oxford University Press.
1956   *The Power Elite.* New York: Oxford University Press.
1959   *The Sociological Imagination.* New York: Oxford University Press.

Mitchell, Jack N.
1978   *Social Exchange, Dramaturgy and Ethnomethodology: Toward a Paradigmatic Synthesis.* New York: Elsevier.

Mitroff, Ian, and Kilmann, Ralph
1978   *Methodological Approaches to Social Science.* San Francisco: Jossey-Bass.

Molm, Linda
1981   "The Legitimacy of Behavioral Theory as a Sociological Perspective." *The American Sociologist* 16:153–166.

Molm, Linda D., and Wiggins, James A.
1979   "A Behavioral Analysis of the Dynamics of Social Exchange in the Dyad."
            Social Forces 57:1157–1179.

Moore, Wilbert E.
1978   "Functionalism." In Tom Bottomore and Robert Nisbet (eds.), *A History of
            Sociological Analysis*. New York: Basic Books: 321–361.

Morris, Charles W.
1934/1962   Introduction. In George Herbert Mead, *Mind, Self and Society*. Chicago:
            University of Chicago Press: ix–xxxv.

Morris, Monica B.
1977   *Excursion into Creative Sociology*. New York: Columbia University Press.

Morse, Chandler
1961   "The Functional Imperatives." In Max Black (ed.), *The Social Theories of
            Talcott Parsons*. Englewood Cliffs, N.J.: Prentice-Hall: 100–152.

Mullins, Nicholas
1973   *Theories and Theory Groups in Contemporary American Sociology*. New York:
            Harper & Row.

Münch, Richard
1981   "Talcott Parsons and the Theory of Action. I. The Structure of the Kantian
            Core." *American Journal of Sociology* 86:709–739.
1982   "Talcott Parsons and the Theory of Action. II. The Continuity of the Develop-
            ment." *American Journal of Sociology* 87:771–826.

Nicolaus, Martin
1974   Foreword. In Karl Marx, *The Grundrisse*. New York: Random House: 7–63.

Nisbet, Robert
1967   *The Sociological Tradition*. New York: Basic Books.

Oksanen, Ernest H., and Spencer, Bryon G.
1975   "On the Determinants of Student Performance in Introductory Courses in the
            Social Sciences." *American Sociologist* 10:103–109.

Ollman, Bertell
1976   *Alienation*. 2nd ed. Cambridge: Cambridge University Press.

Parsons, Talcott
1934–1935   "The Place of Ultimate Values in Sociological Theory." *International Journal
            of Ethics* 45:282–316.
1937   *The Structure of Social Action*. New York: McGraw-Hill.
1949   *The Structure of Social Action*. 2nd ed. New York: McGraw-Hill.
1951   *The Social System*. Glencoe, Ill.: Free Press.
1960   "A Sociological Approach to the Theory of Organizations." In Talcott Parsons
            (ed.), *Structure and Process in Modern Societies*. New York: Free Press:
            16–58.
1964   "Levels of Organization and the Mediation of Social Interaction." *Sociological
            Inquiry* 34:207–220.
1966   *Societies*. Englewood Cliffs, N.J.: Prentice-Hall.
1970   *Social Structure and Personality*. New York: Free Press.
1971   *The System of Modern Societies*. Englewood Cliffs, N.J.: Prentice-Hall.
1974   "Comment on Turner, 'Parsons as a Symbolic Interactionist.'" *Sociological
            Inquiry* 45:62–65.
1977a   General Introduction. In Talcott Parsons (ed.), *Social Systems and the Evolu-
            tion of Action Theory*. New York: Free Press: 1–13.
1977b   "On Building Social System Theory: A Personal History." In Talcott Parsons

(ed.), *Social Systems and the Evolution of Action Theory.* New York: Free Press: 22–76.

Parsons, Talcott, and Shils, Edward A. (eds.)
1951   *Toward a General Theory of Action.* Cambridge, Mass.: Harvard University Press.

Peel, J. J.
1971   *Herbert Spencer: The Evolution of a Sociologist.* New York: Basic Books.

Perinbanayagam, Robert
1981   "Behavioral Theory: The Relevance, Validity, and Appositeness Thereof to Sociology." *The American Sociologist* 16:166–169.

Perrin, Robert
1976   "Herbert Spencer's Four Theories of Social Evolution." *American Journal of Sociology* 81:1339–1359.

Petit, Philip
1975   *The Concept of Structuralism: A Critical Analysis.* Berkeley: University of California Press.

Phillips, Derek
1973   "Paradigms, Falsifications and Sociology." *Acta Sociologica* 16:13–31.
1975   "Paradigms and Incommensurability." *Theory and Society* 2:37–62.

Pollner, Melvin
1979   "Explicative Transactions: Making and Managing Meaning in Traffic Court." In George Psathas (ed.), *Everyday Language: Studies in Ethnomethodology.* New York: Irvington: 227–255.

Pope, Whitney
1973   "Classic on Classic: Parsons' Interpretation of Durkheim." *American Sociological Review* 38:399–415.

Pope, Whitney, and Cohen, Jere
1978   "On R. Stephen Warner's 'Toward a Redefinition of Action Theory: Paying the Cognitive Element Its Due.'" *American Journal of Sociology* 83:1359–1367.

Poulantzas, Nicos
1972   "The Problem of the Capitalist State." In Robin Blackburn (ed.), *Ideology in Social Science.* London: Fontana: 238–253.
1973   *Political Power and Social Classes.* London: Verso.
1974   *Fascism and Dictatorship: The Third International and the Problem of Fascism.* London: NLB.
1975   *Classes and Contemporary Capitalism.* London: NLB.
1976   *The Crisis of the Dictatorships.* London: NLB.

Procter, Ian
1978   "Parsons's Early Voluntarism." *Sociological Inquiry* 48:37–48.

Psathas, George
1973a   "Introduction." In George Psathas (ed.), *Phenomenological Sociology: Issues and Applications.* New York: John Wiley: 1–21.
1979a   "Organizational Features of Direction Maps." In George Psathas (ed.), *Everyday Language: Studies in Ethnomethodology.* New York: Irvington: 203–225.

Psathas, George (ed.)
1973b   *Phenomenological Sociology: Issues and Applications.* New York: John Wiley.
1979b   *Everyday Language: Studies in Ethnomethodology.* New York: Irvington.

Psathas, George, and Waksler, Frances C.
1973   "Essential Features of Face-to-Face Interaction." In George Psathas (ed.),

Phenomenological Sociology: Issues and Applications. New York: John Wiley: 159–183.

Quadagno, Jill S.
1979   "Paradigms in Evolutionary Theory: The Sociobiological Model of Natural Selection." *American Sociological Review* 44:100–109.

Rhoades, Lawrence J.
1981   *A History of the American Sociological Association.* Washington, D.C.: American Sociological Association.

Riley, John, Jr.
1980   "Talcott Parsons: An Anecdotal Profile." *American Sociologist* 15:66–68.

Ritzer, George
1975a   *Sociology: A Multiple Paradigm Science.* Boston: Allyn and Bacon.
1975b   "Sociology: A Multiple Paradigm Science." *American Sociologist* 10:156–167.
1979   "Toward an Integrated Sociological Paradigm." In William Snizek et al. (eds.), *Contemporary Issues in Theory and Research.* Westport, Conn.: Greenwood Press: 25–46.
1980   *Sociology: A Multiple Paradigm Science.* Rev. ed. Boston: Allyn and Bacon.
1981a   *Toward an Integrated Sociological Paradigm: The Search for an Exemplar and an Image of the Subject Matter.* Boston: Allyn and Bacon.
1981b   "Paradigm Analysis in Sociology: Clarifying the Issues." *American Sociological Review* 46:245–248.
1983   *Sociological Theory.* New York: Knopf.

Rose, Arnold
1962   "A Systematic Summary of Symbolic Interaction Theory." In Arnold Rose (ed.), *Human Behavior and Social Processes.* Boston: Houghton Mifflin.

Rosenberg, Morris
1979   *Conceiving the Self.* New York: Basic Books.

Rossi, Ino
1974a   "Intellectual Antecedents of Levi-Strauss' Notion of Unconscious." In Ino Rossi (ed.), *The Unconscious in Culture: The Structuralism of Claude Lévi-Strauss in Perspective.* New York: Dutton: 7–30.
1974b   "Structuralism as a Scientific Method." In Ino Rossi (ed.), *The Unconscious in Culture.* New York: Dutton: 60–106.

Ruse, Michael
1979   *Sociobiology: Sense or Nonsense?* Dordrecht, Neth.: D. Reidel.

Ryan, William
1971   *Blaming the Victim.* New York: Pantheon.

Ryave, A. Lincoln, and Schenkein, James N.
1974   "Notes on the Art of Walking." In Roy Turner (ed.), *Ethnomethodology: Selected Readings.* Harmondsworth, Eng.: Penguin: 265–275.

Salomon, A.
1945   "German Sociology." In Georges Gurvitch and Wilbert F. Moore (eds.), *Twentieth Century Sociology.* New York: Philosophical Library: 586–614.

Scheffler, Harold
1970   "Structuralism in Anthropology." In Jacques Ehrmann (ed.), *Structuralism.* Garden City, N.Y.: Anchor: 56–79.

Schegloff, Emanuel A.
1979   "Identification and Recognition in Telephone Conversation Openings." In George Psathas (ed.), *Everyday Language: Studies in Ethnomethodology.* New York: Irvington: 23–78.

Schenkein, Jim
1979   "The Radio Raiders Story." In George Psathas (ed.), *Everyday Language:
              Studies in Ethnomethodology.* New York: Irvington: 187–201.
Schroyer, Trent
1970   "Toward a Critical Theory of Advanced Industrial Society." In Hans Peter
              Dreitzel (ed.), *Recent Sociology: No. 2.* New York: Macmillan: 210–234.
1973   *The Critique of Domination.* Boston: Beacon Press.
Schutz, Alfred
1932/1967   *The Phenomenology of the Social World.* Evanston, Ill.: Northwestern Univer-
              sity Press.
1962   *Collected Papers I: The Problem of Social Reality.* The Hague: Martinus
              Nijhoff.
1964   *Collected Papers II: Studies in Social Theory.* The Hague: Martinus Nijhoff.
1966   *Collected Papers III: Studies in Phenomenological Philosophy.* The Hague:
              Martinus Nijhoff.
Schutz, Alfred, and Luckmann, Thomas
1973   *The Structure of the Life World.* Evanston, Ill.: Northwestern University Press.
Schwanenberg, Enno
1971   "The Two Problems of Order in Parsons' Theory: An Analysis from Within."
              Social Forces 49:569–581.
Schwendinger, Julia, and Schwendinger, Herman
1974   *Sociologists of the Chair.* New York: Basic Books.
Scimecca, Joseph
1976   *The Sociological Theory of C. Wright Mills.* Port Washington, N.Y.: Kennikat
              Press.
Scott, John Finley
1963   "The Changing Foundations of the Parsonian Action Schema." *American
              Sociological Review* 28:716–735.
Searle, John
1972   "Chomsky's Revolution in Linguistics." *The New York Review of Books*
              18:16–24.
Sewart, John J.
1978   "Critical Theory and the Critique of Conservative Method." *American
              Sociologist* 13:15–22.
Simmel, Georg
1907/1978   *The Philosophy of Money*, Tom Bottomore and David Frisby (eds. and trans.).
              London: Routledge and Kegan Paul.
Simon, Herbert
1957   *Administrative Behavior.* New York: Free Press.
Singelmann, Peter
1972   "Exchange as Symbolic Interaction." *American Sociological Review*
              38:414–424.
Skinner, B. F.
1938   *The Behavior of Organisms: An Experimental Analysis:* New York: Appleton-
              Century-Crofts.
1948   *Walden Two.* New York: Macmillan.
1971   *Beyond Freedom and Dignity.* New York: Knopf.
Skocpol, Theda
1979   *States and Social Revolutions.* Cambridge: Cambridge University Press.
Skotnes, Andor
1979   "Structural Determination of the Proletariat and the Petty Bourgeoisie: A

Critique of Nicos Poulantzas." *The Insurgent Sociologist* 9:34–54.

Slater, Phil
1977   *Origin and Significance of the Frankfurt School: A Marxist Perspective.*
              London: Routledge and Kegan Paul.

Smith, Norman Erik
1979   "William Graham Sumner as an Anti-Social Darwinist." *Pacific Sociological
              Review* 22:332–347.

Smith, T. V.
1931   "The Social Philosophy of George Herbert Mead." *American Journal of
              Sociology* 37:368–385.

Snizek, William E.
1976   "An Empirical Assessment of 'Sociology: A Multiple Paradigm Science.'"
              The American Sociologist 11:217–219.
1979   "Towards a Clarification of the Interrelationship Between Theory and
              Research: Its Form and Implications." In William Snizek, Ellsworth Fuhrman,
              and Michael Miller (eds.), *Contemporary Issues in Theory and Research.*
              Westport, Conn.: Greenwood Press: 197–209.

Snizek, William E., Fuhrman, Ellsworth R., and Miller, Michael K. (eds.)
1979   *Contemporary Issues in Theory and Research.* Westport, Conn.: Greenwood
              Press.

Sorokin, Pitirim
1956   *Fads and Foibles in Modern Sociology and Related Sciences.* Chicago:
              Regnery.

Speier, Matthew
1970   "The Everyday World of the Child." In Jack Douglas (ed.), *Understanding
              Everyday Life.* Chicago: Aldine: 188–217.

Spiegelberg, Herbert
1967   "Husserl's Phenomenology and Sartre's Existentialism." In Joseph
              Kockelmans (ed.), *Phenomenology.* Garden City, N.Y.: Anchor: 252–266.

Staats, Arthur W.
1976   "Skinnerian Behaviorism: Social Behaviorism or Radical Behaviorism?" *The
              American Sociologist* 11:59–60.

Stanfield, Ron
1974   "Kuhnian Scientific Revolutions and the Keynesian Revolution." *Journal of
              Economic Issues* 8:97–109.

Strasser, Hermann
1976   *The Normative Structure of Sociology.* London: Routledge and Kegan Paul.

Struik, Dirk
1964   Introduction. In Karl Marx, *The Economic and Philosophic Manuscripts of
              1844.* New York: International Publishers: 9–56.

Stryker, Sheldon
1980   *Symbolic Interactionism: A Social Structural Version.* Menlo Park, Calif.:
              Benjamin/Cummings.

Szacki, Jerzy
1979   *History of Sociological Thought.* Westport, Conn.: Greenwood Press.

Sztompka, Piotr
1974   *System and Function: Toward a Theory of Society.* New York: Academic
              Press.

Tar, Zoltan
1977   *The Frankfurt School: The Critical Theories of Max Horkheimer and Theodor
              W. Adorno.* London: Routledge and Kegan Paul.

Tarter, Donald
1973   "Heeding Skinner's Call: Toward the Development of a Social Technology."
              American Sociologist 8:153–158.
Thibaut, John, and Kelley, Harold H.
1959   *The Social Psychology of Groups.* New York: Wiley.
Thomas, William I., and Thomas, Dorothy S.
1928   *The Child in America: Behavior Problems and Programs.* New York: Knopf.
Thompson, E. P.
1978   *The Poverty of Theory.* London: Merlin Press.
Thompson, Kenneth
1975   *Auguste Comte: The Foundation of Sociology.* New York: Halstead Press.
Tiryakian, Edward A.
1962   *Sociologism and Existentialism: Two Perspectives on the Individual and
              Society.* Englewood Cliffs, N.J.: Prentice-Hall.
1965   "Existential Phenomenology and the Sociological Tradition." *American Socio-
              logical Review* 30:674–688.
Toby, Jackson
1977   "Parsons' Theory of Societal Evolution." In Talcott Parsons, *The Evolution of
              Societies.* Englewood Cliffs, N.J.: Prentice-Hall: 1–23.
Trivers, Robert L.
1972   "Parental Investment and Sexual Selection." In Bernard Campbell (ed.), *Sex-
              ual Selection and the Descent of Man.* Chicago: Aldine: 136–179.
Troyer, William
1946   "Mead's Social and Functional Theory of Mind." *American Sociological
              Review* 11:198–202.
Tucker, Robert C. (ed.)
1970   *The Marx-Engels Reader.* New York: Norton.
Tumin, Melvin
1953   "Some Principles of Stratification: A Critical Analysis." *American
              Sociological Review* 18:387–394.
Turner, Jonathan
1973   "From Utopia to Where? A Strategy for Reformulating the Dahrendorf Con-
              flict Model." *Social Forces* 52:236–244.
1974   "Parsons as a Symbolic Interactionist: A Comparison of Action and Interaction
              Theory." *Sociological Inquiry* 44:283–294.
1975   "A Strategy for Reformulating the Dialectical and Functional Theories of Con-
              flict." *Social Forces* 53:433–444.
1982   *The Structure of Sociological Theory.* 3rd. ed. Homewood, Ill.: Dorsey Press.
Turner, Jonathan, and Beeghley, Leonard
1974   "Current Folklore in the Criticisms of Parsonsian Action Theory."
              Sociological Inquiry 44:47–63.
Turner, Jonathan, and Maryanski, Alexandra
1979   *Functionalism.* Menlo Park, Calif.: Benjamin/Cummings.
Turner, Ralph
1968   "The Self-Conception in Social Interaction." In Chad Gordon and Kenneth J.
              Gergen (eds.), *The Self in Social Interaction.* New York: John Wiley: 93–106.
Turner, Roy
1970   "Words, Utterances and Activities." In Jack Douglas (ed.), *Understanding
              Everyday Life.* Chicago: Aldine: 161–187.
1974a   "Words, Utterances and Activities." In Roy Turner (ed.), *Ethnomethodology:
              Selected Readings.* Harmondsworth, Eng.: Penguin: 197–215.

Turner, Roy (ed.)
1974b   *Ethnomethodology: Selected Readings.* Harmondsworth, Eng.: Penguin.
van den Berg, Axel
1980   "Critical Theory: Is There Still Hope?" *American Journal of Sociology*
             86:449–478.
van den Berghe, Pierre
1963   "Dialectic and Functionalism: Toward Reconciliation." *American Sociological
             Review* 28:695–705.
1974   "Bringing Beasts Back In: Toward a Biosocial Theory of Aggression."
             American Sociological Review 39:777–788.
Veltmeyer, Henry
1978   "Marx's Two Methods of Sociological Analysis." *Sociological Inquiry*
             48:101–112.
Venable, Vernon
1945   *Human Nature: The Marxian View.* New York: Knopf.
Wagner, Helmut
1964   "Displacement of Scope: A Problem of the Relationship Between Small Scale
             and Large Scale Sociological Theories." *American Journal of Sociology*
             69:571–584.
Wallerstein, Immanuel
1974   *The Modern World-System: Capitalist Agriculture and the Origins of the Euro-
             pean World Economy in the 16th Century.* New York: Academic Press.
1980   *The Modern World-System II: Mercantilism and the Consolidation of the Euro-
             pean World-Economy, 1600–1750.* New York: Academic Press.
Warner, R. Stephen
1978   "Toward a Redefinition of Action Theory: Paying the Cognitive Element
             Its Due." *American Journal of Sociology* 83:1317–1349.
Weingart, Peter
1969   "Beyond Parsons? A Critique of Ralf Dahrendorf's Conflict Theory." *Social
             Forces* 48:151–165.
Weinstein, Eugene A., and Tanur, Judith M.
1976   "Meanings, Purposes and Structural Resources in Social Interaction." *Cornell
             Journal of Social Relations* 11:105–110.
Whyte, William F.
1961   "Parsons' Theory Applied to Organizations." In Max Black (ed.), *The Social
             Theories of Talcott Parsons.* Englewood Cliffs, N.J.: Prentice-Hall: 250–267.
Williams, Robin
1980   "Talcott Parsons: The Stereotypes and the Reality." *American Sociologist*
             15:64–66.
Wilson, Edward O.
1975   *Sociobiology: The New Synthesis.* Cambridge: Harvard University Press.
1978   Foreword. In Arthur L. Caplan (ed.), *The Sociobiology Debate.* New York:
             Harper & Row: xi–xiv.
Wilson, Thomas P.
1970   "Normative and Interpretive Paradigms in Sociology." In Jack Douglas (ed.),
             Understanding Everyday Life. Chicago: Aldine: 1–19.
Zeitlin, Irving M.
1968   *Ideology and the Development of Sociological Theory.* Englewood Cliffs, N.J.:
             Prentice-Hall.
Zimmerman, Don
1978   "Ethnomethodology." *American Sociologist* 13:5–15.

Zimmerman, Don, and Pollner, Melvin
1970   "The Everyday World as a Phenomenon." In Jack Douglas (ed.), *Under-standing Everyday Life*. Chicago: Aldine: 80–103.
Zimmerman, Don, and Wieder, D. Lawrence
1970   "Ethnomethodology and the Problem of Order: Comment on Denzin." In Jack Douglas (ed.), *Understanding Everyday Life*. Chicago: Aldine: 285–298.
Znaniecki, Florian
1934   *Method of Sociology*. New York: Farrar and Rhinehart.
1936   *Social Actions*. New York: Farrar and Rhinehart.

NAME INDEX

Abbott, Carroll, 258n
Aberle, D. F., 98
Abrahamson, Mark, 72, 73, 96
Abrahamsson, Bengt, 250
Abrams, Philip, 31–33, 35
Adorno, Theodor, 54
Agger, Ben, 116, 124, 125
Akers, Ronald, 260
Allport, Gordon, 53
Althusser, Louis, 65, 128, 129,
    130–135, 137, 141, 412–143, 283
Anderson, Perry, 132
Andreski, Stanislav, 12, 13
Antonio, Robert J., 121
Appelbaum, Richard, 129, 142–143

Back, Kurt, 259
Baldwin, Alfred, 82
Baldwin, Janice, 234n
Baldwin, John, 234n
Balibar, Etienne, 132
Ball, Richard A., 269–270, 272
Baran, Paul, 64, 143–145
Barash, David, 65, 275
Bauman, Zygmunt, 126, 127
Beeghley, Leonard, 268n
Bellah, Robert, 77
Beniger, James R., 239, 259
Berger, Peter, 61, 62, 92, 193, 205, 206,
    208–212, 224
Bergson, Henri, 202, 205
Bernstein, Eduard, 117
Bierstedt, Robert, 192
Birnbauer, J. S., 239
Bittner, Egon, 62, 226
Blalock, Hubert, 306
Blau, Peter, 59, 231, 252–256, 259, 287,
    288, 289–293, 308
Bleich, Harold, 120
Blum, Alan, 206, 213
Blumenstiel, Alexander, 205
Blumer, Herbert, 54, 59, 158, 160–161,
    166, 171–172, 177–178, 179–181
Borricaud, François, 79n
Bosserman, Phillip, 306
Bottomore, Tom, 288–289
Braverman, Harry, 64, 145–149
Brawley, Eleanor, 239

Bredemeier, Harry C., 259
Brentano, Franz, 205
Brinton, Crane, 43
Brown, Charles R., 258n
Buckley, Walter, 63, 268n, 269, 270,
    271–272
Burger, Thomas, 23
Burgess, Ernest W., 46, 47
Burgess, Robert, 234–237
Burris, Val, 128, 129, 142, 280, 284
Bushell, Don, 234, 235–236, 237, 239

Campbell, Colin, 92n
Caplan, Arthur L., 273, 275
Carnegie, Andrew, 42
Carter, Ellwood B., 29
Chadwick-Jones, J. K., 259
Charon, Joel, 159, 169
Chekhov, Anton, 42
Chua, Beng-Huat, 228
Cicourel, Aaron, 62, 227–228, 285, 286
Cohen, Percy, 96, 97, 98, 99
Coleman, James, 57, 62, 107
Colfax, J. David, 64
Collins, Randall, 59, 81, 107–111, 298
Comte, Auguste, 7, 12–13, 26, 33, 39, 41,
    42, 44, 49, 72–73
Connerton, Paul, 120, 126
Cooley, Charles Horton, 43, 47–48, 49, 158,
    167, 171, 204, 267
Coser, Lewis, 57, 62, 103, 105, 287–288
Craib, Ian, 63, 293, 294–295
Crosbie, Paul V., 258n
Culler, Jonathan, 278
Curelaru, M., 301, 303

Dahrendorf, Ralf, 58, 100–105
Darwin, Charles, 35
Davis, Kingsley, 56, 71, 74, 84, 85,
    98
de Bonald, Louis, 10, 12,
de Maistre, Joseph, 10, 12,
Demerath, Nicholas, 72
Descartes, René, 9
Dewey, John, 47, 159, 167
DiTomaso, Nancy, 143
Dobb, Maurice, 149
Douglas, Jack, 63, 186, 187, 293

SUBJECT INDEX

Slavery, 89, 91–92
Social and Cultural Dynamics, 50
Social behavior. *See* Behavior
Social Behavior: Its Elementary Forms, 59,
   241, 246
Social Construction of Reality, The, 61, 62,
   208–212
Social Darwinism, 33. *See also* Survival of
   the fittest
Social definition. *See* Definitions
Social facts. *See* Facts, social
Social objects, 168
Social physics, 12
Social system, 78–80. *See also* Parsons,
   Talcott (*Name Index*)
Social System, The, 52, 63
Socialism, 11, 20, 21, 23, 28, 151
   rise of, 7
Socialization, 79–80, 88, 99, 140, 165, 167–
   168, 200, 207, 223–224
Societal functionalism, 72
Society, 166, 256, 258
Society of Symbolic Interaction, 158*n*, 298
Sociobiology, 65, 265–266, 273–278
Sociobiology: The New Synthesis, 273, 274,
   276
Sociocultural systems, 270, 271
Sociological Imagination, The, 57
Sociological Society of London, 31
Sociology
   creative, 60–63, 66, 293
   environmental, 65
   industrial, 238
   Italian, 35–36
   lexical, 303
   meta-, 300–302
   phenomenological. *See* Phenomenology
   semantical, 303–304
   substantive. *See* Weber, Max (*Name
   Index*)
   syntactical, 304
Sociology: A Multiple Paradigm Science,
   275*n*, 300, 302–305
Sociology and Modern Systems Theory, 63,
   269
Sociology of Marx, The, 64
Sociology of Sociology, A, 301
Solidarity, 106
Sorbonne, the, 15
Sorokin Award, 150, 290
Soviet Union. *See* Russia
Spain, 153
Specialization, 147–148
Species-being, 135, 136

Speech. *See* Conversation
Spendthrift, miser and, 29
Sports, 123
Stage, *See also* Dramaturgy; Musical theater
State. *See specific theories and theorists*
States and Social Revolutions, 153–156
Statistics, 32, 49, 223
Status, 24, 78, 94, 119, 176, 288, 291, 308.
   See also Exchange Theory
Stigma, 176
   discreditable, 176
   discredited, 176
Stigma, 176
Stimulus proposition, 248
Stimulus/response. *See* Exchange theory
Stranger, the, 29
Strasbourg, University of, 30
Stratification, 24, 56, 84–86, 87, 94, 95, 98,
   108–110
Structural functionalism, 13, 34, 50, 54, 57,
   58, 64, 71–99, 142–143, 161, 232, 233,
   273, 289, 298, 304
   and analysis of poverty, 93–96
   and conflict theory. *See* Conflict theory
   and evolutionary theory, 82–84
   and the functional prerequisites of a society, 86–88
   historical roots of, 72–74
   Homans and, 243–245, 246
   major criticisms of, 96–100
   peak and decline of, 55–56
   and theory of stratification, 84–86
Structural Marxism, 128–143, 283–284
Structuralism, 65, 66, 213, 227–228, 266,
   278–287. *See also* Macrostructural
   theory; Structural functionalism; Structural Marxism
Structure of Scientific Revolutions, The, 301–
   302
Structure of Social Action, The, 15, 36, 51,
   76, 90
Structure of Sociological Theory, The, 115–
   116
Structures. *See* Structural functionalism
Students, 239. *See also* Breaching experi-
   ments
Studies in Ethnomethodology, 62
Studies in Symbolic Interaction, 298
Subjective-objective continuum, 306–309
Subjectivity, 234*n*
Subordination, 101, 102
Substantive sociology. *See* Weber, Max
   (*Name Index*)
Success proposition, 247–248

About the Author

George Ritzer is Professor of Sociology at the University of Maryland in College Park. Author of *Toward an Integrated Sociological Paradigm, Sociology: A Multiple Paradigm Science, An Occupation in Conflict,* and *Working: Conflict and Change,* and coauthor of *Sociology: Experiencing a Changing Society* (an introductory textbook), he has also written numerous articles for professional journals. In 1980–1981 Professor Ritzer served as Fellow in Residence at the Institute for Advanced Studies in the Netherlands.

A Note on the Type

The text of this book was set on the Editwriter in a computer version of Times Roman, designed by Stanley Morison for *The Times* (London) and first introduced by that newspaper in 1932.

Among typographers and designers of the twentieth century, Stanley Morison has been a strong forming influence as typographical adviser to the English Monotype Corporation, as a director of two distinguished English publishing houses, and as a writer of sensibility, erudition, and keen practical sense.